EXTREME LAKELAND

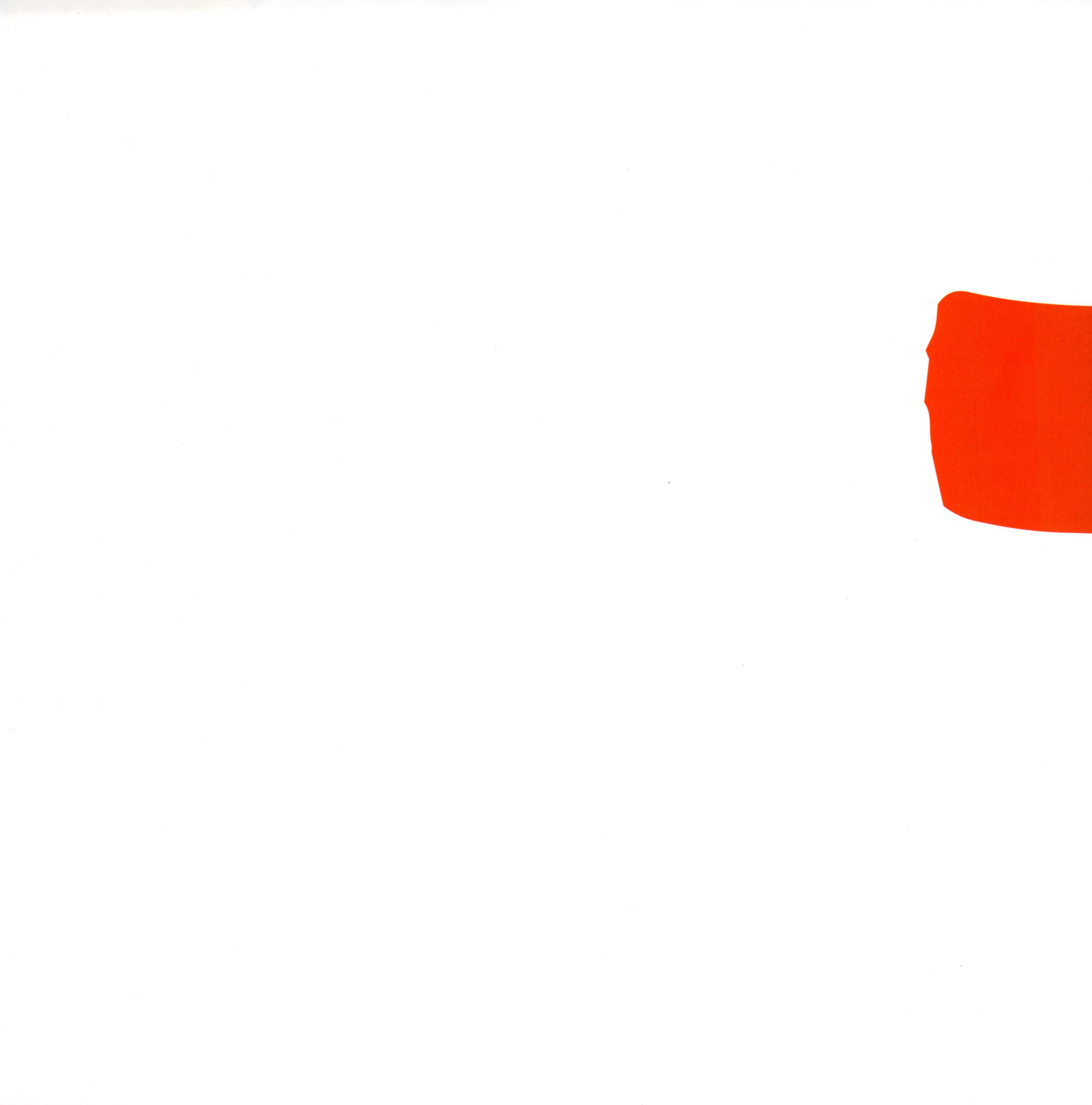

NADIR KHAN & TOM McNALLY

EXTREME LAKELAND

A PHOTOGRAPHIC JOURNEY THROUGH LAKE DISTRICT ADVENTURE SPORTS

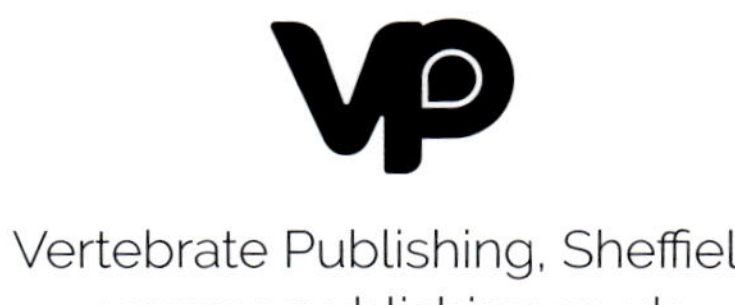

Vertebrate Publishing, Sheffield
www.v-publishing.co.uk

NADIR KHAN & TOM McNALLY

EXTREME LAKELAND

First published in 2022 by Vertebrate Publishing

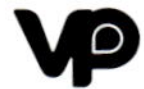

VERTEBRATE PUBLISHING
Omega Court, 352 Cemetery Road, Sheffield S11 8FT, United Kingdom.
www.v-publishing.co.uk

A CIP catalogue record for this book is available from the British Library.

ISBN: 978-1-83981-125-8 (Hardback)

10 9 8 7 6 5 4 3 2 1

Design and production by Jane Beagley.
www.v-publishing.co.uk

Vertebrate Publishing is committed to printing on paper from sustainable sources.

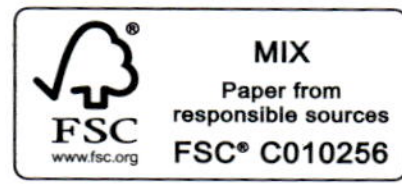

Printed and bound in China by Latitude Press.

CONTENTS

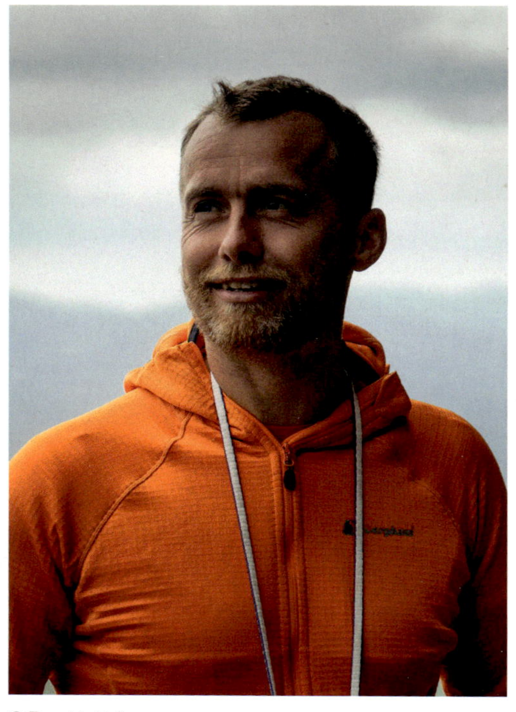
© Tom McNally

FOREWORD

LEO HOULDING

Stumbling through the darkness, exhausted and shivering with cold, my head torch illuminated nothing but the dense, wet mist that ripped past on wind that chilled through to the bone.

Completely disorientated, verging on seasick, in the white-out I could hardly tell if I was going up or down, never mind east or west. The only way I knew I was on the right path was thanks to the remarkable half-metre accuracy of the GPS, my eyes glued to the bright screen watching the red arrow sway either side of the blue dotted line while sore feet squelched through boggy ground.

Having already been on the go for over twenty hours, covered twenty-five miles of rough terrain and climbed thirty-eight pitches with severely insufficient food or water intake, wearing all my layers and carrying no emergency equipment and with no communications, I was acutely aware of the precariousness of the situation. With any hope of rescue a long way off, a sprained ankle or twisted knee could easily and quickly result in hypothermia or worse.

But this time I wasn't on a major expedition to some remote greater range, I was just down the road from home, somewhere between Pillar Rock and Great Gable in the Western Lakes. It occurred to me that I'd first been up here when I was a child not much older than my daughter who was tucked up in bed not twenty miles away.

The Lake District 'Classic Rock Round', a thirty-four-mile, 4,300 metres of ascent, sub-twenty-four-hour jaunt around the fifteen Lakeland climbs featured in Ken Wilson's iconic book *Classic Rock*, certainly isn't a picnic, but I hadn't anticipated the day leading into such a serious predicament.

Our complete lack of preparation, having not done any of the climbs or inspected any of the routes in advance, meant Anna Taylor and I knew we wouldn't be vying with Will Birkett or Tom Randall for a heroic sub-twelve-hour record.

But the climbs are well within our capabilities and our presumed general familiarity with the fells made an on-sight round a tempting prospect in what would most likely be the last fine-weather spell of the year.

The short October days certainly didn't help but it was the far-worse-than-forecast weather that forced us to abort our attempt three quarters of the way around at Pillar Rock, the most isolated point of the round, and left us stumbling through the darkness, deeply grateful to the GPS, taking extra care to avoid an incident.

Then out of the fog a uniquely colloquial saviour, a barbed-wire fence, appeared like a lifeboat through the swell, offering an easy line to follow down to safety. Soon enough we dropped below the cloud base and out of the wind, eventually hitting the road at Honister Pass.

As a glorious dawn brought with it the warmth and colour of a perfect autumn Lakeland day we slogged the last six miles down the road through Borrowdale to the car that was parked at Shepherd's Crag. It was here that I had climbed my first multi-pitch route, *Little Chamonix*, thirty years earlier. A smile grew across my face as I considered the irony of having been on the edge of an epic so close to home after a lifetime of extreme expeditions to the most hostile natural environments across the globe.

I was born a stone's throw from the foot of those fells, in Penrith, the gateway to the Northern Lakes. It was here in 'the loveliest spot that man hath found', as Wordsworth put it, that I discovered a passion for outdoor adventure that would evolve into a profession as a climber and a life of extreme adventure that has led me to the wildest experiences in places I never dreamed existed, at the most remote ends of the Earth – from skydiving high into the Canadian Arctic, to discovering lost worlds in the depths of the Amazon rainforest, and from snow-kiting thousands of miles at breathtaking speeds to reach a mile-high cliff in Antarctica, to bouldering in 1920s alpine gear at the top of Mount Everest.

I owe a deep debt of gratitude to these Lakeland fells that I once again call home.

My journey on this adventurous path began with family forays on to the gentler fells, Blencathra and Catbells, and weekends wild camping in the woods of Borrowdale and becks of Swindale when I was little more than a toddler, kindling a love of living in nature, of being feral in the wild.

But walking uphill is tiring and my young self was soon bored of the majestic views. It wasn't until my dad and I progressed from the well-trampled trails of the classic Wainwrights on to the jagged scrambles of Striding Edge on Helvellyn and Pinnacle Ridge on St Sunday Crag that these rolling, sheep-covered hills became a much more enticing proposition.

Once you start needing to use your hands to ascend, getting to the top becomes a much more engaging endeavour. As the flanks grow steeper, the consequences of a mistake grow higher and the element of risk comes into play.

Then a friend introduced me to rock climbing proper. A brave new world of vertical walls, high exposure, specialist equipment and real danger. That was the pivotal moment when I found the meaning of my life and have hardly looked back since.

As the stakes grow higher, fear and adrenaline enter the game and these humble, green hills beloved of poets and painters take on an entirely different persona. Viewed through the right prism, armed with the necessary gear and skills, the Lakes becomes a big kids' playground created by Mother Nature to allow those who can to push themselves in directions others don't even know exist. This is Extreme Lakeland.

In the three decades since discovering this world of adventure and extreme sports I've been thrilled to enjoy most of the activities captured within this book. Many I encountered for the first time here in the Lakes, while others I was introduced to elsewhere and have yet to practise on my doorstep as pictured here.

I left the Lakes in search of bigger game and greater scale straight after finishing school. The appetite for adventure I developed here has served me well on countless missions throughout seasons spent in many of the world's finest adventure playgrounds – Chamonix in the Alps, Yosemite in California, Patagonia in South America – and dozens of major expeditions to the greater ranges and beyond.

Throughout those decades of travel I imagined I would settle in one of these glamorous adventure hubs. The sun-kissed walls of the western USA, Alpine delights of Europe or rustic wilderness of Patagonia were all tempting, and I seriously considered putting down roots in all of these places. But as I matured and began to figure out what I truly valued the most, the subtle beauty of this little patch of North-West England consistently came out on top.

On becoming a parent and the plethora of new dimensions and complications that brings to life I realised that, for me at least, I can think of no better place to raise a family and to call home.

Yes, it rains a lot! Yes, the crags are small and the approaches long. Yes, some winters the snow and ice are sparse.

But when the conditions do align – those long spells of sunny high pressure when all the high crags are dry and the trails become dusty underfoot; when the ice does form and the snow settles, and the north faces come alive with tools in hands or skis on feet; when the rivers are in spate, or the thermals and winds harmonise for a sublime day of flying – I could not agree with ol' Wordsworth more that this is indeed 'the loveliest spot that man hath found'.

At least that's what I felt walking down Borrowdale on my tired legs in that crisp autumn sunrise after surviving that aborted attempt at the Classic Rock Round.

Welcome to Extreme Lakeland. Enjoy it!

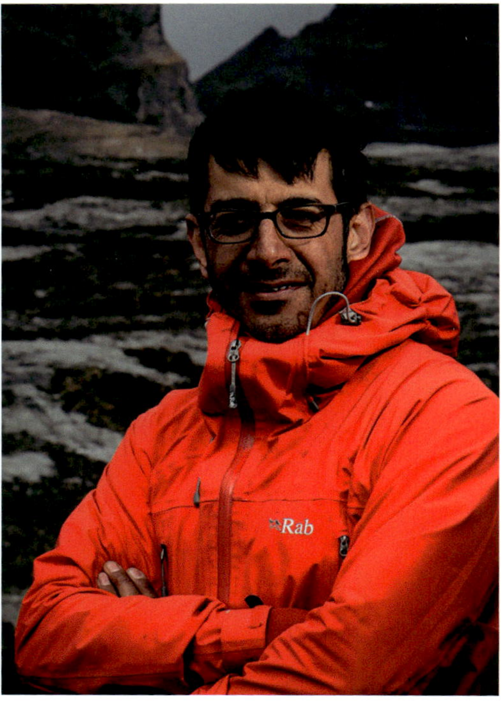

© Nadir Khan Collection

INTRODUCTION

NADIR KHAN

Adventure sports photography has always been a passion, a companion, a familiar touchstone telling me who I am, how I relate to the world around me as we spin on our little planet in space. And we all need a sense of who we are. It grounds us and gives us reference points. But for me a lot of those certainties have seemed to change and shift as I've got older. Priorities change and what once seemed like absolutes now seem less certain.

We live in an image-obsessed world, where style means more than substance and the appearance of a life well lived has more value than actually living. In this self-obsessed, social-media world that we now inhabit, it seems counterintuitive to bring out a book celebrating 'the image'. But the purpose of this book isn't just to celebrate the summit shot, the happy face, the celebratory fist bump or the Instagram shot to make your friends envious. As we all know, life isn't made up of snapshots of victory and triumph. Life goes on when the cameras are switched off, so while not sexy or envy-inducing, these images actually say more about who we are as people than the mountaintop moments of glory.

I hope in this book you will glimpse behind 'the brave face' and see people being honest about who they are. There are short stories from people talking about battling ill health, juggling family life, dealing with mental health and the one none of us can escape, getting older.

This book is a celebration of life, of lives well lived, in all their messy glory. It's a celebration of a community of climbers, runners, walkers, mountain bikers and paddlers. It's a celebration of joy, of the privilege to live in a land where movement is free and one can go about one's business, pleasure and sport relatively free from mortal danger, in an age where so many in distant lands do not have that privilege.

And it's a celebration of connections. All the athletes photographed in this book will know of each other, or have climbed or biked or paddled with each other, such is the network of people that make up the adventure landscape in the Lake District. And it's connections that help us to feel human, to feel love and to feel we belong to each other in many ways. Especially coming as it does during a time when connections and closeness have been threatened

and tested to breaking point. I hope that this book inspires you to seek out parts of the Lakes that you've not visited or to plan some new adventure, and to share those adventures with people you love and care about and create memories to cherish and yes, to get that next Instagram shot!

This book is a successor to *Extreme Scotland: A photographic journey through Scottish adventure sports*. That book took six years to complete, mostly while living in the south of England in a previous incarnation of life. If I was going to do another book, I felt it would be more productive to work with a collaborator, someone whose style complemented my own but also who could give a unique view of the land and people. I had come across Tom McNally's work just as I was finishing the first book and when the publishers gave the green light to start *Extreme Lakeland* I already had in mind who I wanted to work with. The fact that Tom had the same idea after seeing *Extreme Scotland* sealed the deal so to speak, and the result is what you have in your hands.

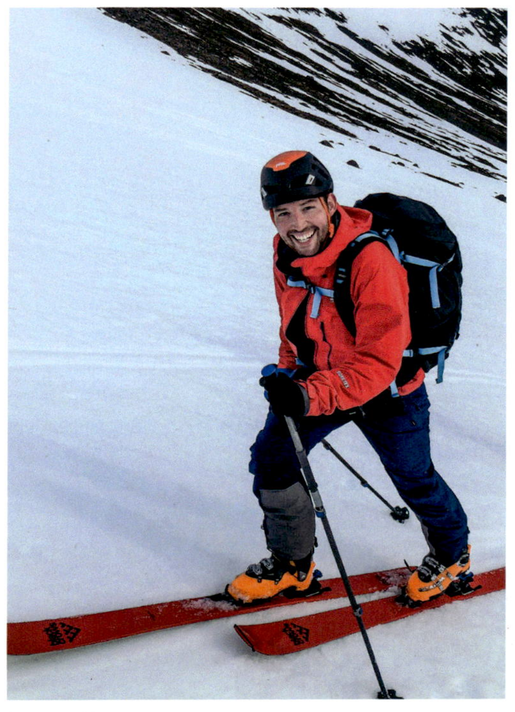

© Bruno Skinner

INTRODUCTION

TOM McNALLY

The Lake District, cornerstone of the English Romantic movement and home to Wordsworth, Wainwright, Peter Rabbit, fell walking, sheep farming, great pubs, excellent food, odd place names, and millions of visitors enjoying all of the above. Delve beyond these first impressions, however, and a far more nuanced and complex landscape emerges, disconnected from the somewhat sedate and 'natural' place many perceive, one in fact heavily shaped by industry and with a rich history of exploration, exhilaration and risk at its very heart.

Since moving here around ten years ago I have always wanted to embark on a photographic project exploring our contemporary interactions with this unique landscape, one that reaches beyond the quaint, well-trodden stereotypes. As an outdoors person I've always been inspired by the Lake District as a forge of adventure, steeped in heritage thanks to the legendary exploits of such historical figures as Walter Parry Haskett Smith, Bentley Beetham, Millican Dalton, the Abraham brothers and George Mallory. Today their legacy is perpetuated by a vibrant outdoor community operating not only at the cutting edge of 'traditional' outdoor activities such as climbing and kayaking, but also more eclectic pursuits such as BASE jumping and slacklining. *Extreme Lakeland* seeks to document these diverse sports and just some of the amazing people who undertake them.

There have been many obstacles to overcome in its completion. The challenges presented by Covid-19 lockdowns have been significant, and my own personal recovery from the illness was a bit more character-building than I would have liked. Its lingering and strange effects reduced my activity levels for over a year – not ideal when trying to shoot images of predominantly mountain sports. The positive outcome is that these limitations forced my hand creatively, compelling me to consider at length the efficiency of each shoot and how to achieve the very maximum visual impact from every location.

Living in the national park afforded me the flexibility needed for some of the 'set-piece' images – namely the luxury of being able to plan (and wait for) the magical alignment of location, subject and light. As such there are a few pictures that took years to actually realise. In contrast my collaborator, Nadir, living in Scotland, was sometimes forced to adopt a more fluid approach, making the long journey south, and despite our best-laid plans was faced with unpredictable weather conditions and/or a lack of subjects. Despite this, his photographs are stunning and perhaps more authentic to the true Lake District outdoor 'experience' many of us know and love!

I would like to say a huge and heartfelt thanks to all the people you see (and don't see) on the following pages – to those who put up with my tens of 'one last shot' at the end of a tiring day, often ignoring discomfort, hunger and hypothermia; to those who put themselves in mortal danger all in the name of a good picture; to those who did all of the above and didn't make the final cut; to those who looked after my children at short notice when I spotted an opportunity too good to miss before disappearing out to 'work'; and of course to my wonderful wife, Louise, and the boys, Edward and Oscar. *Extreme Lakeland* would not have been possible without every single one of you. Thank you.

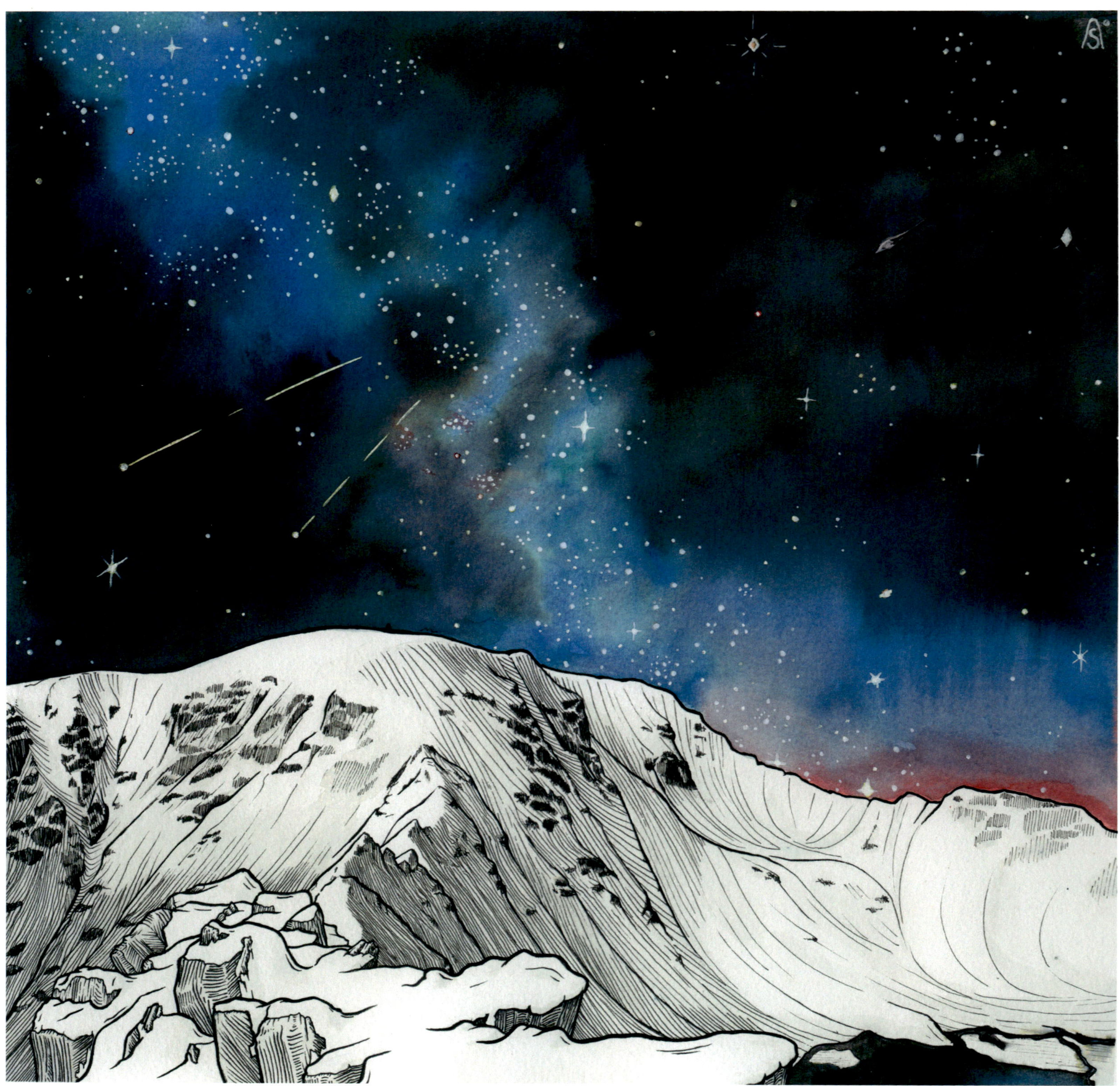

WINTER

« *Striding Edge.* © Anna Sharpe

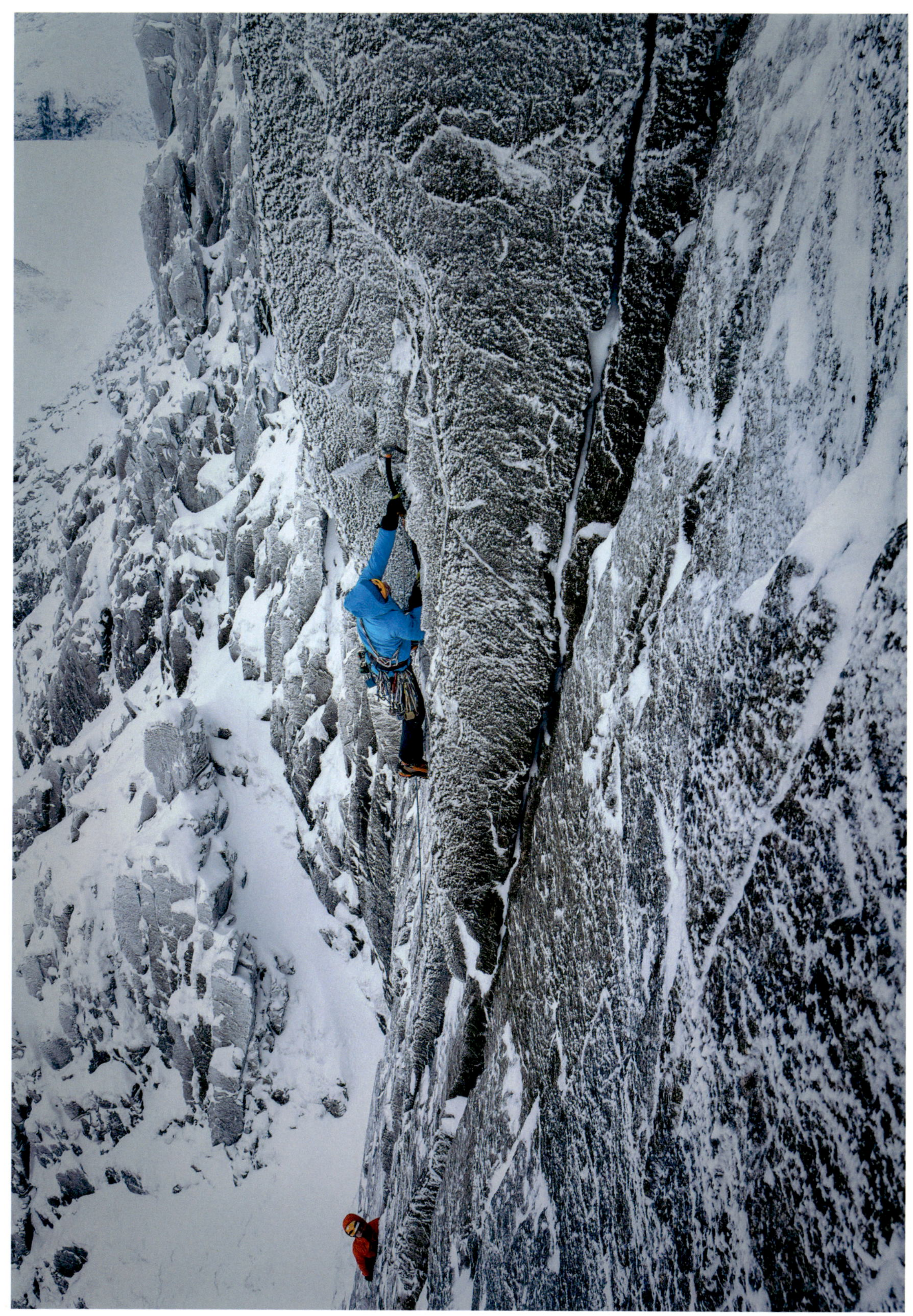

WINTERCEPTER

BY NADIR KHAN

It's 5 a.m. and I'm crunching through fresh snow to the car parked at the end of the lane. The snow is heavier than forecast and the car is covered in an icy crust. I'm wondering how the drive up to Borrowdale is going to be.

The camera bag is thrown in to the back of the four-wheel drive. The forecast is good but I'm driving through spindrift and deep snow to meet Matt and Adam just outside Kendal. The drive should be forty-five minutes to the parking place at Seathwaite from where we'll set off, but in these conditions gritting has been sporadic or non-existent, and the boys seem to think there's a big difference between North Lakes and South Lakes councils' urgency to maintain the roads. In the end the journey time is more like two hours, driving at about twenty miles per hour and occasionally side-slipping, unintentionally, around blind corners.

Finally we get to the parking spot. Vitamin I (ibuprofen) caps are taken, bags checked and loaded, and we head off. I have more body fat in my little finger than these two young lads have between them and I'm older than their ages put together. Self-doubt, aches and pains and general creakiness are creeping into my bones and leave me wondering how long I can keep going in the world of young guns and super-psyched athletes.

Adventure photography is something I've done since university, even through the years of having a family, career and the various twists and turns of life. But the last two months have been turbulent. Moving to Edinburgh full time after living in the south of England for thirty-two years, leaving all I had known behind me, has left me feeling lost, empty and very alone.

I'm walking up behind Adam and Matt and surprise myself by actually keeping up with them and not being half an hour behind. Sweat drips down my back and I wonder how windy it will be when I change into a dry base layer. I'm kicking myself as I only have one pair of gloves with me that are warm enough to keep the cold and wind out, and I can feel sweat building up inside them.

We get to the top of Gable Crag and I drop an abseil line down the side of the route that they're climbing – *Wintercepter* (VII, 8), a hard mixed testpiece. My gloves have now frozen into cardboard and I'm abseiling down the line as they get ready to set off. The climbing is slow and steady, as Matt tries to find gear in thin cracks, and clear away ice and snow to find ledges and grooves for picks and crampon points to purchase.

I'm eyeing up my single abseil line. I have rope protectors on the edges but an experience from 2017 at Gogarth when my abseil line was cut almost in half leaves me feeling on edge. As a photographer, you spend a lot of time on an abseil line, as compared to a climber. As Adam climbs up, I jumar up the rope, the seesawing action causing the rope to rub up and down unhelpfully against the rock.

I focus on the composition, keeping an eye on any facial expressions or body positions that speak of the energy of the climb. Stupidly I had decided to keep my crampons off for the jumaring and I get little purchase against the icy cliffs with my non-active foot. I watch my rope as it scrapes against the rock walls.

Matt is at the crux and I hold my breath, expecting him to take a fall as he shouts to Adam, 'Watch me here!', so tenuous do the moves seem to be. But somehow he's through the crux sequence and around the corner and I breathe a sigh of relief for him but also that I can get off this damn abseil line.

Note to self: from now on, always drop in with two lines.

« Matt Foot leading on *Wintercepter* (VII, 8) Great Gable, belayed by Adam Simpson. © Nadir Khan

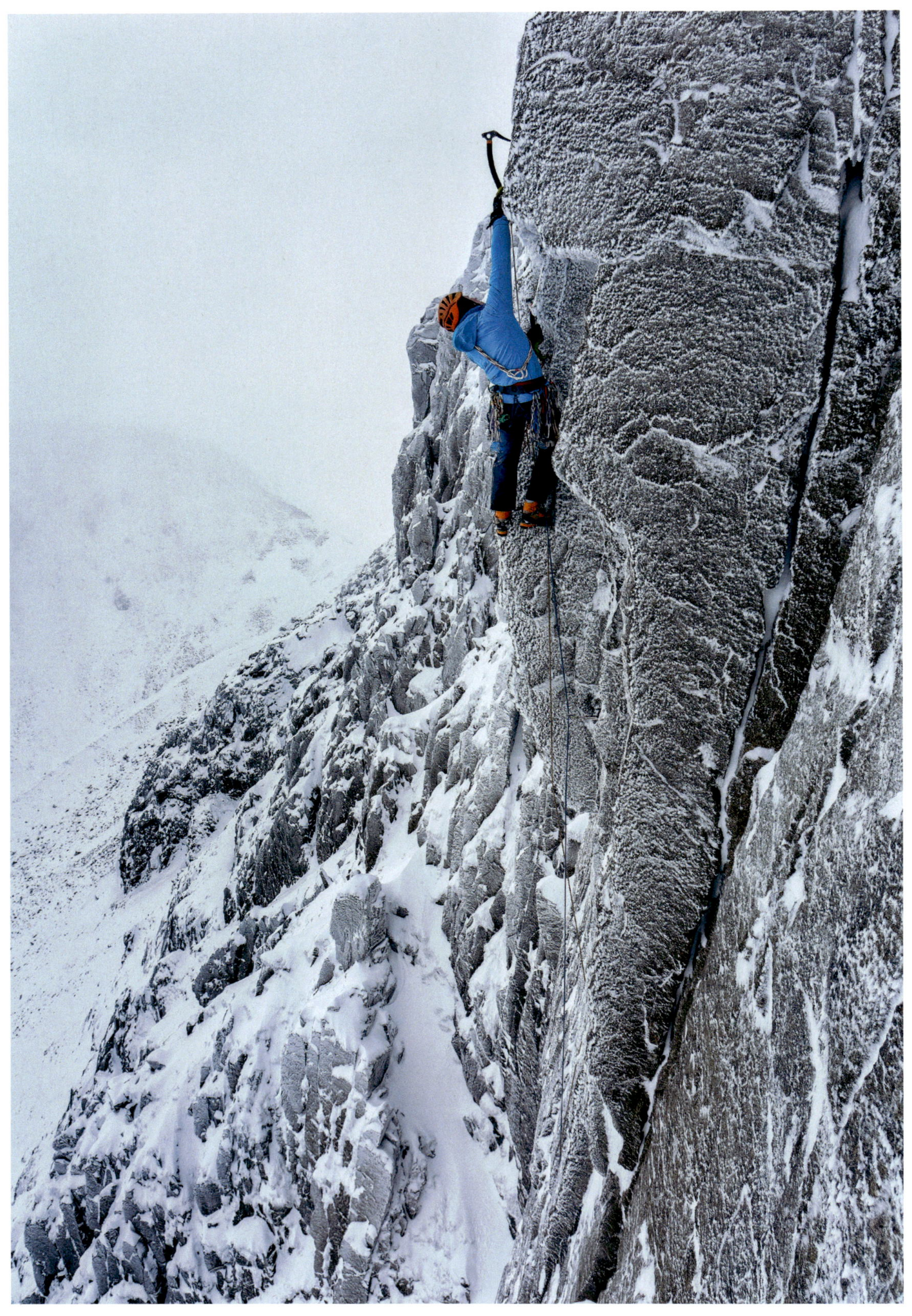

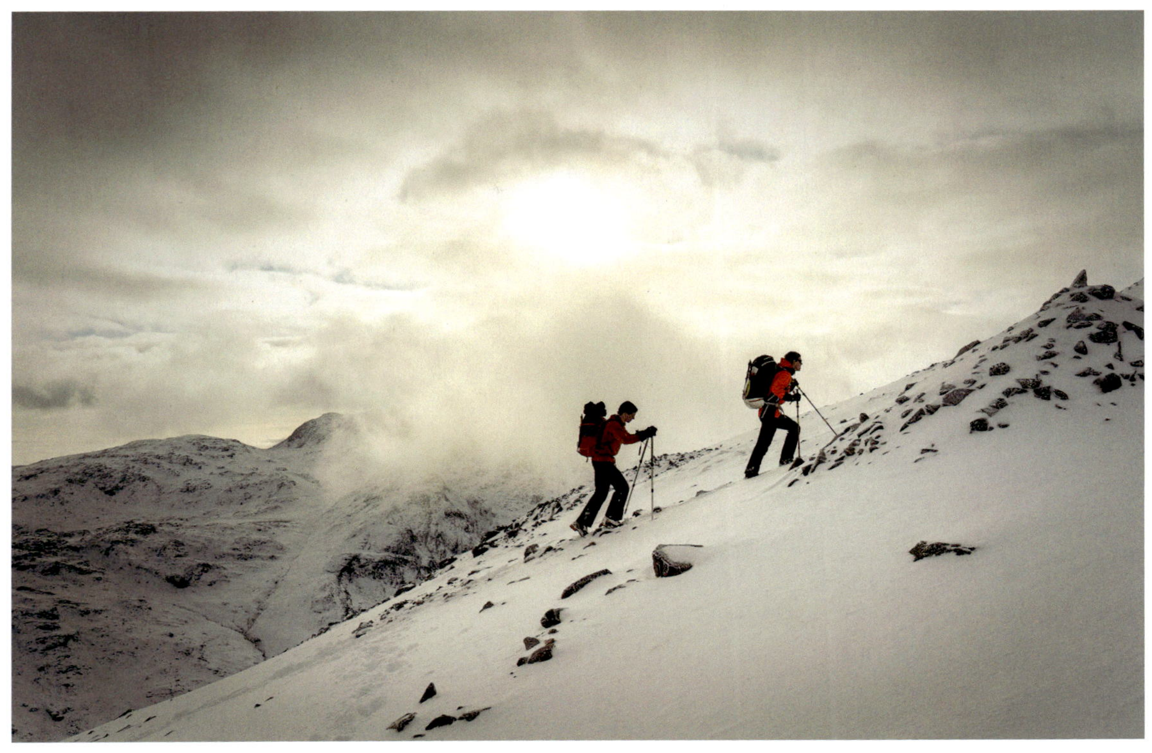

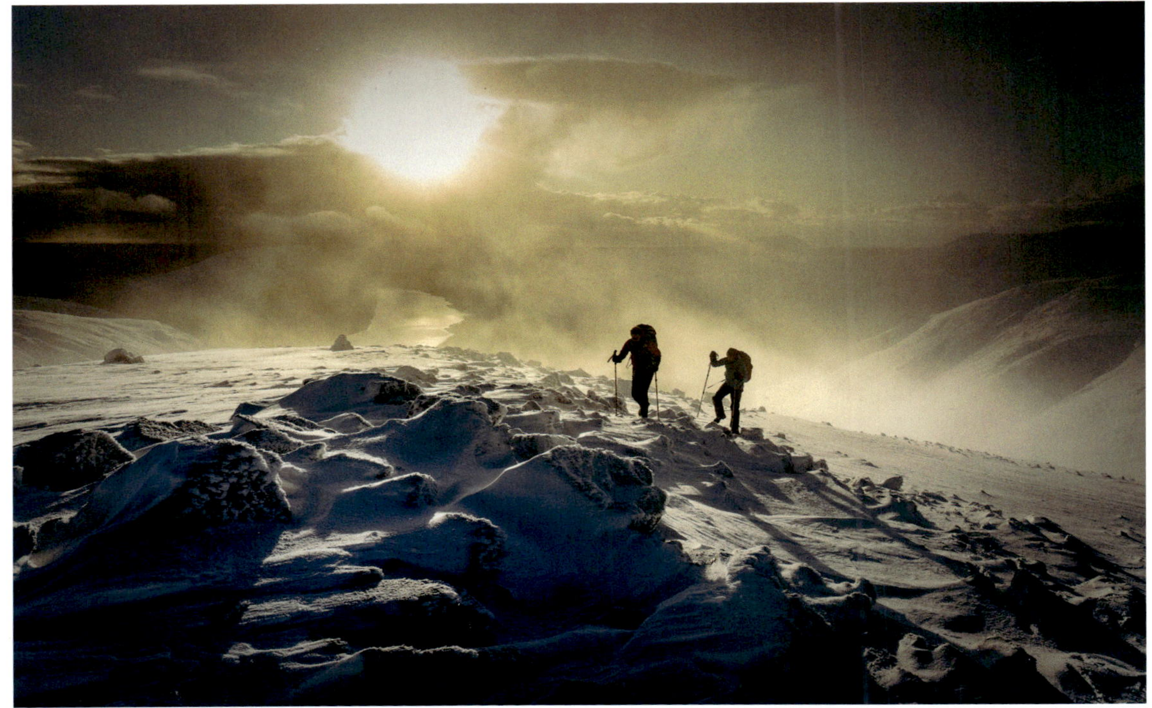

Matt and Adam on the slopes of Great Gable. © Nadir Khan

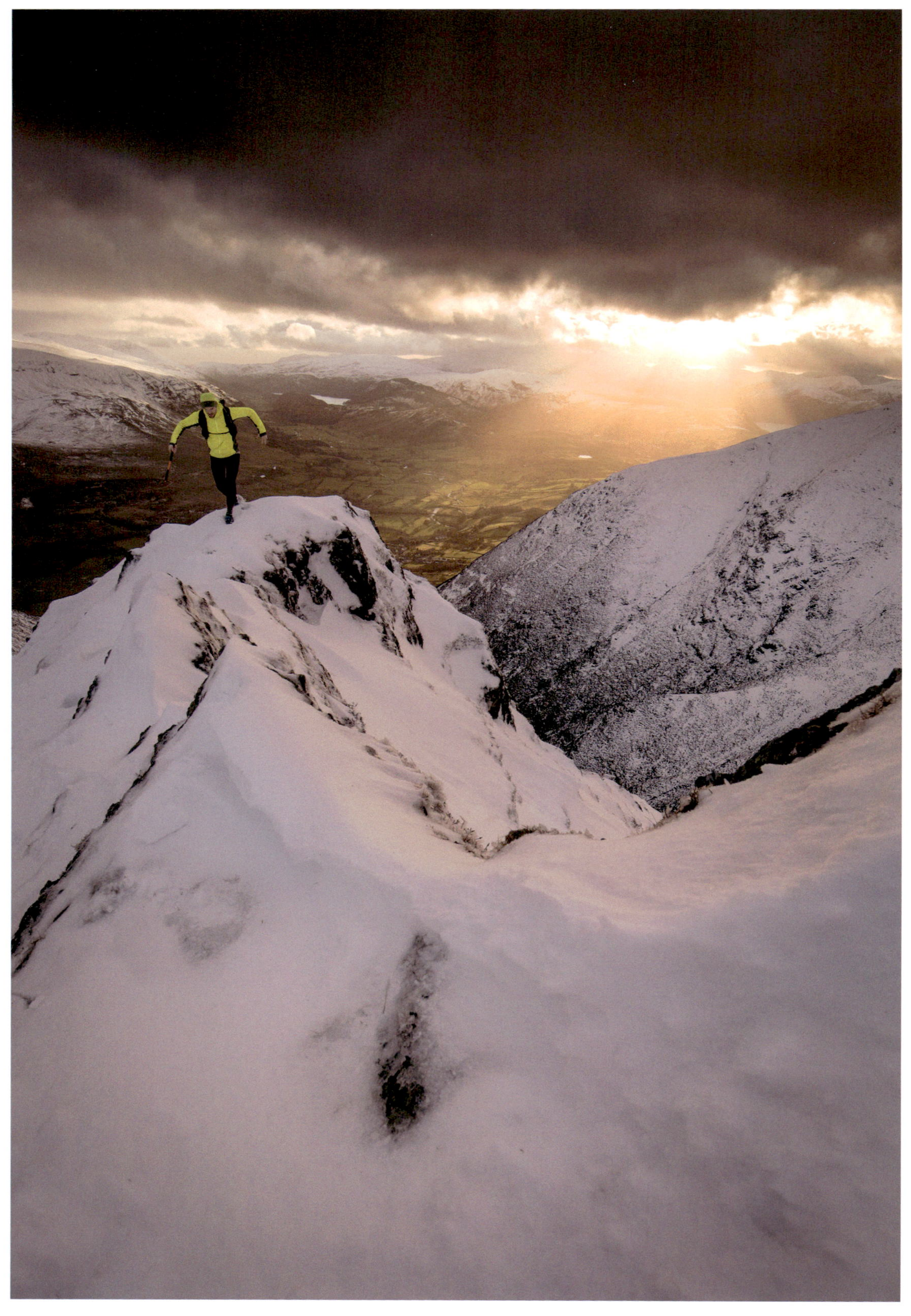

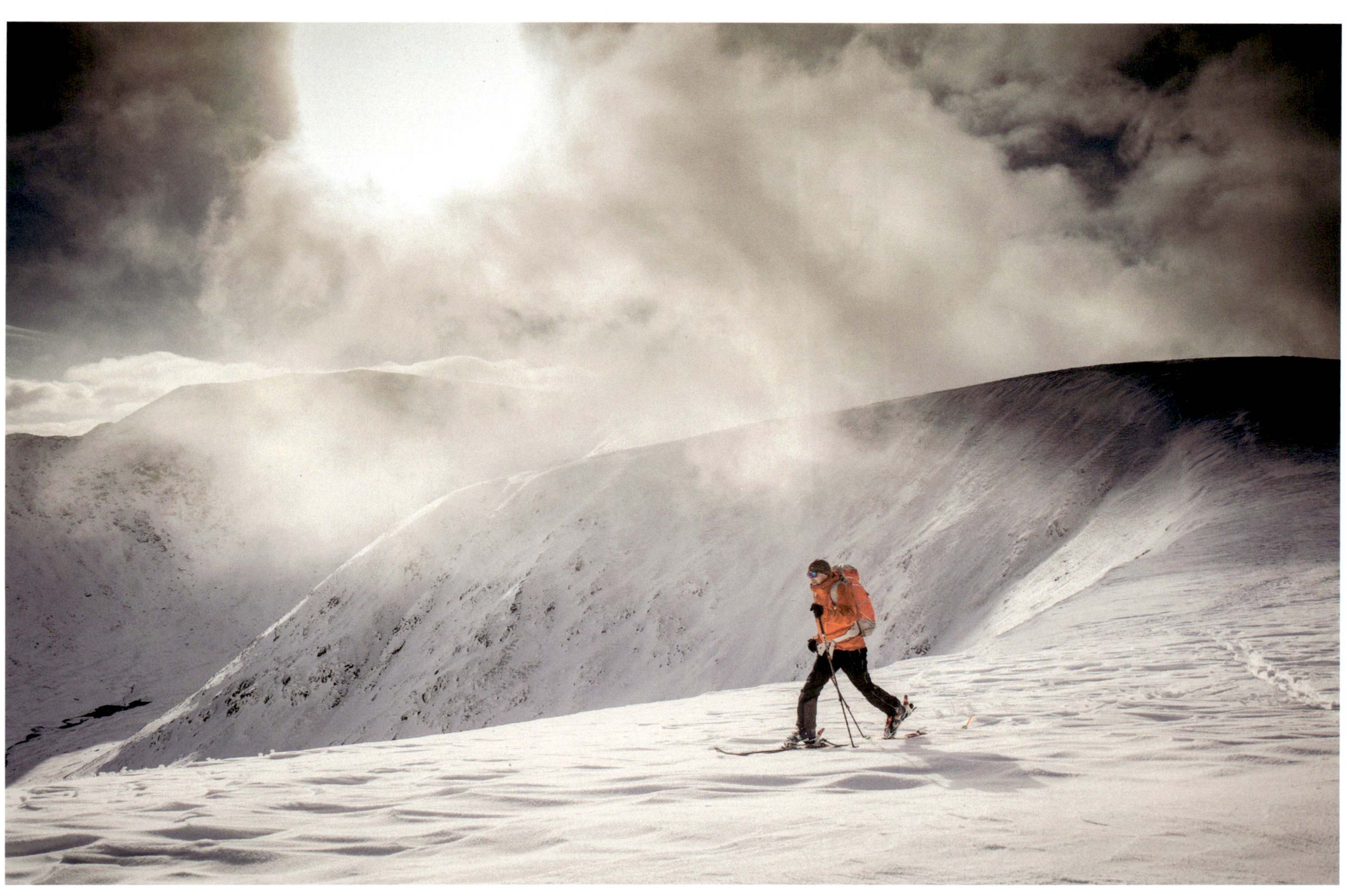

Matt Eaves ski-touring on Helvellyn. © Tom McNally

<< Dava Waterhouse on Hall's Fell Ridge, Blencathra. © Tom McNally

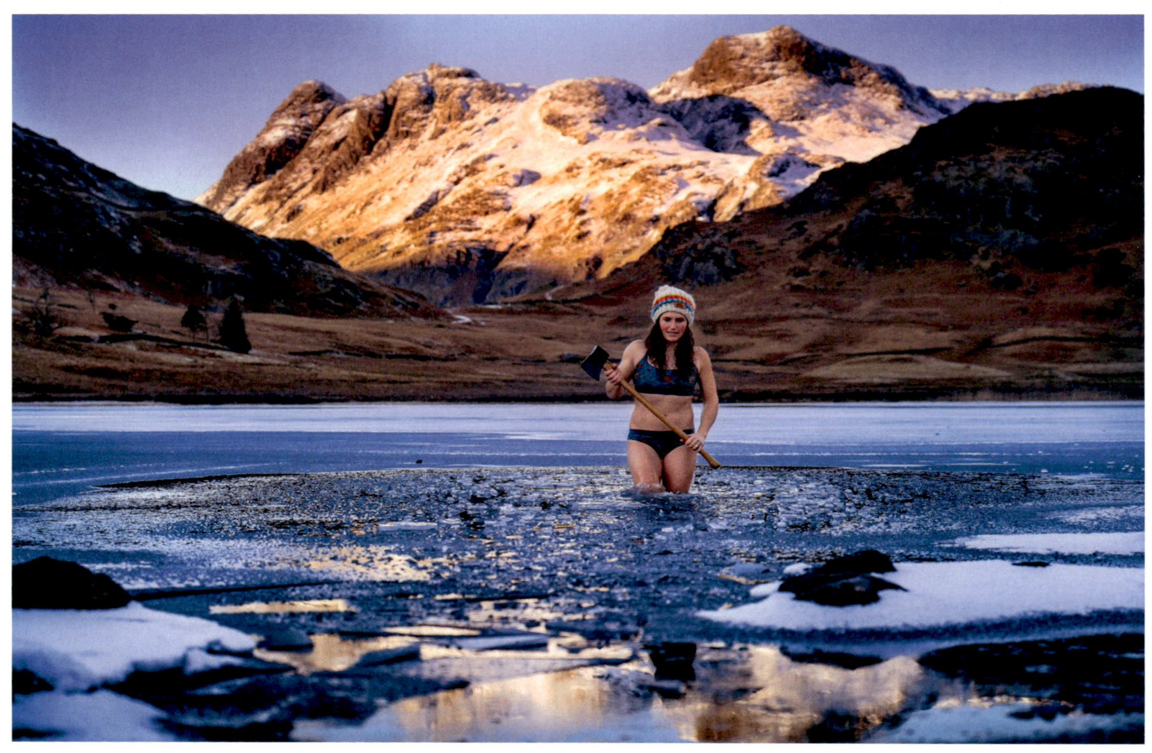

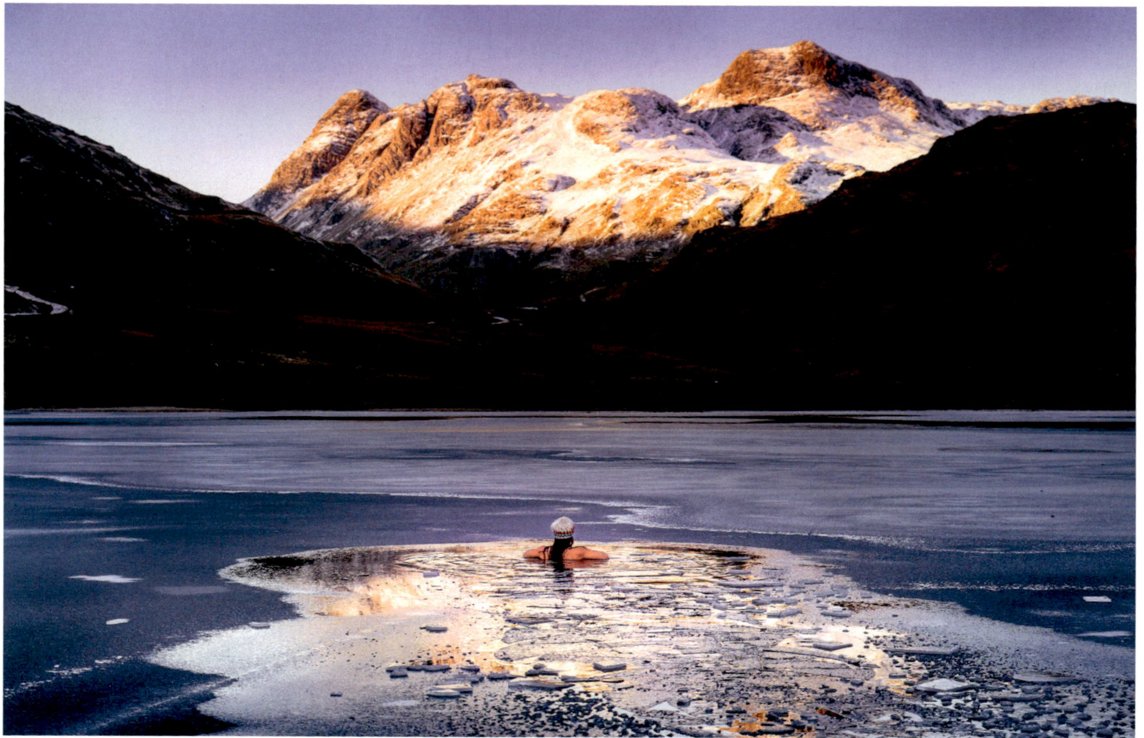

Becki Vale enjoying an icy dip at Blea Tarn. © Tom McNally

LETTING GO

BY GILLY McARTHUR

All you can do in very cold water is let go.

Let go of the day before or the day ahead. Of the ego and of any expectation of what is going to happen in the next moments when the sharp cold takes her grasp.

That's certainly my experience of it all, over the last six years of shedding my outer suit and just submitting to the kinaesthetic perception of the icy nip of winter.

It's a meditation, a portal to a dreamlike state of involuntary attention to now. The water is so familiar yet every time its properties are so unswervingly unique it brings me back to what it means to feel alive.

When I meet folks at the water's edge in winter (usually when I'm in a state of undress) the common and curious question is, 'Is it cold?' followed by, 'You're mad, I could never do that', and my reply is always, 'Yes, it's cold!' then, 'How do you know it's not for you? Have you ever given it a try?'

There are so many things in life, as we get older, that we close off from because society or our brains (shaped to be a certain way by years of unconscious routine and formulae) tell us that it's 'not for us' – and isn't that a shame?

By doing new things and opening up to new experiences we can develop new neural pathways to be happier, to explore this wonderful world in new ways and to find a new freedom.

Life will, at some point, deliver hammer blows of sadness and dreams deferred. Expecting life to be anything but this is folly. These hard times, however, don't need to change the whole life story to black.

For me, being totally present in nature, in a body of water, gently sews new stitches in the tapestry of my story. The dark patches of grief and sadness that life has placed there are joined with other vibrant colours; the bright colours need the dark to sparkle off.

Tiny intricacies year on year follow the same pattern of birth, growth and death. The sap rises in the trees; the leaves unfurl, play host to life, and by autumn they are withering. The wonder of it all is so beautiful, so breathtaking.

By accepting this ultimate truth of life, and its cycle of renewal, we can discover more joy in living. There's a harshness, a beauty and a wonder we have sometimes just ceased to notice.

Perhaps we have forgotten what plump raindrops really feel like on our naked skin and what grainy rough pebbles and spongy moss really feel like between our toes. We have forgotten how soft and animal-like we really are, in all the trappings of our twenty-first-century bodies, with waterproofing and wick-away; of adornments and egos; of technology and rules on how we assess risk. We are subtly bombarded with how we need to look to be valid and how we should feel and act. It's not nature's way.

So as summer slips effortlessly and quietly into autumn and the leaves begin to let go from the branches, we can open up to possibilities to do the same.

Find opportunities to strip things back. Discover that adventures don't have to be far away; the best ones sometimes happen in our minds. Give it a go. The water does nothing but be itself, and in that simplicity we can find ourselves, awakening to life as we find it now.

I'll be up high with my axe this winter again, chipping away at the bodies of water we all really are.

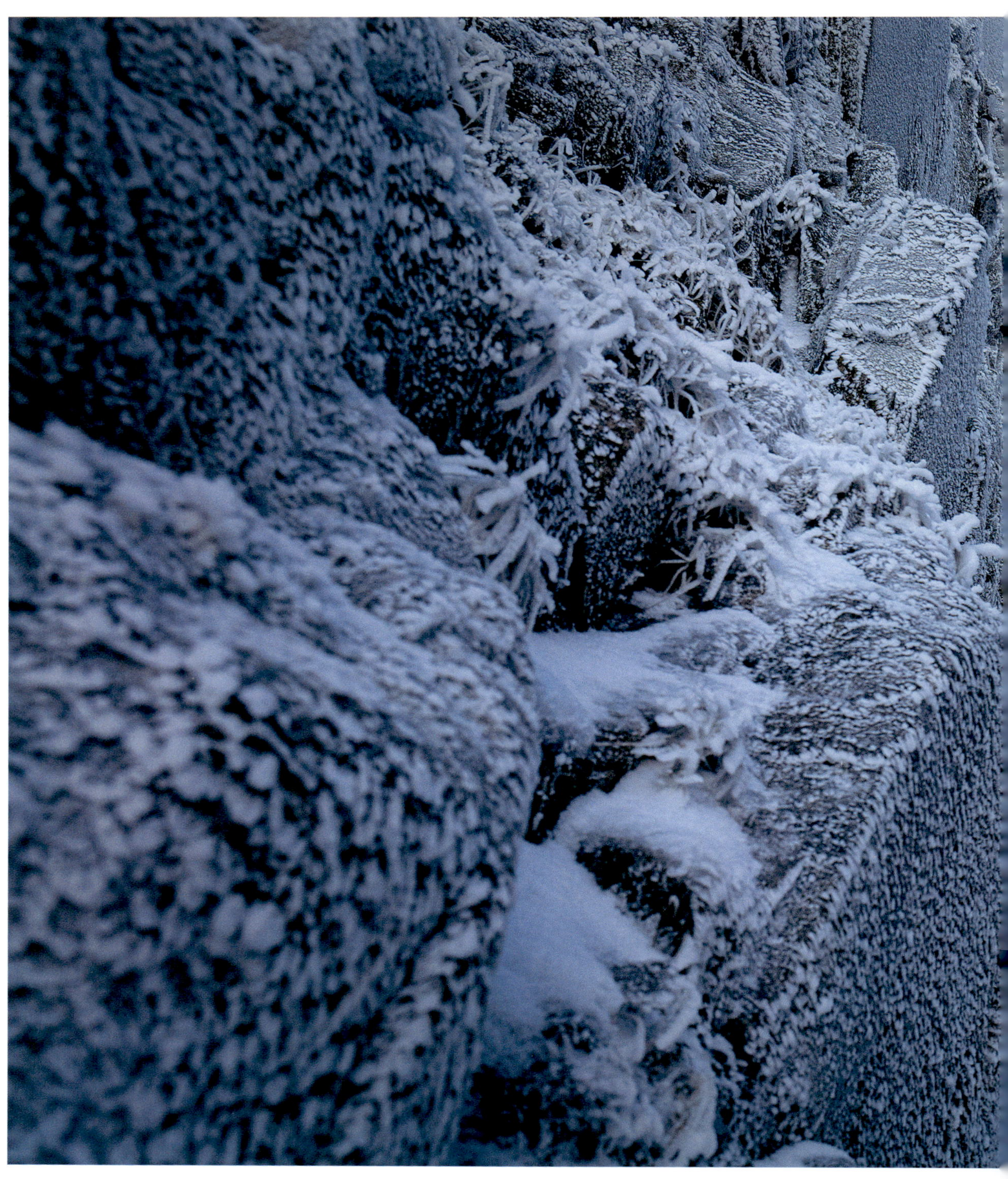

James Austrums on *Window Gully* (III), Great End. The rime on the rocks creates an other-worldly feel to this image.
© Nadir Khan

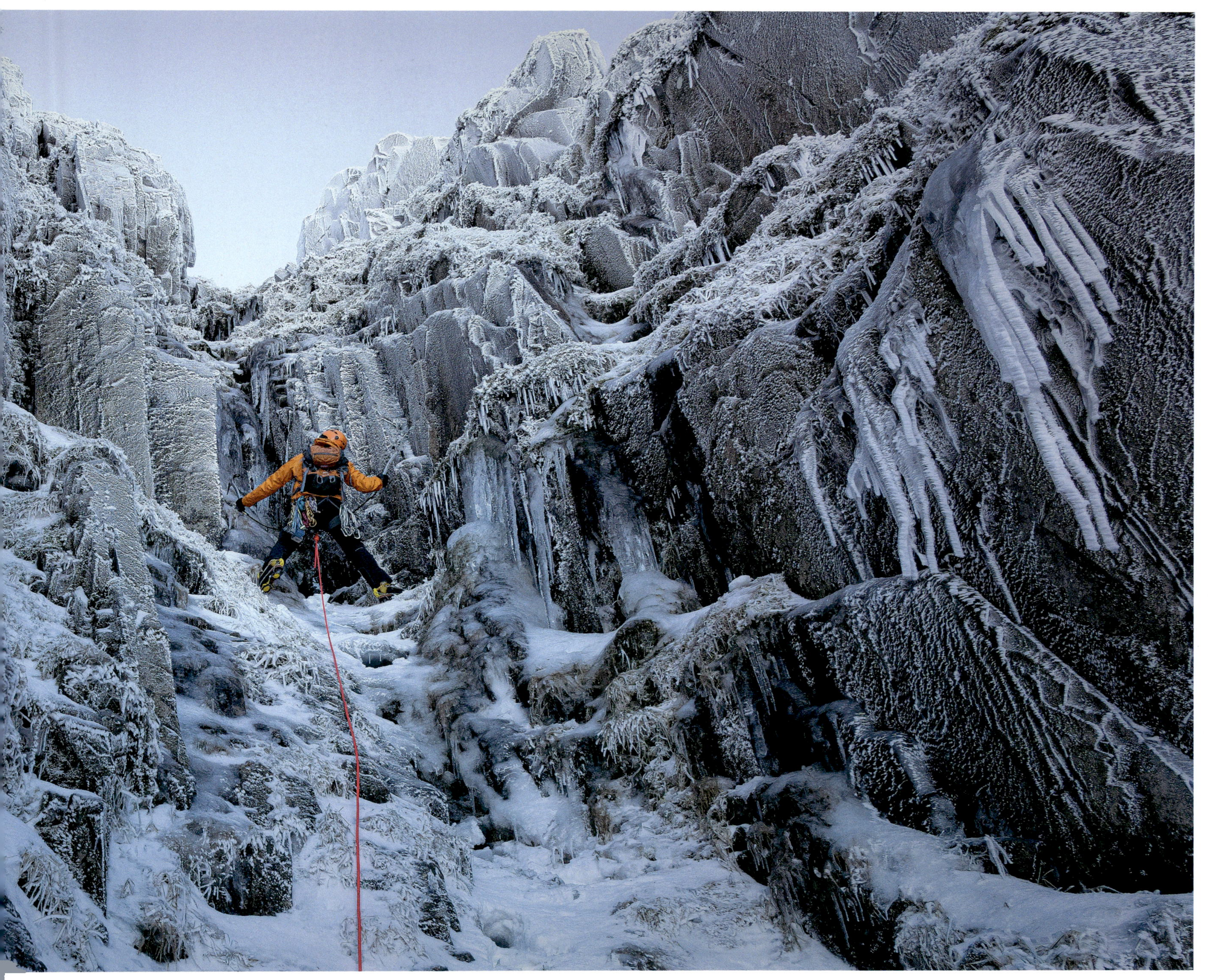

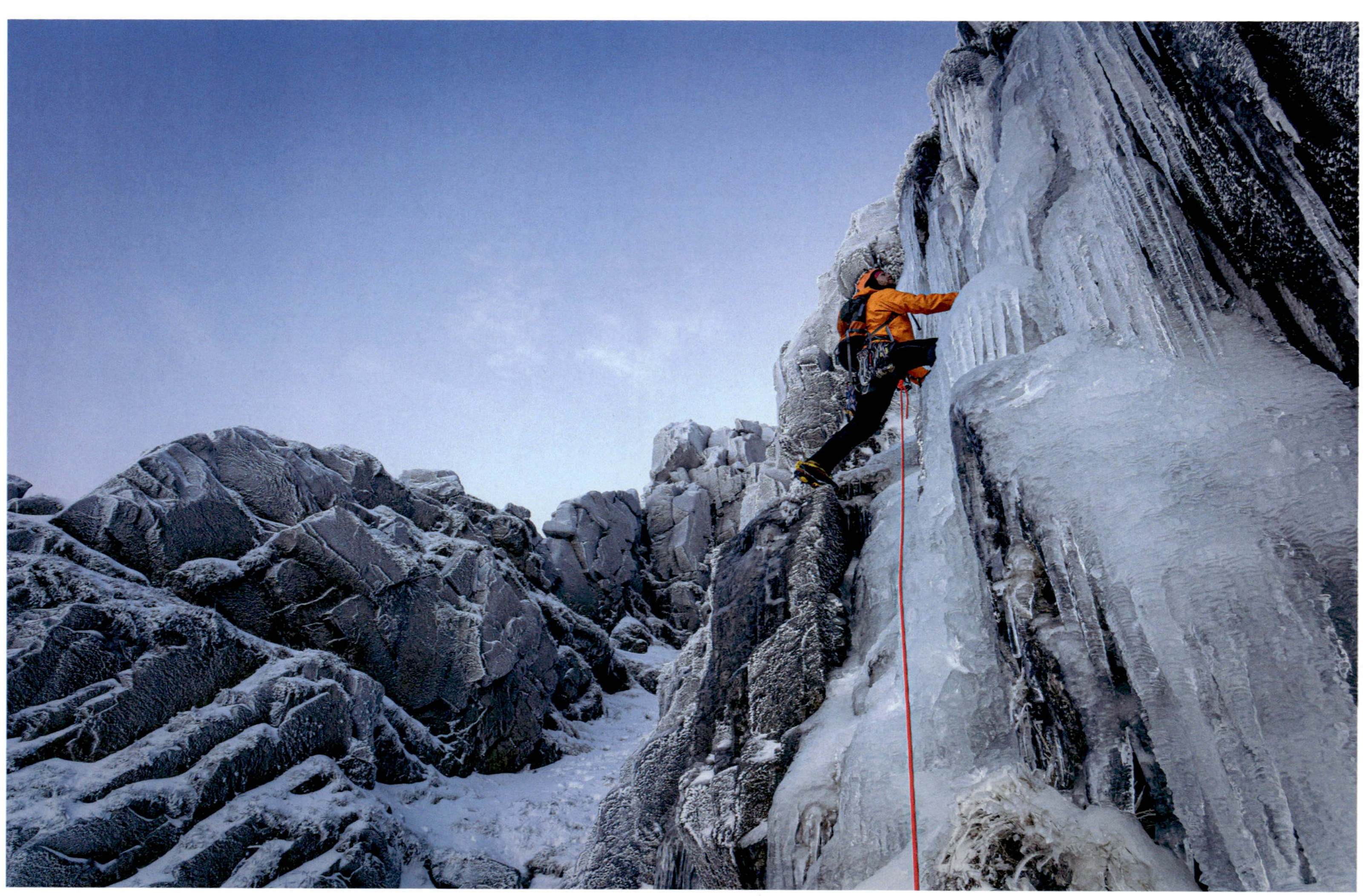

James on the IV ice pitch of *Window Gully*. © Nadir Khan

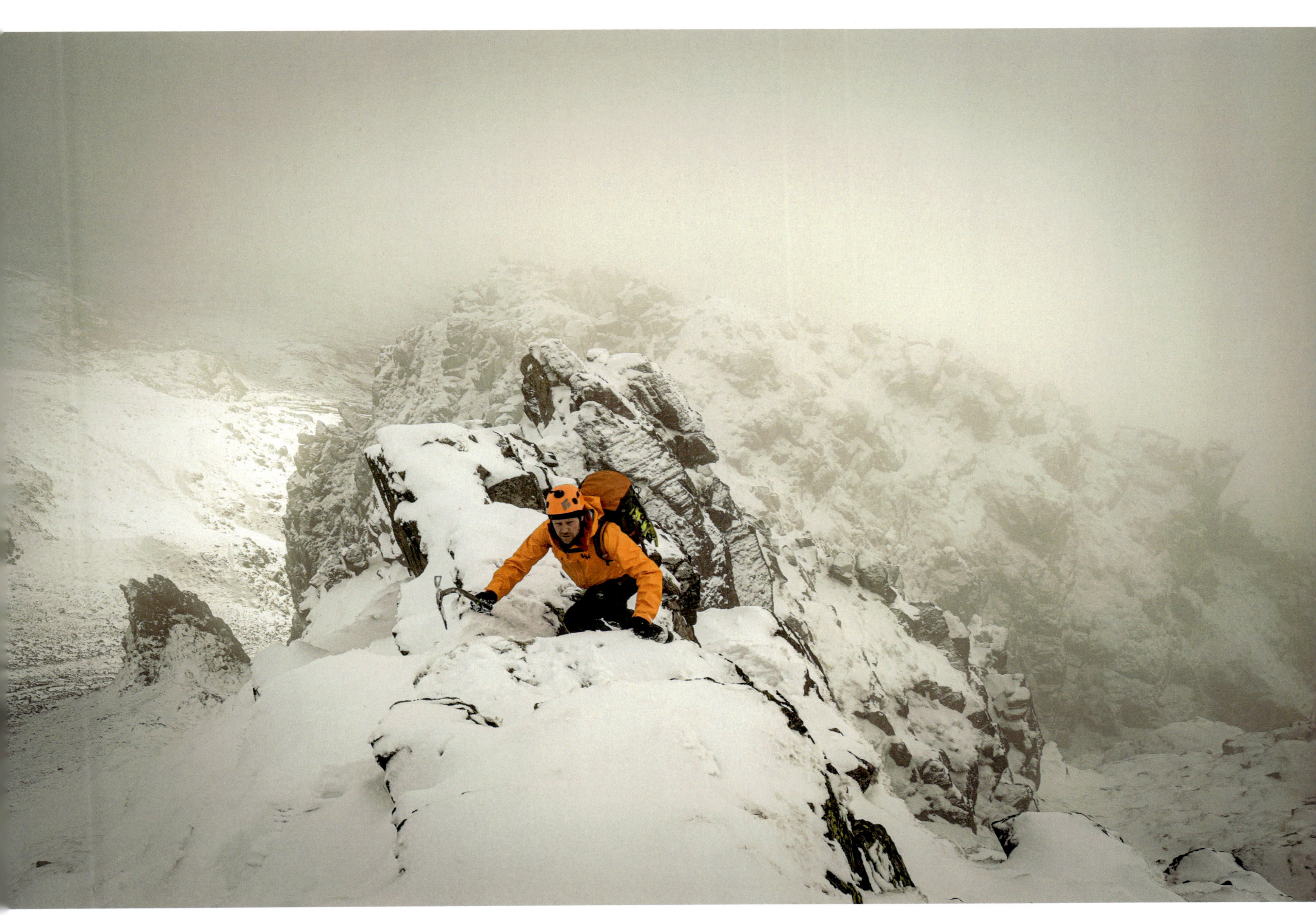

James on the final slopes of Needle Ridge on Great Gable. © Nadir Khan

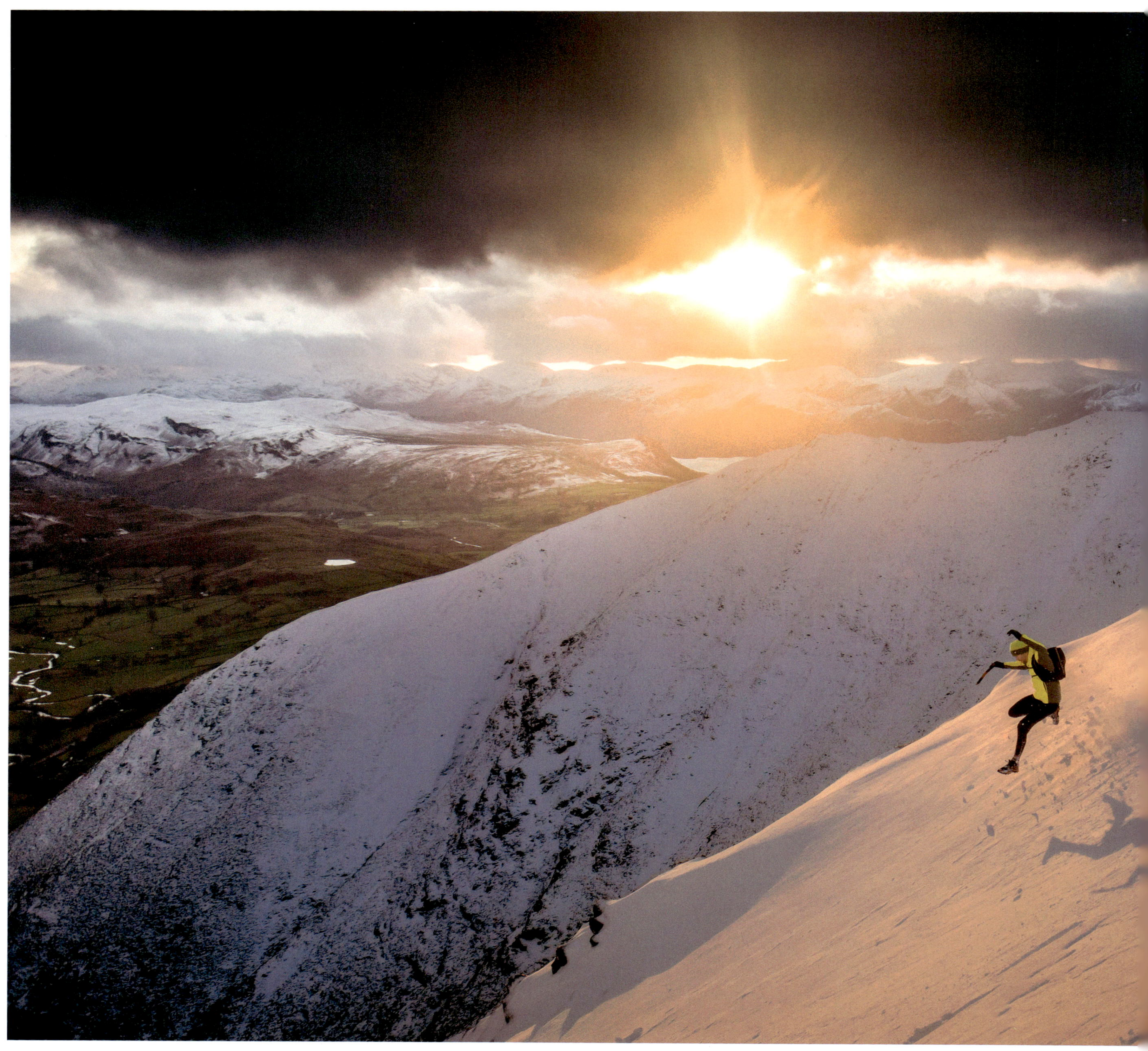

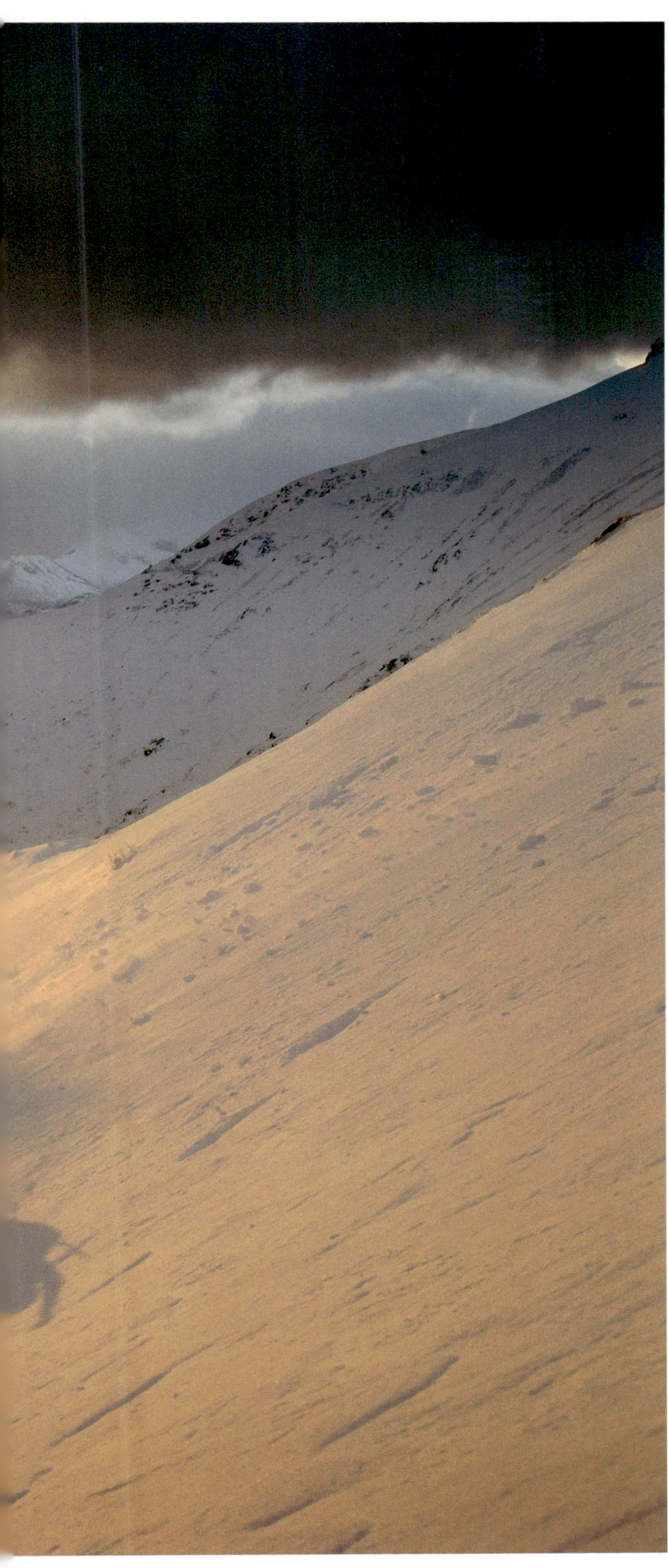

« Dava Waterhouse descending Hall's Fell Ridge, Blencathra. © Tom McNally

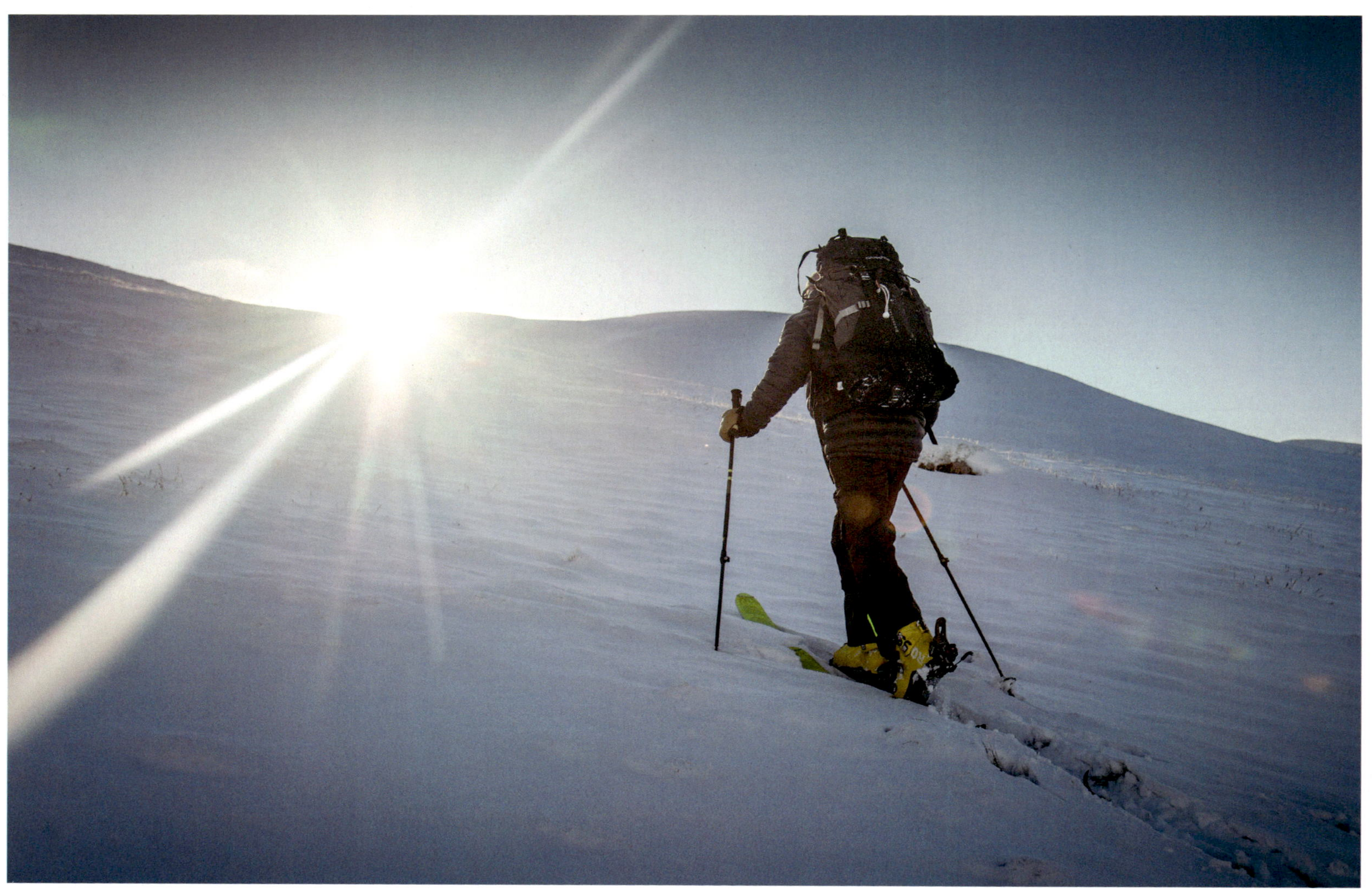

Gordie Oliver skinning up to the Lake District Ski Club on Raise. © Tom McNally

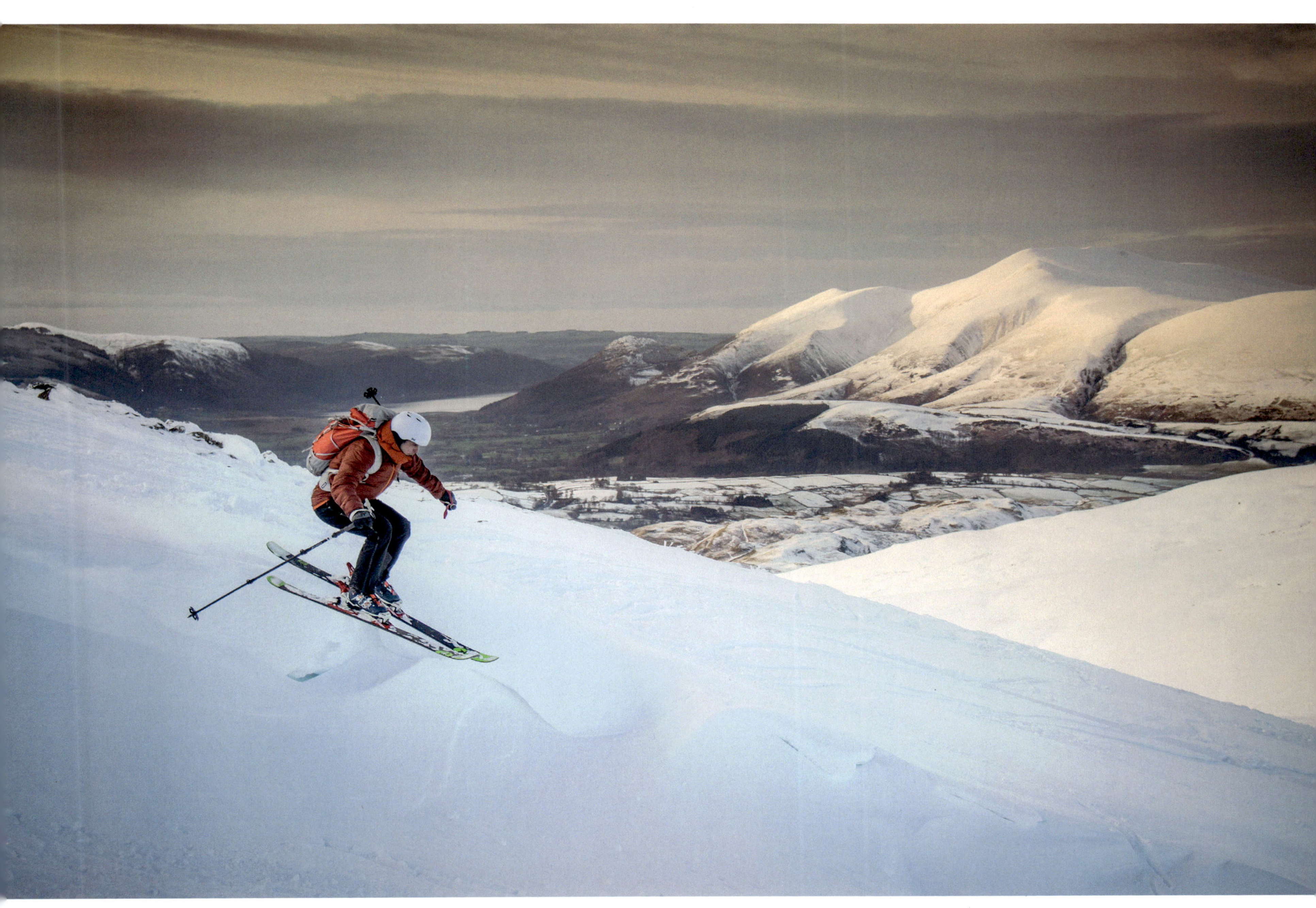

Matt Eaves enjoying one last lap on Raise. © Tom McNally

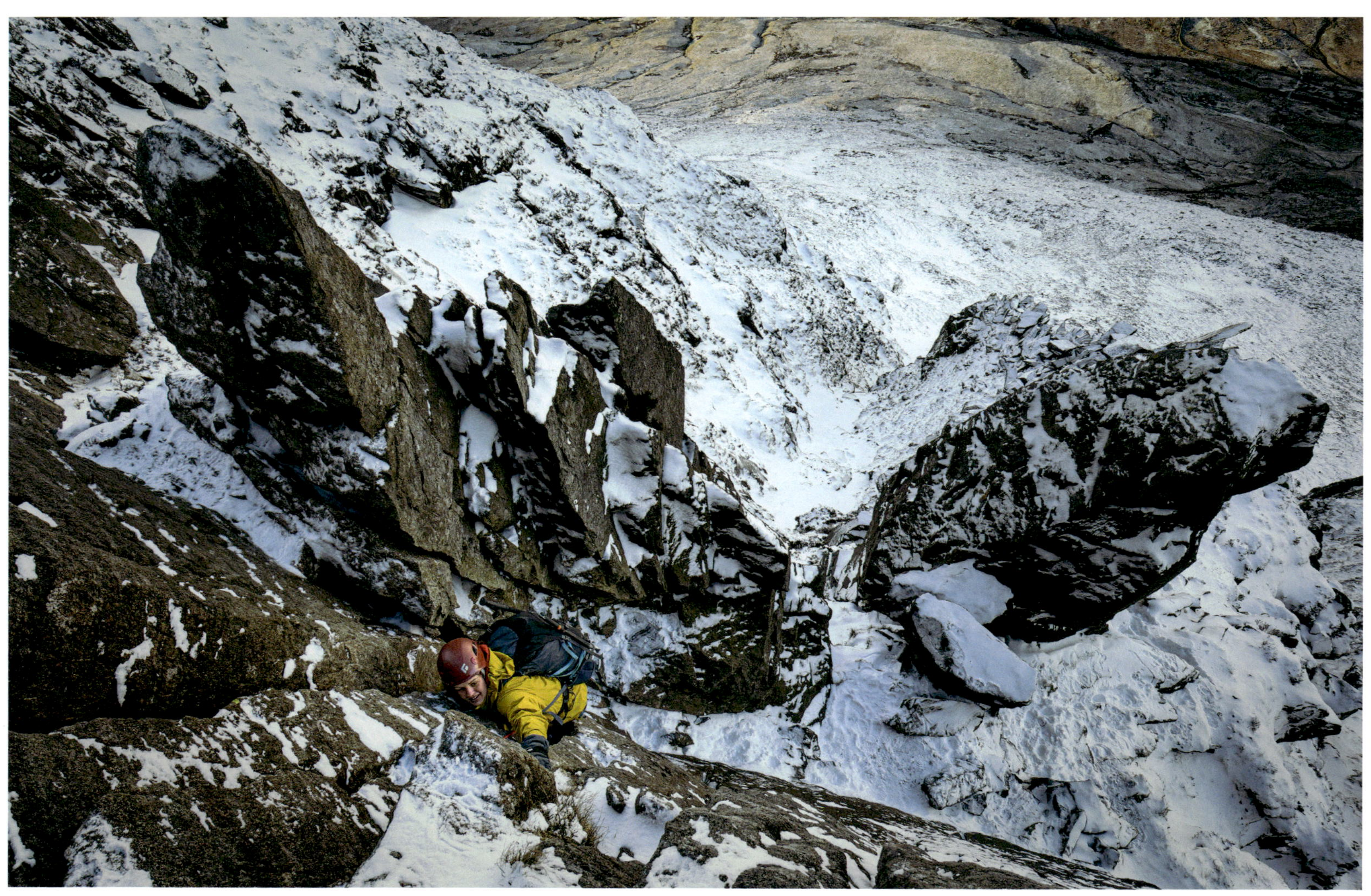

Chelsey Robinson (left) and Anna Sharpe on Pinnacle Ridge, St Sunday Crag. © Nadir Khan

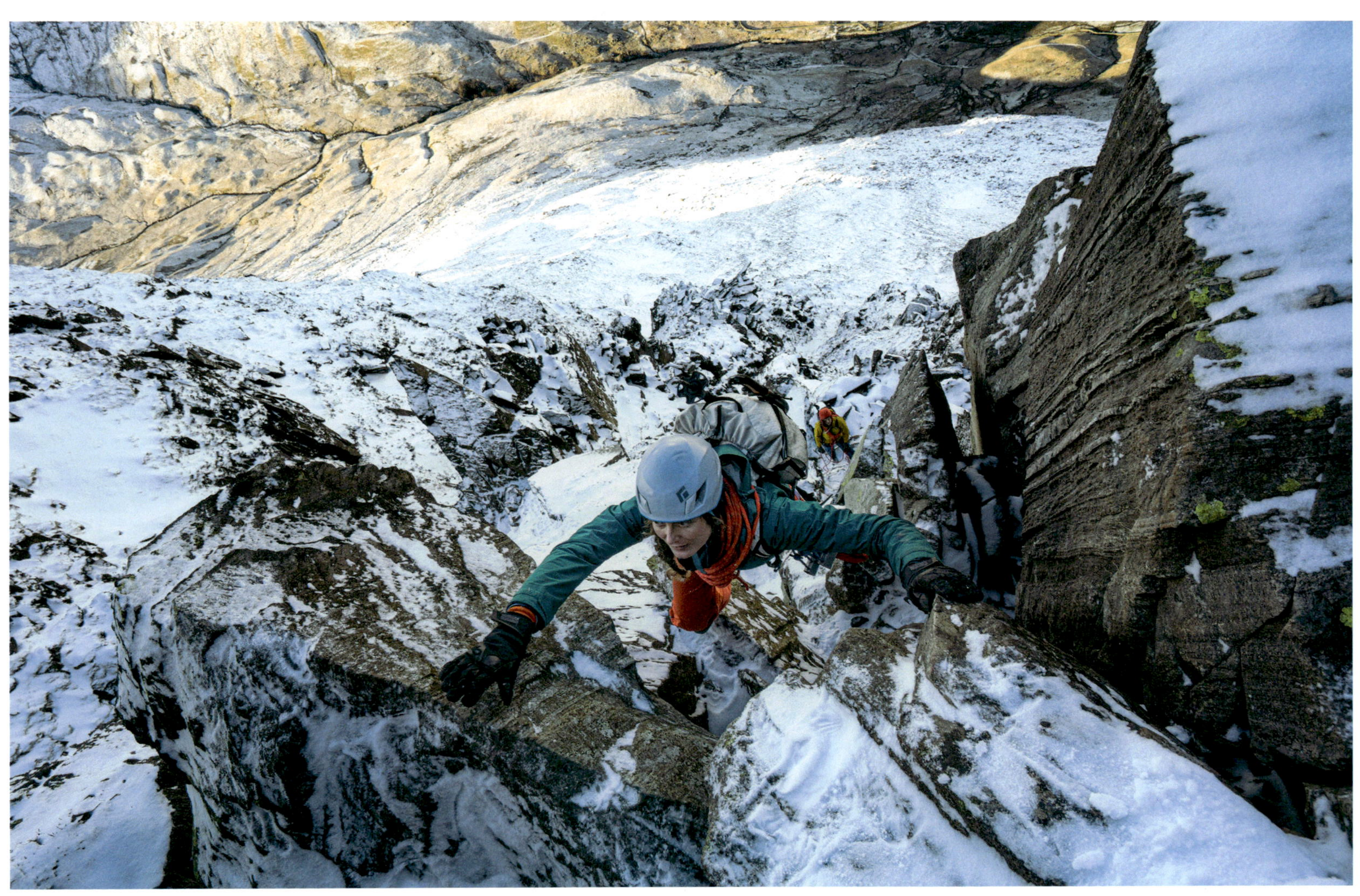

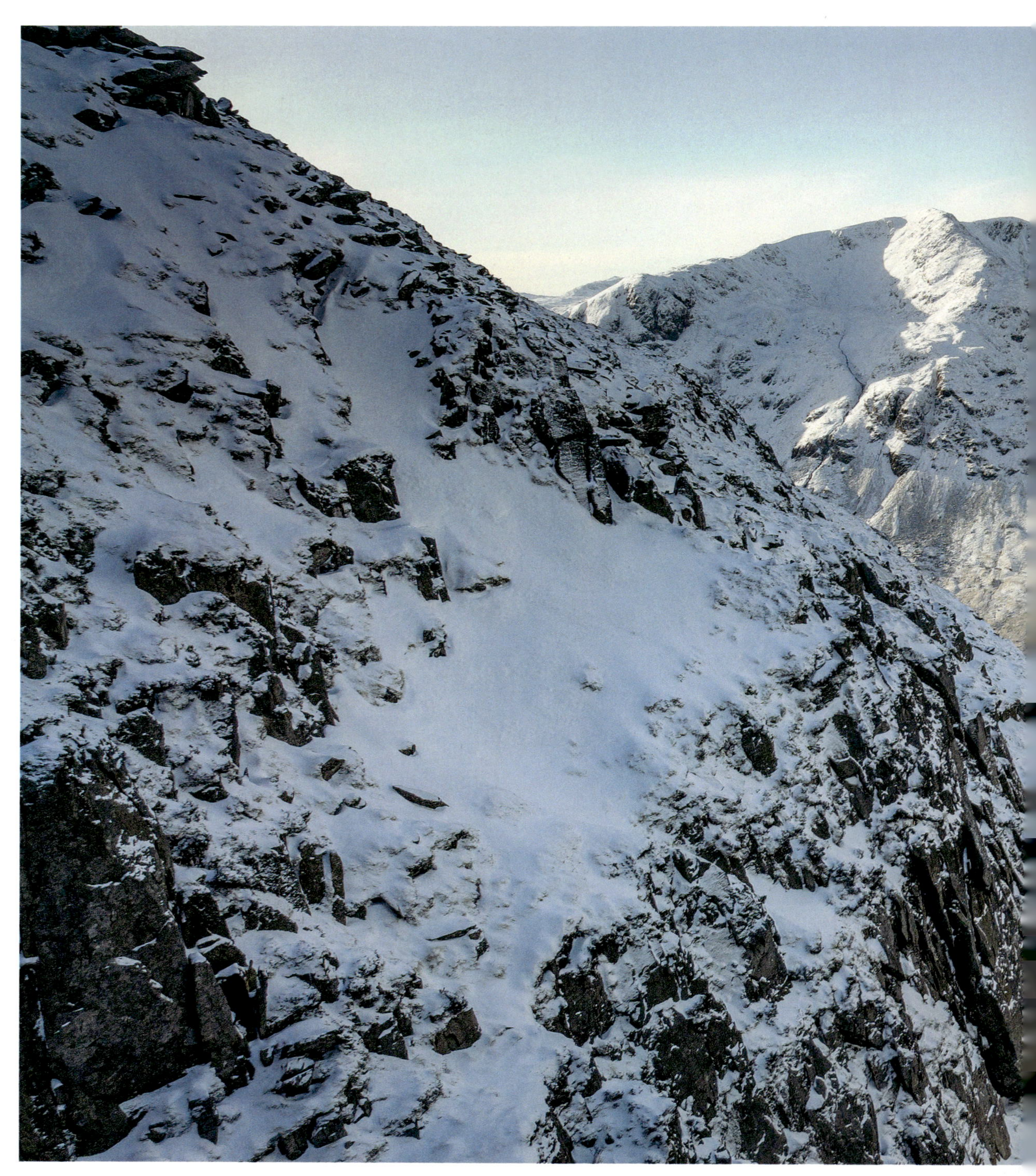

Anna and Chelsey on the final pinnacle of Pinnacle Ridge
on a bluebird February day. © Nadir Khan »

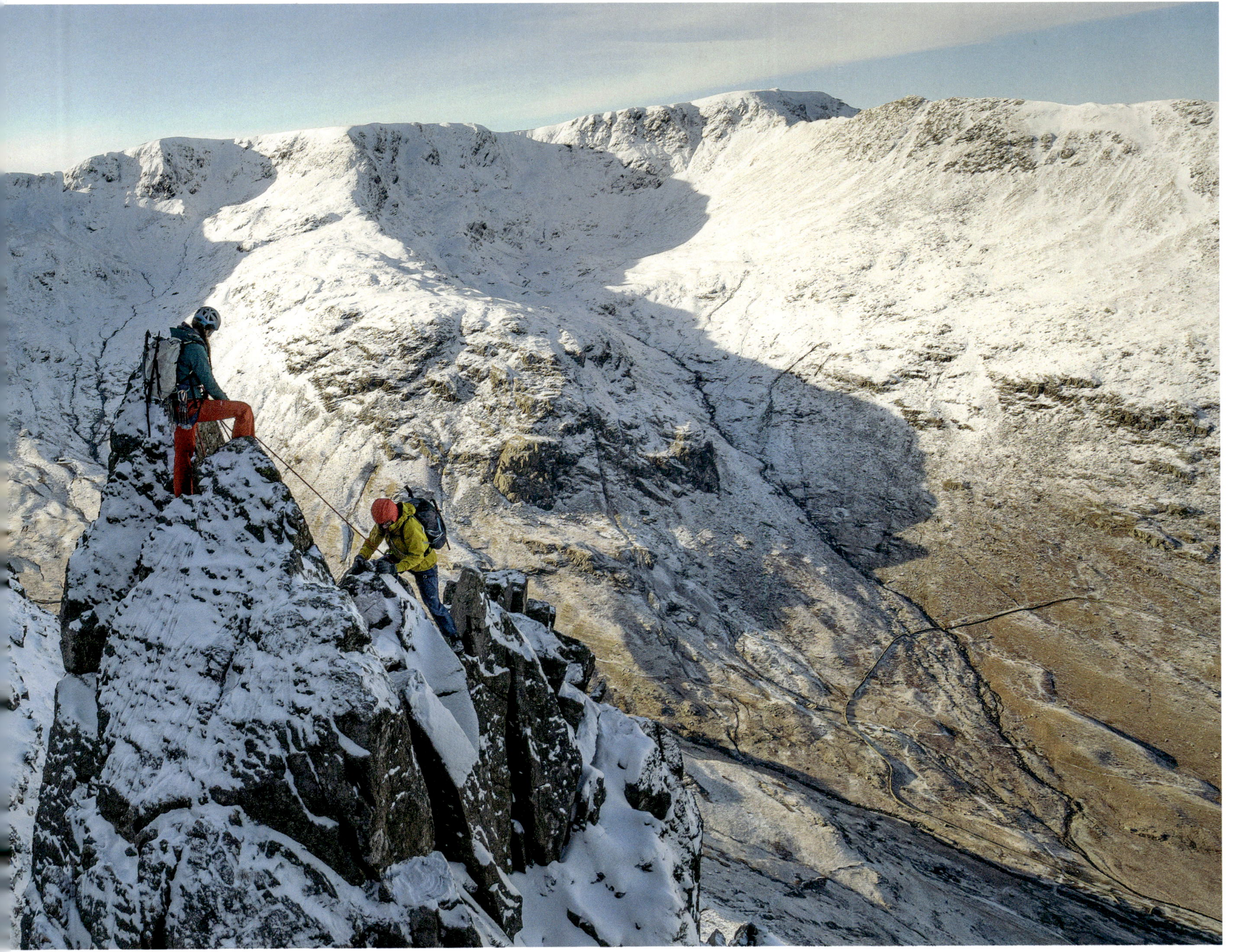

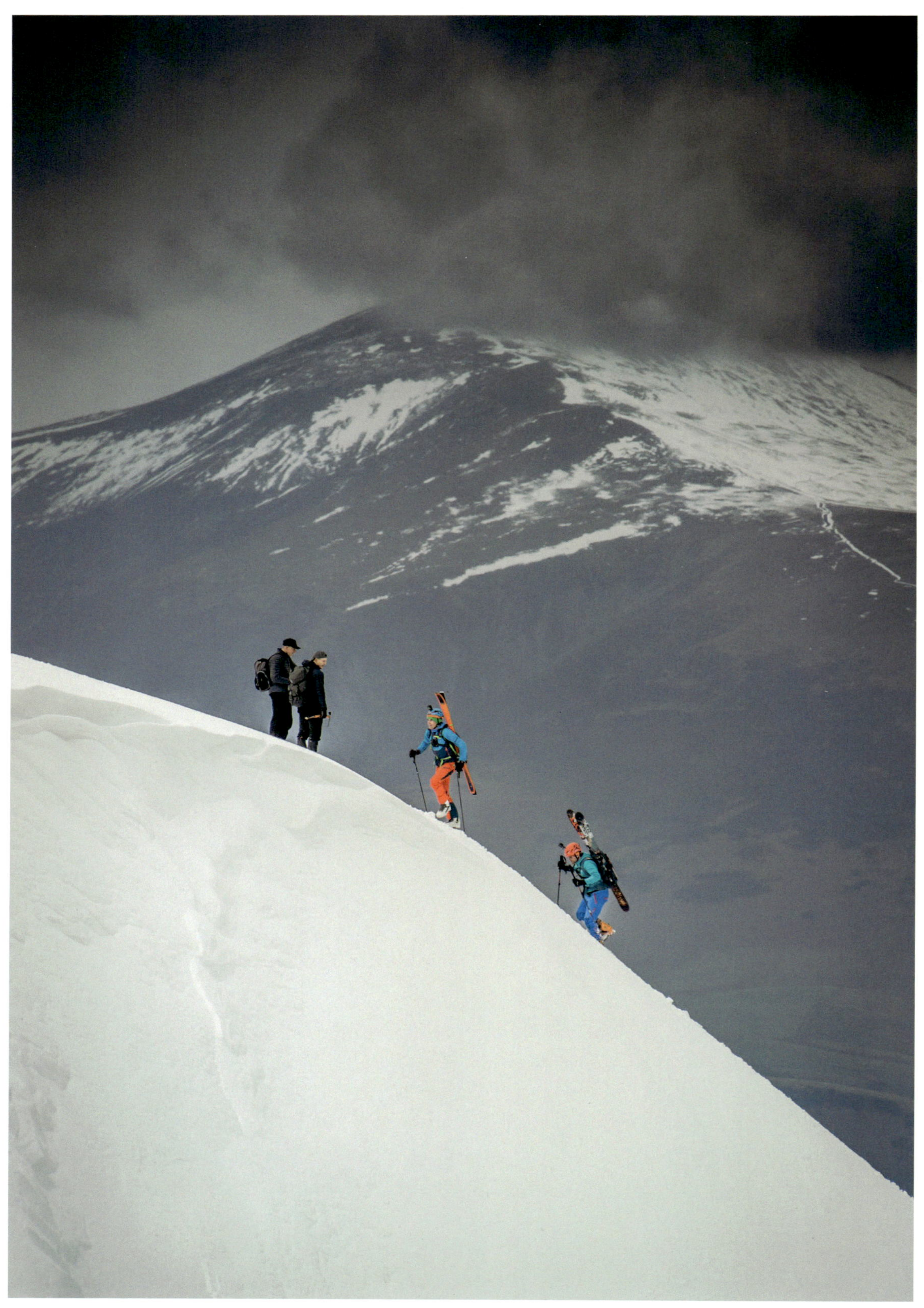

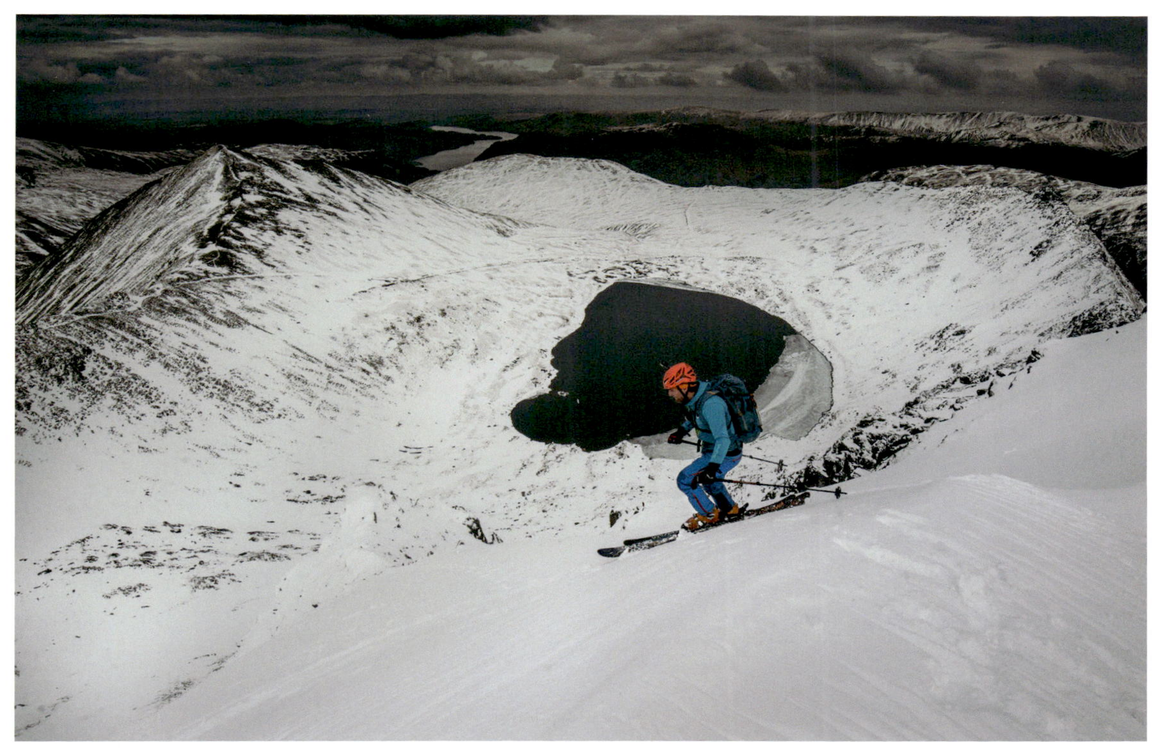

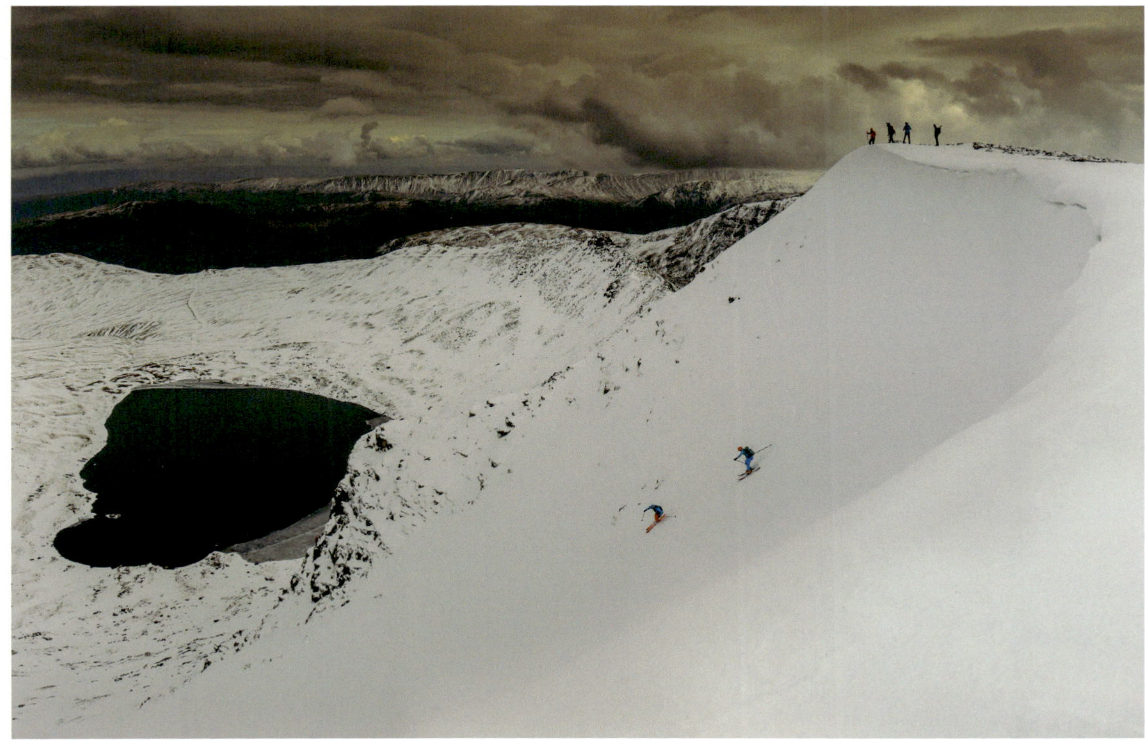

Paddy and Charles descend the Red Tarn headwall, Helvellyn. © Tom McNally

« Charles Sproson and Paddy Cave near the top of Swirral Edge, Helvellyn. © Tom McNally

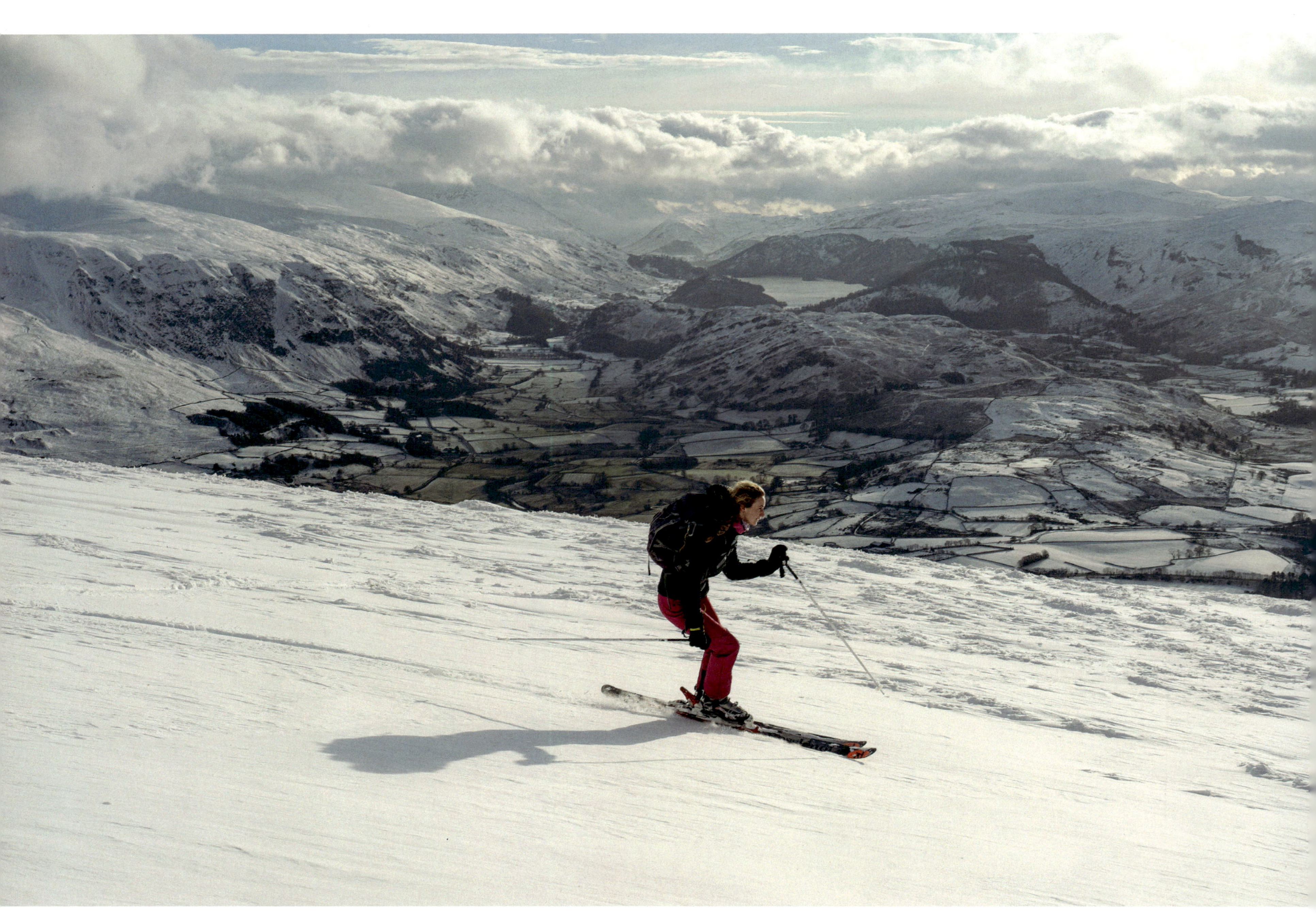
Ski-touring on Blencathra. © Nadir Khan

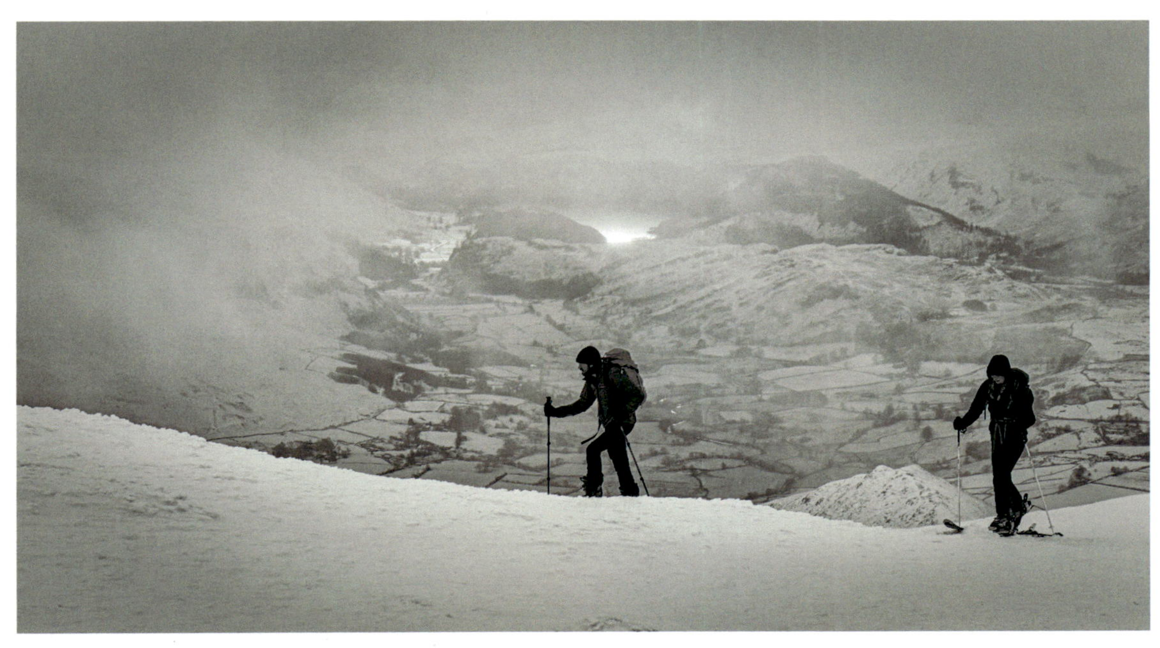

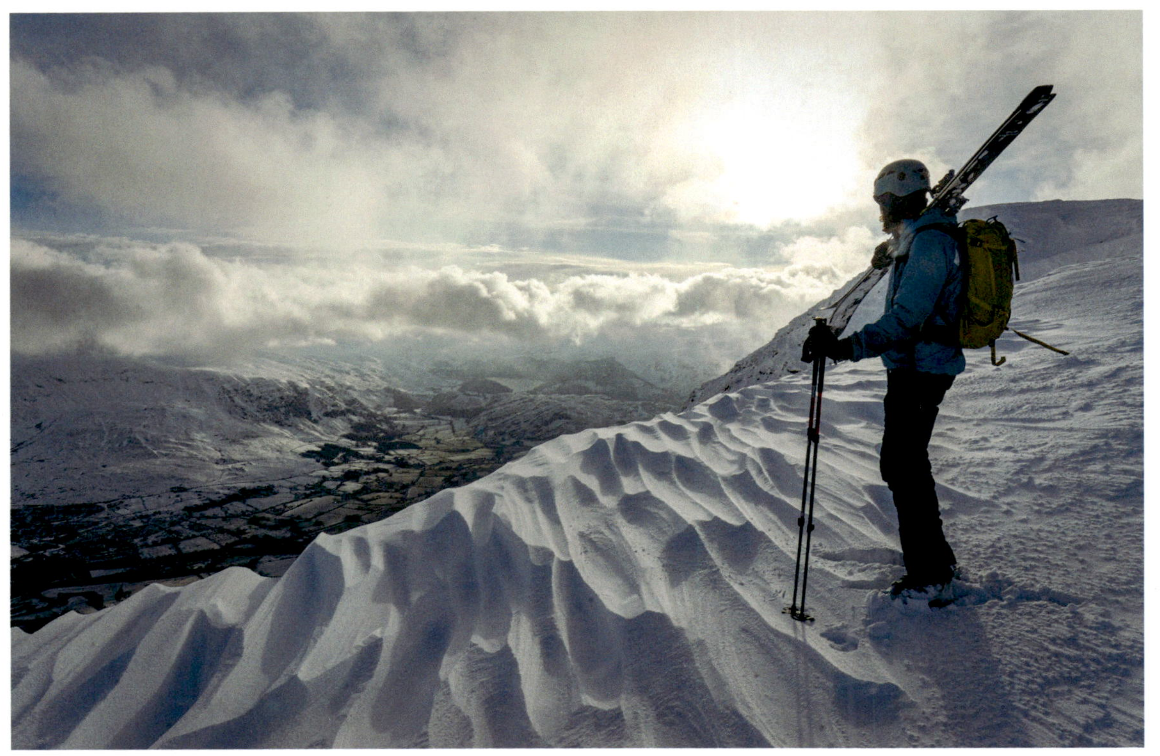

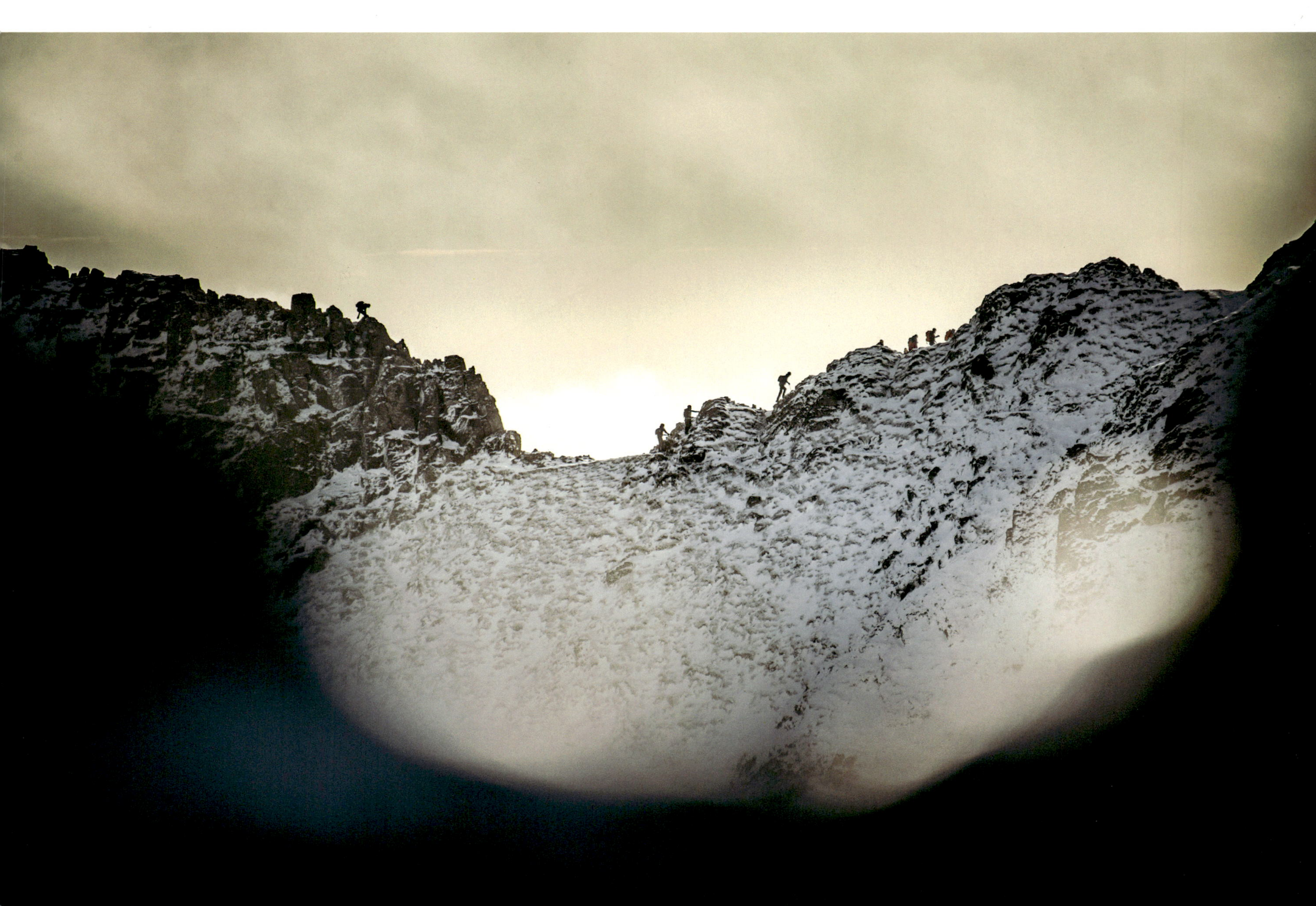

A procession of walkers negotiate Striding Edge, Helvellyn. © Tom McNally

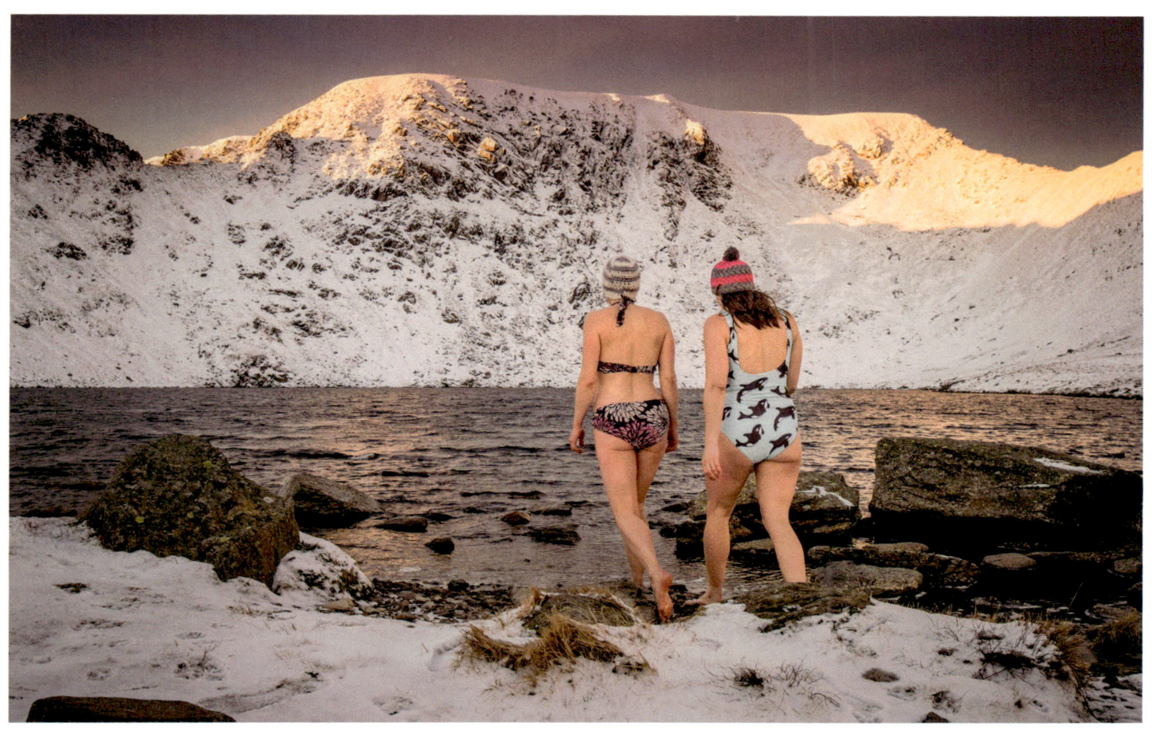

Joanne Richardson and Christine Davies take a refreshing morning dip in Red Tarn, Helvellyn. © Tom McNally

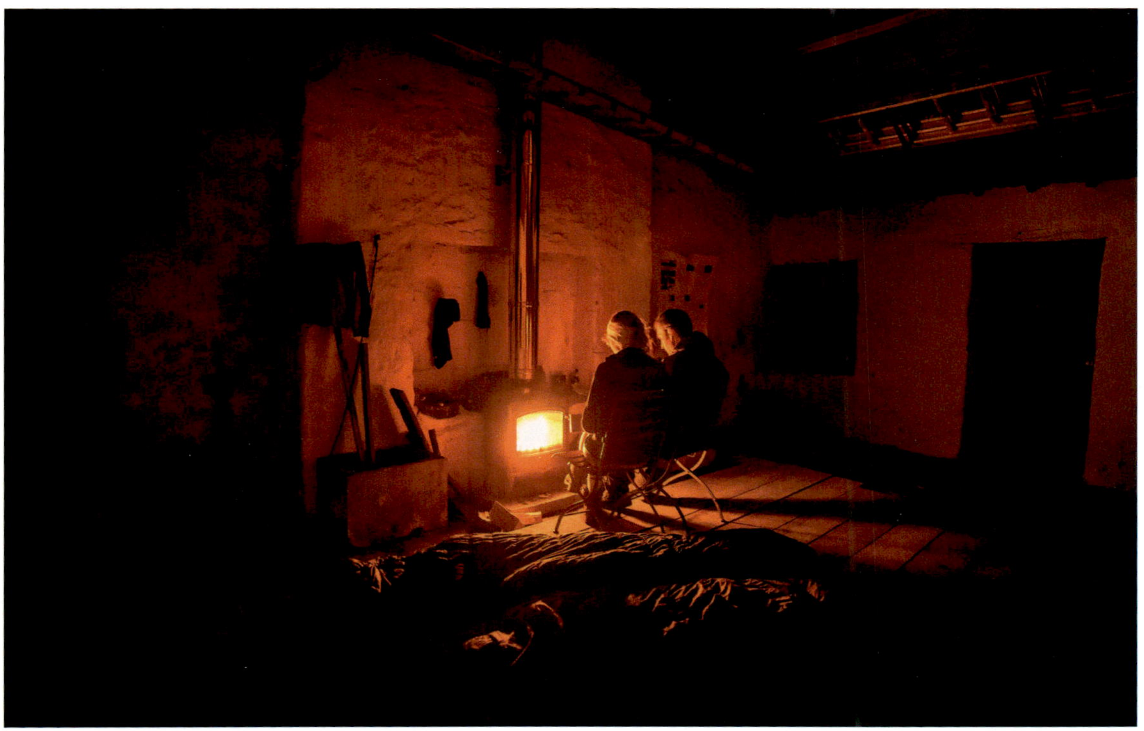

Tom and Louise McNally enjoy a cosy evening in Dubs Hut near Honister (image captured with a tripod and self-timer). © Tom McNally

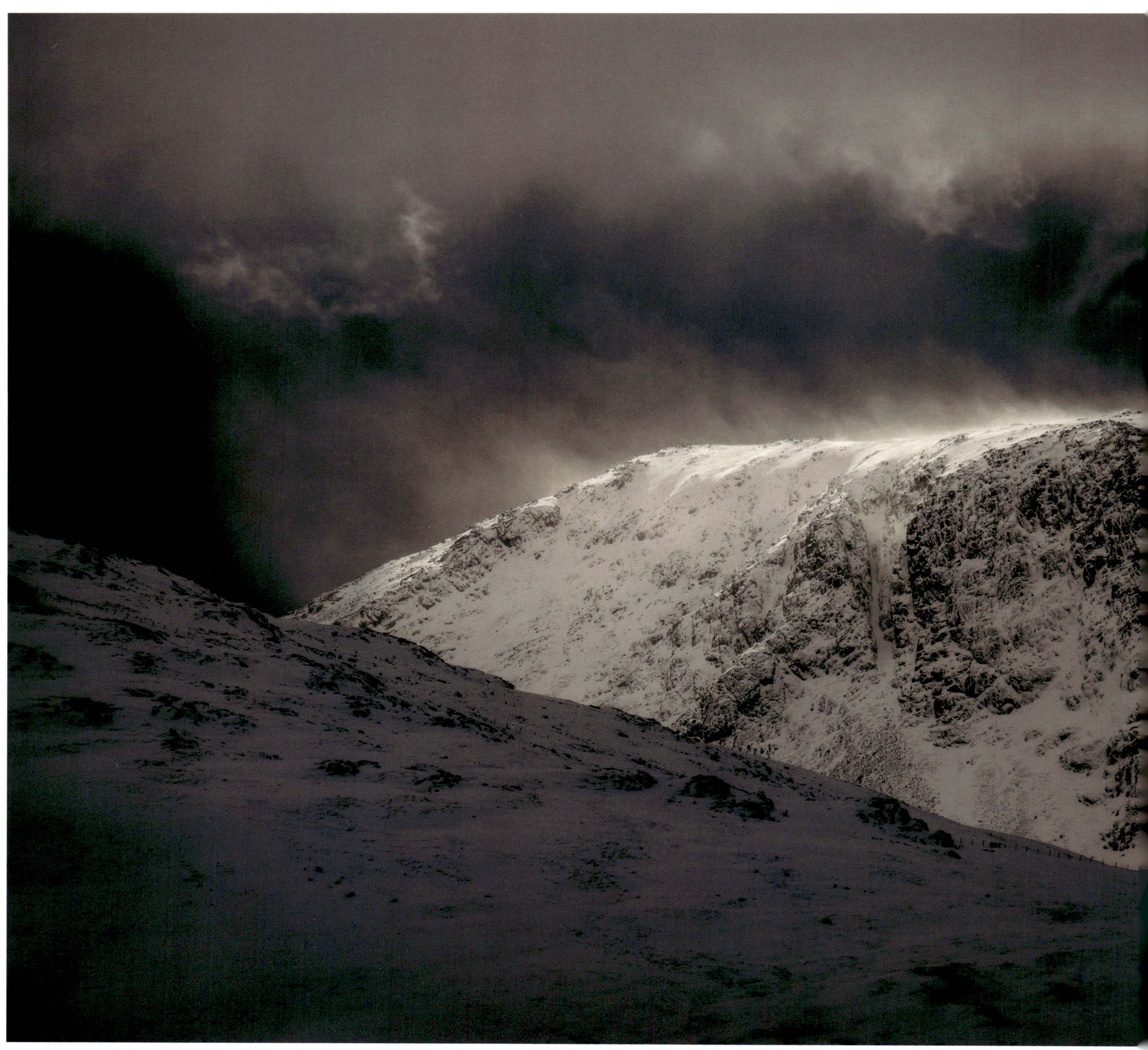

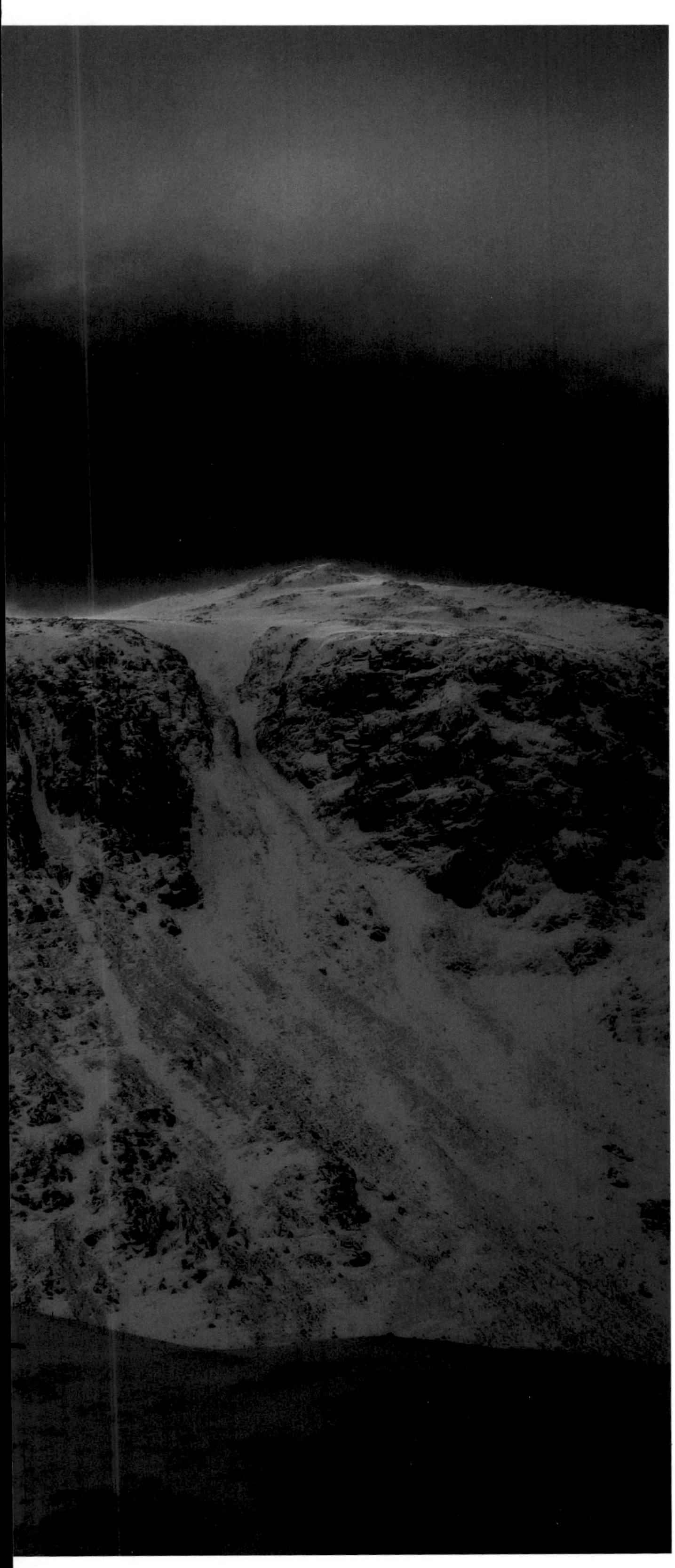
« Full winter conditions on Kirk Fell. © Tom McNally

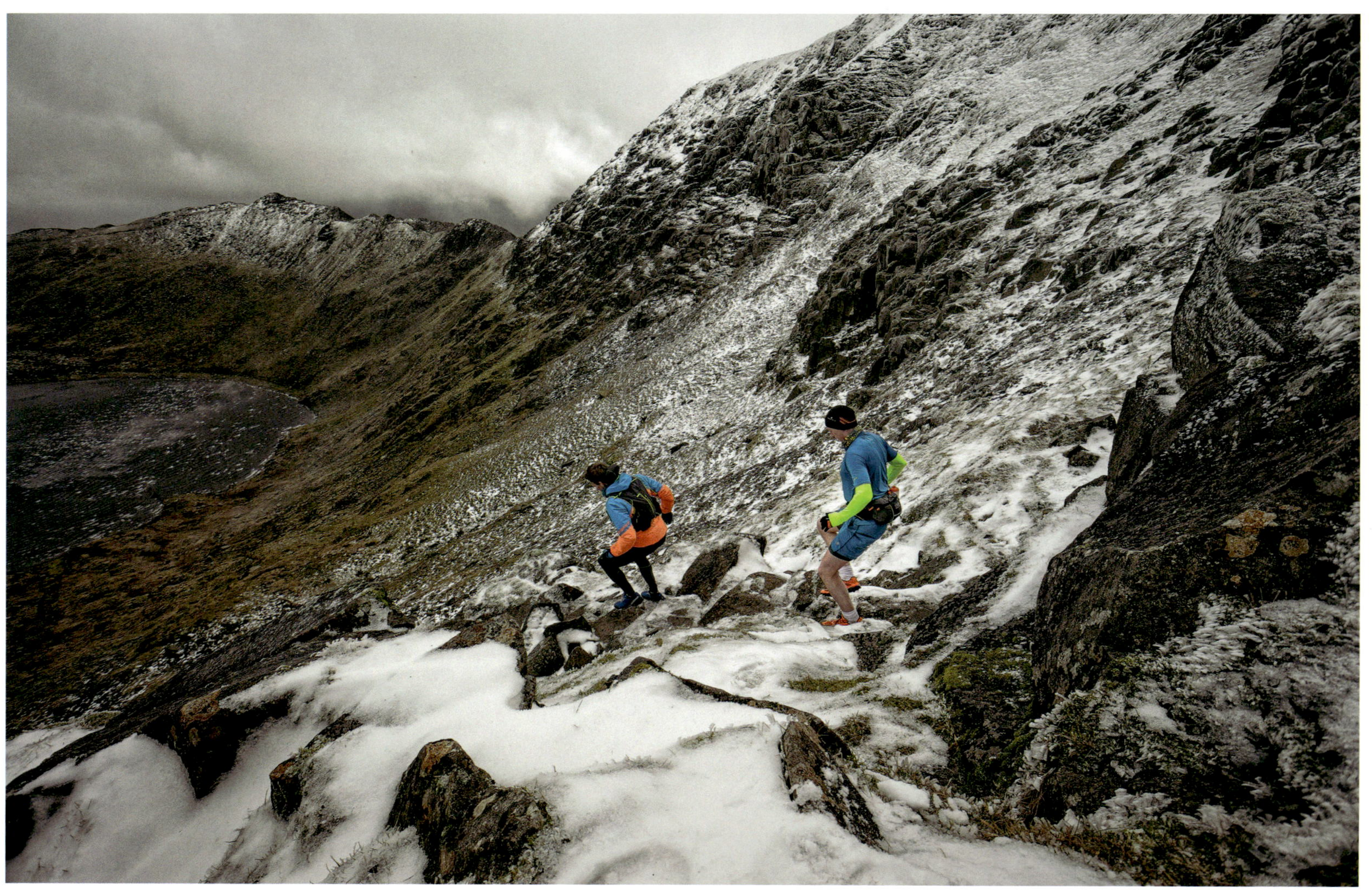

Runners on Swirral Edge, Helvellyn. © Nadir Khan

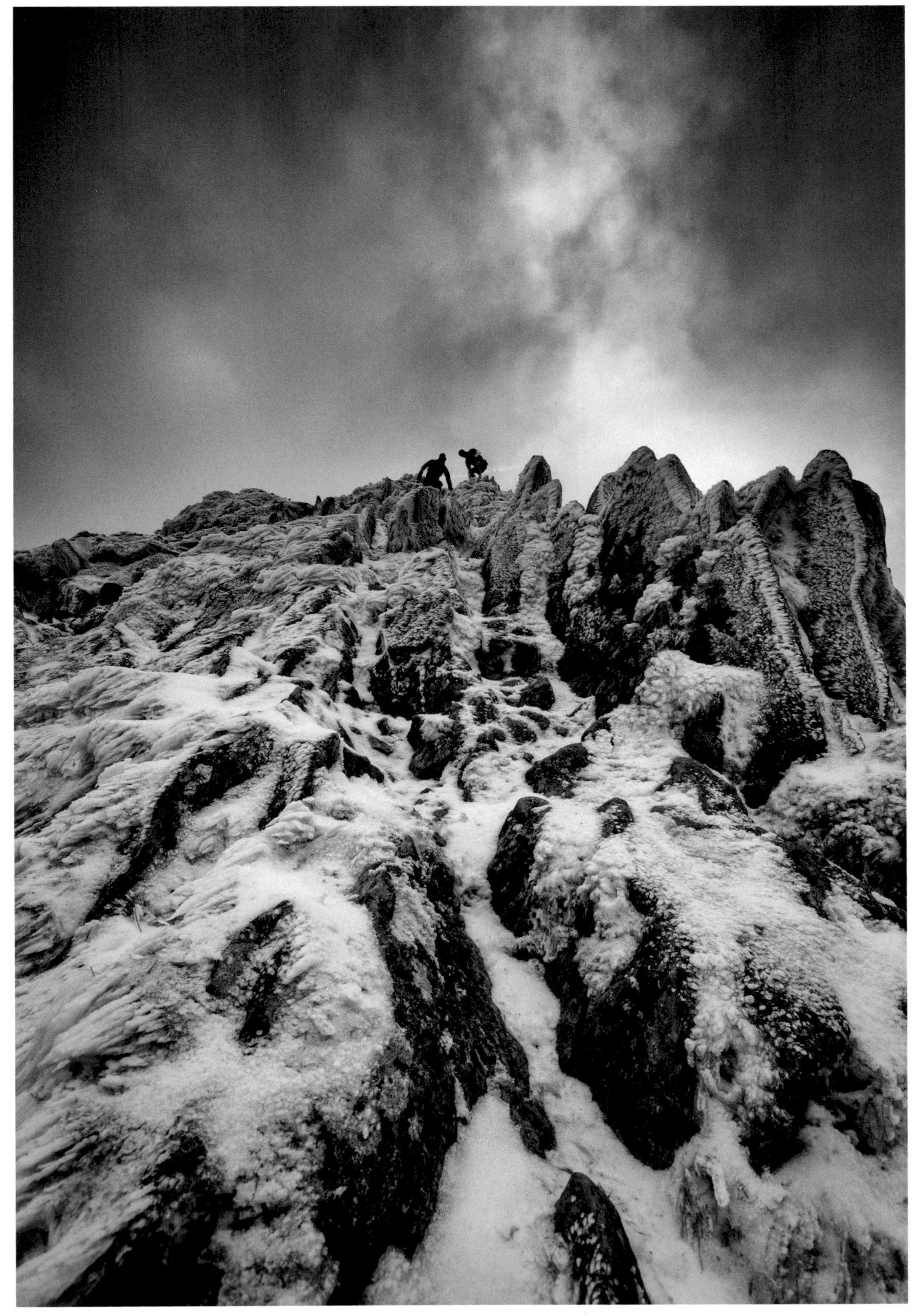

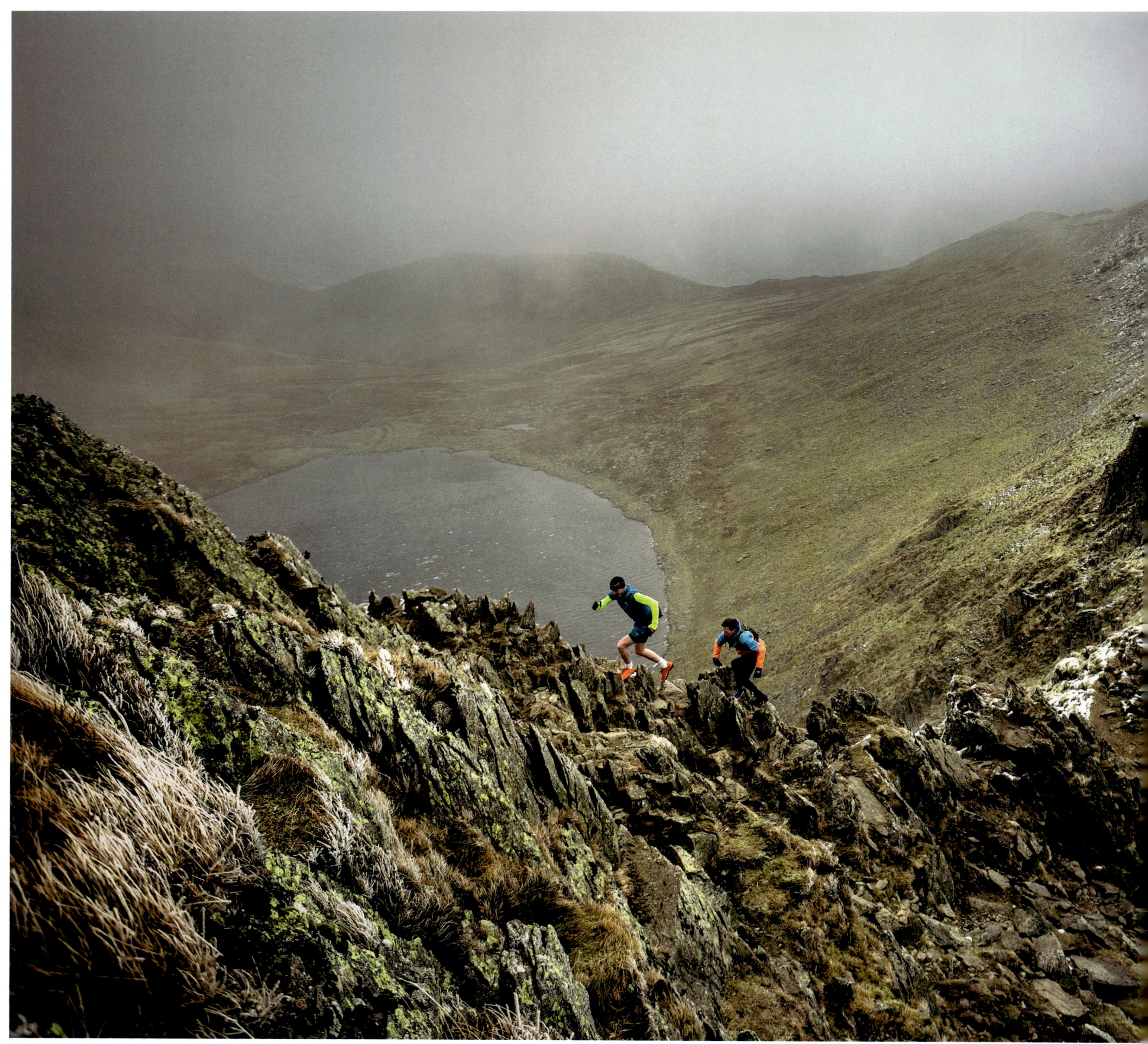

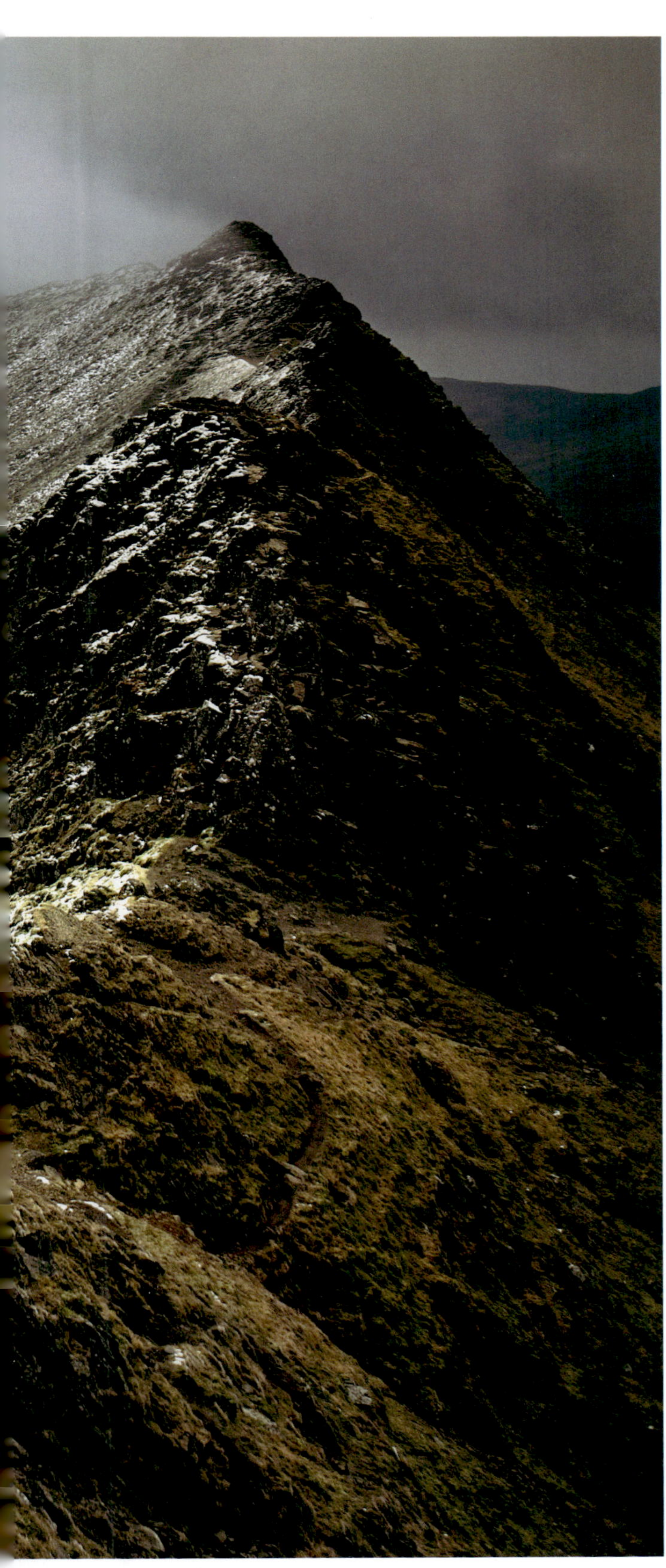

« Matty Jackman and Neil Davies on Striding Edge, Helvellyn, in early December
as the first snows of winter make their appearance. © Nadir Khan

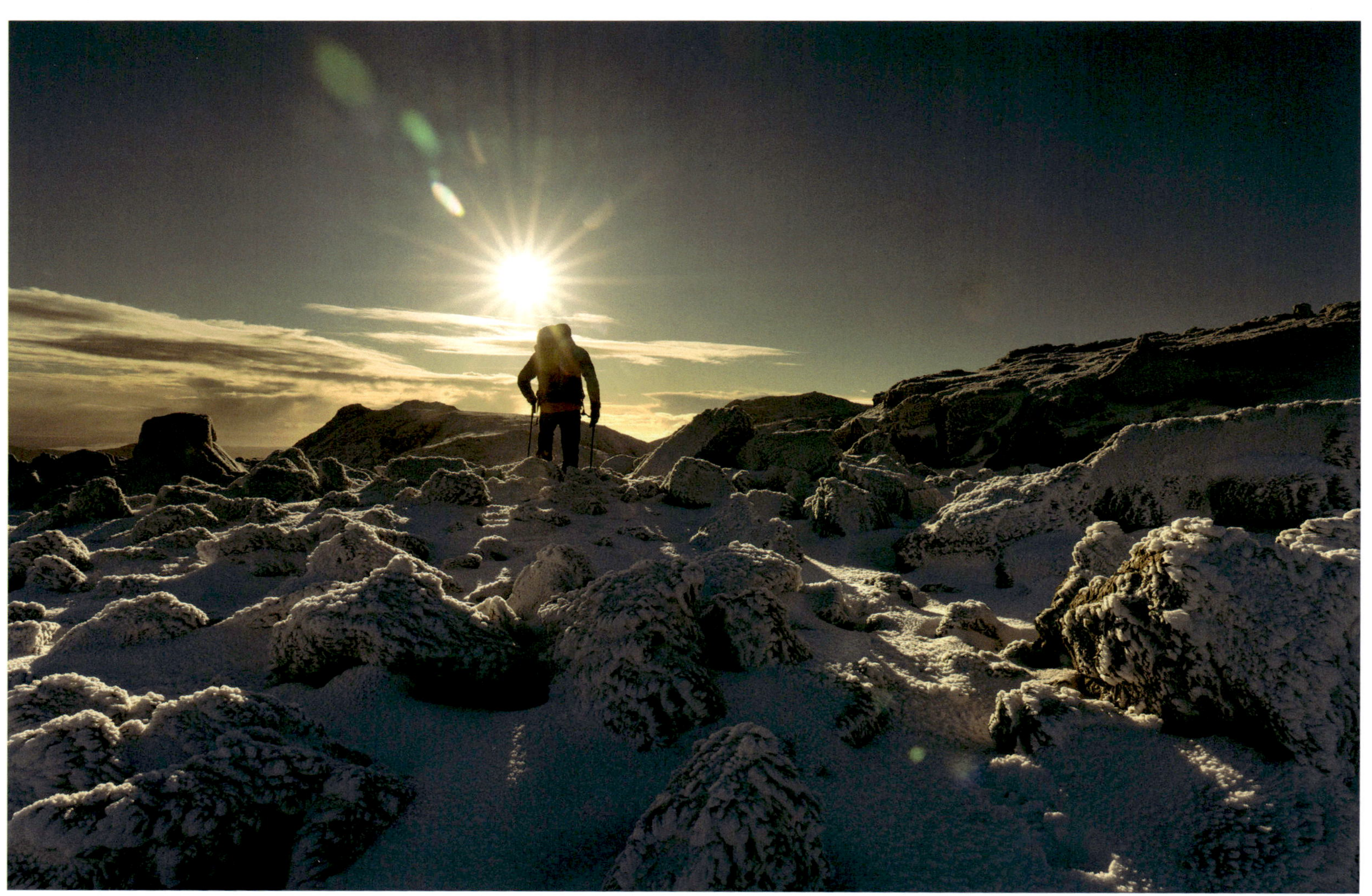
James Austrums on the summit of Great End. © Nadir Khan

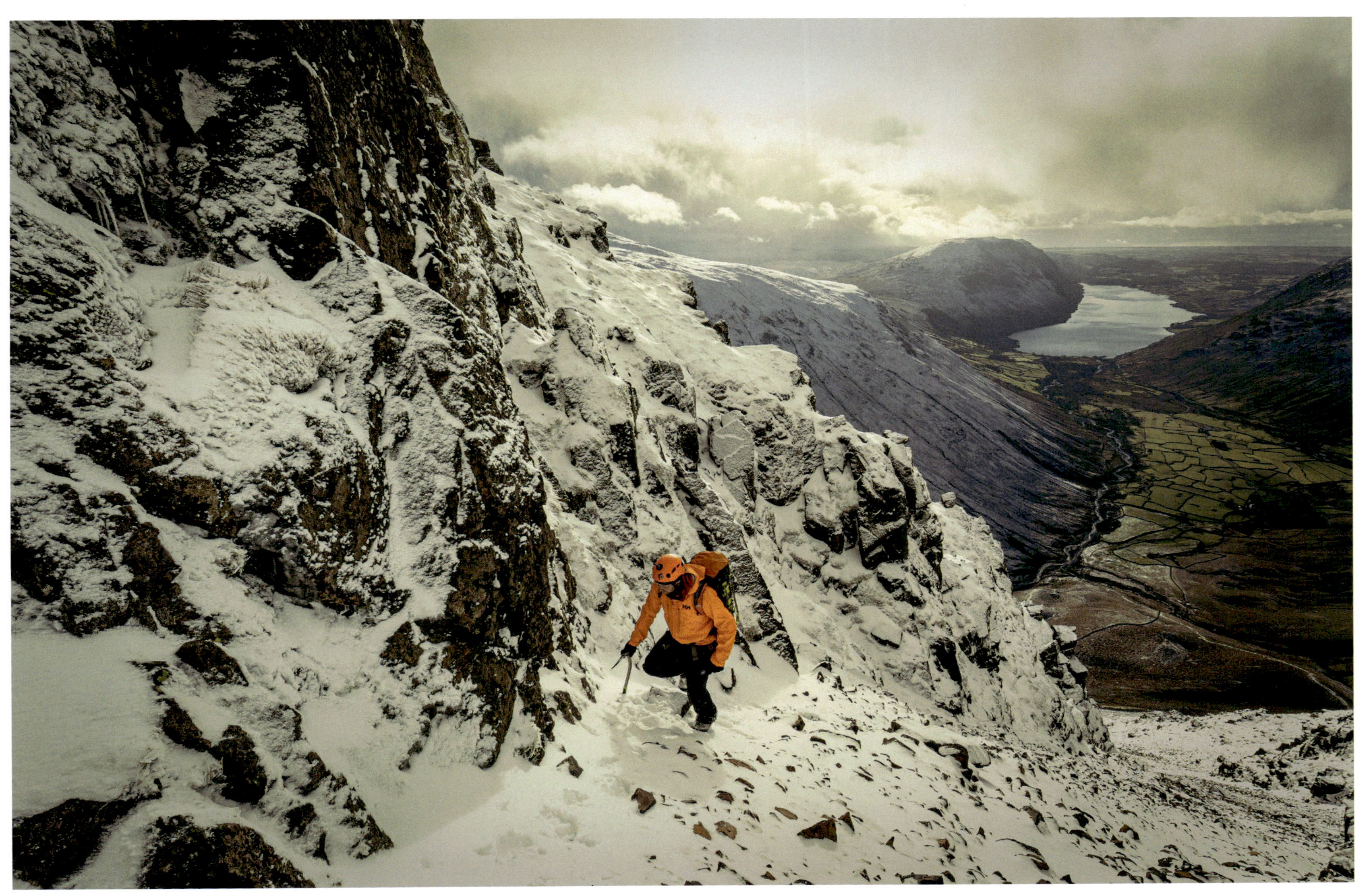

Approaching Great Gable from Wasdale Head, Wast Water beyond. © Nadir Khan

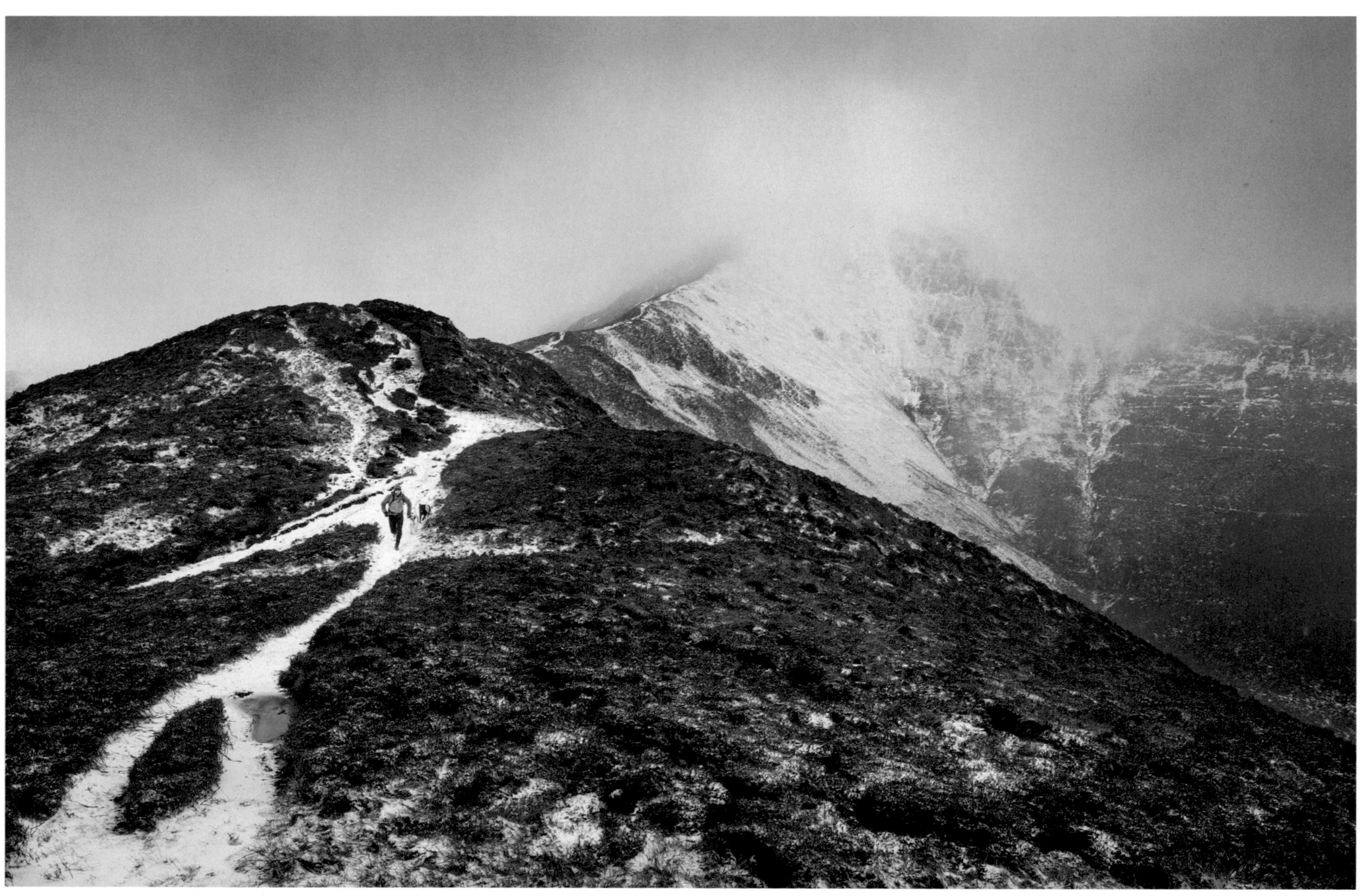

Matt Le Voi descending from Grisedale Pike. © Tom McNally

Justin Kyme-Oliver enjoying the via ferrata at Honister Slate Mine. © Tom McNally »

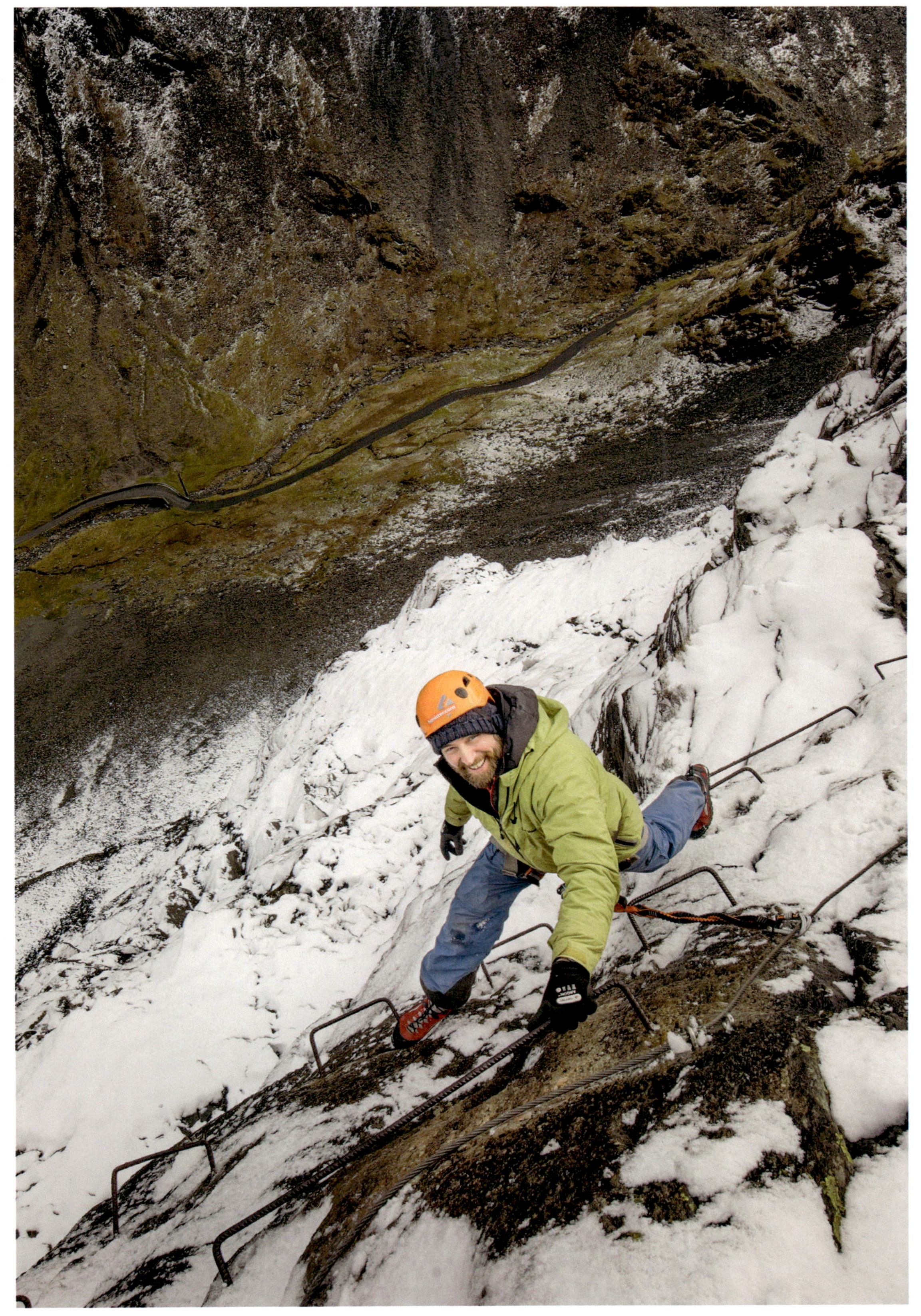

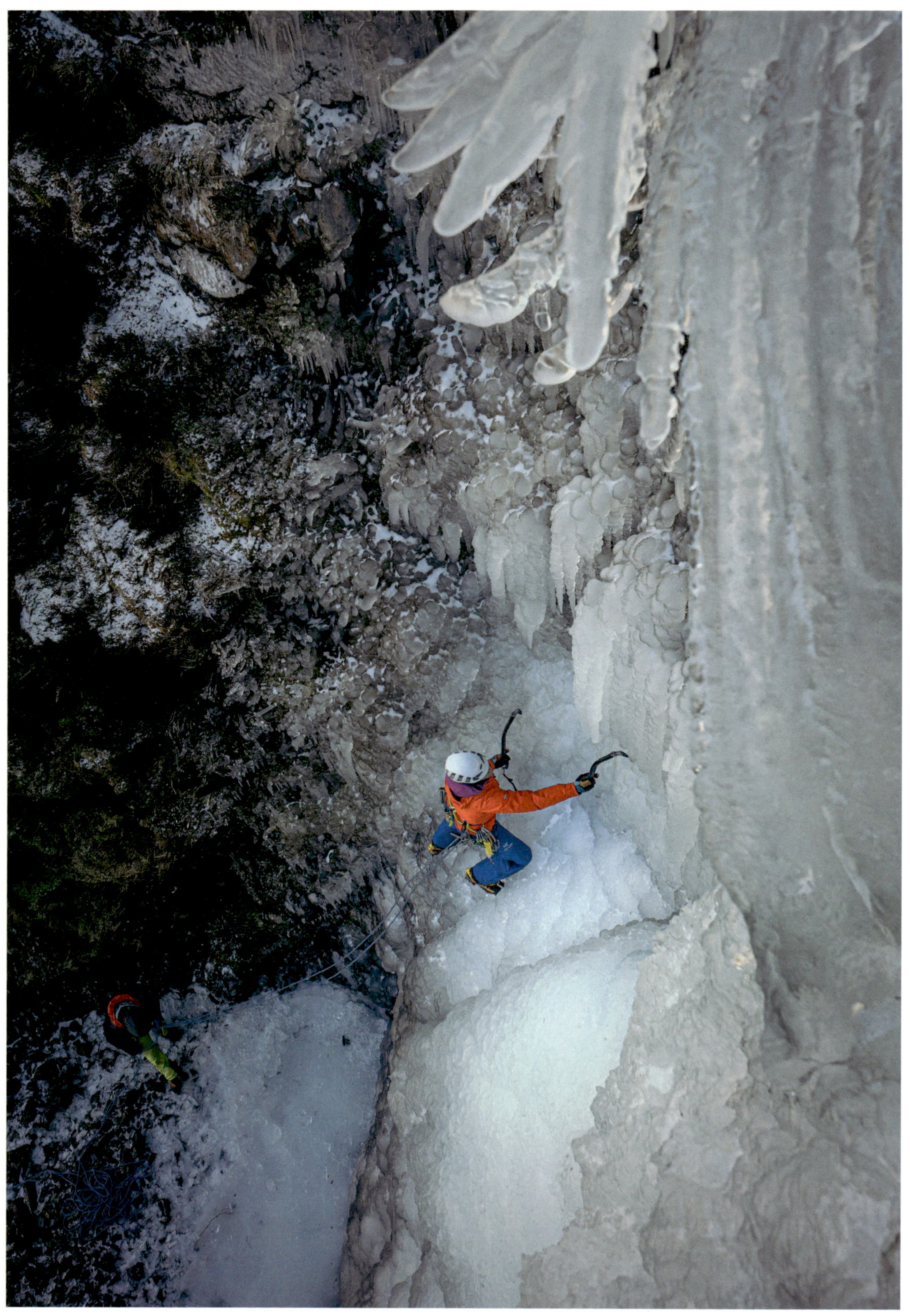

Katie Frances leads the *Quarry Fall* ice pillar (V) at Honister Quarry Falls. © Nadir Khan

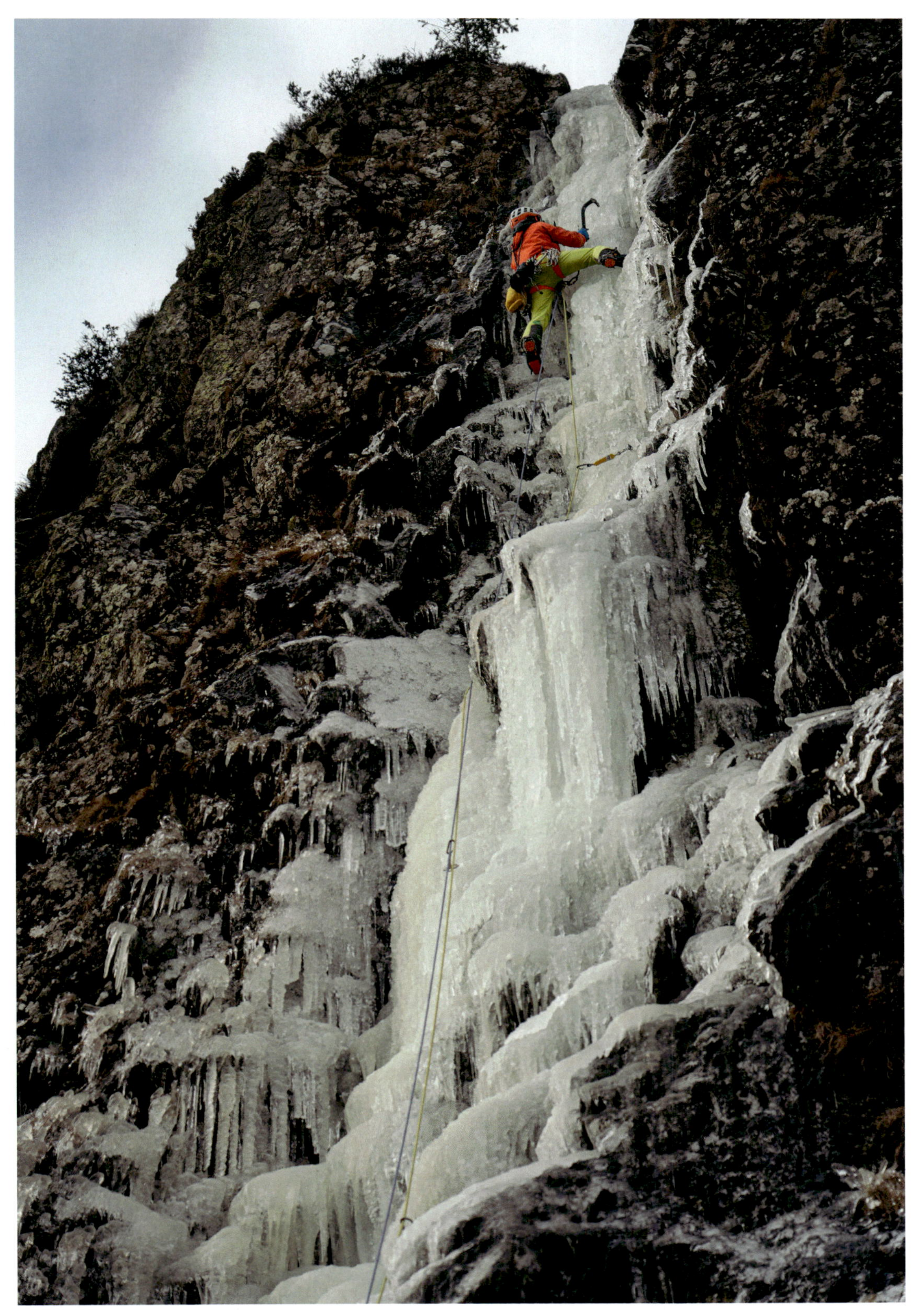

Joe Dobson on *Shoulthwaite Gill* (V) near Thirlmere. © Nadir Khan

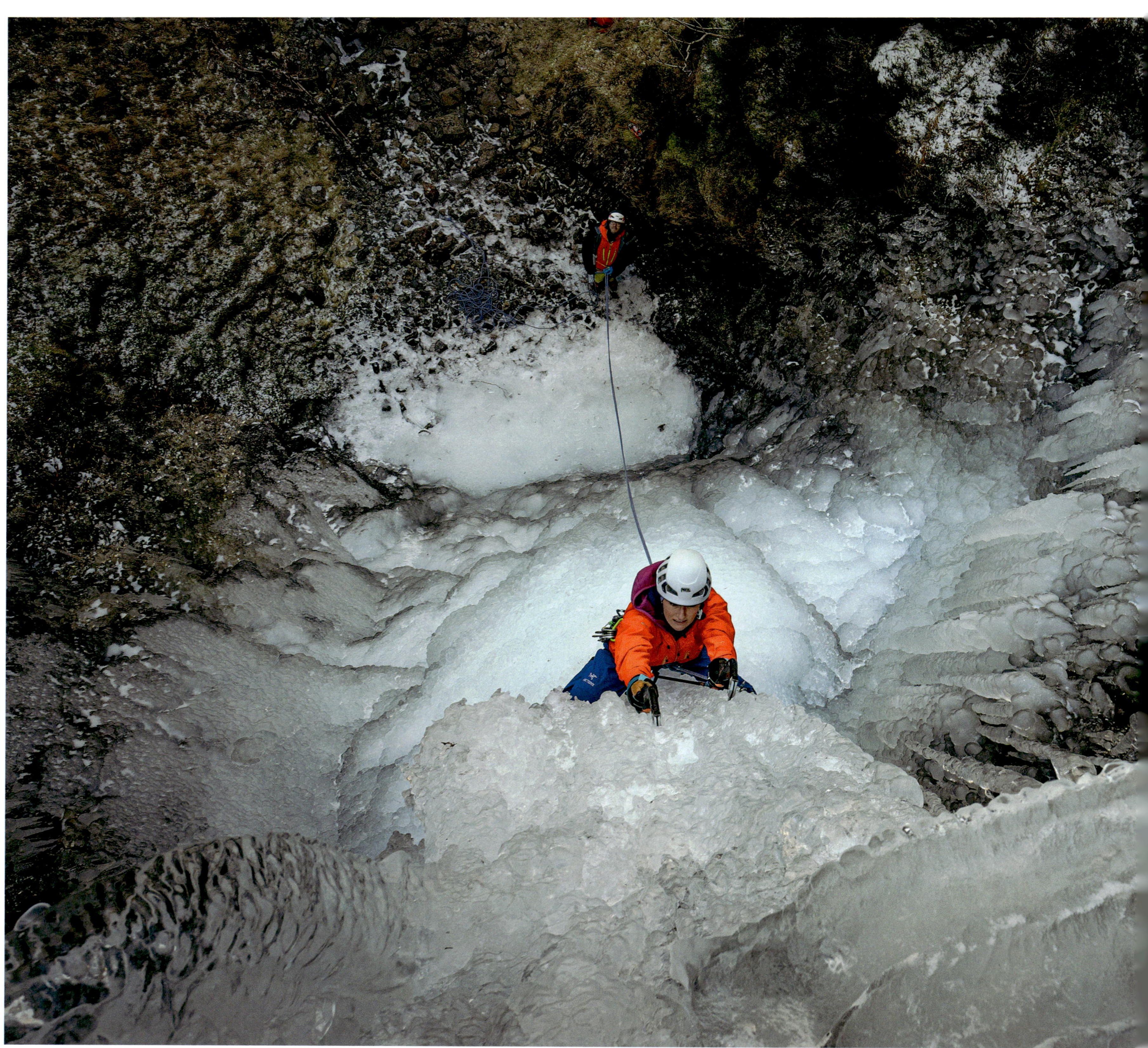

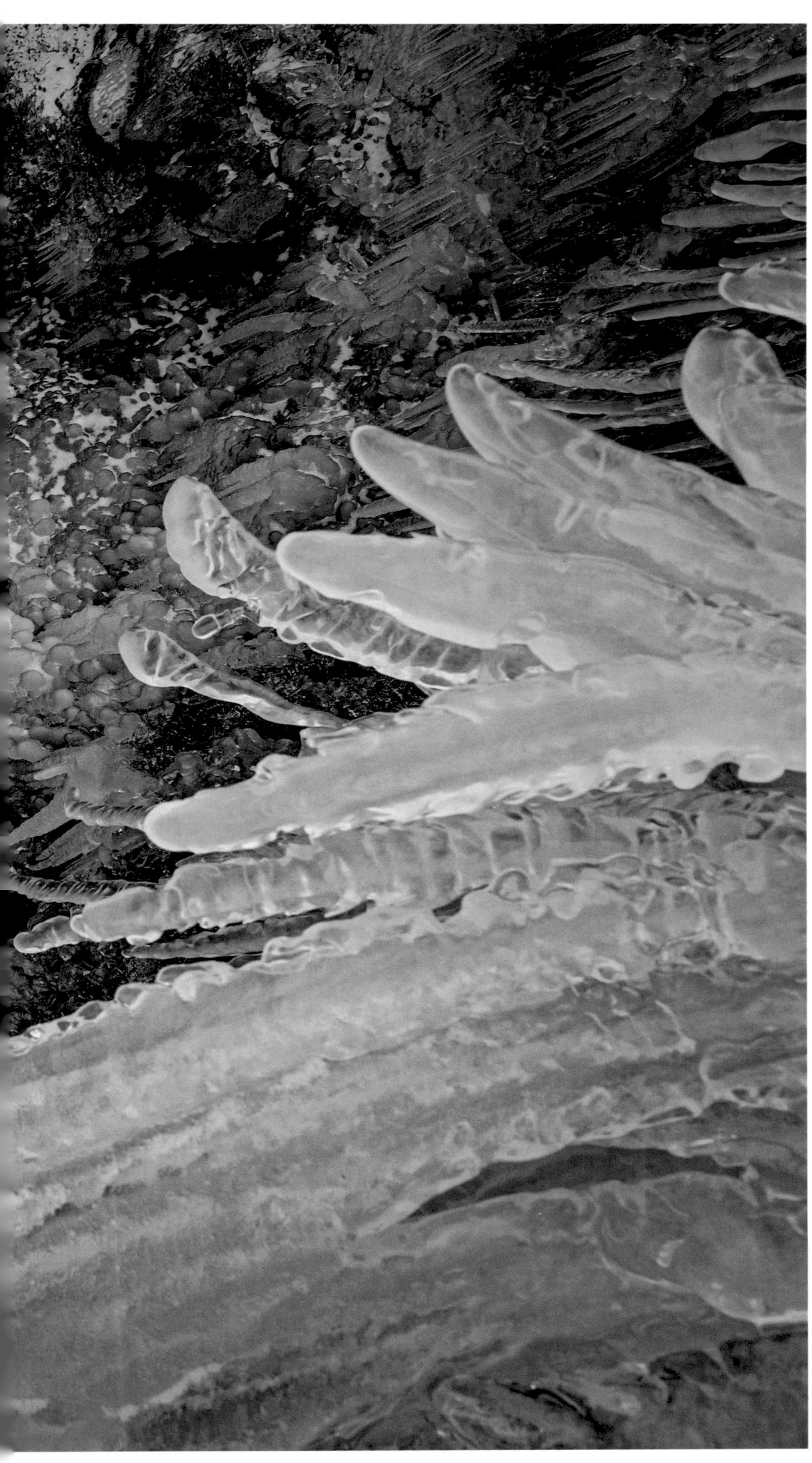

« Another angle of Katie Frances leading *Quarry Fall* (V).
This fragile and steep ice pillar came into condition during
a prolonged cold snap in February 2021. © Nadir Khan

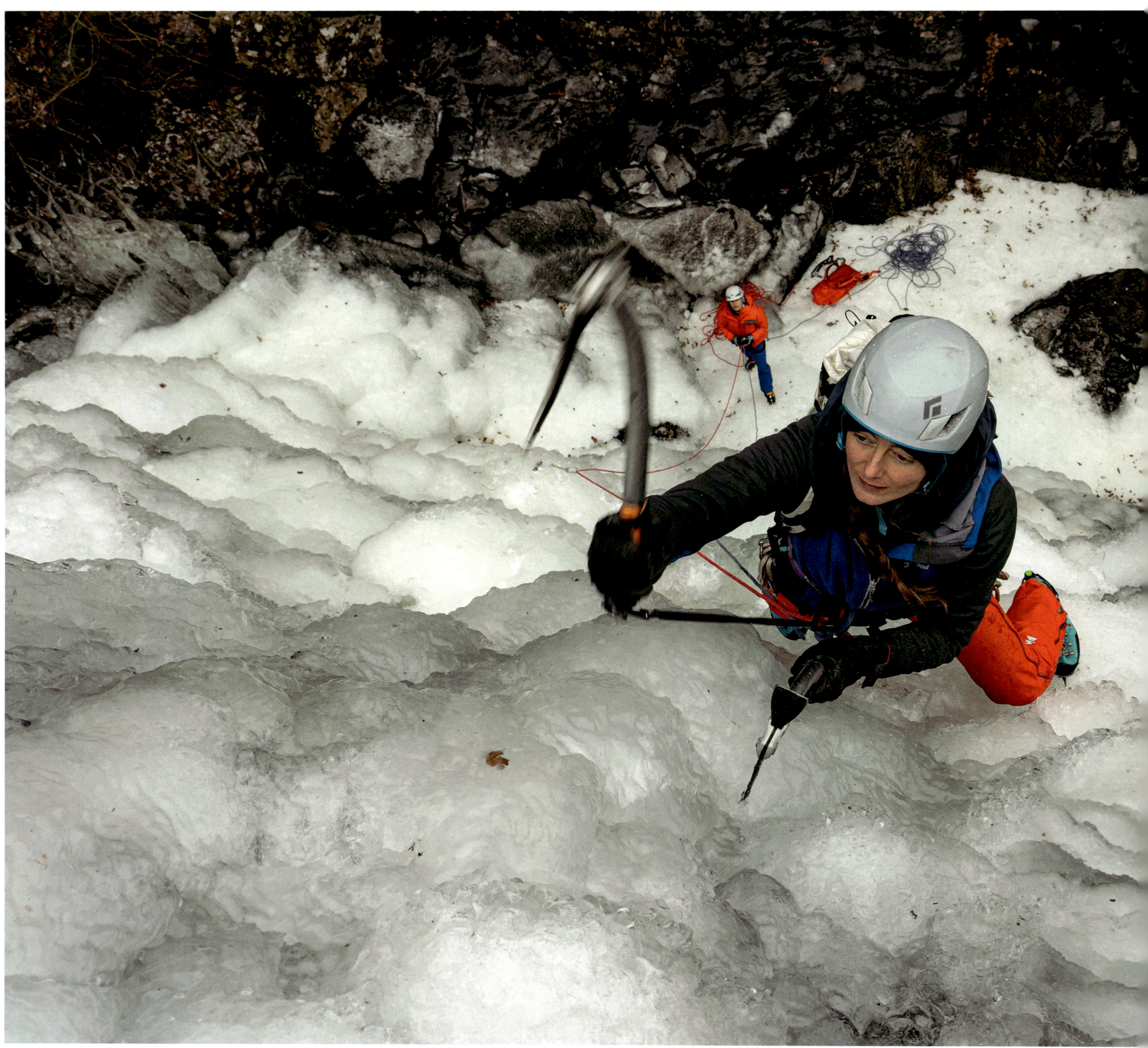

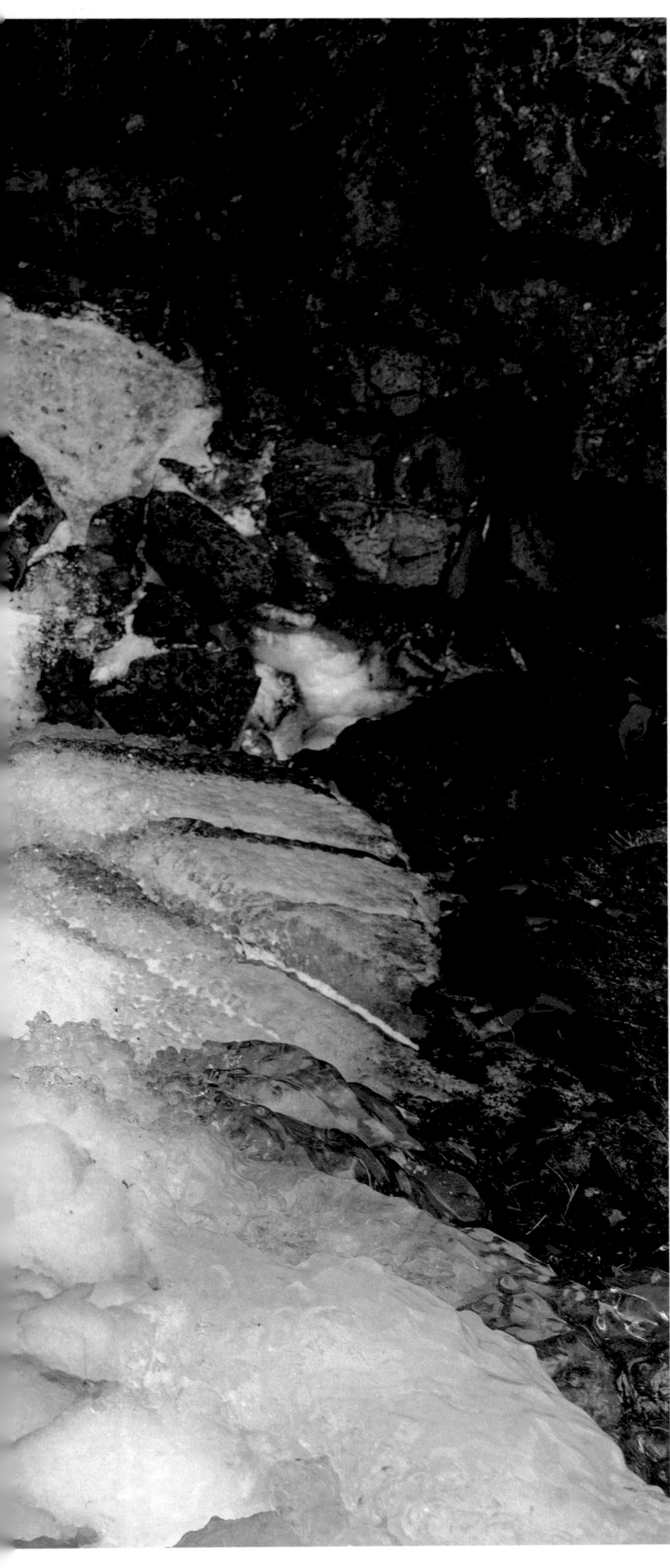

« Anna Sharpe on *Launchy Gill* (III) above Thirlmere. © Nadir Khan

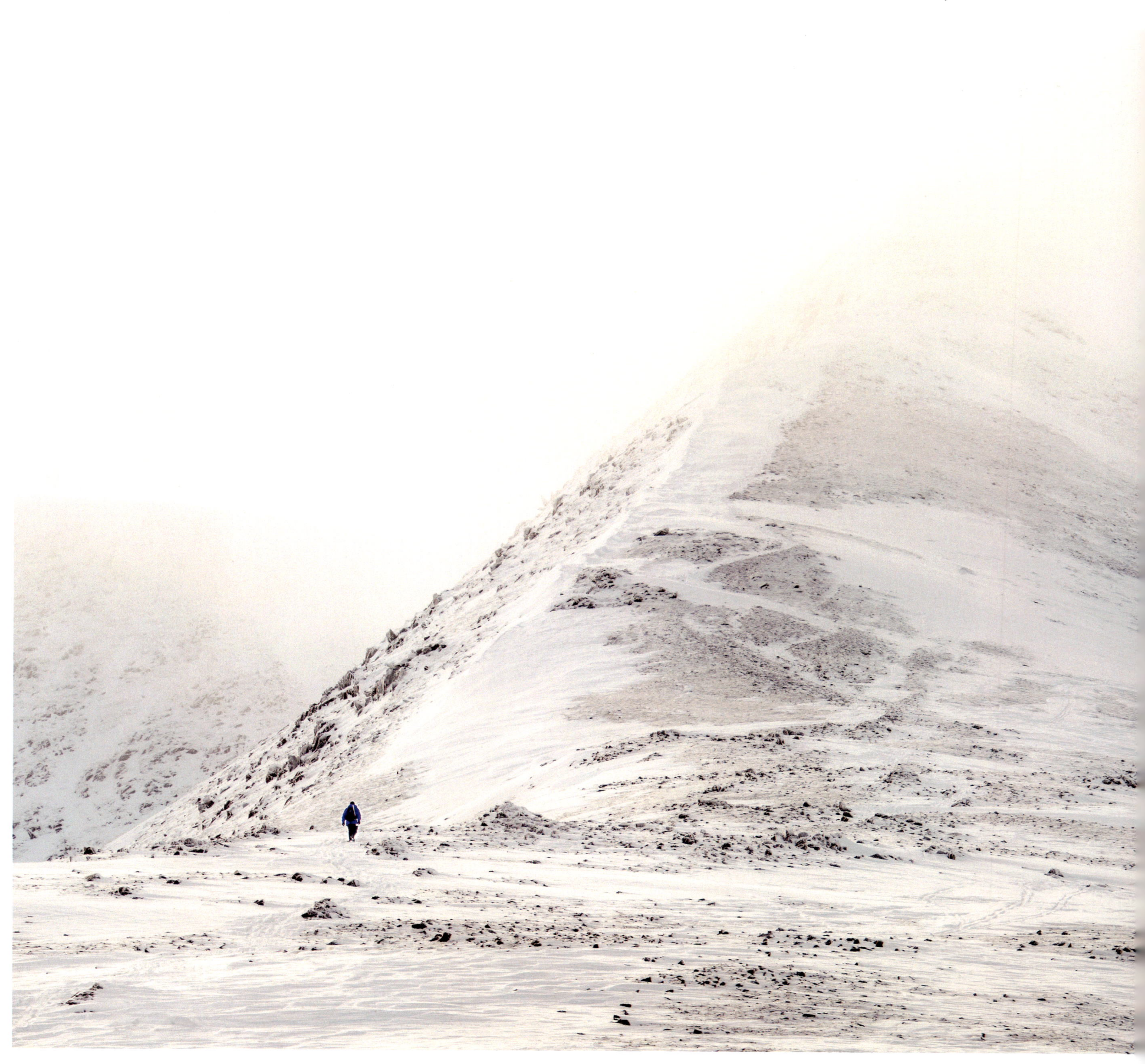

« A walker ascends into the mist on Lower Man, Helvellyn. © Tom McNally

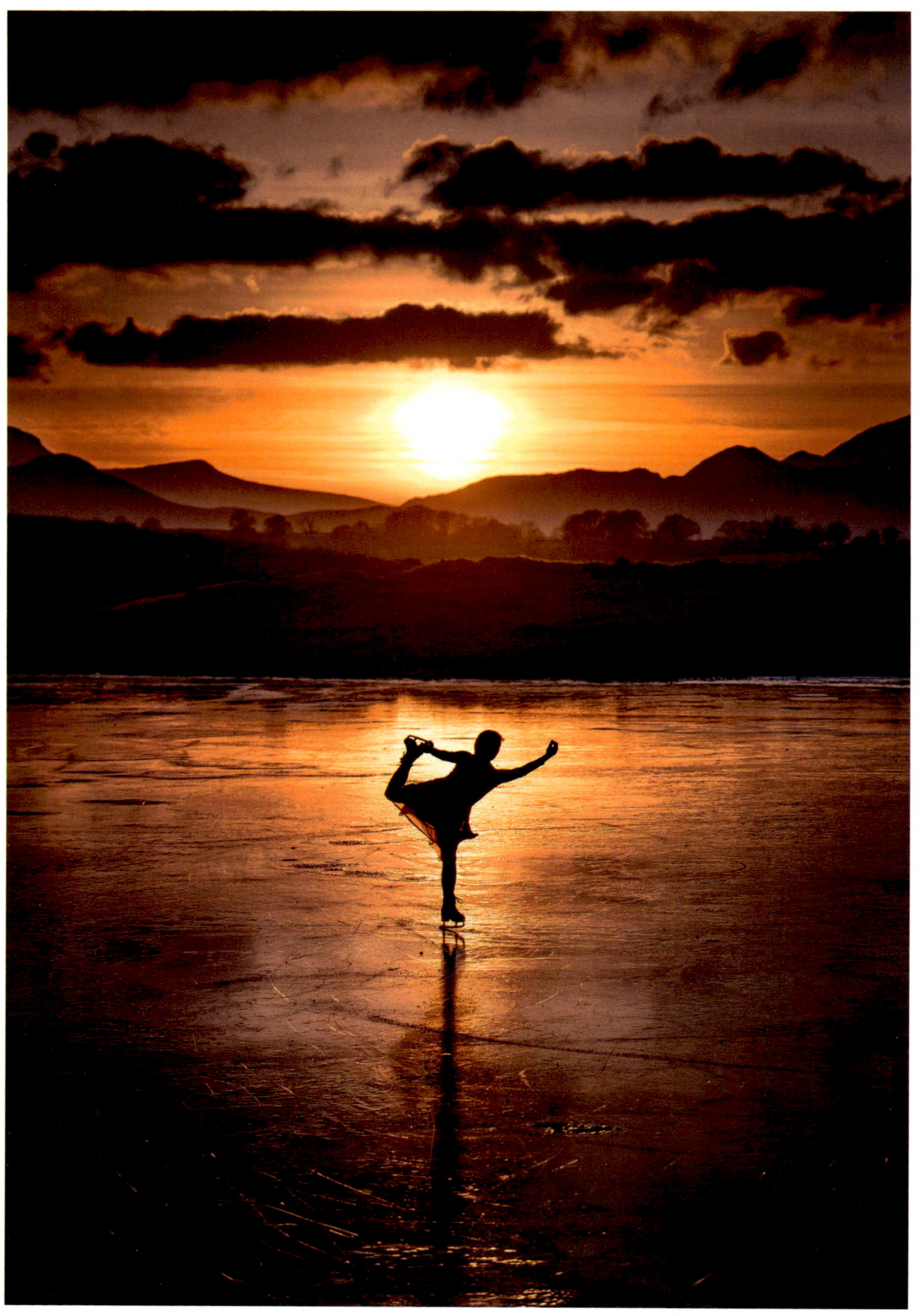

Figure skater Esther Newton on Tewet Tarn. The cold snap during February 2021 was the first time some Lakeland tarns had frozen in a decade. © Tom McNally

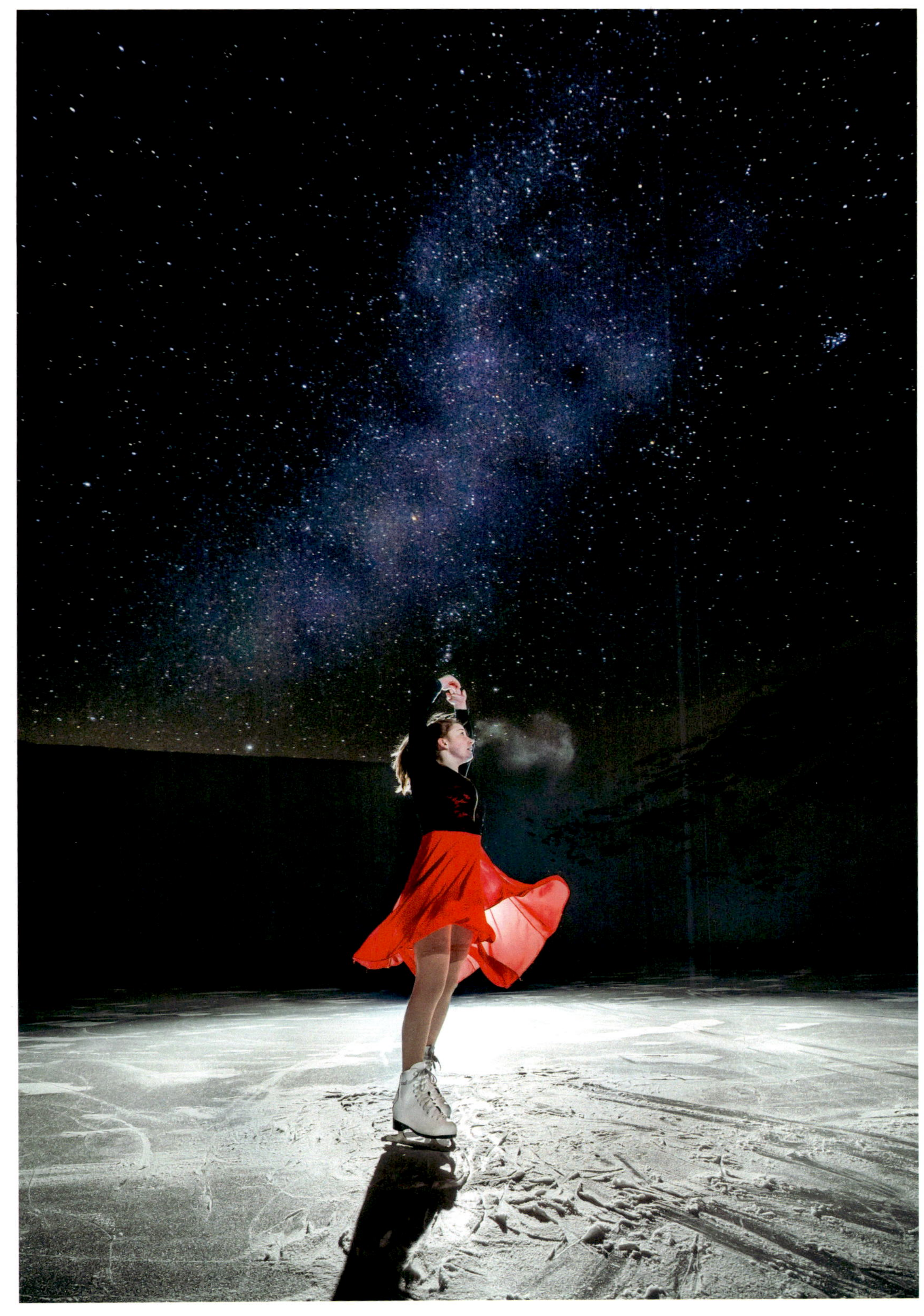

Esther performs under the stars on Scales Tarn, Blencathra (a single 30-second exposure was used to capture the night sky, while strobes froze Esther in action). © Tom McNally

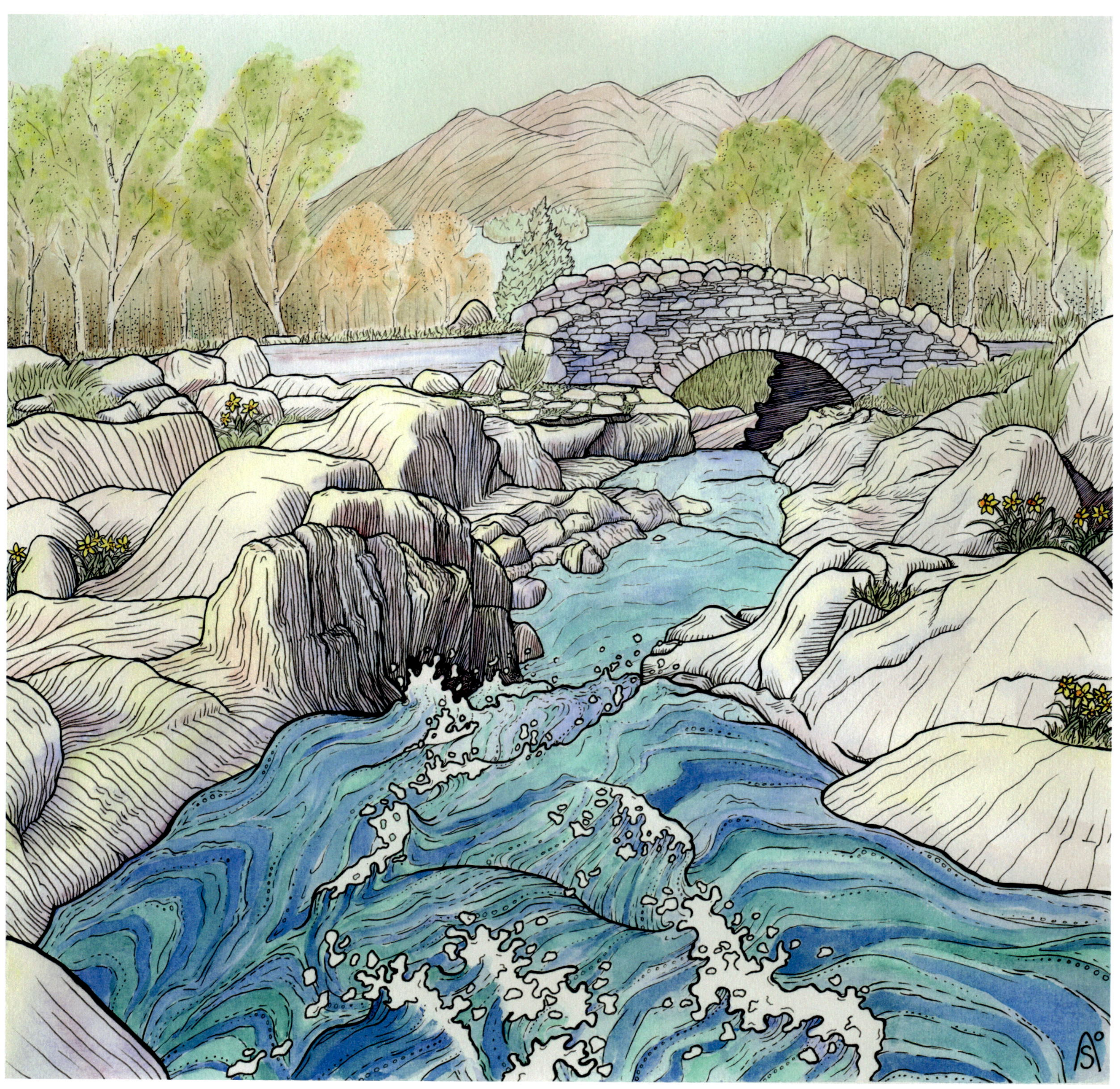

SPRING

« *Ashness Bridge.* © Anna Sharpe

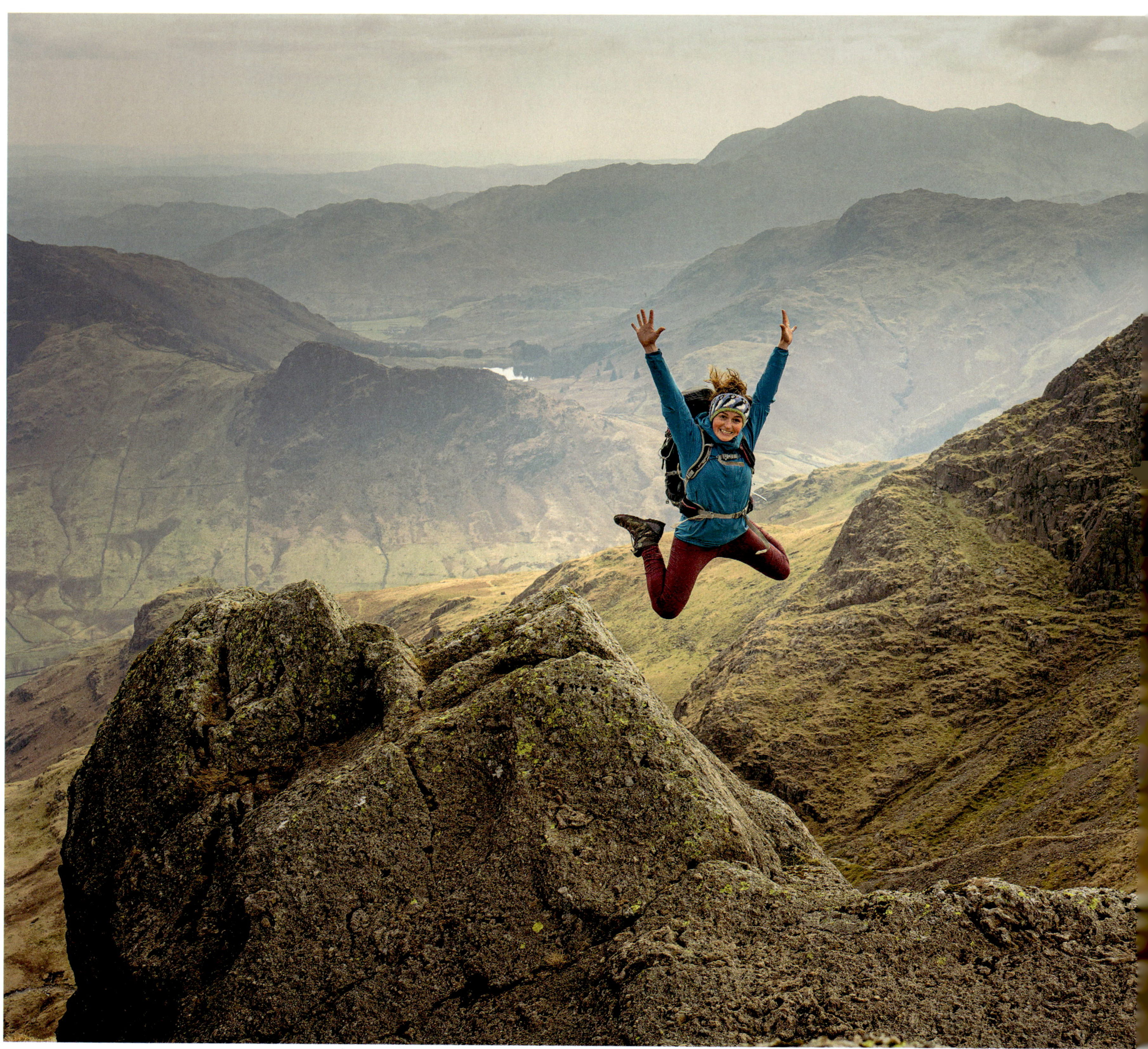

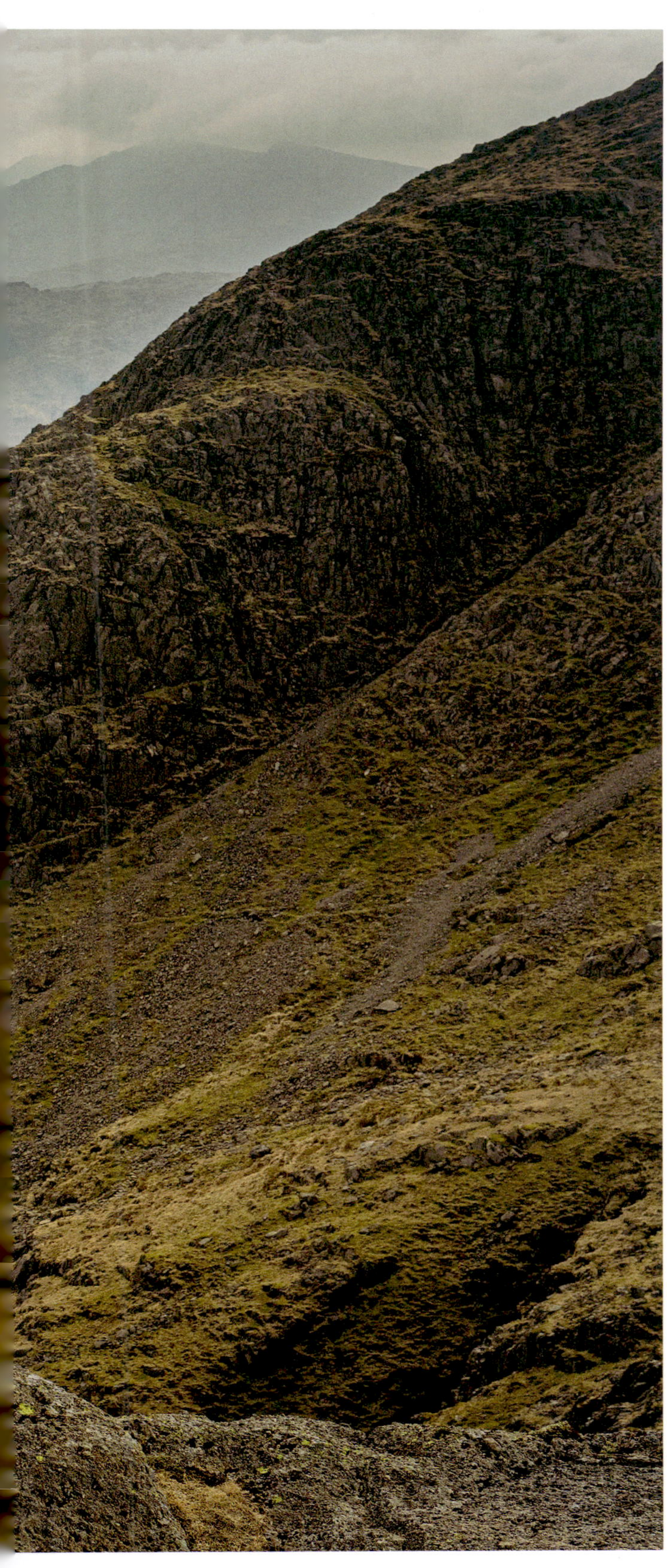

« Becki Vale leaping with joy at the top of Jack's Rake, Pavey Ark. © Nadir Khan

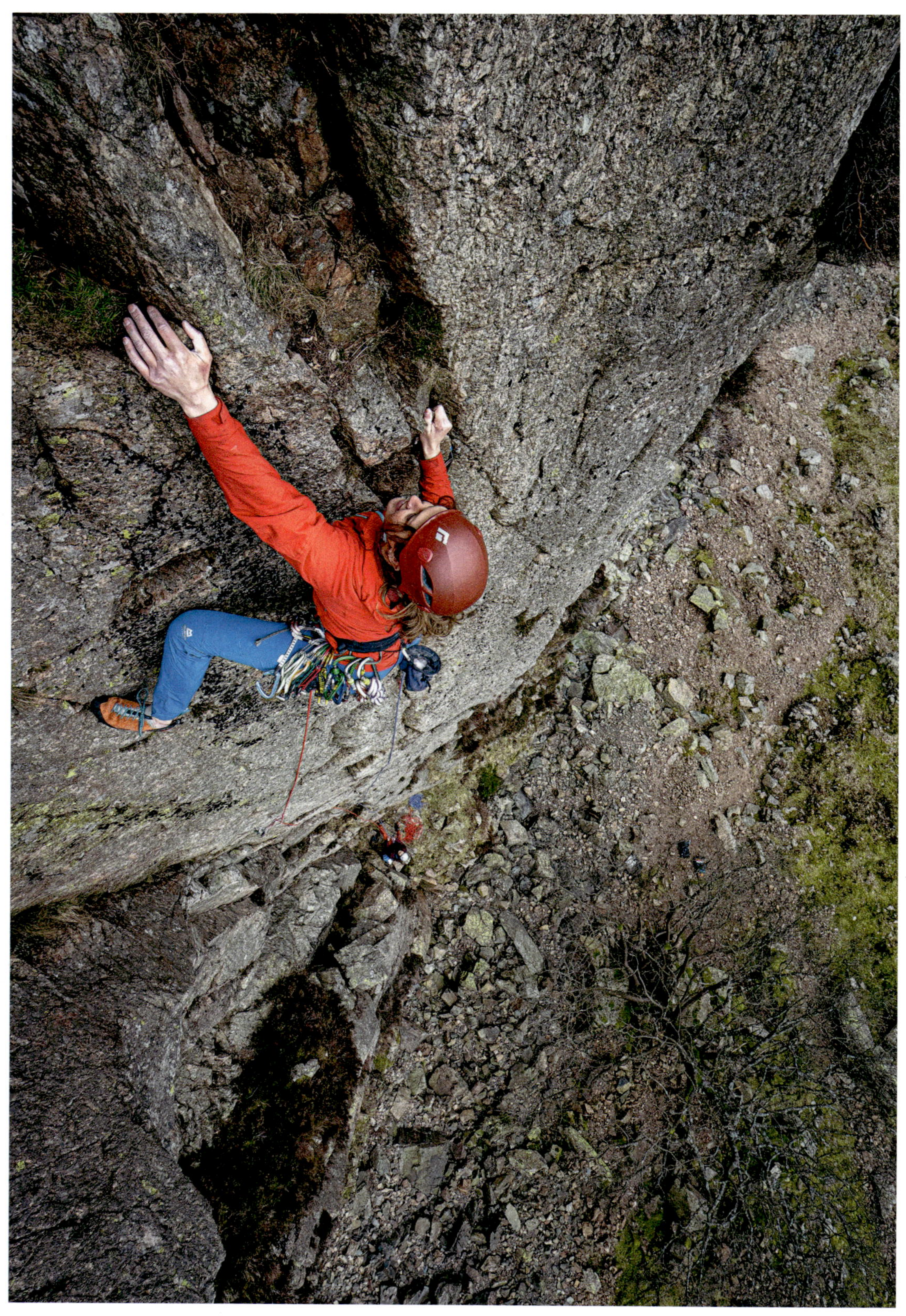

Chelsey Robinson on the first pitch of *Slip Knot* (VS 4b), White Ghyll. © Nadir Khan

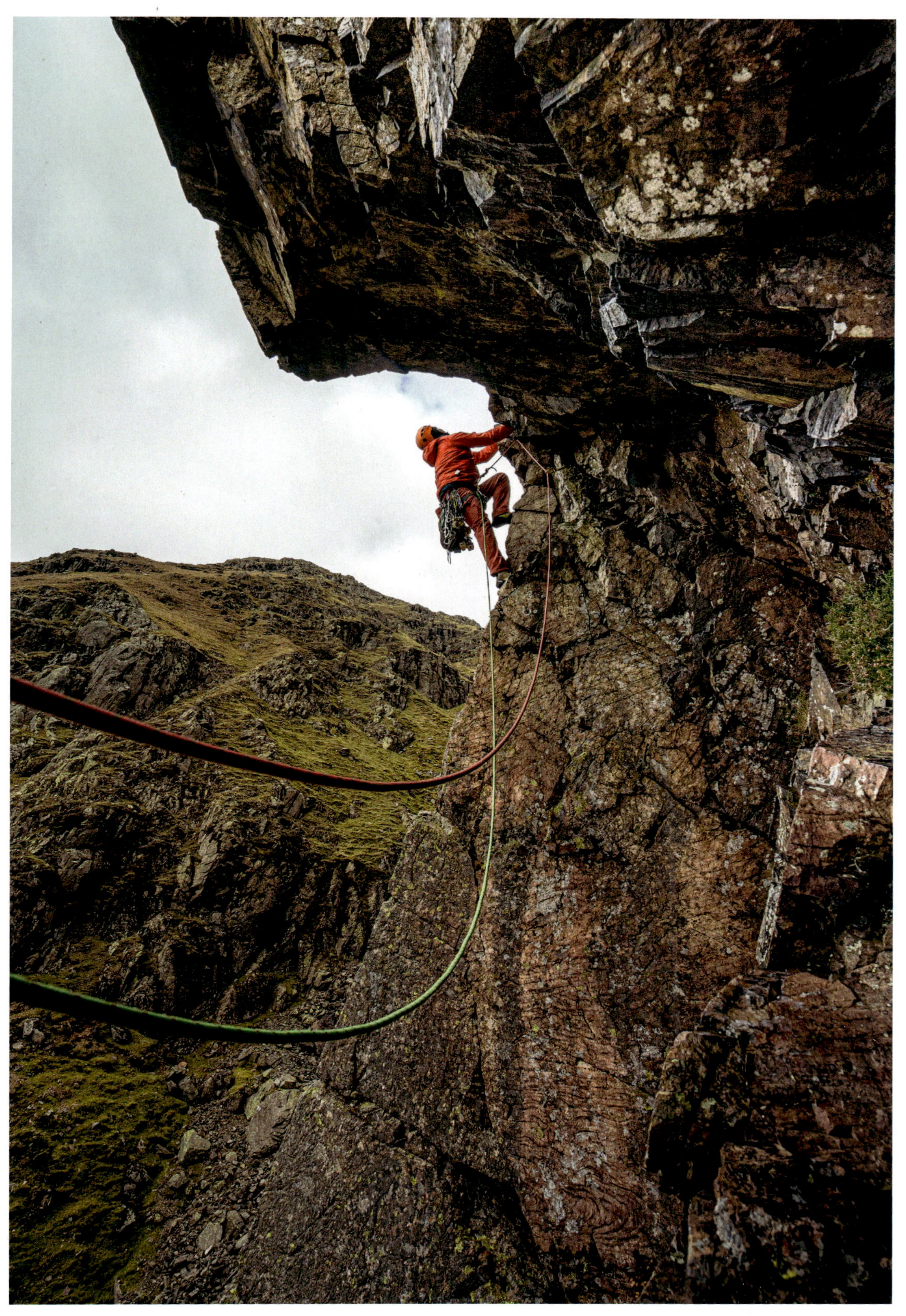

James Austrums on the second pitch of *Slip Knot*. © Nadir Khan

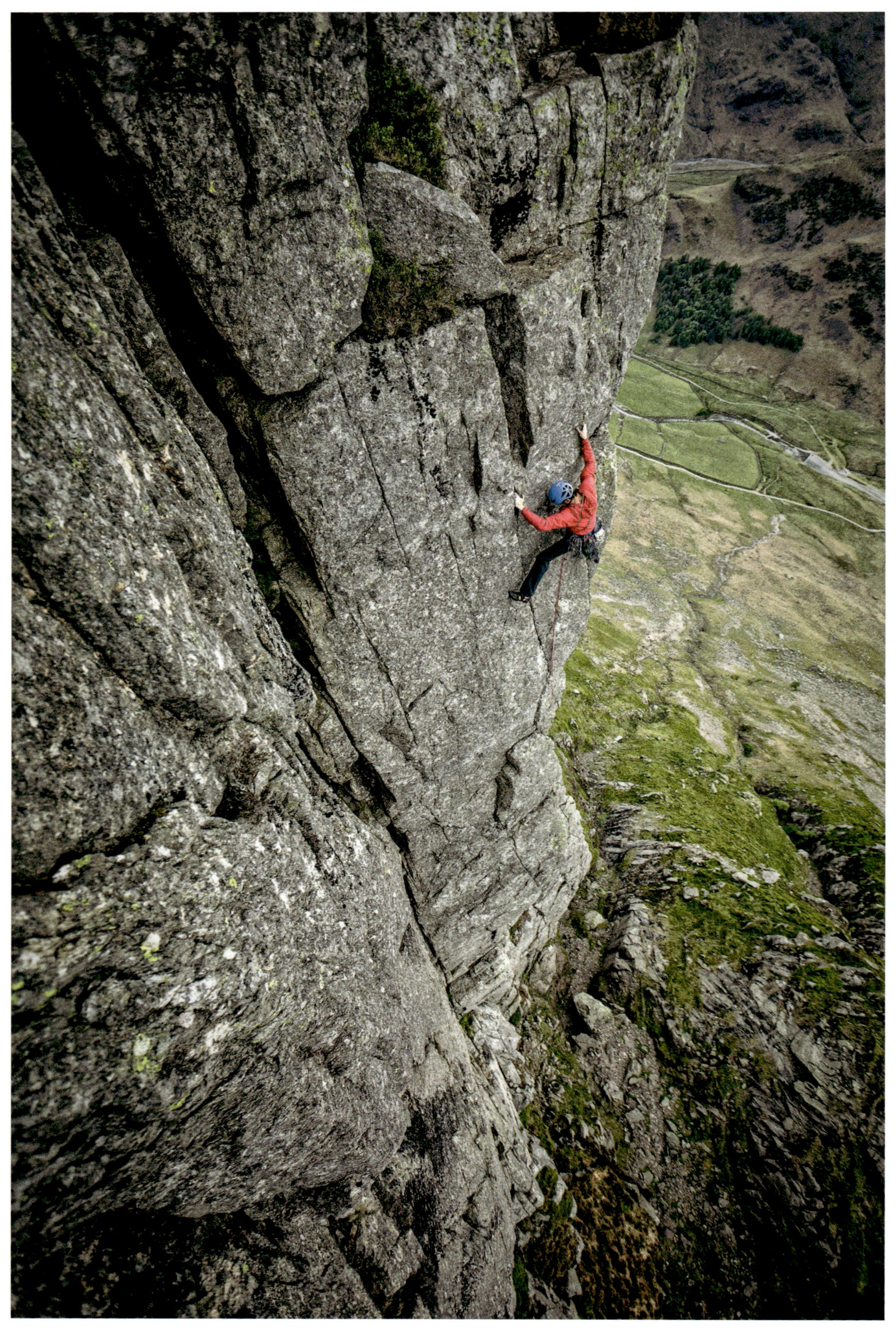

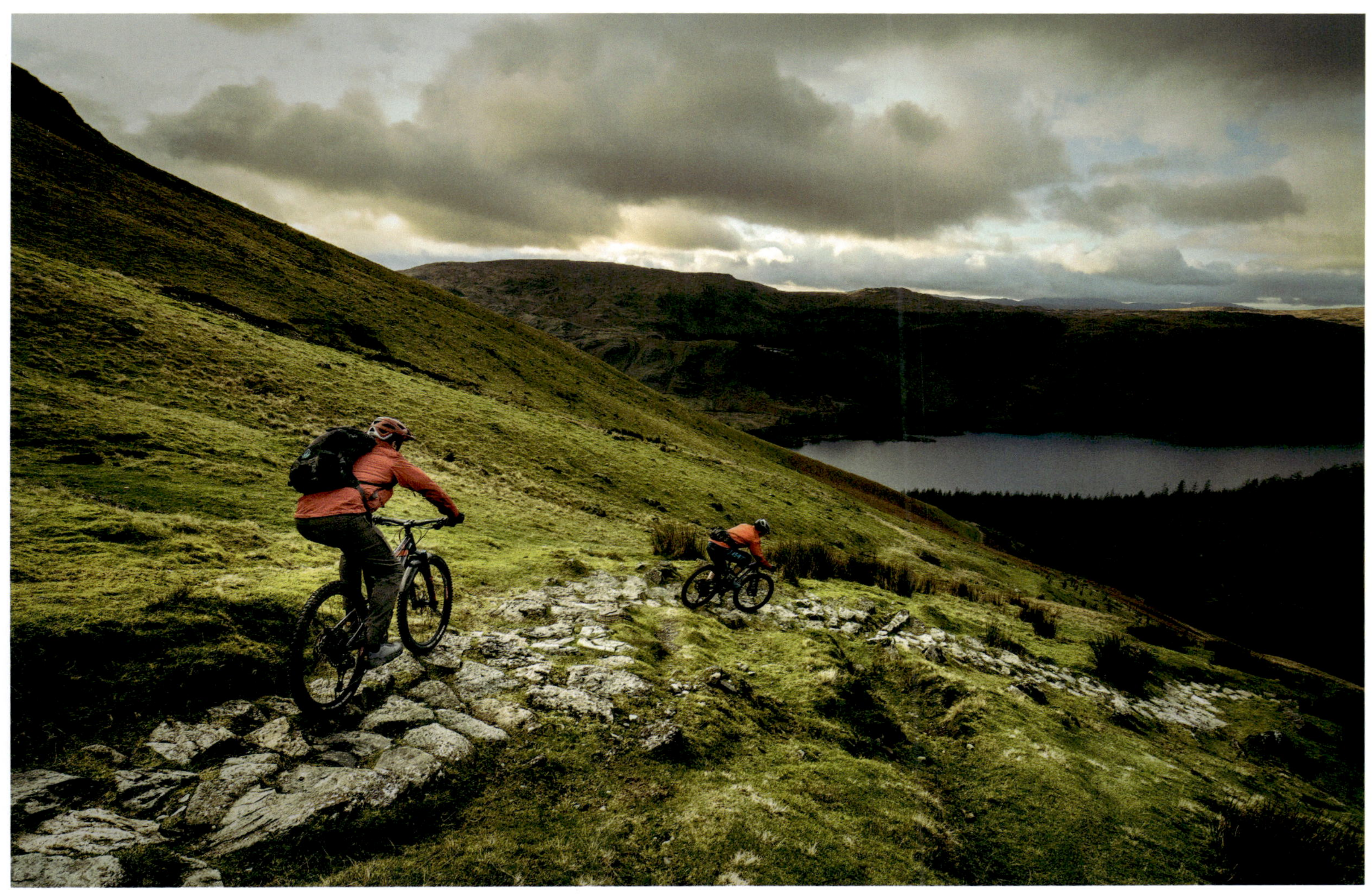

Dan Stringer and James Vincent on the rocky descent to Thirlmere from Helvellyn. © Nadir Khan

« Scott William Quinn on *Gimmer String* (E1 5b), Gimmer Crag. © Nadir Khan

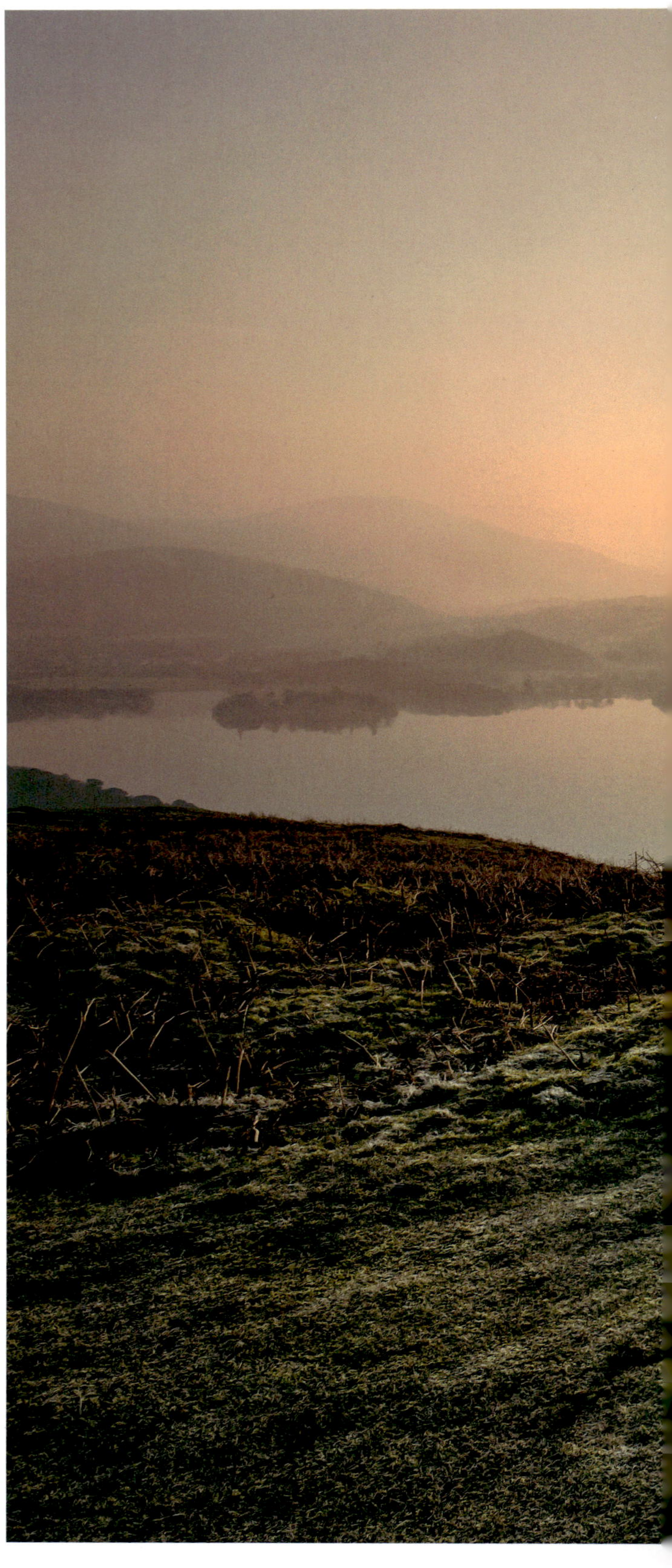

Watching the sunrise over Derwent Water. © Nadir Khan »

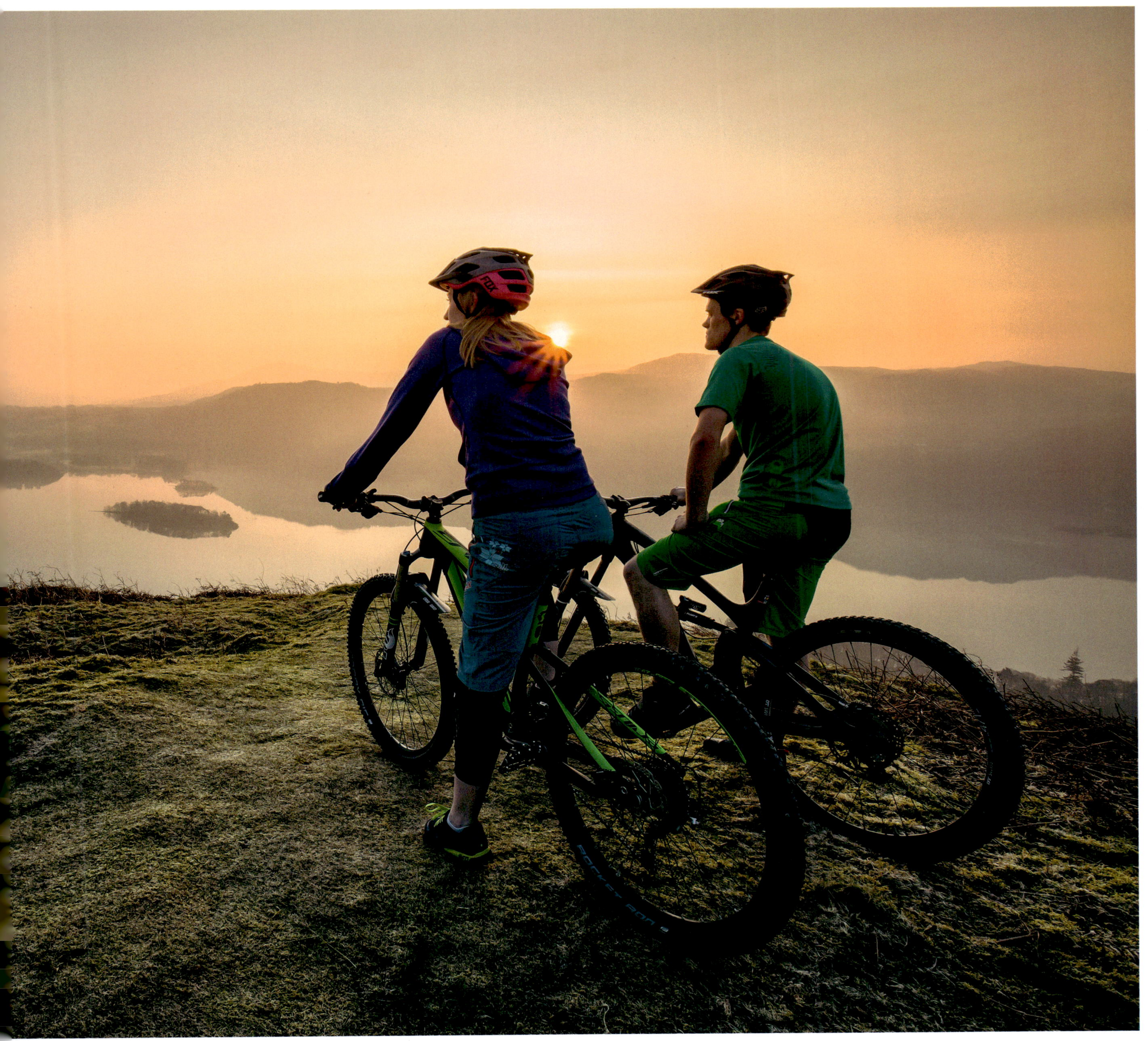

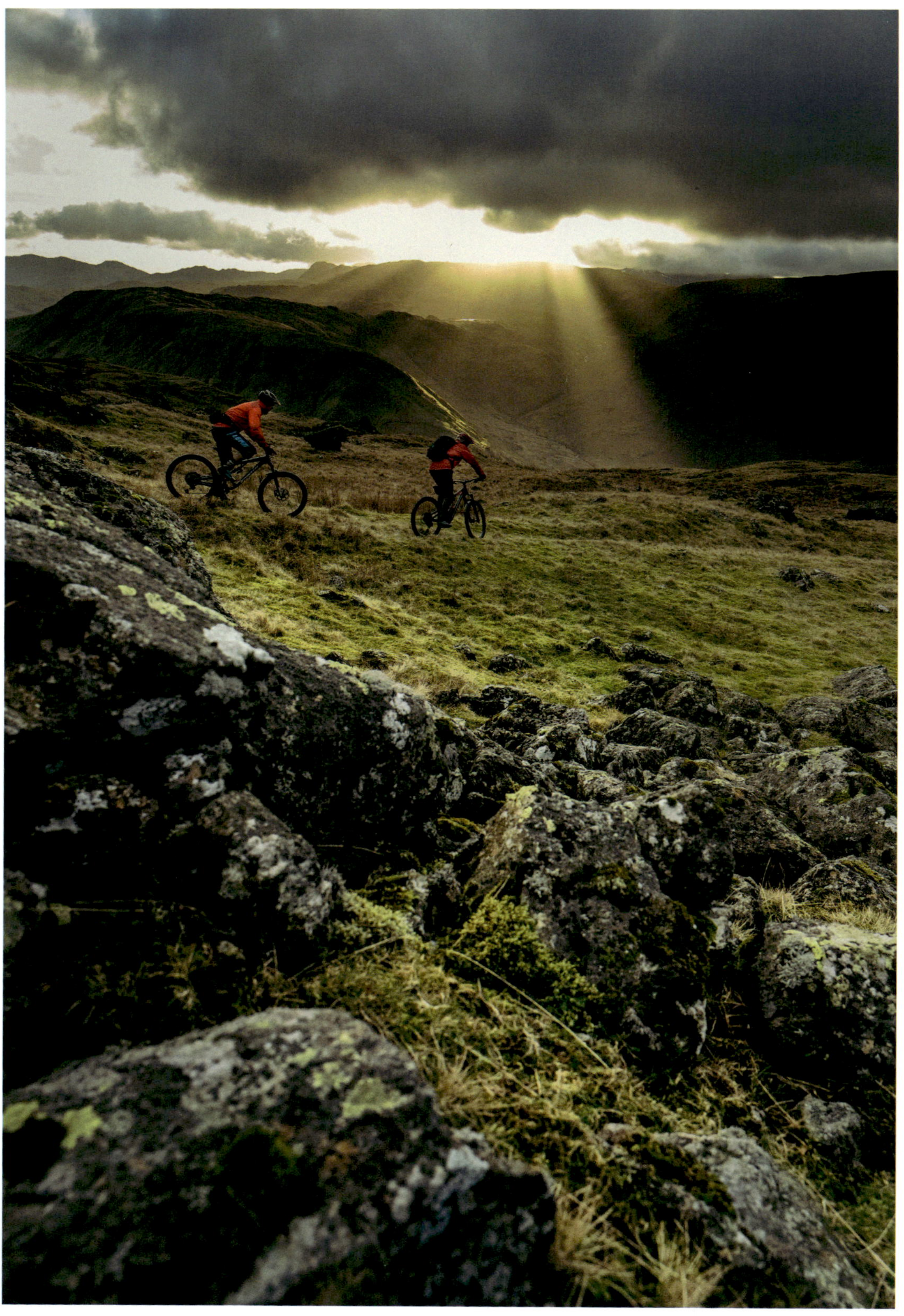

Dan Stringer and James Vincent at the beginning of the technical descent from Hellvelyn to Thirlmere. © Nadir Khan

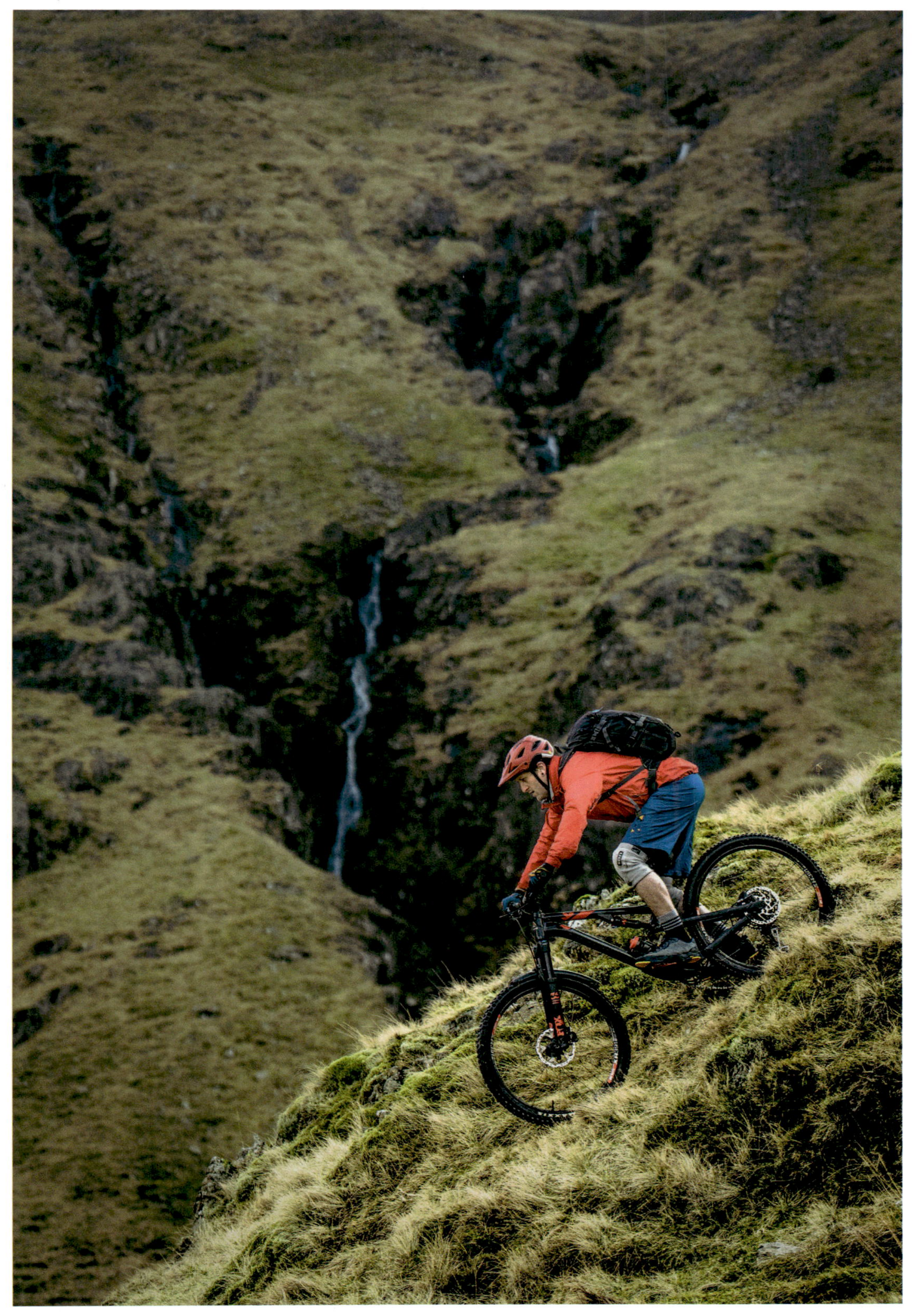

Dan Stringer descending from the Black Sail Pass. © Nadir Khan

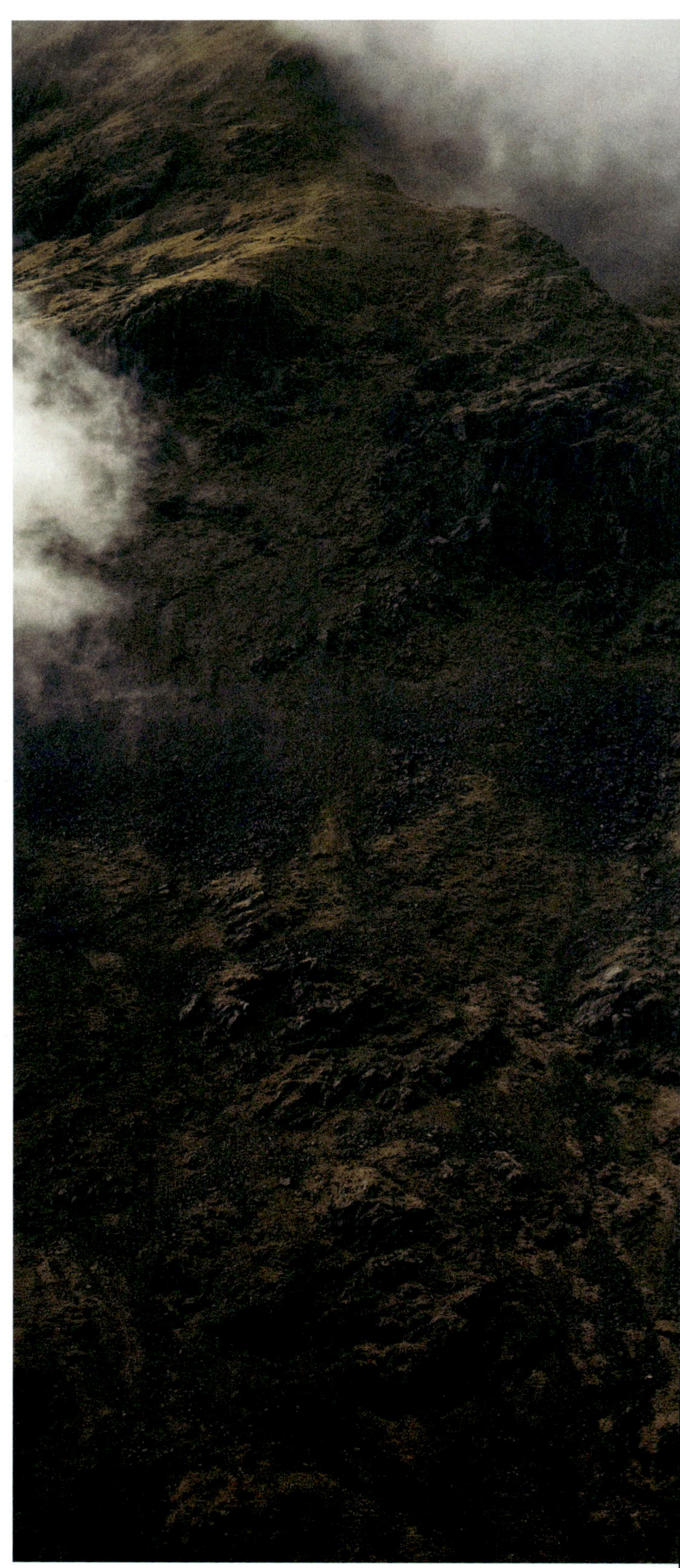

Dan Stringer amid dramatic clouds against a background
of Scoat Fell and Red Pike. © Nadir Khan »

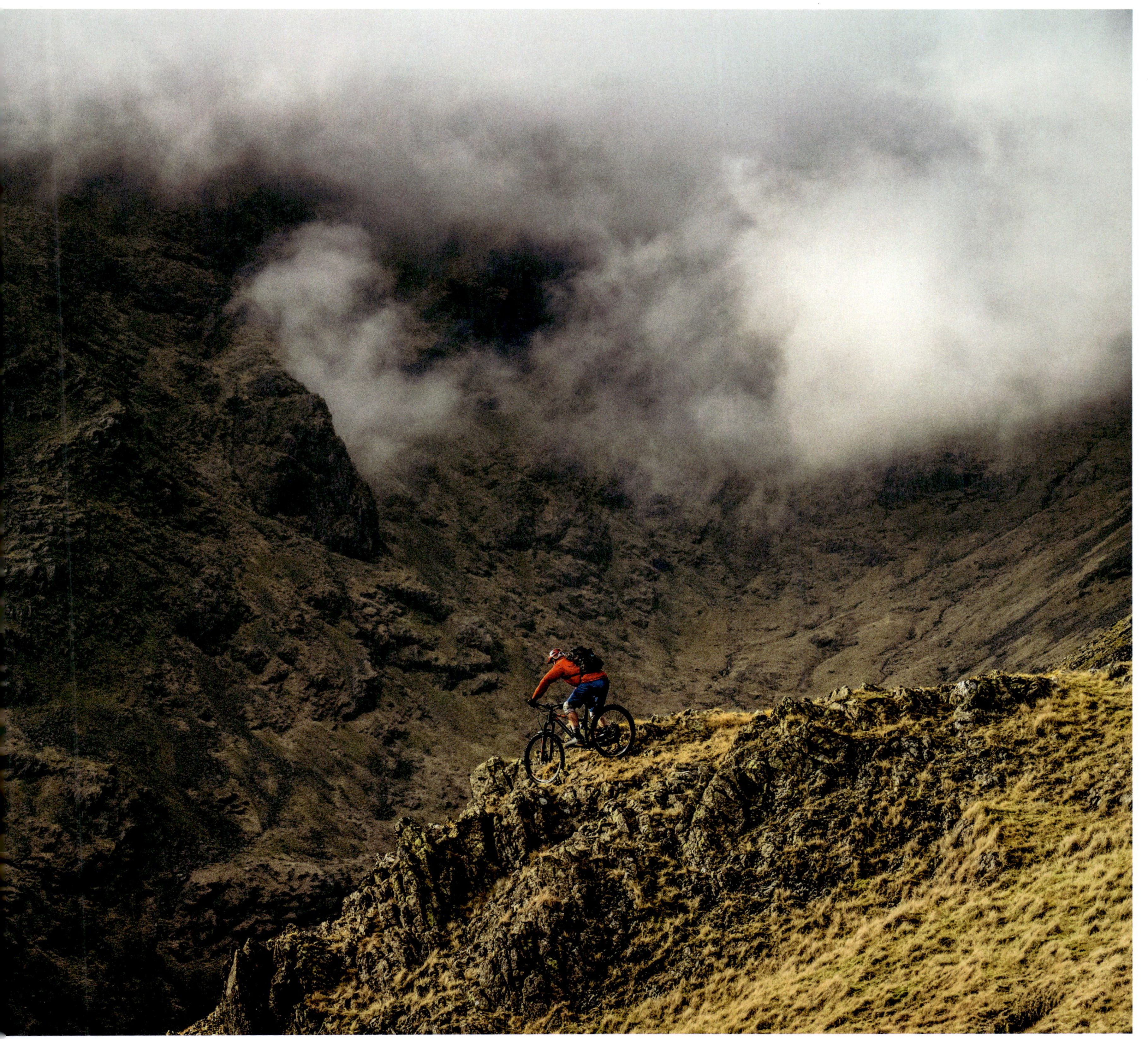

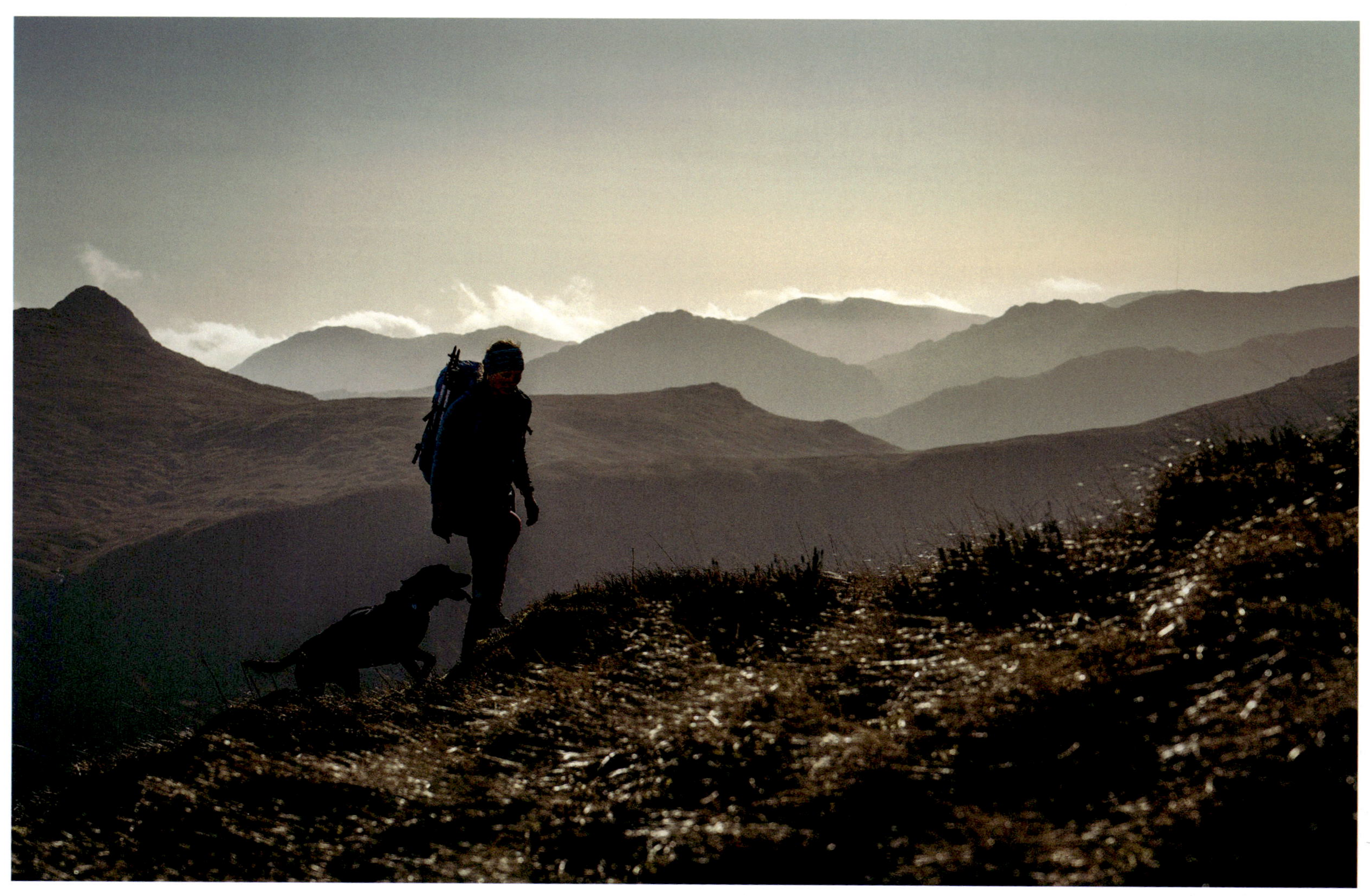

Katy Forrester on the approach to and climbing on Cam Crag Ridge in the Langstrath valley. © Nadir Khan

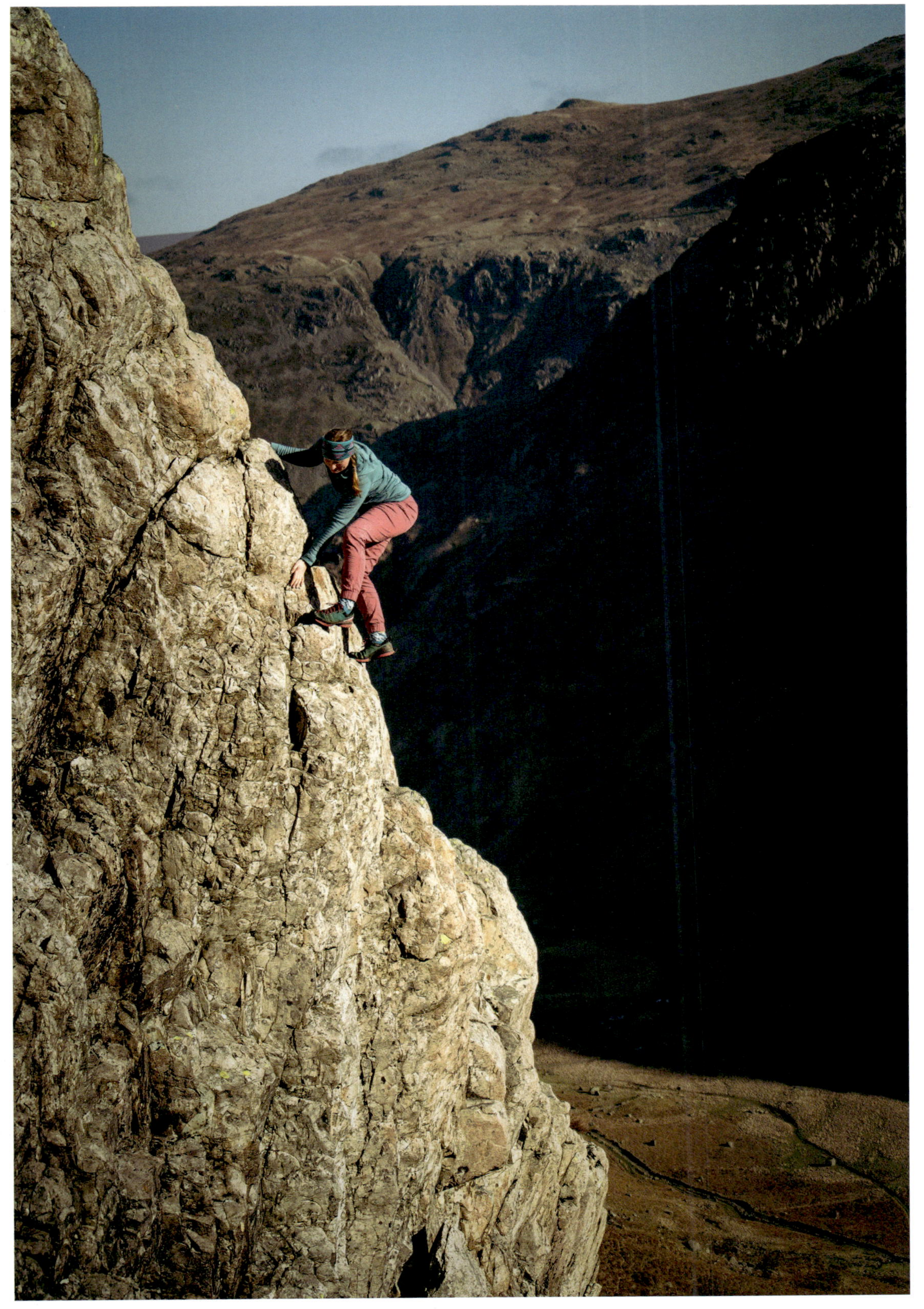

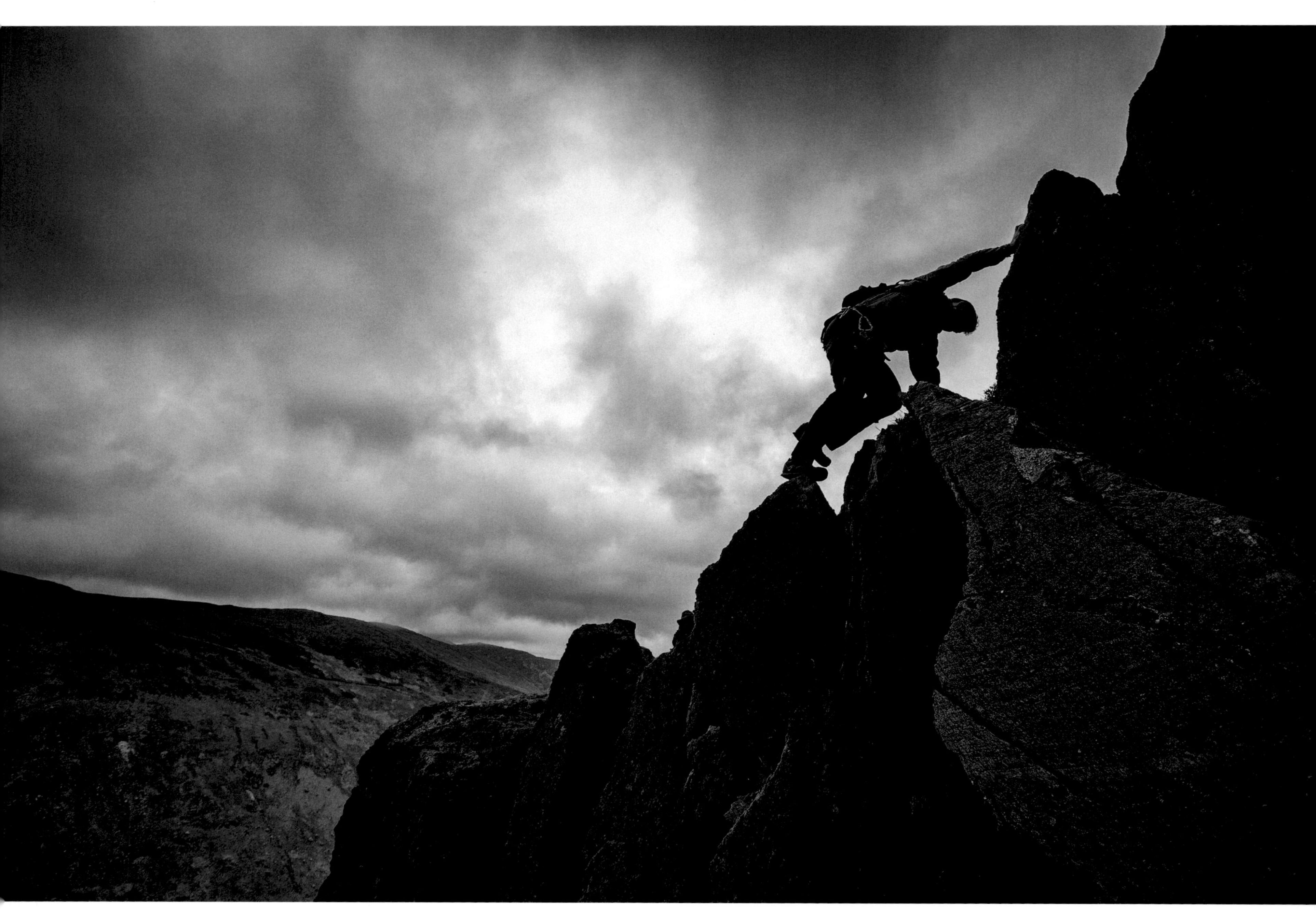

Scrambling on Pinnacle Ridge, St Sunday Crag. © Nadir Khan

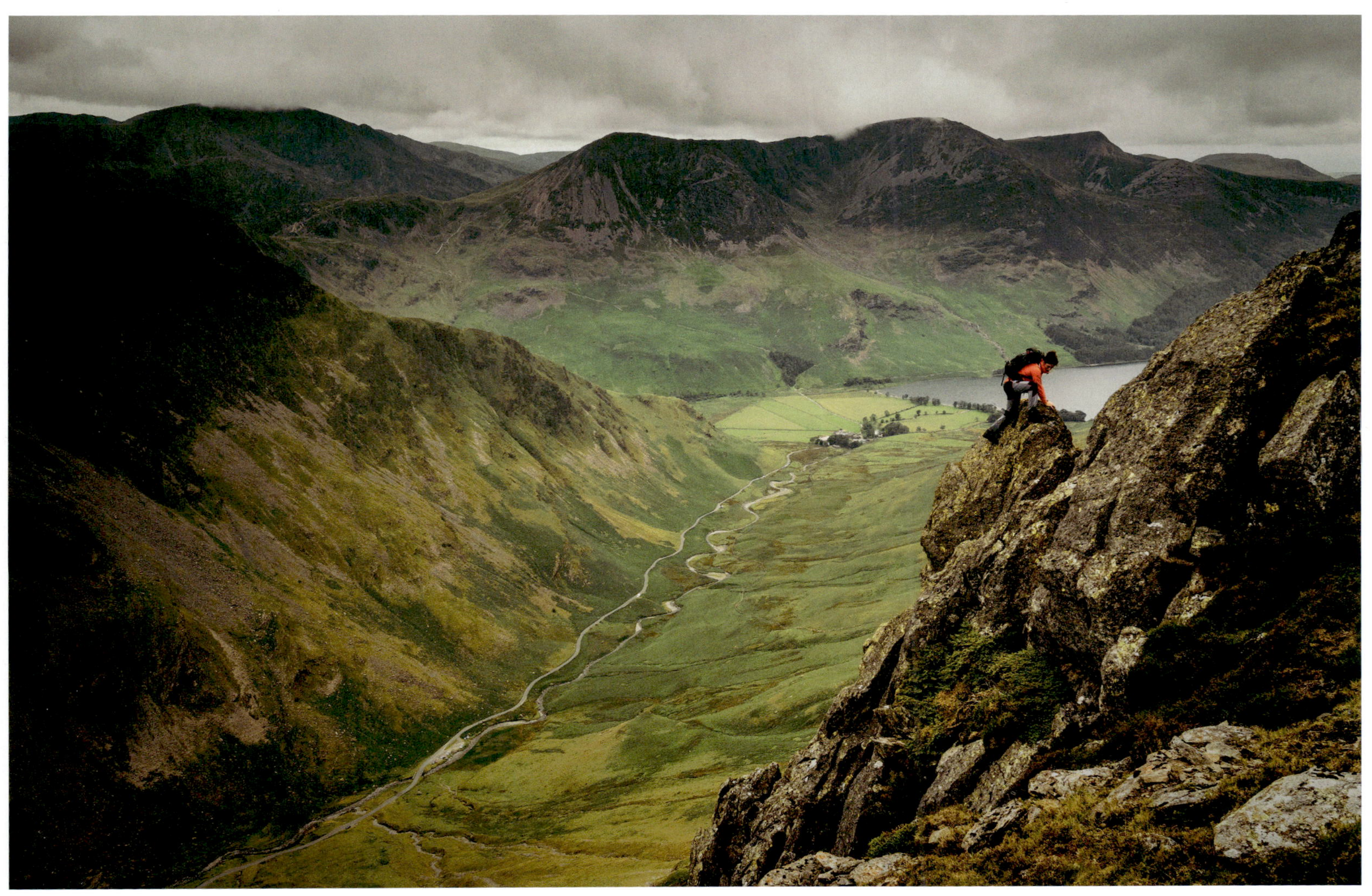

Becki Vale on Robinson with Buttermere beyond. © Nadir Khan

THE 'ONLY' WORD

BY JON SPARKS

It's only a Grade 1 scramble, but the wind seems to get stronger with every metre we rise. As the ridge gets a bit steeper, a bit more continuous, a flurry of hail rattles on the rock. Hands, already stiff and awkward, start to numb.

At an easing, an almost-ledge, I half-crouch, braced against the rock. When Bernie joins me, we have one of Those Conversations. *Do we, don't we … ?*

We go on, but we could easily have made a different decision. A degree or two colder, a little more wind, another scour of hail … We go on, and almost immediately face a couple of trickier moves. Nothing crazy, but the holds aren't quite the stonking jugs you might expect on a Grade 1 – at least they don't feel that way with chilled hands. And, let's be honest, hands that are out of practice too.

A reach, a lean, a subtle side-step to unlock the problem; the precise anatomy of the moves is immaterial. It's the feeling that counts. The commitment to continue in the face of steep rock, cold, wind, lack of practice and – in my case at least – general decrepitude. It's only a Grade 1 scramble, but for me, on this day, in these conditions, there's not much of the 'only' about it.

Perspective is everything. Some might dismiss a Grade 1 scramble as too trivial to mention; others might think we were crazy to be out there at all, when there were snug coffee shops and pubs in Coniston half an hour away.

I have my own perspective now. Once, I might also have thought of this route (*Long Crag Buttress*) as no more than a light-hearted romp. But then came a time, not so very long ago, when I would have struggled even to reach the foot of the rock.

Age comes into it, of course, but when I hit sixty I didn't think I was doing too badly. Rock climbing had rather taken a back seat, but only because bikes had taken over. Road, gravel, MTB … I was probably fitter, and certainly more technically adept, at sixty than I had been at forty. I even celebrated, if that's the word, by doing my first triathlon. Only a 'sprint' distance, and I was dead slowest in the pool, but still …

Then Fate, Chance, Nature – whatever you want to call it – served up a double whammy. First, cardiac arrhythmias (atrial flutter and atrial fibrillation), resulting in alarming episodes when my heartbeat went haywire. A trip in an emergency ambulance and two ablations later, I was arrhythmia-free, but *something* wasn't right. Walking or cycling, even on the level, my speed dropped, and going up any kind of hill I was reduced to crawling pace. I'll never forget going up the lovely, but very modest, Hampsfell at a pace that wouldn't have looked out of place at 8,000 metres.

It took longer than maybe it should have to work out that the culprit wasn't my heart. But, once we did, answers weren't long in coming: I had cancer. This explained my debilitating lethargy; I had severely depleted haemoglobin levels. Specifically, I had a variety of non-Hodgkin's lymphoma (even more specifically, Waldenström's macroglobulinaemia; is that a disease or a tongue-twister?).

Lesson 1: just because you have one health condition, it doesn't make you immune to others. It's all too easy to 'fit' new symptoms to an existing condition, to overlook the possibility that they're a pointer to a new issue. Lesson 2: the NHS is bloody brilliant.

That was then. Now, at another comfortable ledge, I pause and look out: the rooftops of Coniston village, the glinting waters of the lake, and the dark mass of Grizedale Forest (full of mountain bike memories) shrouding the rise beyond. In the far distance, mere hazy suggestions, the Howgills and the Yorkshire peaks. A wide world, and a stark contrast with the way my world contracted when I was at my lowest ebb.

In the few days following each round of chemotherapy, I hardly stirred from the house. Between those episodes, I kept walking and kept riding, even if it was just a few slow miles to a local cafe for eggs Benedict. I keep recalling some words from John Hunt's essay on Gimmer Crag in Ken Wilson's *Classic Rock*. In the summer of 1939, as war-clouds gathered, 'we went climbing every day, with a desperate, unspoken wish to hold on to things we loved while the world threatened to fall apart'. I was struck by that when I first read it, but it resonates more deeply now. Every mile on the bike, however slow, every step along the canal towpath,

every move on rock, however easy, was also my way
of holding on to things I love.

And now, moving up again, I'm holding on to
cold, hard rock. There are streaks of black moss and
splatters of lime-green lichen. Clean, weathered rock
is mostly mouse-back grey; but in the secret places,
where a flake has recently spalled off, the raw rock
is a startling, almost cranberry, pink. Cold, and hard
– and utterly wonderful. A reconnection.

The wind is still buffeting, but the hail has relented.
My hands are chilled but functioning, though I'm
constantly searching for the luxurious jug-handle
holds that surely should be there, but surprisingly
often aren't. This may be 'only' a Grade 1, but not
every move can be reduced to grab and heave.
Subtlety – the hallmark of Lakeland rock – is still
called for. So it's good to find not just that some
strength has returned but that muscle memory is
present and correct too. Given half a chance, the
body remembers the gentle transfer of weight, the
intuitive feel for when the best way over is actually
the way round.

Many years ago, I wrote, glibly, 'With most things
in the outdoor life, the most interesting place is
around the edge of the comfort zone.' That's come
to seem more and more true over time, and a quick
text search on my computer suggests I've flogged
it almost to exhaustion. And yet here we go again
… In fact I believe it more strongly than ever, not
in spite of but because of recent experience. I've
been through a phase when my comfort zone shrank
dramatically, but I was still picking and poking at
whatever limits there were.

And Bernie, who'd watched me struggle many
times, is watching me now. Not making a song and
dance about it, just quietly keeping an eye on me as
I pick a line up a little groove and out on to a knobbly
slab. I'm hardly aware of it as I focus on my moves,
but if she's more anxious than she seems – well, she's
seen me blue-lighted to A & E; she's seen me receive
the attentions of the crash team after reacting badly
to one of the chemo drugs. I could hardly blame her
if she wanted to wrap me in cotton wool, but she's
here and getting on with living, same as I am.

Carpe diem has always seemed a good
philosophy, but it has even more force when you've
confronted the possibility that it could all be taken
away.

Just as beauty is in the eye of the beholder,
'Extreme' is in the eye, and the arms and legs and
feet and fingers – and, above all, in the mind. Only
you know where the limits of your comfort zone are.
(Of course, if you never push those limits, at least a
little bit, you'll also never really know.) Extreme is
not necessarily confined to E9 7a, or Class VI, or
Double Black Diamond. For me, all those things
aren't Extreme, they're impossible. For me, even
thirty years ago, Extreme was leading the wall pitch
of *Central Pillar* (E2 5b) on Esk Buttress. I looked
across at *The Cumbrian* (E5 6b) and knew it would
always be beyond me. And even then I was pretty
much OK with that.

Long Crag Buttress is only a Grade 1 scramble,
but doing it at all was an affirmation. And for this
body, this mind, on that day, in that weather, it was
definitely flirting with the edge of the comfort zone;
there was not much 'only' about it.

To paraphrase Master Yoda:

'Do. Or do not. There is no only.'

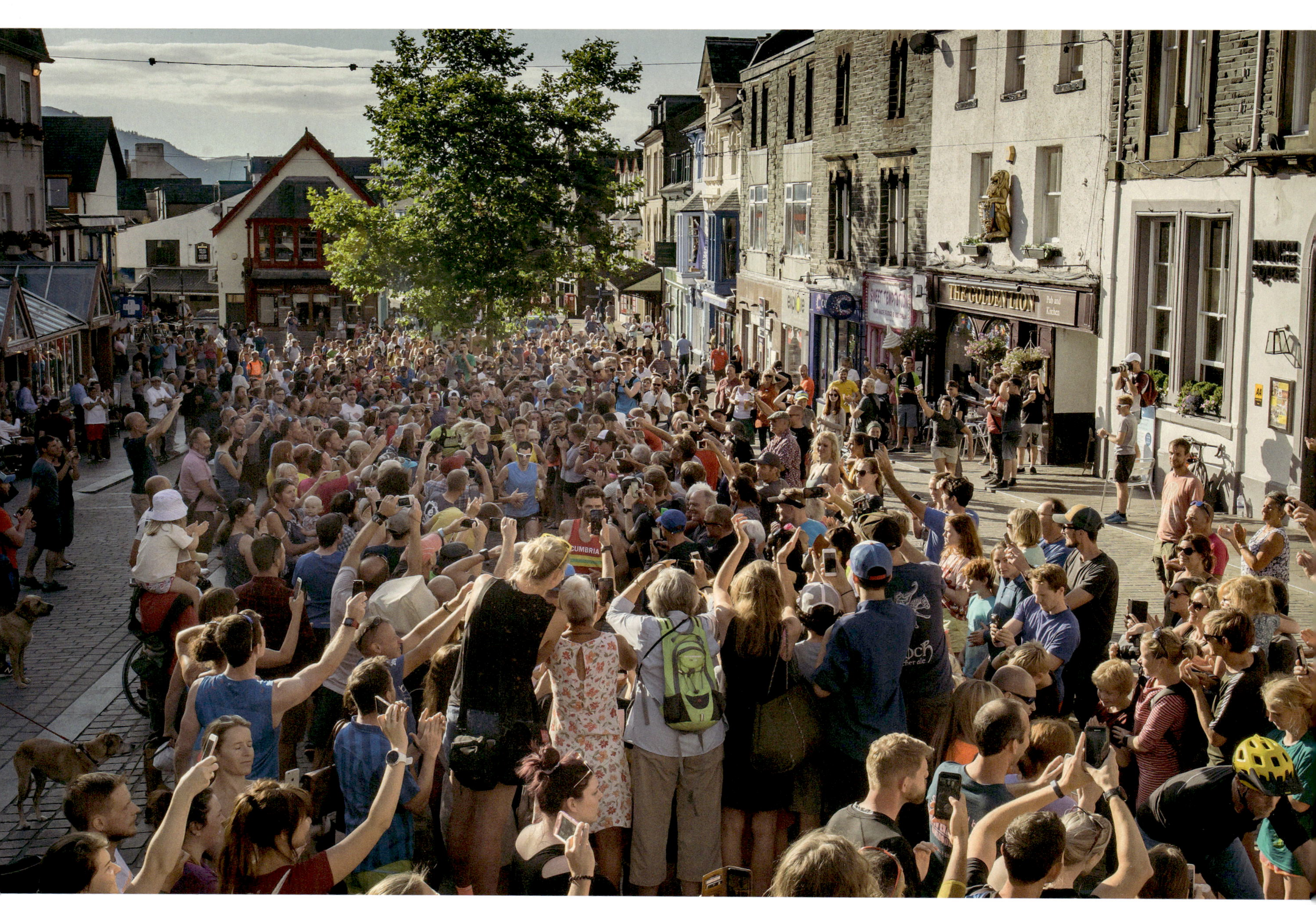

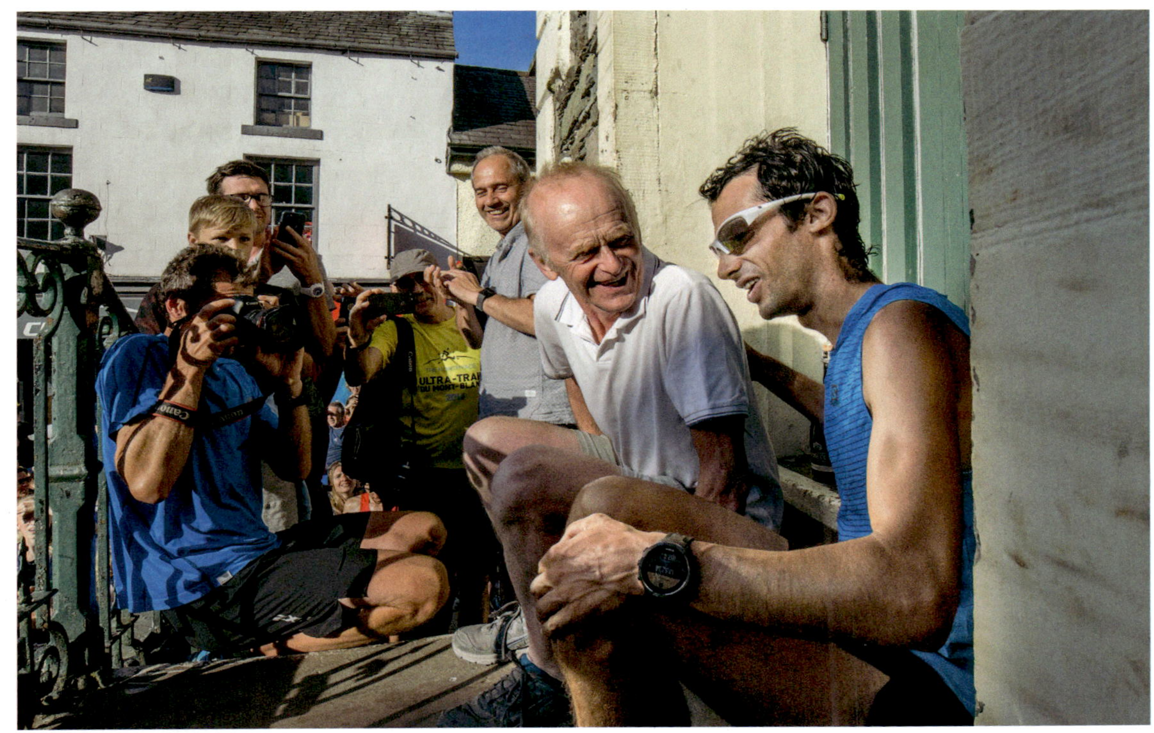

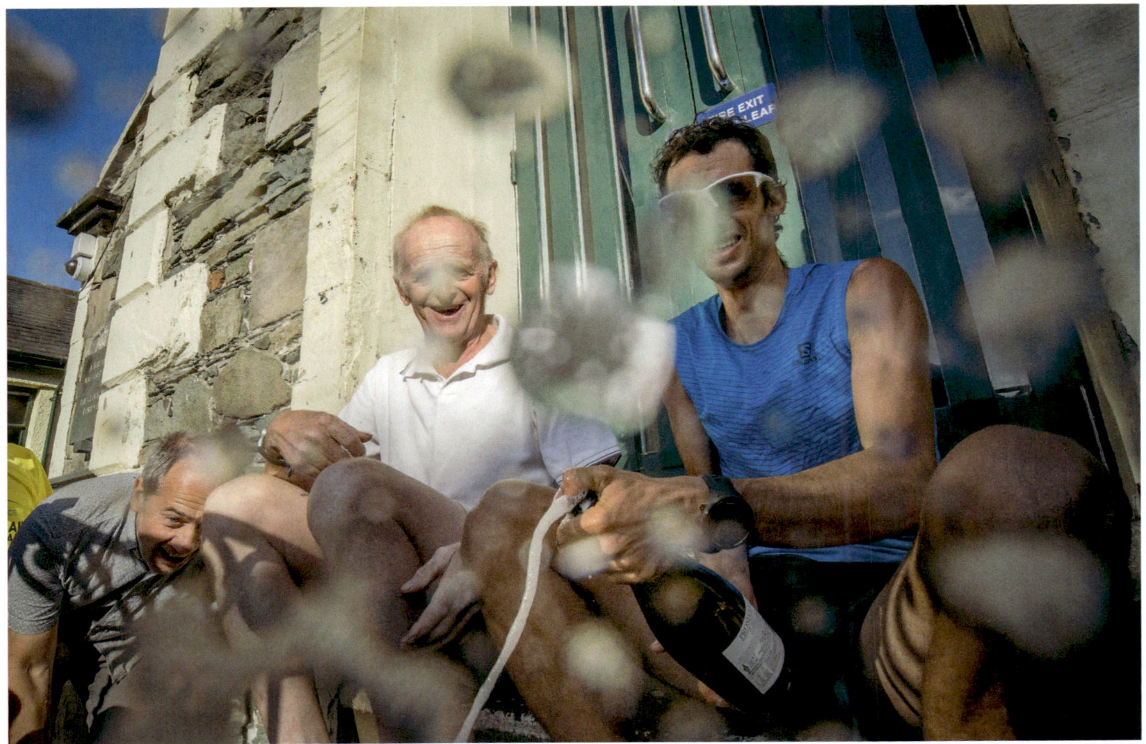

July 2018: Kílian Jornet arrives in Keswick to break the long-standing record for the Bob Graham Round by over an hour, finishing in a time of 12 hours and 52 minutes. He is met and congratulated by the previous record holder, Billy Bland. This legendary fell-running challenge starts and finishes at Keswick's Moot Hall and traverses 42 summits over 66 miles (106 kilometres) of difficult mountain terrain with 26,900 feet (8,200 metres) of ascent. © Tom McNally

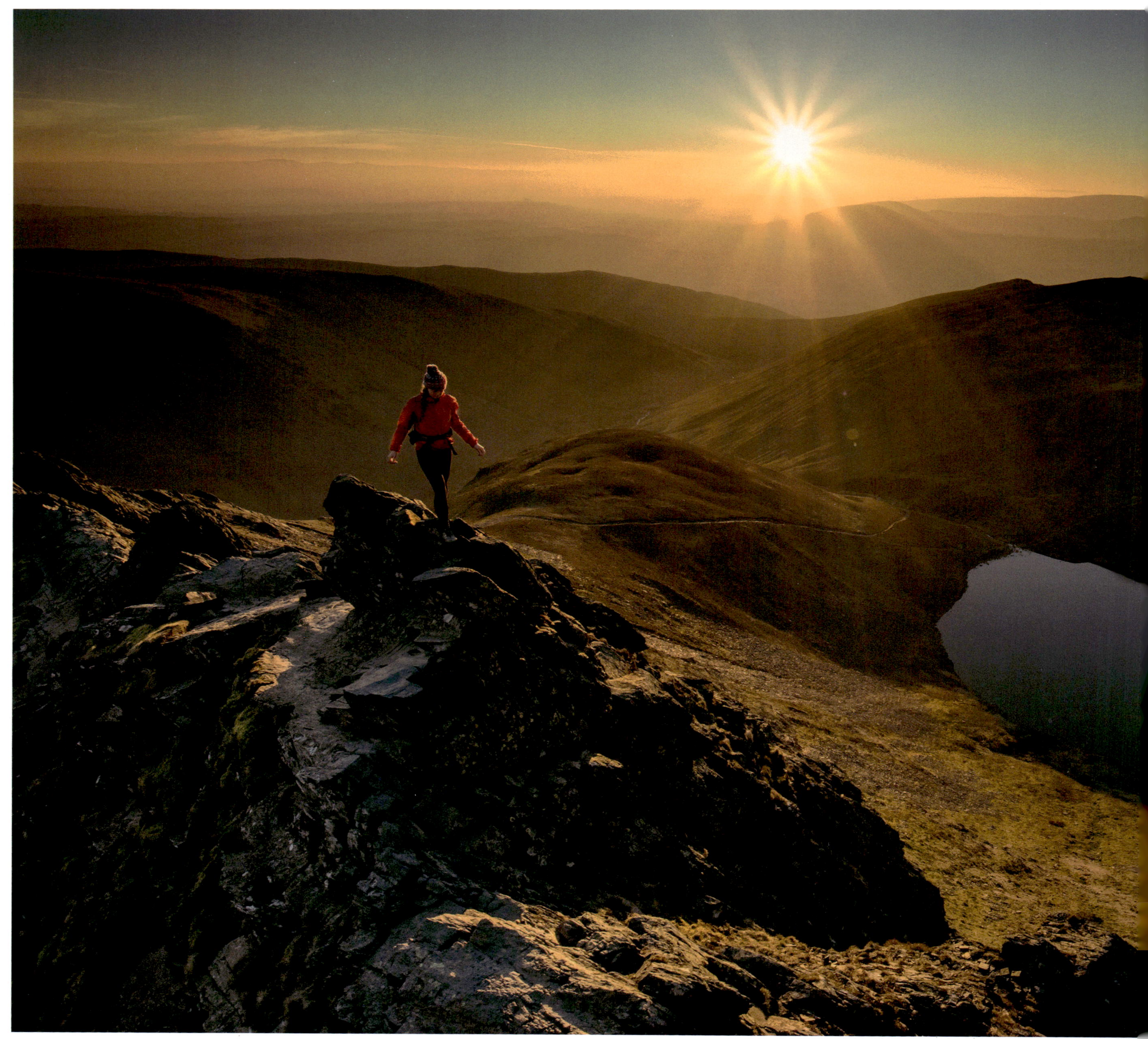

« Helen Fairlamb ascends Blencathra's Sharp Edge at dawn.
  © Tom McNally

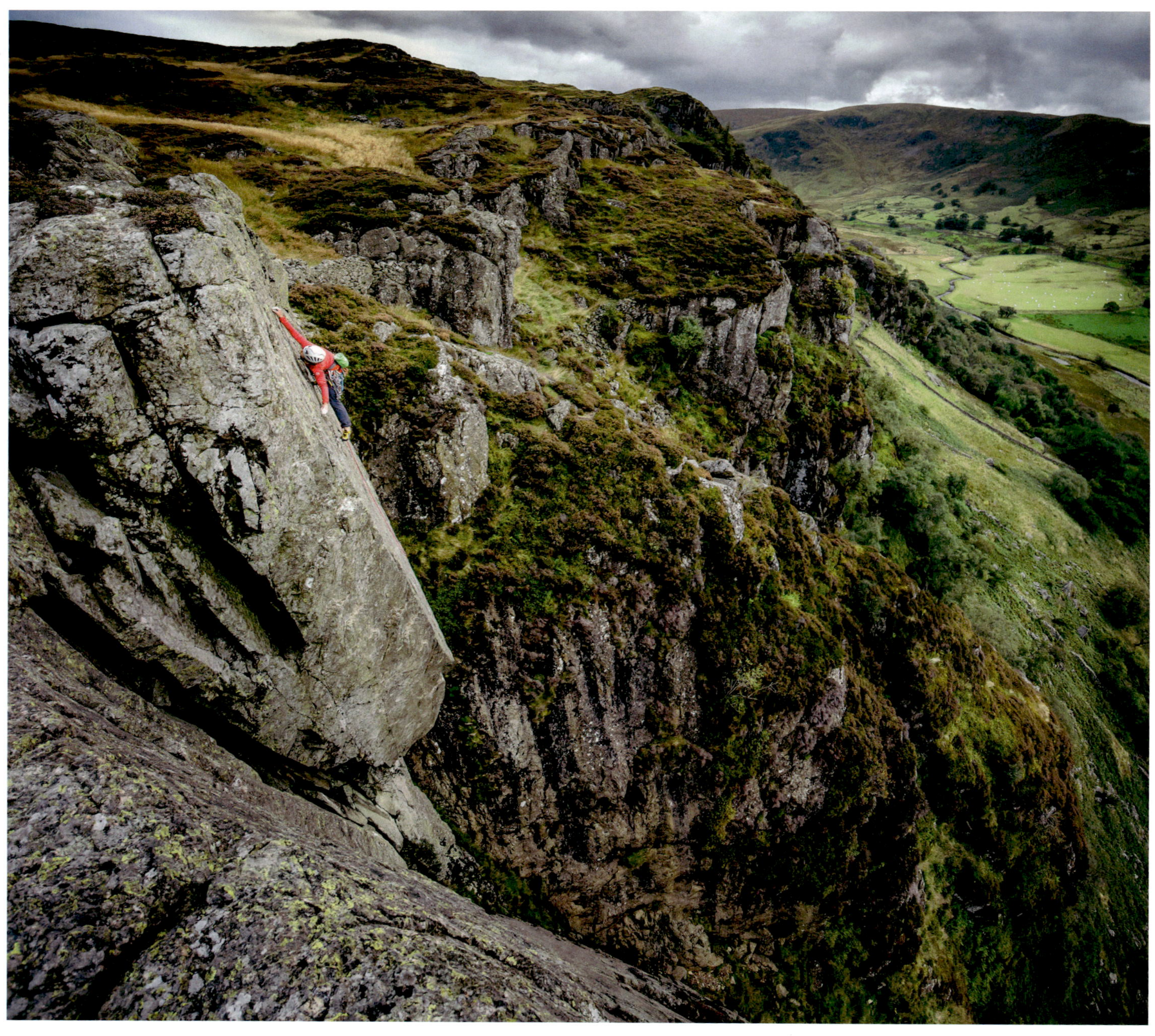

Esther Foster on the final moves of *One Step Beyond* (E4 6a), Gouther Crags. © Tom McNally

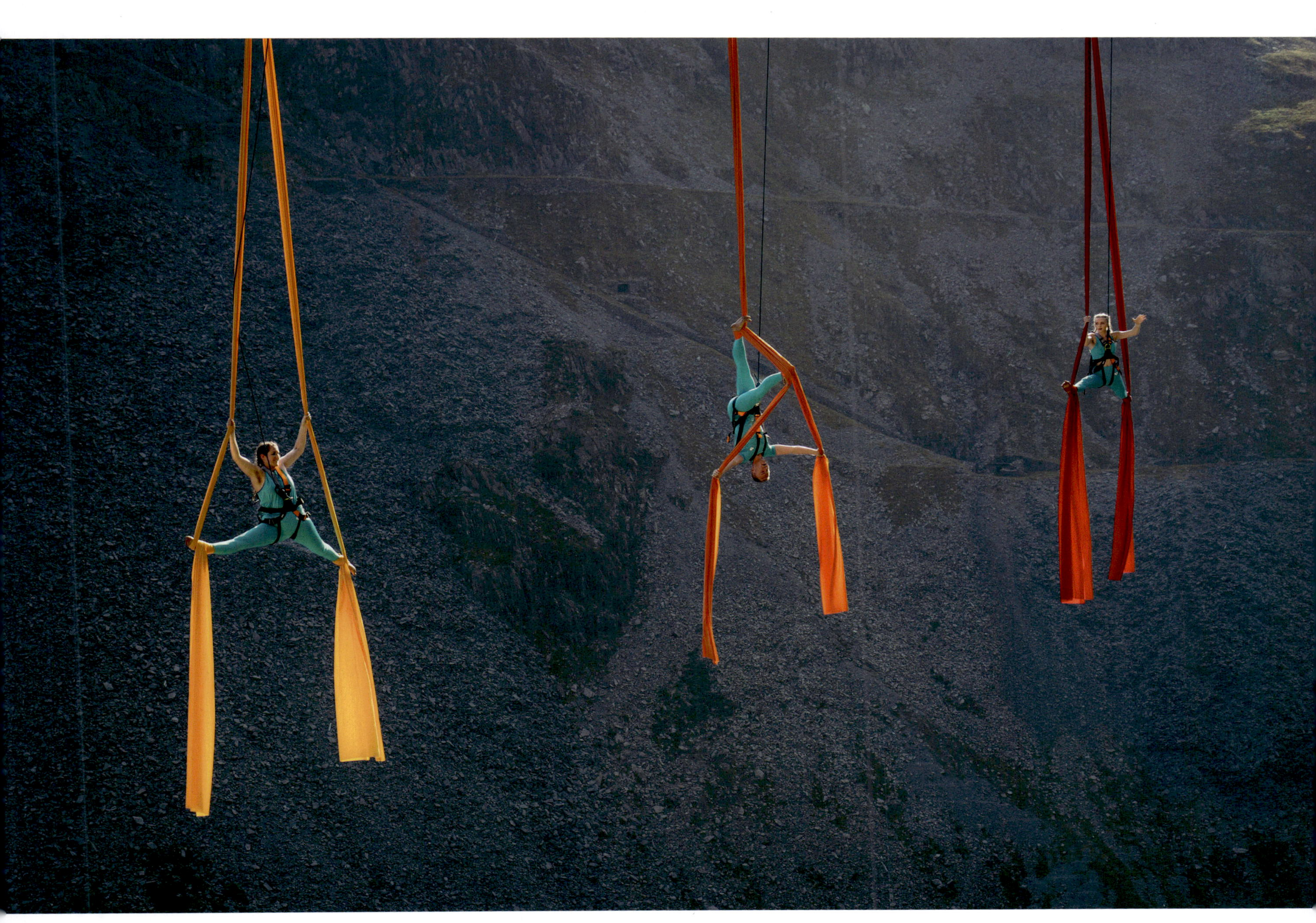

Aerial dancers Georgi Thorns, Jamie Hall and Hannah Tattersall perform
300 metres (1,000 feet) above the valley floor at Honister. © Tom McNally

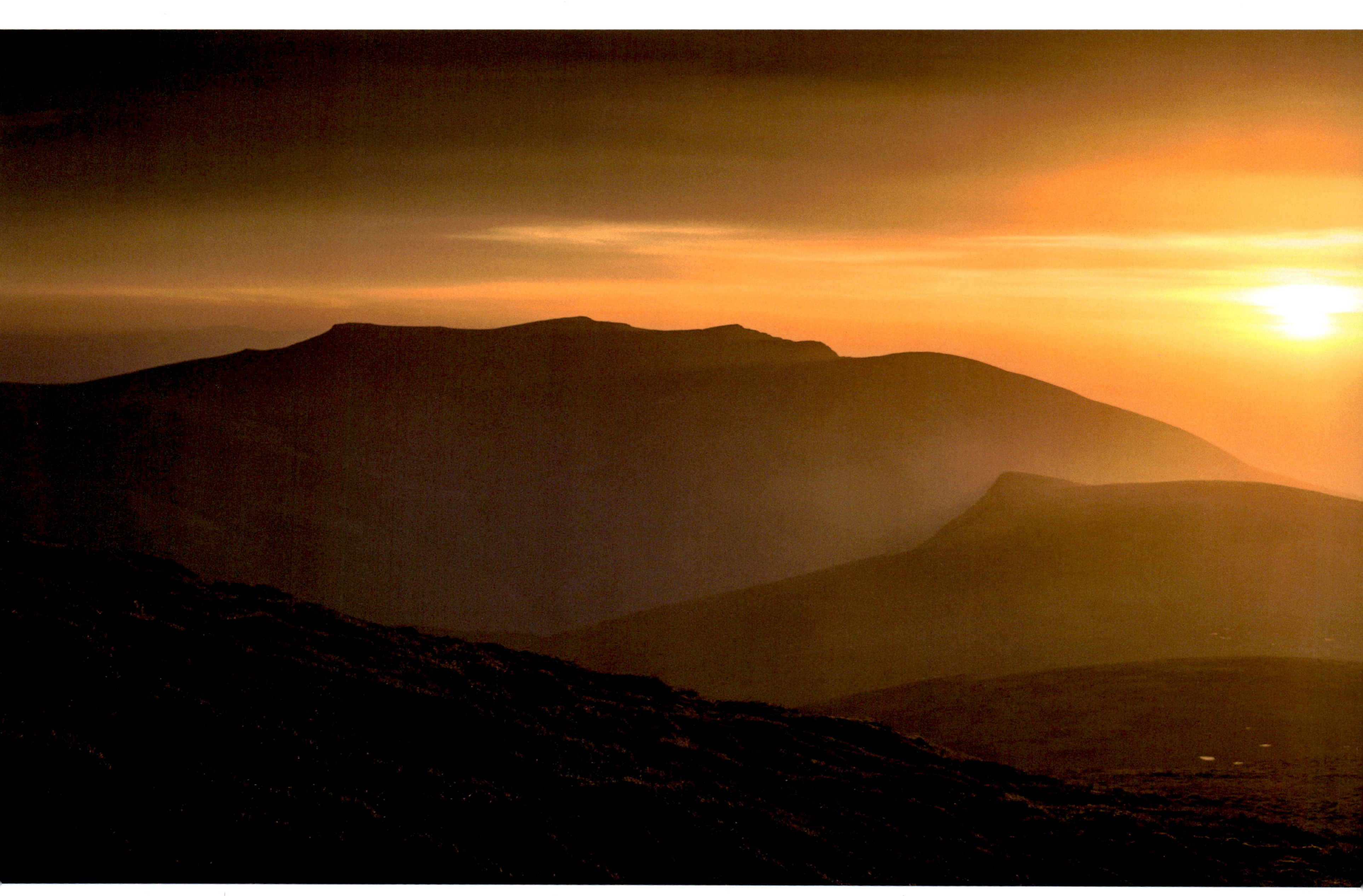

Mountain bikers Dan Stringer, Trevor Morton and Simon May enjoy sunrise from Little Man, Skiddaw. © Tom McNally

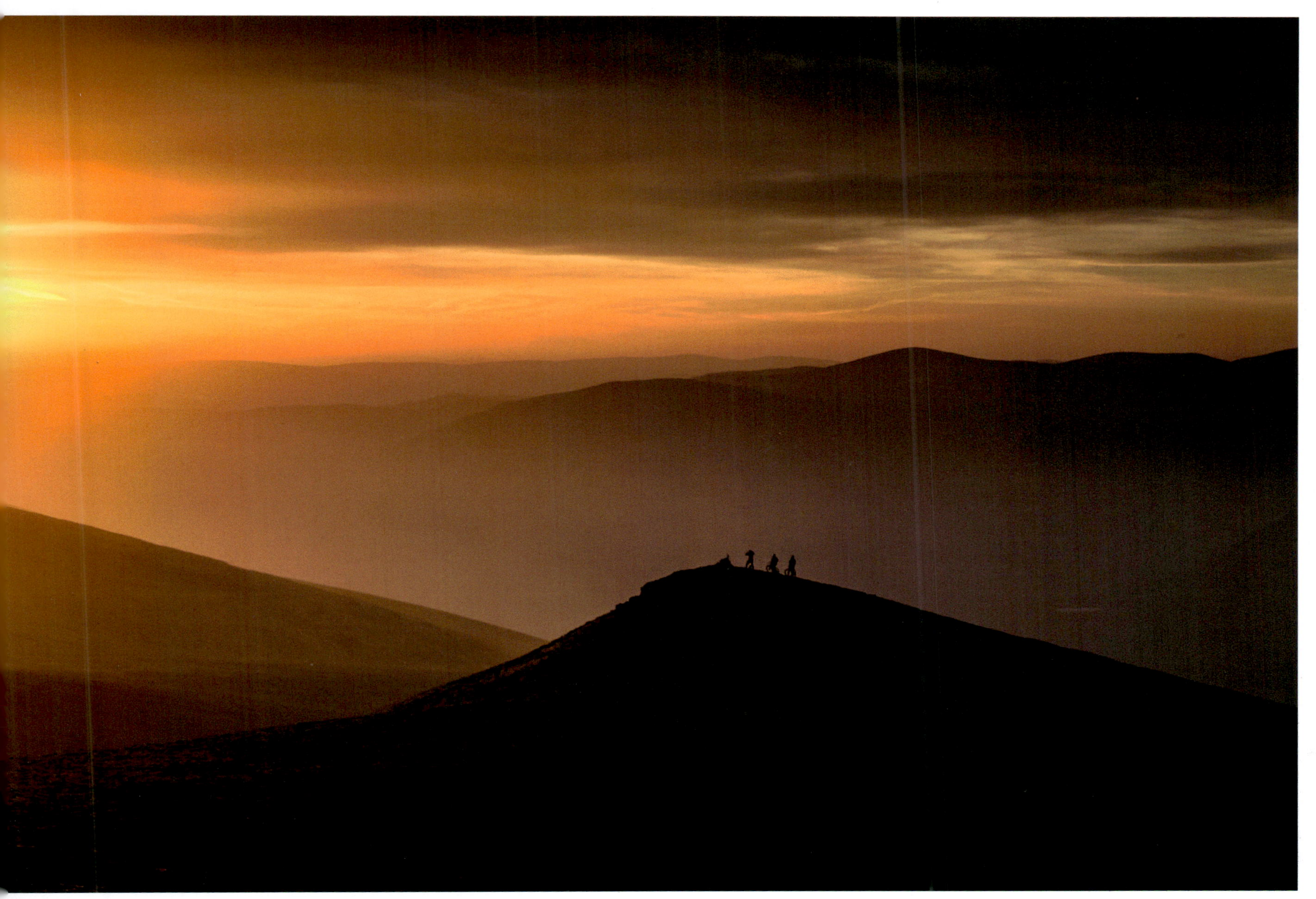

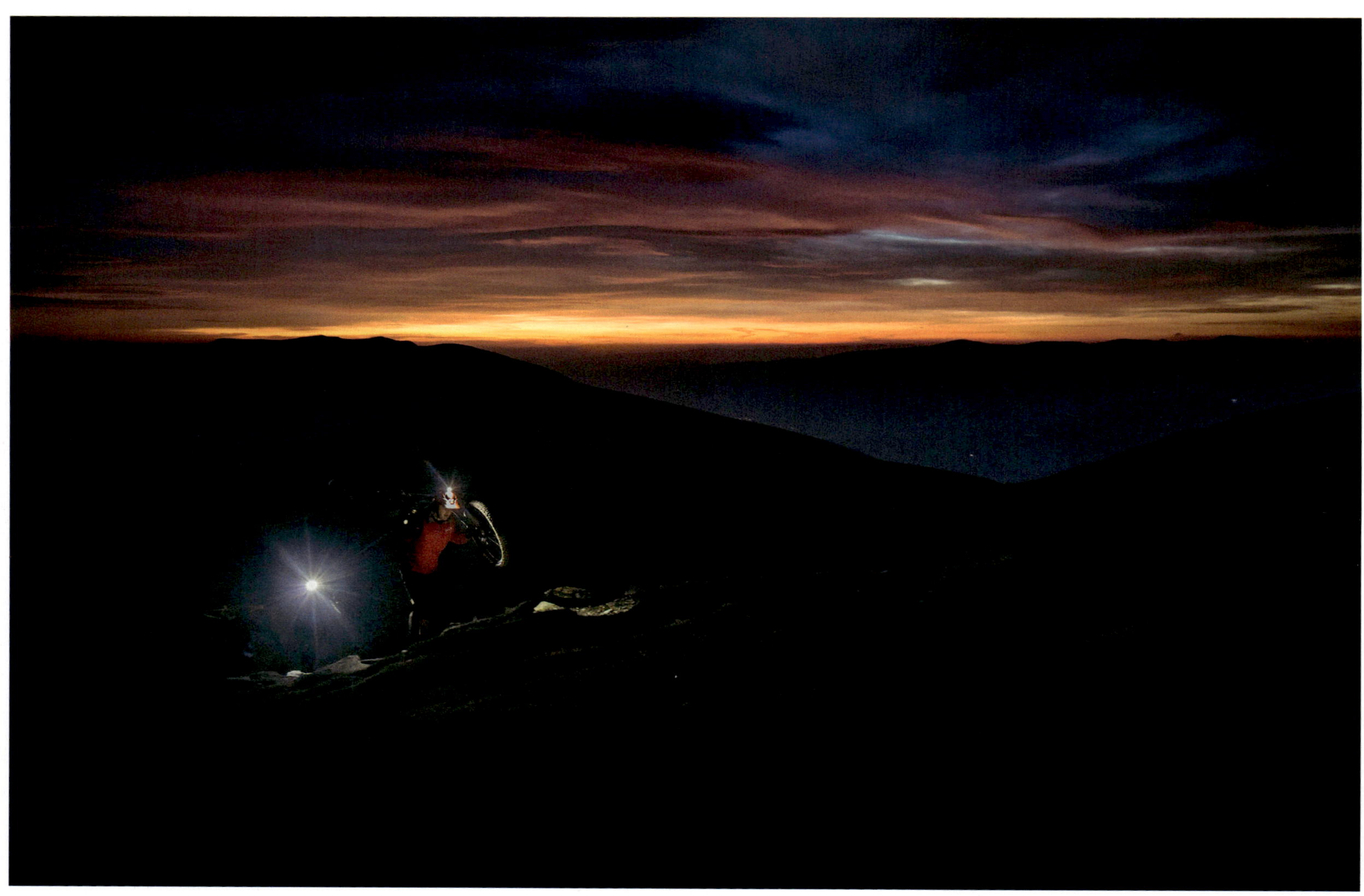
Dan Stringer ascends Skiddaw. © Tom McNally

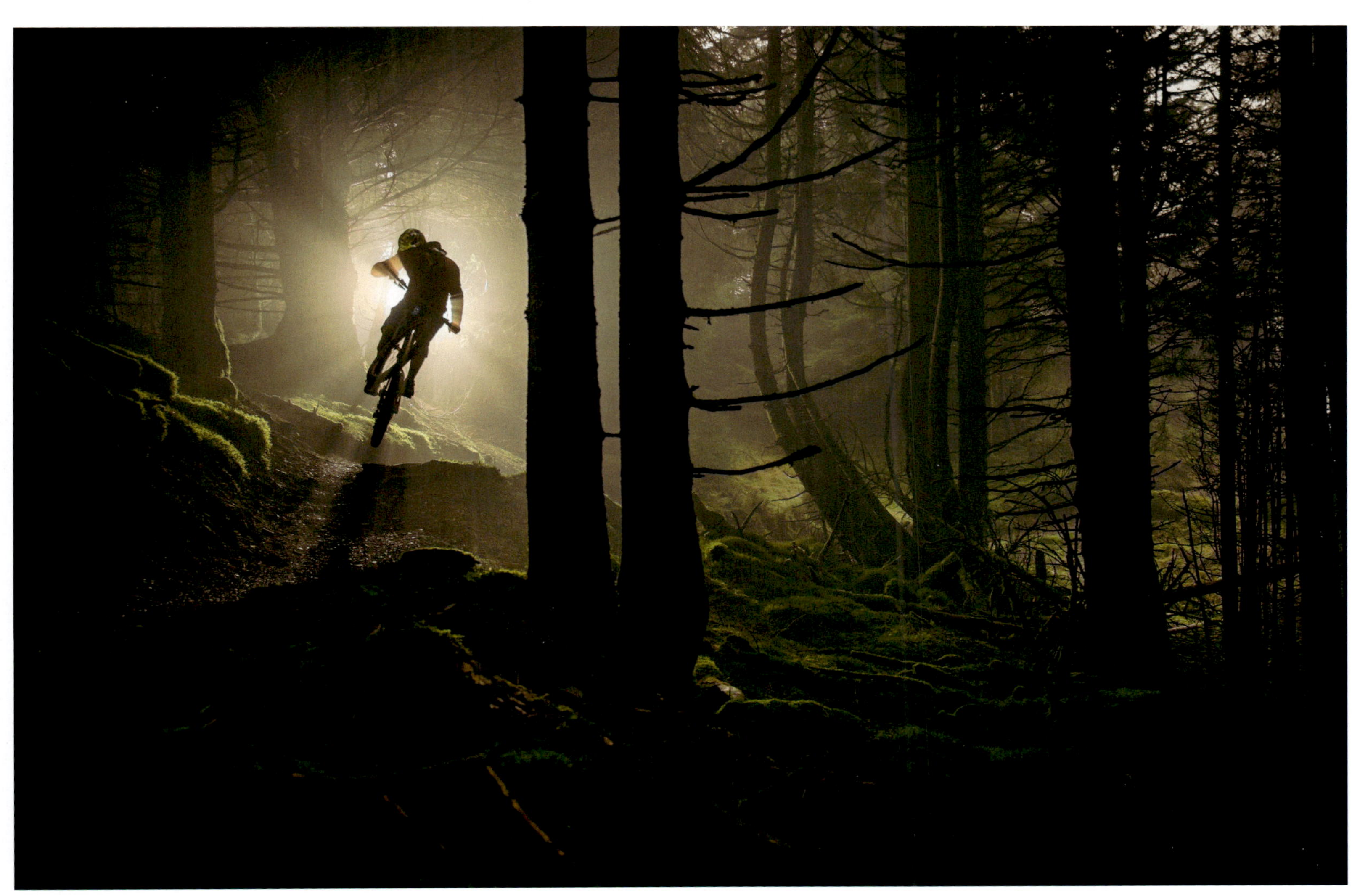

Dava Waterhouse enjoying a misty morning on the trails at Whinlatter Forest. © Tom McNally

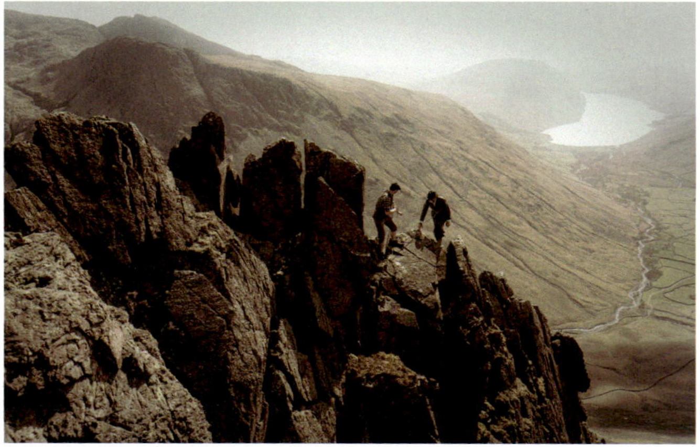

© Nadir Khan

ON THE SHOULDERS OF GIANTS

BY TOM McNALLY

Two pairs of feet quickly clapped across sunlit slate flagstones and swerved through a whitewashed gate, a pair of teenage boys chattering about the great adventure on which they were about to embark. Coiled over the shoulder of one was a washing line 'borrowed' from the yard, unbeknownst to their mother. It wasn't the first time this dubiously thin cord had been pressed into service as a makeshift climbing rope, a lifeline securing them together as they scrambled around on rock outcrops close to their Keswick home. Emboldened with success they now set out for the precipitous mountain crags of Pillar Rock, home to some of the longest and steepest climbs in England.

After a long, hot walk over the fells, they finally reached the base of this enormous cliff, sweaty and breathing heavily from the approach. Undeterred by the great, grey tower of rock looming over them, they began to tie the washing line round their waists. A loud shout rang out, echoing around the crags. They were not the only climbing party there that day. A small group of men made their way across to them, moving quickly over the steep ground. Noticing their efficient progress, impressive moustaches, robust tweeds and stout rope the brothers were quickly in awe of these obviously experienced mountain men.

On seeing the washing line and apparent lack of other suitable equipment and knowledge, other climbers might have laughed them from the mountain. Instead, this group of men, Alpine Club

members no less, recognised the same enthusiasm and commitment with which they were drawn to the mountains. Lending them a spare rope they proceeded to advise the boys on their first day's 'proper' climbing.

This event marked the beginning of one of the most significant partnerships in climbing history. The year was sometime around 1890 and over the next thirty years, George and Ashley Abraham chalked up an impressive list of bold climbs, not only in the Lake District but also Wales, Scotland and the Alps. Many of these were first ascents and remain classic routes to this day. The pair were often described as 'fearless' and were extremely determined. One famous photograph depicts them precariously balanced on a steep rock face, George standing on Ashley's shoulders in an effort to circumvent a blank section. It is possible that their names, like so many of their contemporaries, might have only been recorded in climbing guidebooks, were it not for the fact that their additional talents placed them firmly at the forefront of another field.

George Perry Abraham, father of George and Ashley, was an established photographer with a large bespoke studio in Keswick, earning a decent income from landscape postcards and portraiture. Judging by George Jnr's stint at the Manchester Art School and the high quality of his paintings, he had originally aspired to paint the Lakeland landscape instead of photographing it. Despite this, both he

and his younger brother followed their father into the family business.

Fusing the parallel passions of climbing and photography must have seemed an obvious creative pursuit and from the outset George and Ashley photographed their activities on the crags. There is even an image from 1890 of George and another brother, Sidney, clinging precariously to the side of Sharp Edge, the rope joining them said to be the fabled washing line.

In 1895, while at Wasdale Head, they were introduced to one of the most talented climbers of the era, Owen Glynne Jones. He was planning a book and proposed the brothers provide images with which to illustrate the text. They must have worked quickly as *Rock-Climbing in the English Lake District* was published to great acclaim just a year and a half later. Unfortunately it was not well received by all. Some members of the climbing establishment felt the publicity to be somewhat sensationalist and that profiting from climbing was poor form. Untroubled by such sensitivities, George and Ashley understood the commercial value of exciting content, and many of their images were undoubtedly thrilling, depicting climbers (often George) delicately poised above heart-stopping drops. They also wrote about their exploits in detail, although by modern standards their tone is more understated than sensational. One account, in *Beautiful Lakeland* (1912), of freezing rain turning Napes Needle into a 'huge inverted icicle' while they were on the summit is particularly memorable:

It was an unpleasant dilemma, but we got out of it in the following manner. The strongest man of the party lowered first one and then the other of us, swinging round and round on the rope end like a spider at the end of its clew, until we reached the neck between the Needle and the mountain. Then the last man tied his rope round the top of the rock and came down hand over hand for about twenty feet, when off slipped the rope from the top and he came tumbling down on to us. Beyond a severe shaking he was no worse, and this, with a bruised shoulder where his boot struck me as his body flew through the air, was all the damage sustained in our escapade.

Those who know the location can appreciate the true severity of this particular 'escapade'.

With Ashley behind the lens, Owen Glynne Jones and George forged one of the strongest climbing partnerships of the era and had been planning an ambitious attempt on Kangchenjunga. Sadly, in 1899 OGJ was killed in a fall on Dent Blanche in the French Alps. Despite this blow, George and Ashley's work continued apace. They published prolifically but while their books and articles detailed many of their climbing exploits, they revealed little of their photographic approach. What we do know comes from those who worked with them. One thing is sure: they were true masters of their craft.

Eschewing modern compact cameras of the time, Ashley and George favoured the far superior results afforded by an Underwood large-format plate camera, wilfully accepting the logistical and technical challenges presented by its use in precarious locations. Indeed, it is recorded on more than one occasion that after emerging from under the dark cloth, temporarily blinded by the increase in brightness, the photographer promptly fell off the stance on which he was perched. Luckily these falls were always held in check, the photographer 'none the worse but for some slight bruising' from the rope.

Perhaps unsurprisingly they became two of the first proponents of motoring in the Lake District, driving their heavy photographic equipment as far as possible before the awkward burden of camera, tripod and glass plates (ten-kilograms-plus) was shouldered by Ashley's tall, fifteen-stone frame. Their safety record on the rock was unblemished, but a broken collarbone sustained in a car accident by George attests that the same cannot be said for the road.

In contrast, their approach to photography was unwaveringly patient and methodical. Like all great photographers they understood the vital importance of good light to the rendering of a scene and were happy to wait for it. With the greater distances involved while working in the Alps they often employed porters who apparently, upon seeing the camera and tripod deployed, instinctively knew there would be time for a nap. They also rarely used a light meter, an unimaginable feat for many photographers, emphasising their considerable technical abilities.

Many think that image manipulation is a modern development but for George and Ashley it was commonplace, both in the taking of their photographs and the printing of them. When photographing landscapes they sometimes employed their nieces to hold up flowers, better framing the edge of a scene, and even chased cattle into the edge of lakes to provide interest to a composition. In their climbing images they soon realised that white jumpers stood out against the rock far better than tweeds and were criticised for tilting the camera to exaggerate the steepness of some climbs. In the darkroom, scenes were often 'enhanced' and dramatic skies were transplanted from separate exposures – a practice still frowned upon by purists today.

Whatever the ethical concerns, it is obvious that George and Ashley were completely focused on one thing: making the very best images they could. Shrewd businessmen, they became extremely successful, using lecture tours to promote their work, and even brought picture-postcard sets to Britain, appropriating the idea while on a trip to Zermatt, using many of the exact same Lakeland locations which now draw so much attention on platforms such as Instagram. Right up until the end of their careers they remained modest about their contributions to both climbing and photography and, following in the footsteps of those Alpine Club men, were always willing to offer help to those venturing on to the crags.

Some argue that the Abraham brothers were the first true 'adventure sports' photographers. A better term might be 'influencers', using their bold climbs and stunning photography to both make a living and open people's eyes to beautiful landscapes and the possibilities of adventure. Whatever the case, we owe them much. The groundbreaking techniques they pioneered are the mainstay of photographers the world over. Just like the combined climbing tactics they employed, the images we now make are taken standing on their shoulders.

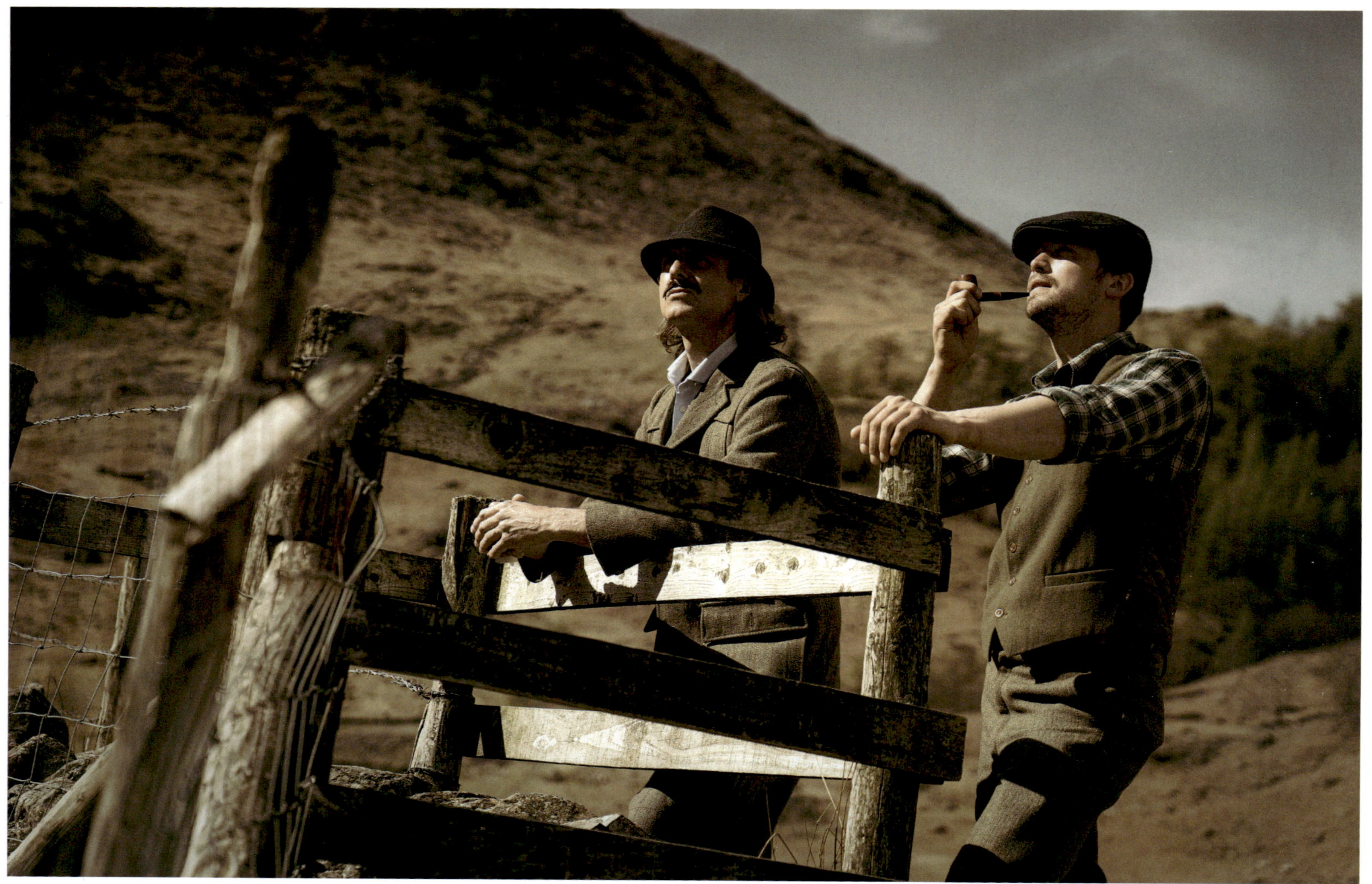

Antony McPhillips and Lyndon Chatting-Walters in Victorian costume for the film
Standing on the Shoulders of Giants, which celebrates the work and legacy of George
and Ashley Abraham. © Nadir Khan

Antony on the start of *Innominate Crack* (VS 4b), Kern Knotts. © Nadir Khan »

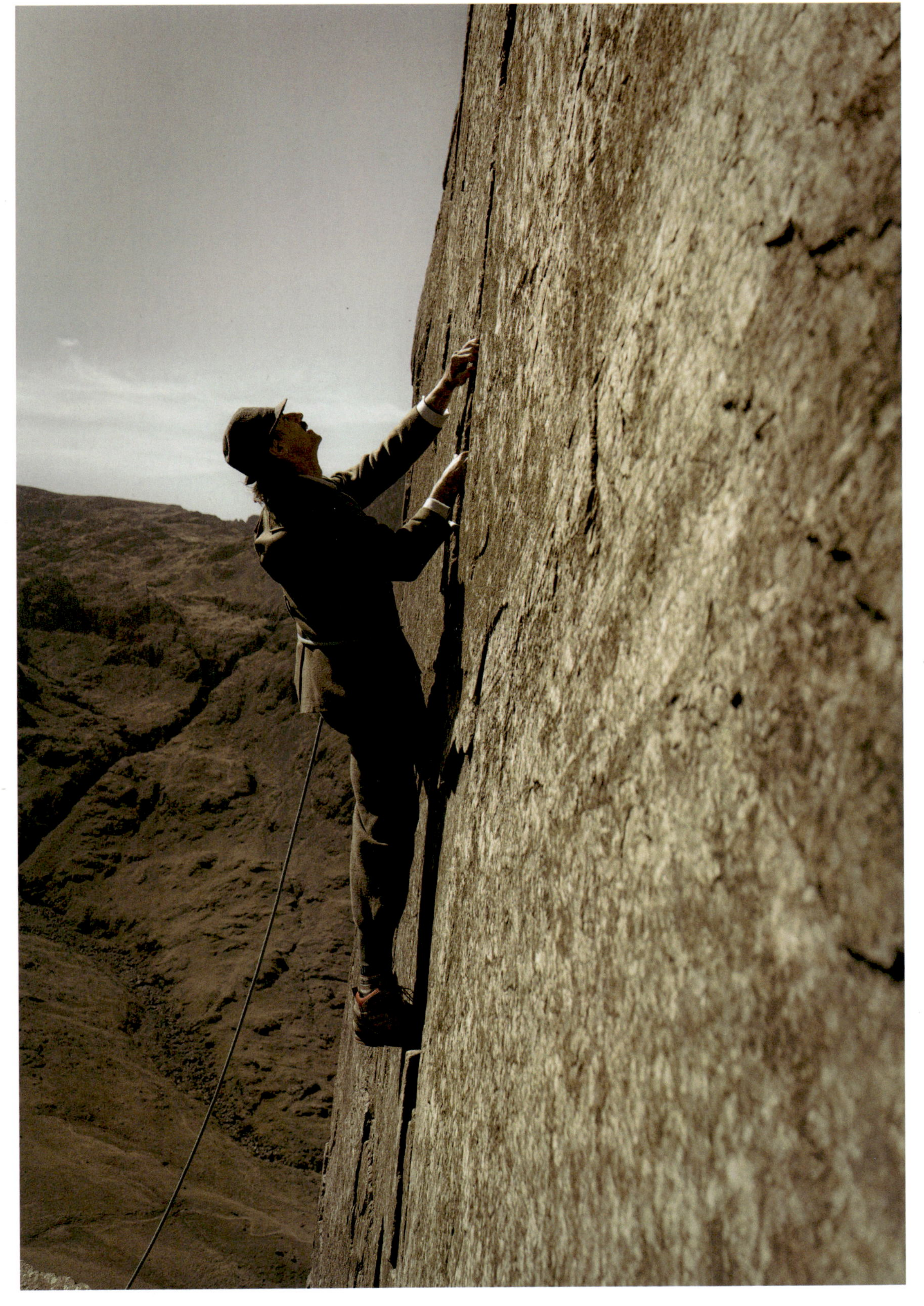

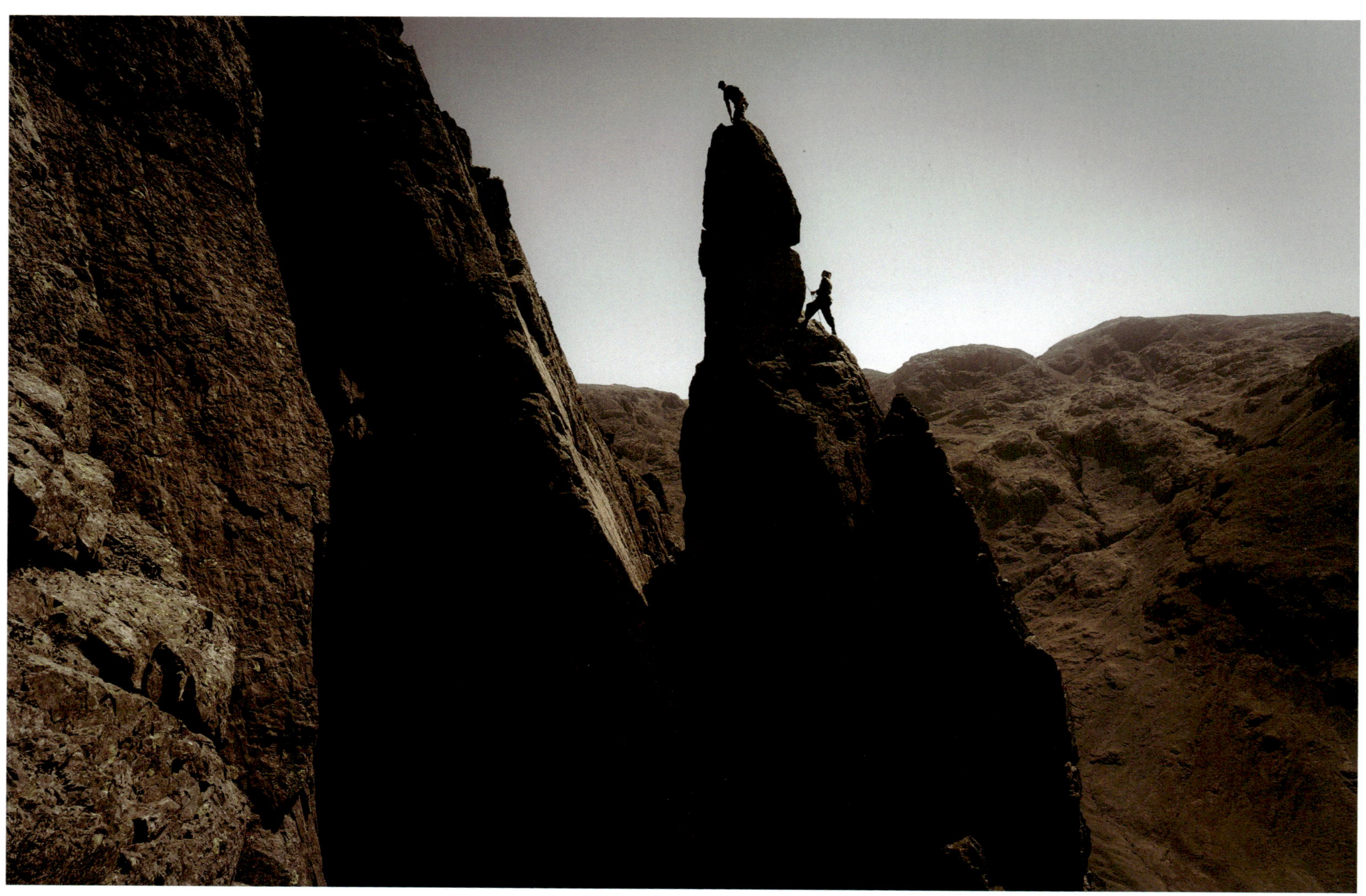

Antony and Lyndon on the iconic Napes Needle. © Nadir Khan

Needle Ridge. © Nadir Khan »

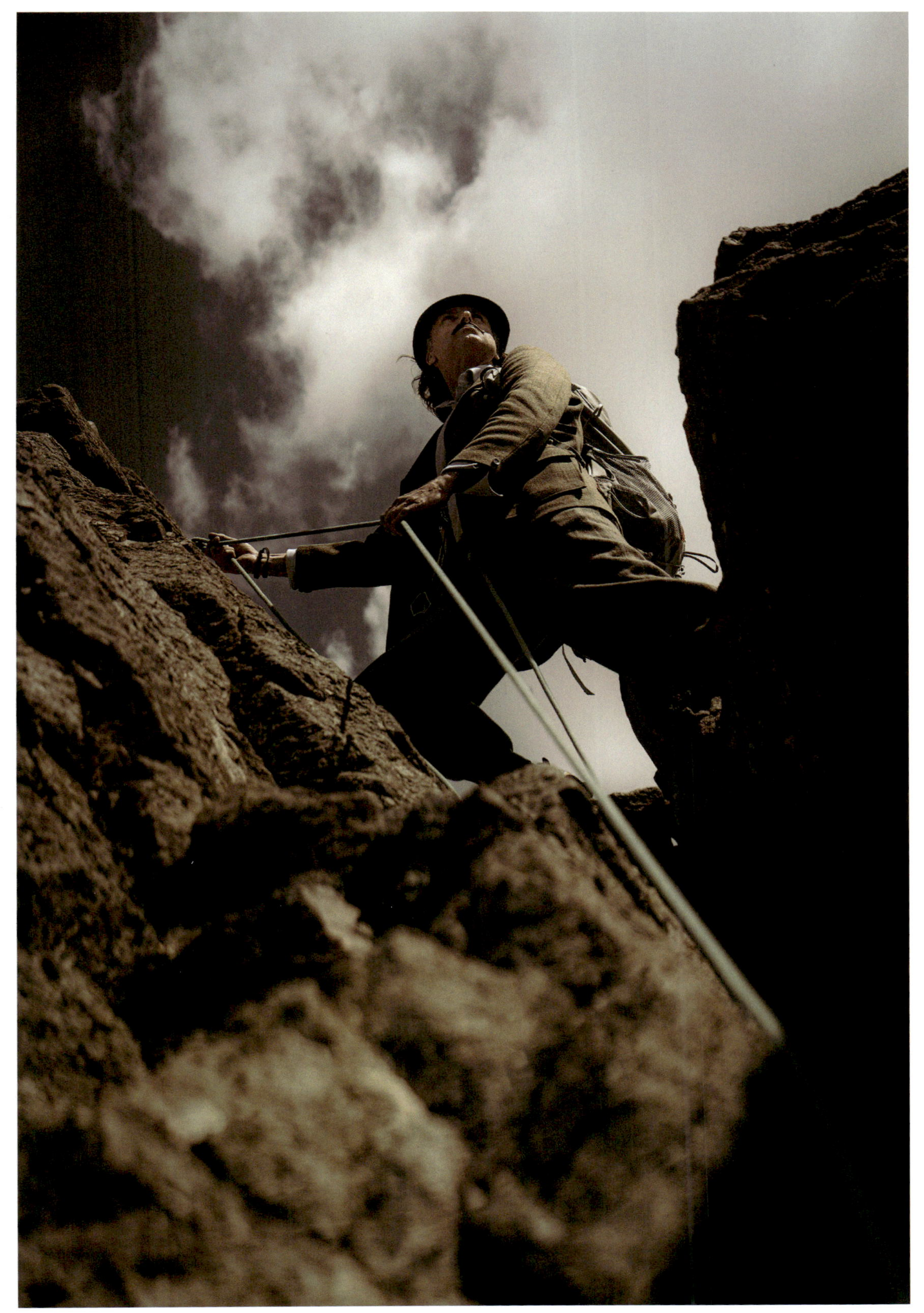

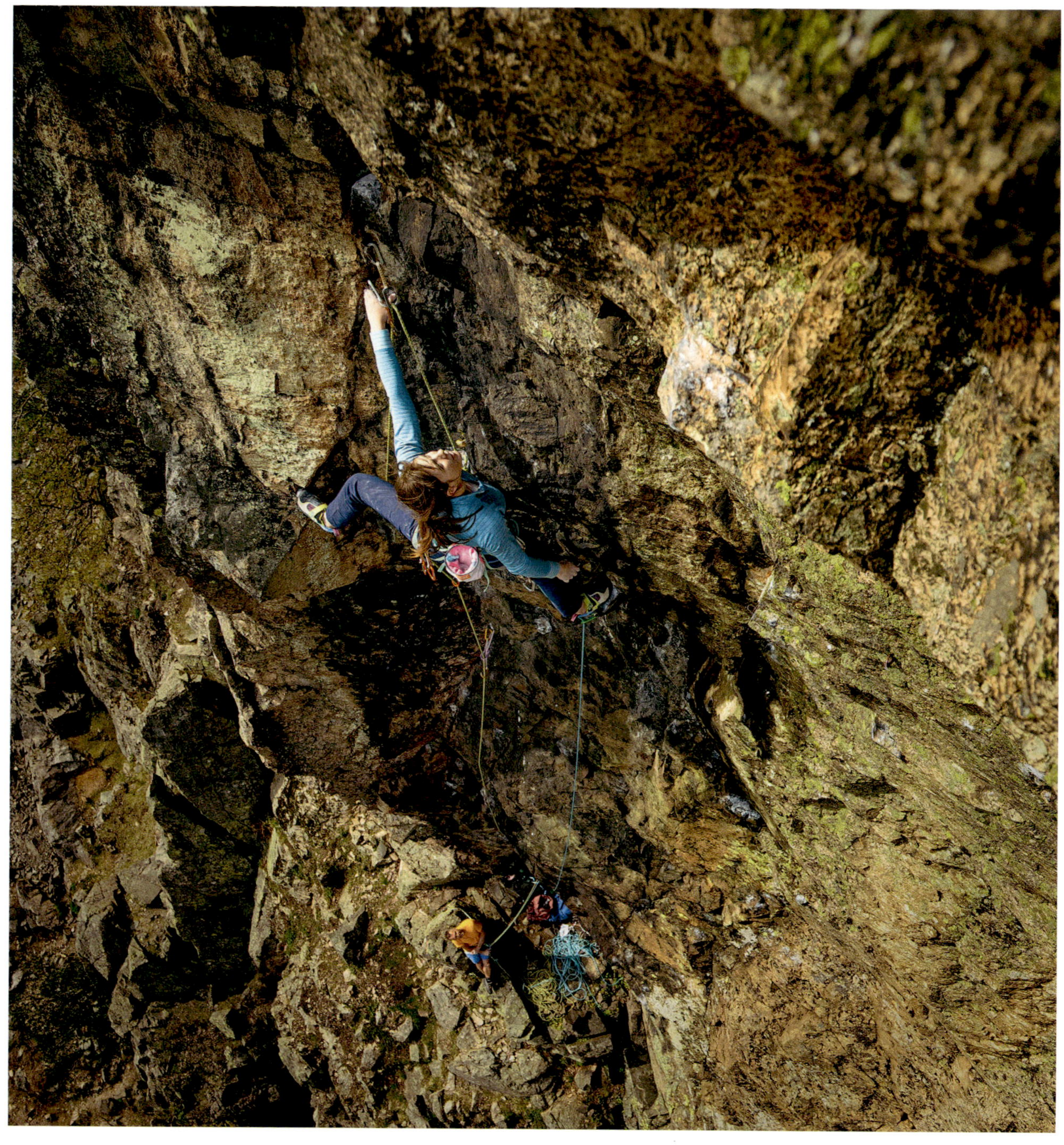

Anna Taylor on *Trilogy* (E5 6a), Raven Crag, Langdale. © Nadir Khan

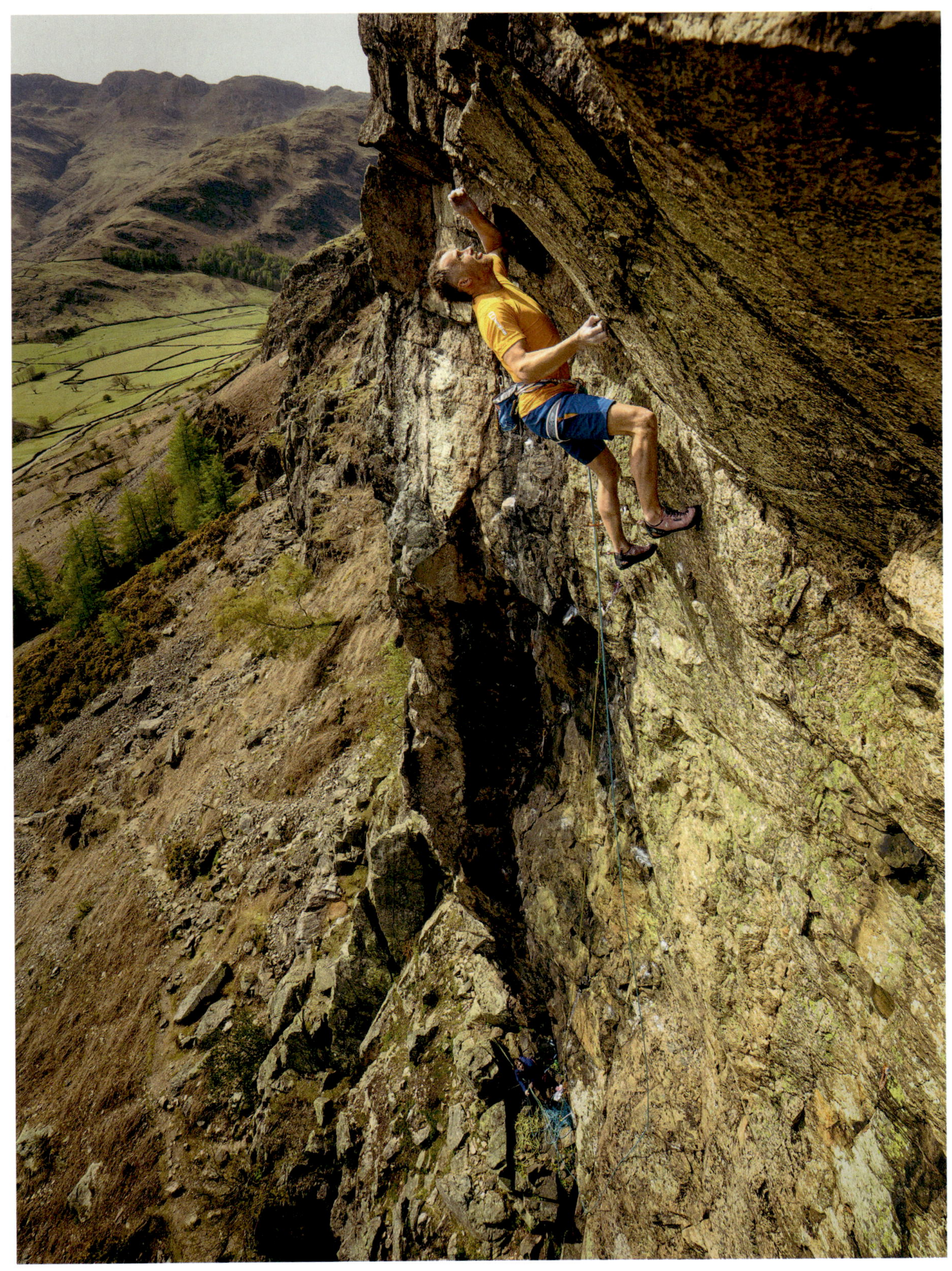

Leo Houlding on *Eulogy Direct* (E8 6c), Raven Crag, Langdale. © Nadir Khan

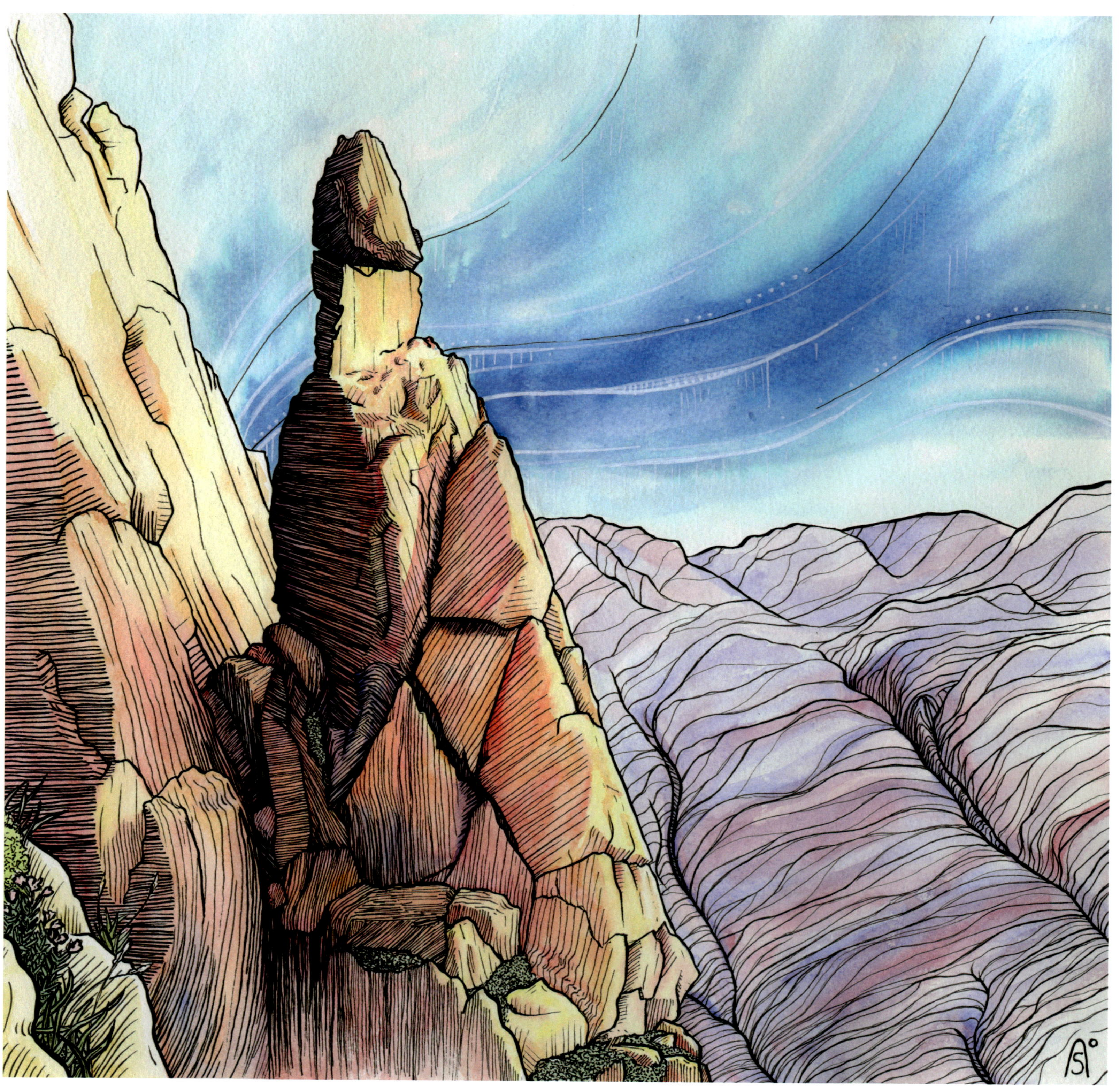

SUMMER

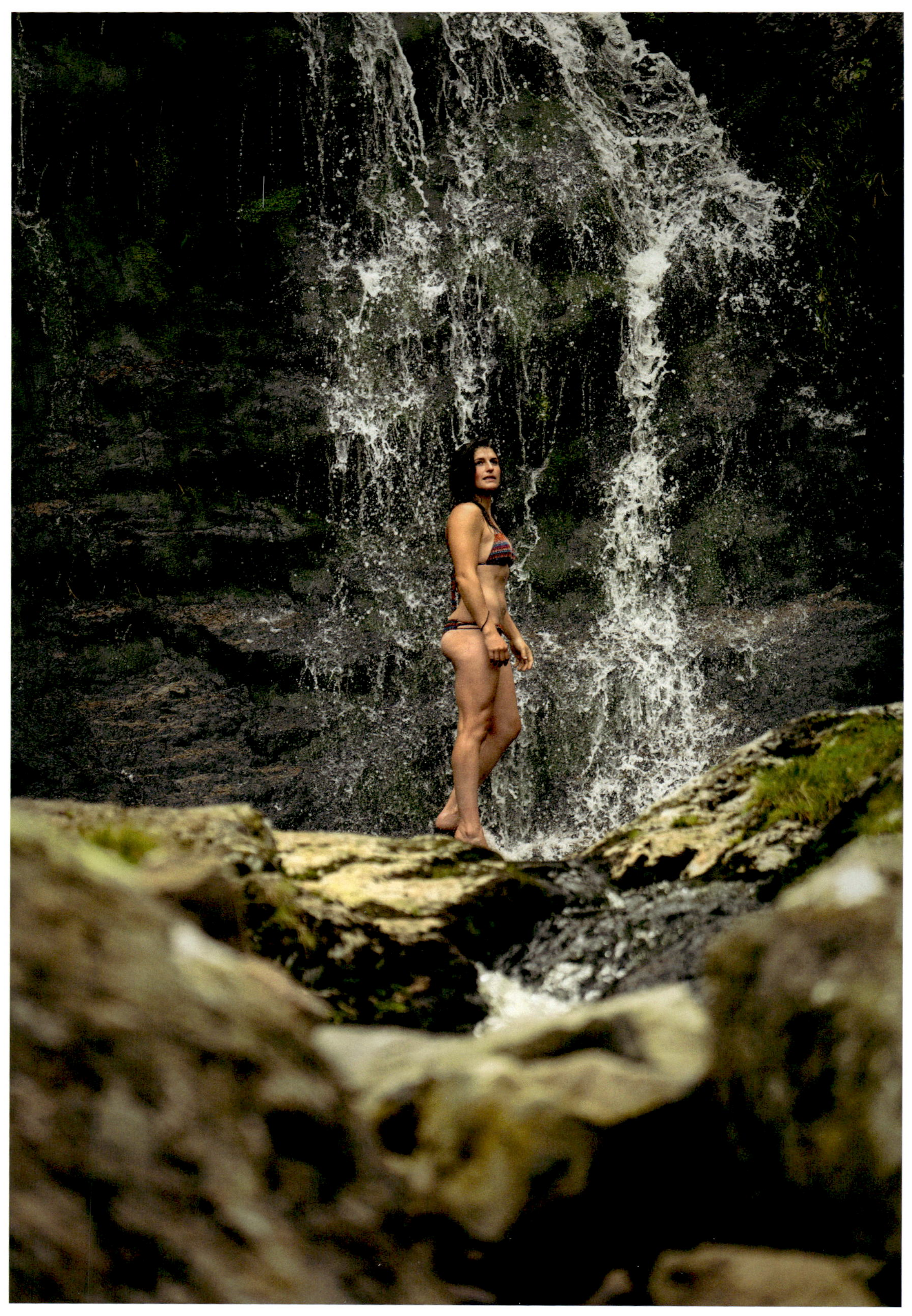

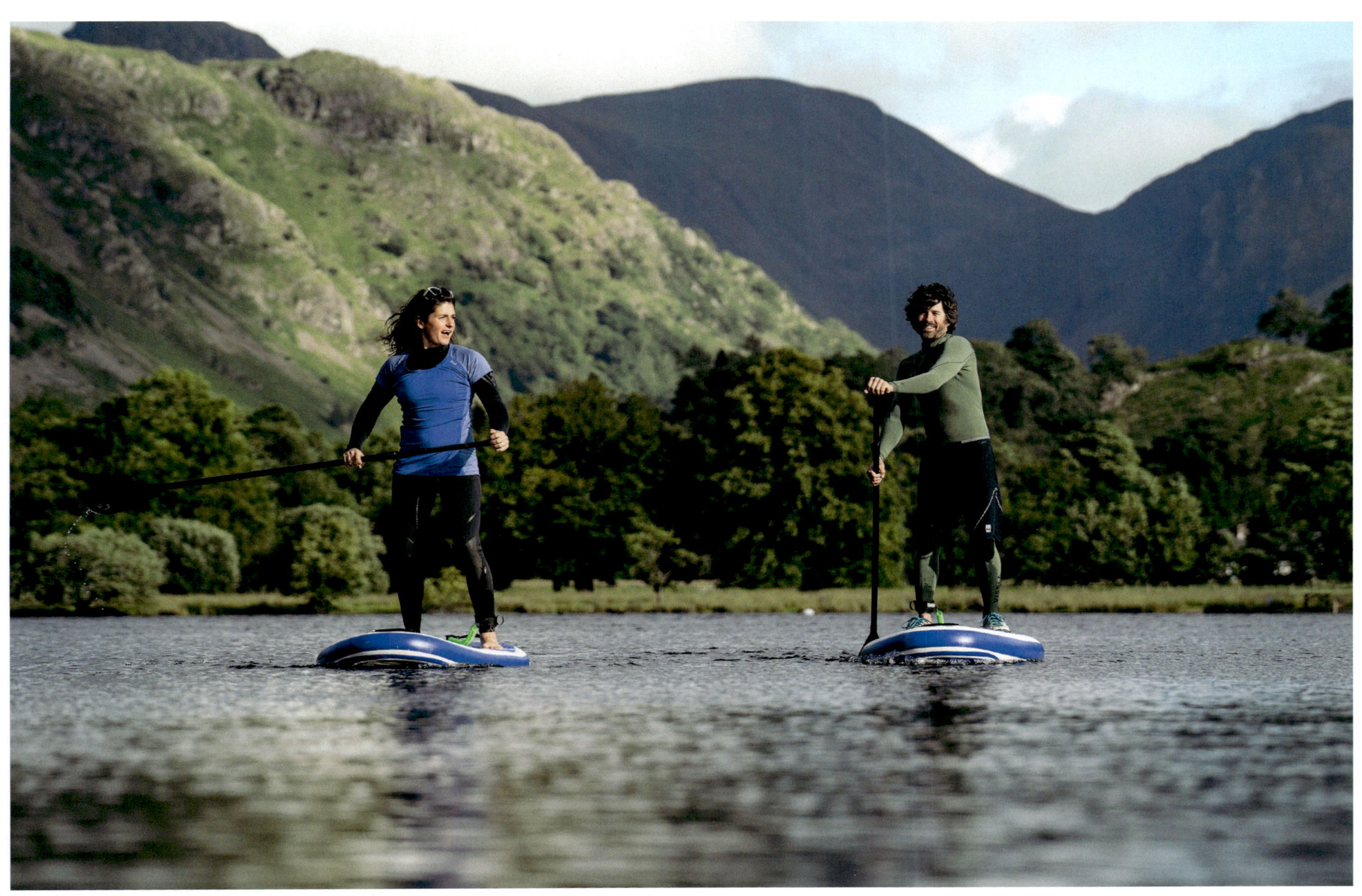

Into the Outside's Becki Vale and Dan Fylan-Smith stand-up paddleboarding on Ullswater. © Nadir Khan

« Becki Vale taking an early cold-water dip in Moss Force waterfall.
© Nadir Khan

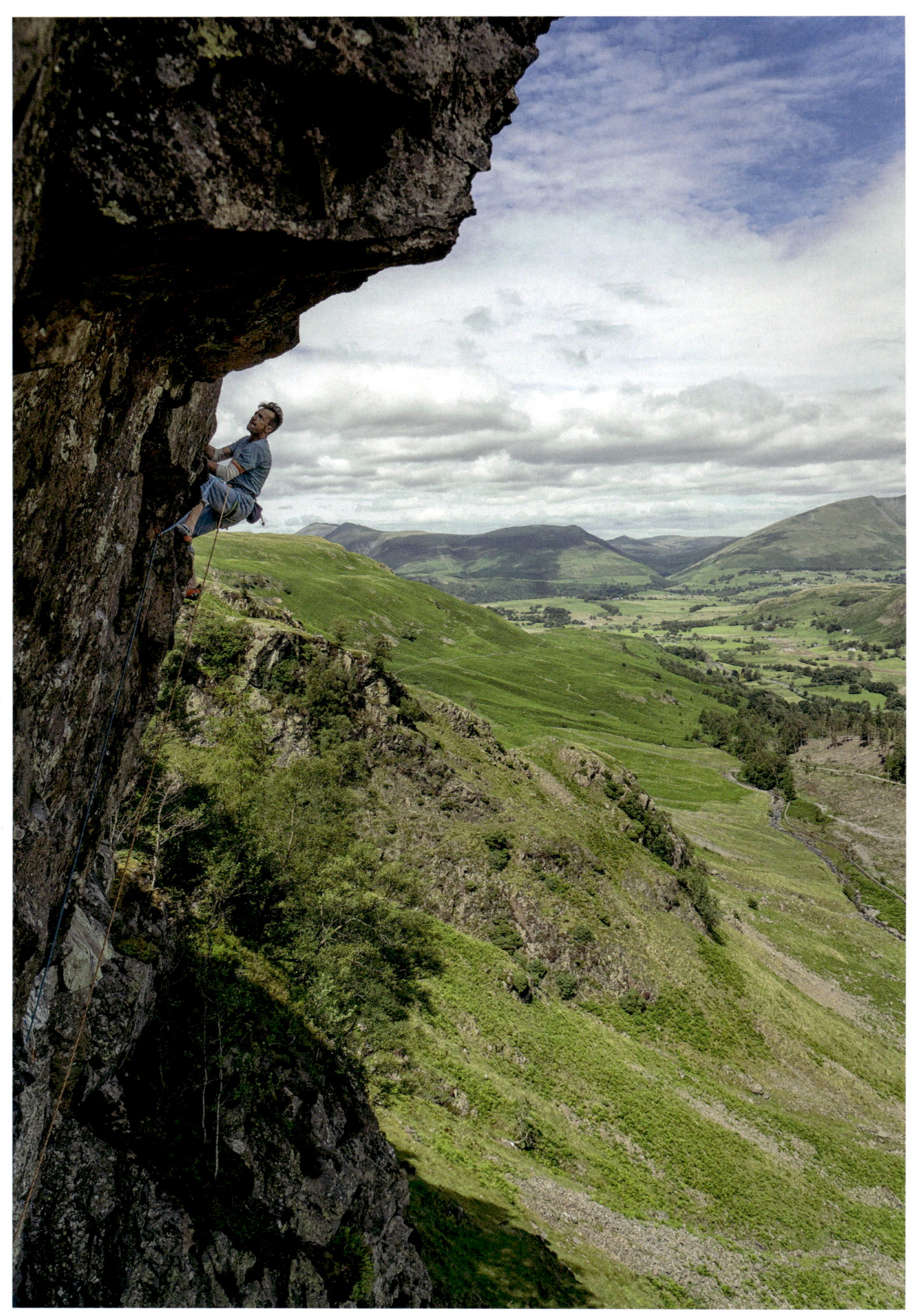

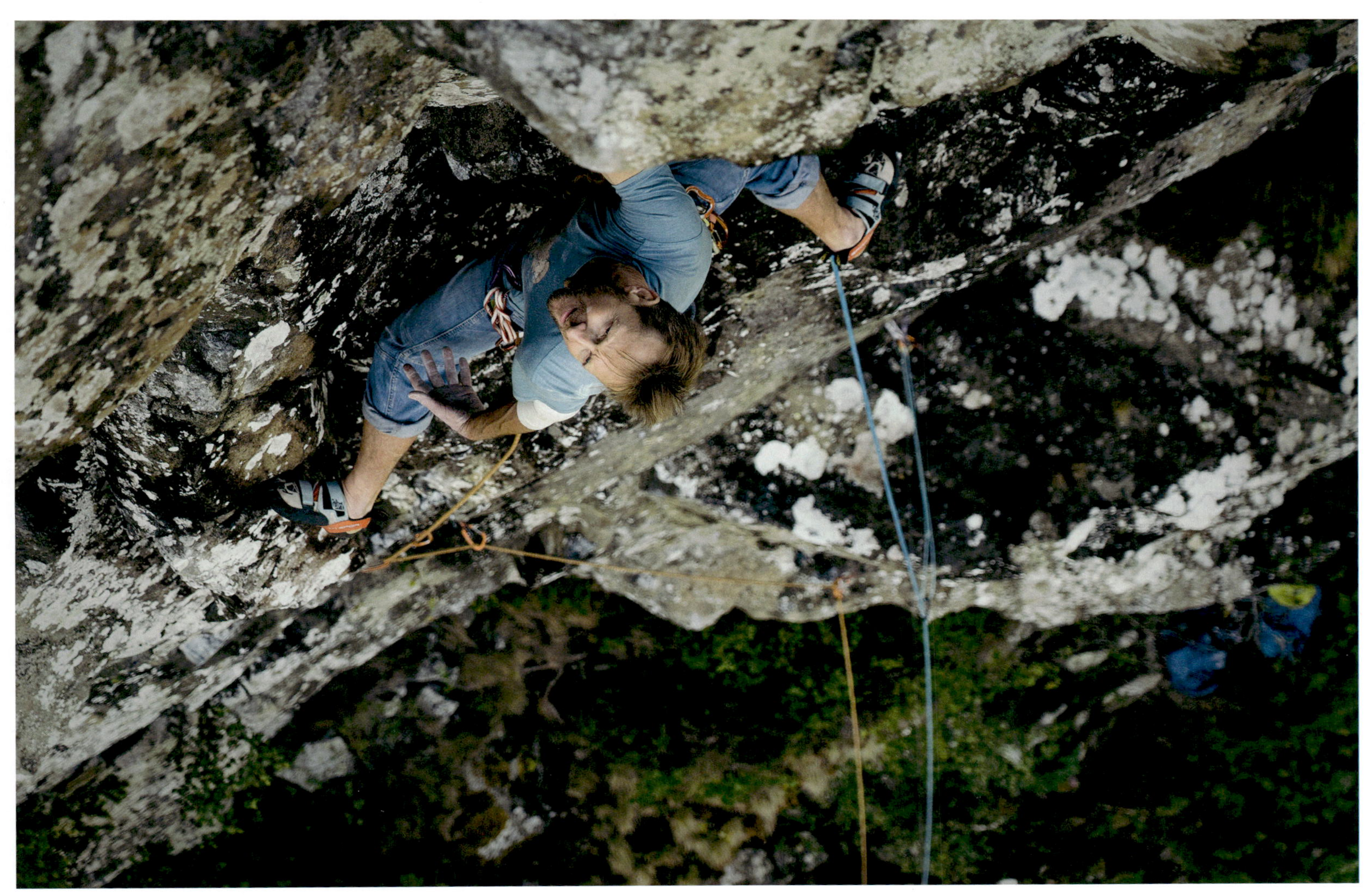

Andy Mitchell on *Way Out West* (E8 6c), Iron Crag, near Thirlmere. © Nadir Khan

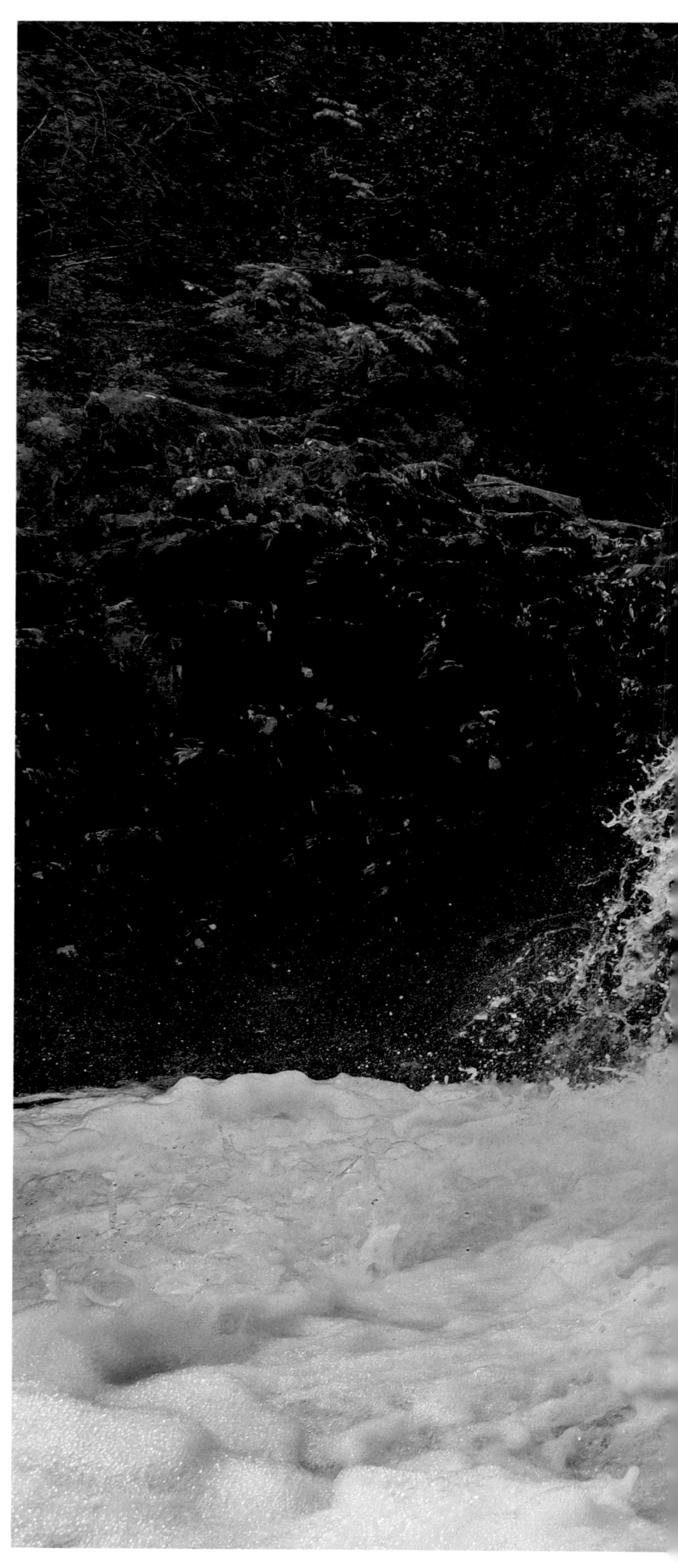

Dan Fylan-Smith running Skelwith Force (grade V). © Tom McNally »

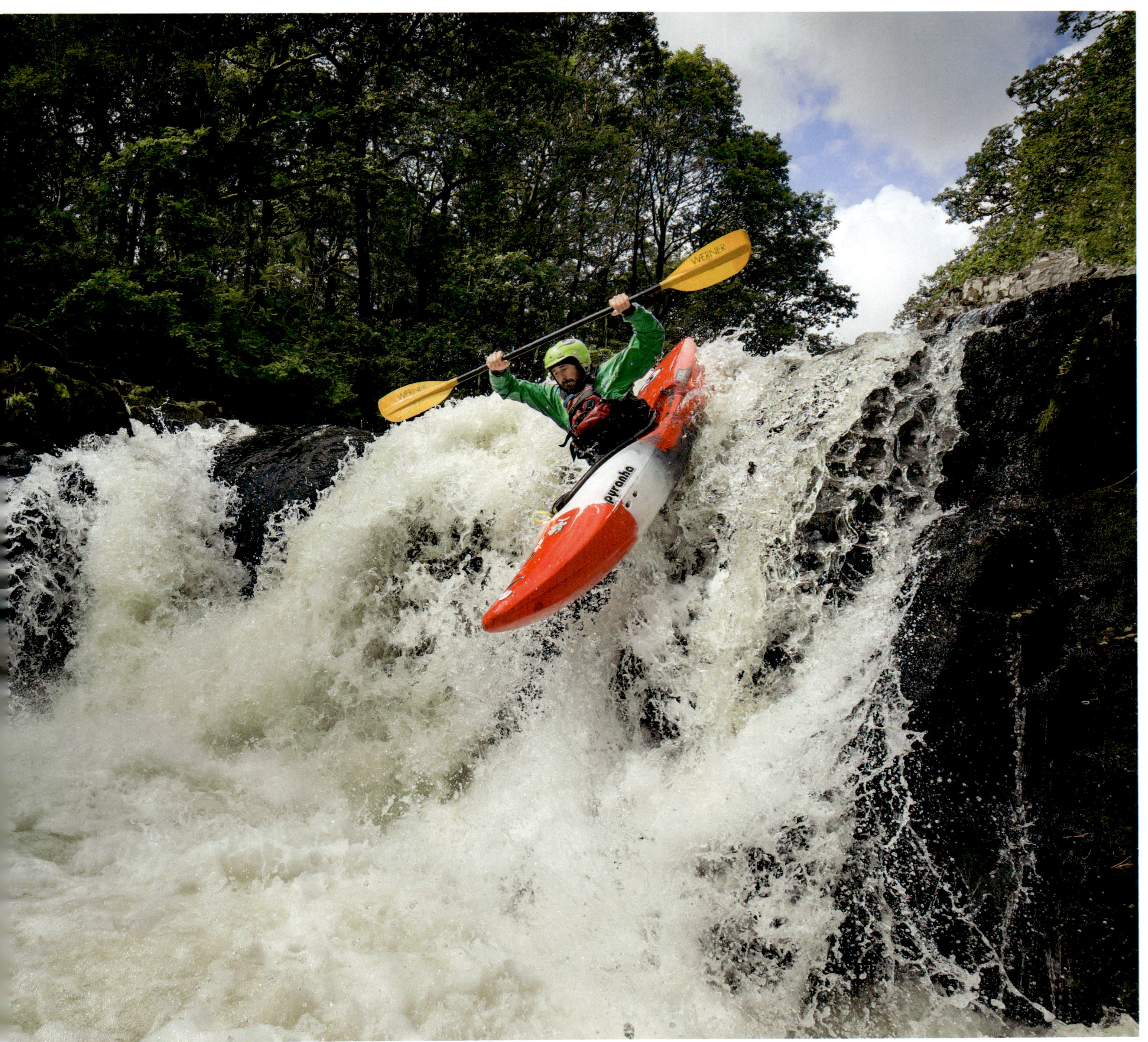

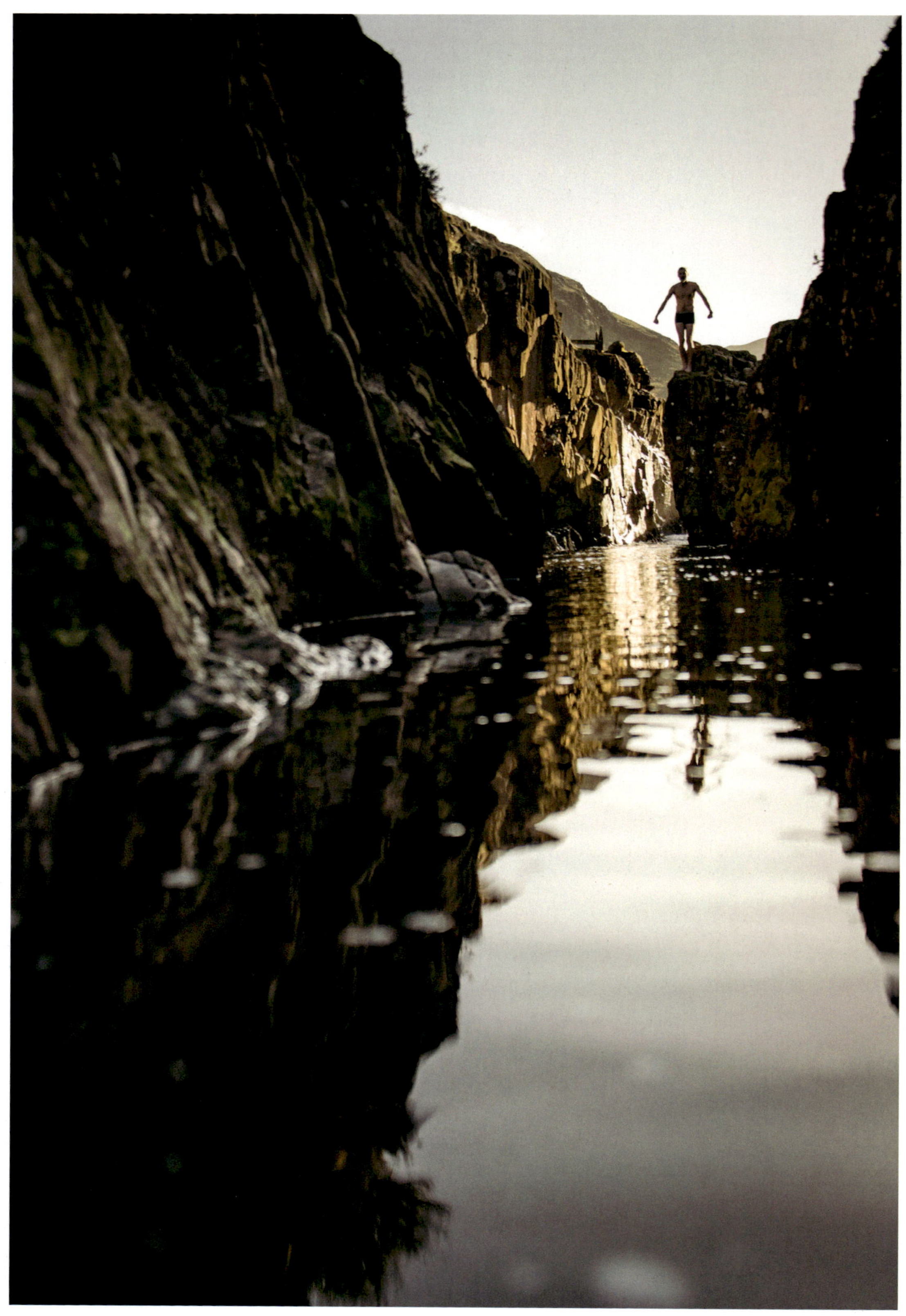

Matt Sharman about to take the plunge into Black Moss Pot in the Langstrath valley. © Tom McNally

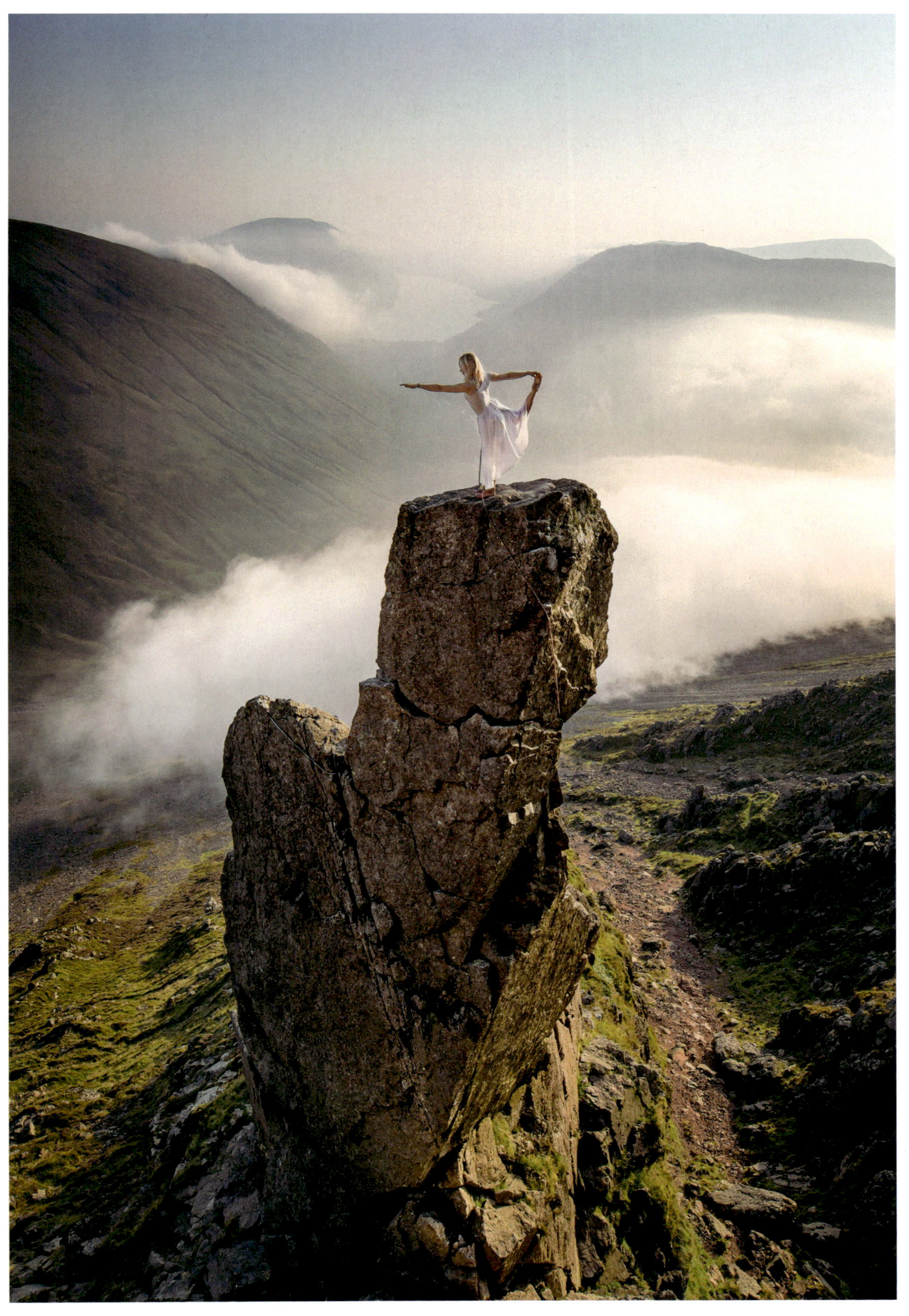

Dancer and climber Eliza Sandford performs on top of Napes Needle, Great Gable. © Tom McNally

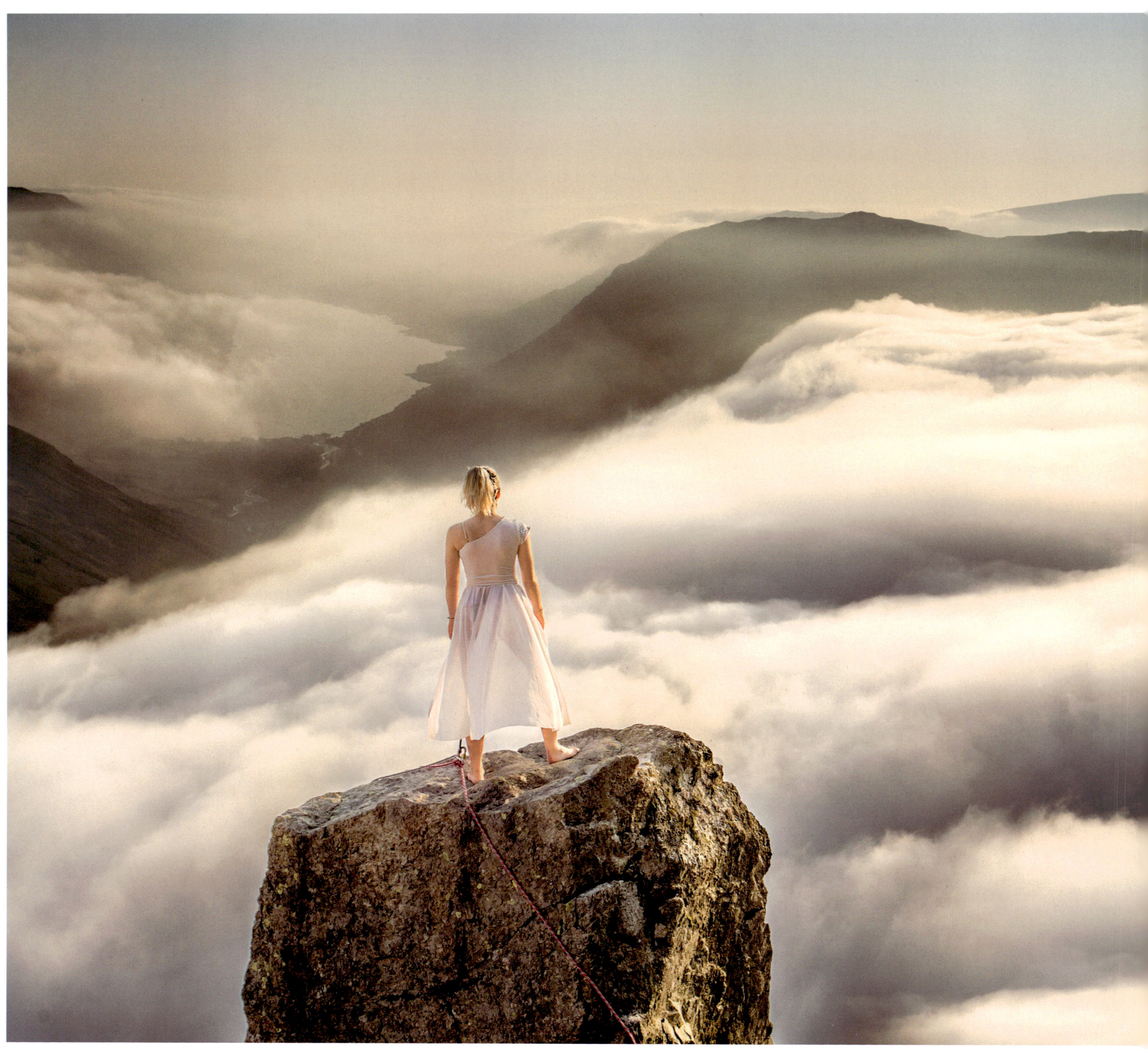

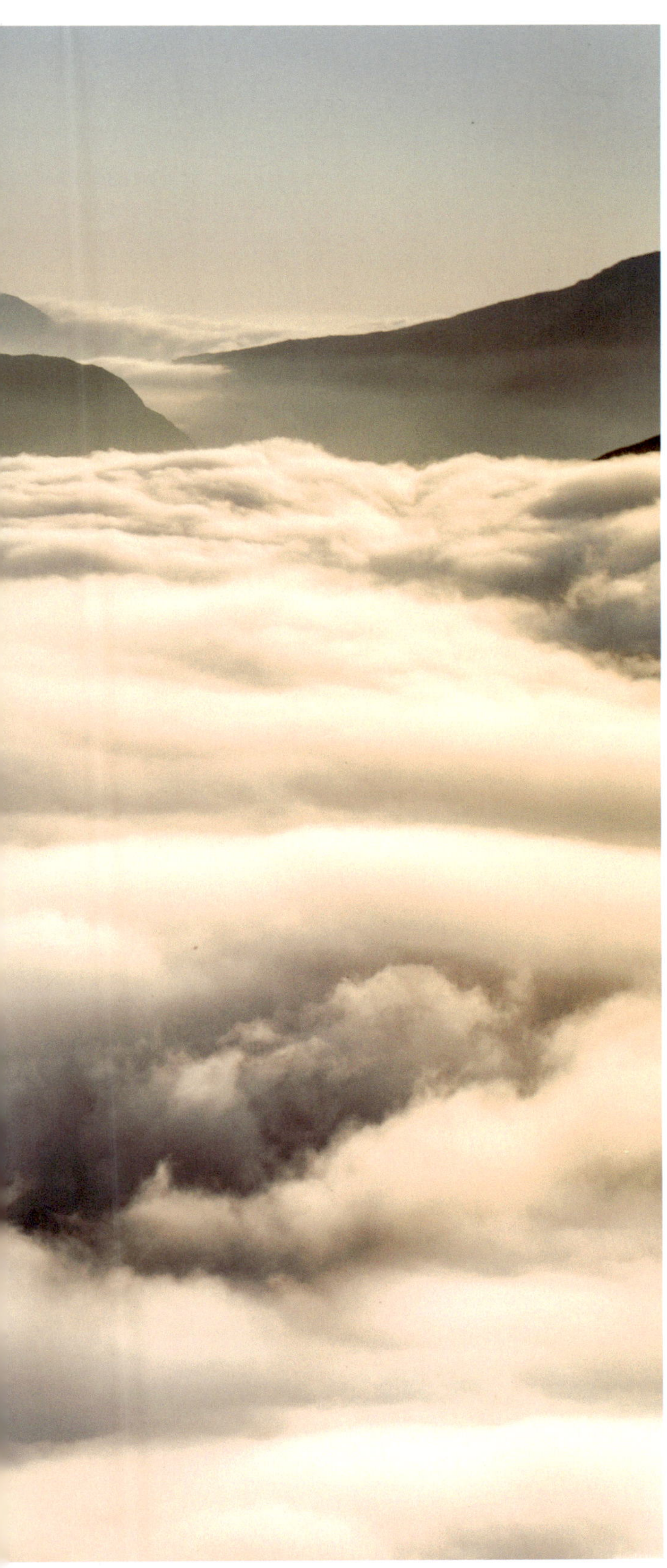

« From the summit of Napes Needle, Eliza enjoys a spectacular cloud inversion
rolling off the sea into the western valleys. © Tom McNally

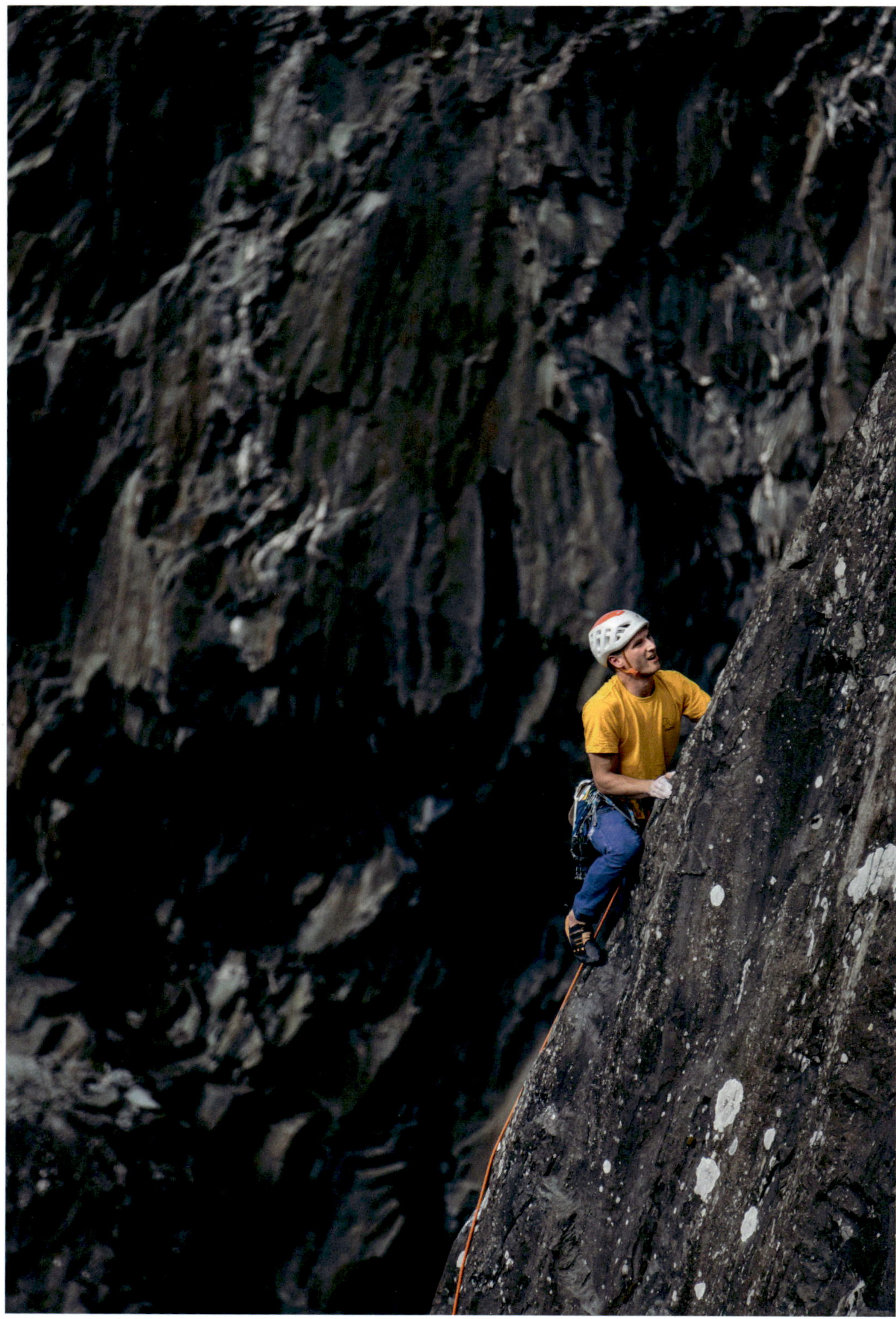

Theo Moore eyes up the rather bold finish to *Malice in Wonderland* (E4 5c), Hodge Close Quarry. © Tom McNally

I want to love you, Hodge Close Quarry, but you aren't making it easy.

It's late snow and an early Easter. Friday's forecast is for showers and cold. What's the only thing any good in showers? Slate. I haven't done any up here in the Lakes.

Skel's been before; he doesn't rate it. 'The bolts have all been chopped. Or something. I just remember it being really shit.' But Garry is happy to ignore him, and it's Garry's van. Sabrina and Tracey want to try some low-grade sport routes.

At the end of the road from Yewdale we get out, and everyone raids their pack for extra jackets. Bloody hell. That freezing wind.

We walk around the edge of the quarry, surrounded by fir trees, looking into a big deep pool the colour of broken flint. There are huge tunnel entrances below. A path drops down into Parrock Quarry, which leads to Hodge. Parrock hasn't been popular for a long time. The rock looks loose; brambles shoot barbed wire out of cracks; lichen and moss are recolonising.

In the All Weather Gym, bolts have had their hangers stripped; they're rusted or loose. Easy sport routes are now harrowing. *Northumbrian VS* in the other tunnel just turns out to be hard; I need a better warm-up. But I don't dare risk those bolts, uninspired by a climb called *Broken Pelvis*.

The best bit so far is the double tunnel system; they are so big they don't feel like tunnels. More like walking under a motorway flyover made of faceted slate instead of poured concrete. Water droplets fall

HODGE CLOSE QUARRY

BY PETER GOULDING

from the ceiling, catching the light. In the right-hand tunnel is the 'diving board'. It looks like a bit of the Tyne Bridge – massive girders and big rivets jutting into the water of the pool. We shuffle along it like penguins, out over the lake. Families in waterproofs stop to watch us uncoil our ropes, but our show is disappointing, and they don't stay for long.

So far it's a bust. I'm not enjoying it. Skel keeps laughing, but there's no humour to it. Sabrina and Tracey have fixed grins. Along the edge of the pool, we look for signs of rockfall on the cliff walls. The climbs feel way beyond my grade. Not today.

I feel like crying. A precious free weekend, all those miles away from home, and my idea turns out to be a shit one.

My partner was keen for me to go climbing this weekend. I could have stayed at home with her and my young son, with the heating on. I haven't been out climbing since last October, sinking into the routine of work (climbing wall twice a week), then Christmas, then work.

'Yeah, of course. Go on. We'll be alright. I'll take him out for the day and he can get a model.'

My son still likes it when I put him to bed and stroke his hair while he goes to sleep. If I'm not there he gets anxious and wants me to phone.

'It's not very dangerous what I do,' I tell him.

'Yes it is, Dad,' he says. 'You have to drive there.' *Yep*, I think. I can hear myself telling him the driving is a bigger risk than the climbing.

I do want to stay and play Lego with my son. On evenings and Saturdays I watch TV with him.

He comes running in to tell me if there's some climbing on CBBC. I love these times, sitting with him, and it hasn't occurred to me to work out how many of them I'll have left before he doesn't really want to spend his time with me any more.

Between the good bits, I go to work, tidy up and wait for something to happen. My routine is boring, but when the routine is broken – like the heating breaking down – I get frustrated. Get away from the flatlands, scare myself silly and blow all the pressure off. When I come home again, I'm different, with my patience back. Once I've recovered from the drive, for a short while I enjoy how simple it is to make a cup of tea, or a sandwich, when I like.

We all head up on to the road and round the rim of the quarries. At the far end of Hodge a little rabbit trail leads down. Brambles, tussocks of grass and young trees have grown up around a path, a scar of slate waste that twists through ramps of boulders. It is not what I'm here for, but I'm trying to find some adventure, save something from the day. It's still cold, though.

Among the trees are wrecked cars. Years ago they'd been rolled off the top of the quarry, trundled for the thrill. They haven't been burnt, all the paint is still on, but everything a spanner could loosen has been stripped.

There are great climbs along the left-hand side: *First Night Nerves, Main Event*. Some of them start from an abseil access, but we hadn't planned to do that and no one feels like it. The grades are high. I haven't done E3, and that's where the quality

seems to start; *Malice in Wonderland* looks good. One exception: *Behind the Lines*, an HVS corner system. But HVS is a nasty grade for me; I've had horrendous experiences on climbs where the moves are easy. I'm just too cold, no bottle.

Near the pool edge there are a few bolted lines. *Cafe Boys Do Their Thong* has a sport grade of F5. While I'm climbing that, Skel and Garry start up *Oiling the Lawnmower*.

'I'll drop you a rope,' shouts Garry. 'We'll climb it as a three.'

Oiling the Lawnmower is lovely. Positive holds and a nice little dance over the water, then up through the creases. I wish I'd led this. It isn't like the Welsh slate I've climbed; it has a grainy texture, enough to smear on, tints of red-purple.

While Skel leads off, I turn out and look over the water. In a different mood, I'd be buzzing. The top – a grassy ledge then a crappy corner – isn't great. But topping out feels better than the faff of rethreading your rope through the chains of single pitch. We trail around and walk back down to pick up our bags.

Down at the bottom, Sabrina hasn't managed to get past the long move near the first bolt of *Cafe Boys*. She can't quite reach, and has tried again and again. I feel stupid for telling her *Cafe Boys* would be good. Tracey isn't keen either. We walk back out, past the wrecked cars and other climbs we don't try.

Hodge Close Quarry did nothing wrong. It's a hole in the ground. It needs another chance from me. Shit days are just bad days. Be honest about them.

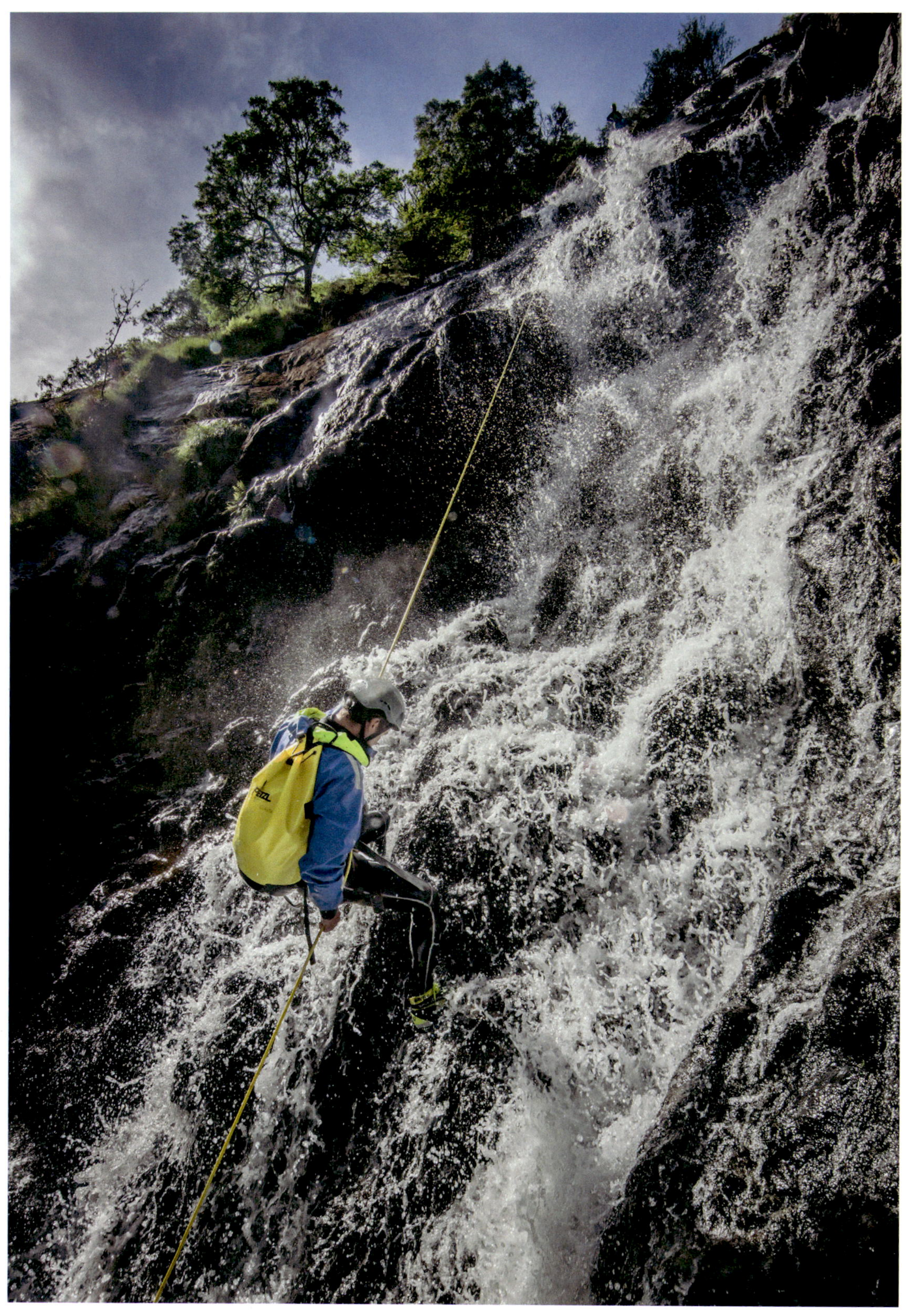

Matt Eaves enjoys the big pitch on Sourmilk Ghyll on a hot day in Borrowdale. © Tom McNally

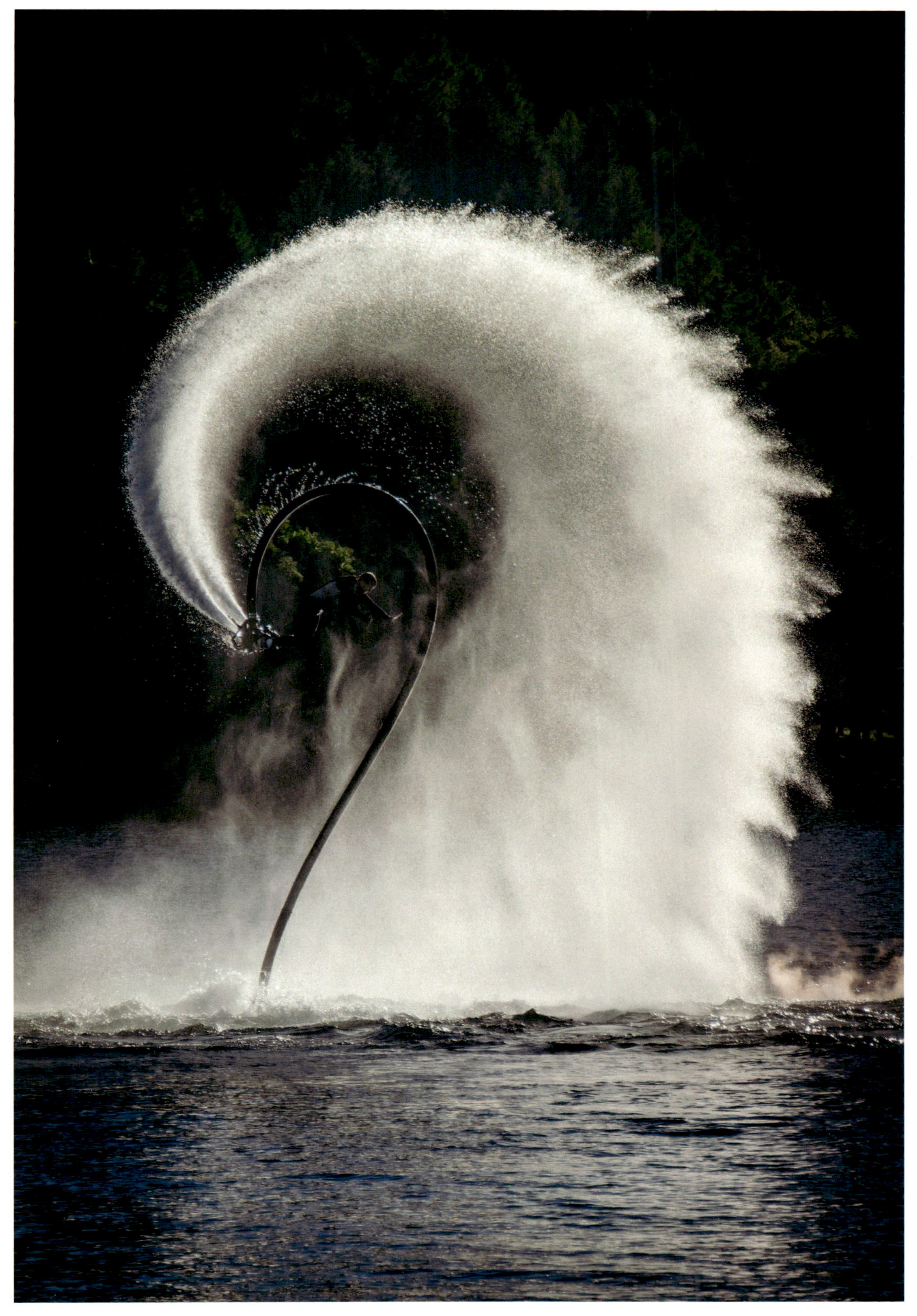

'Jet Boot John' Hayden-Gibb doing his thing at the Buttermere Bash paragliding festival. © Tom McNally

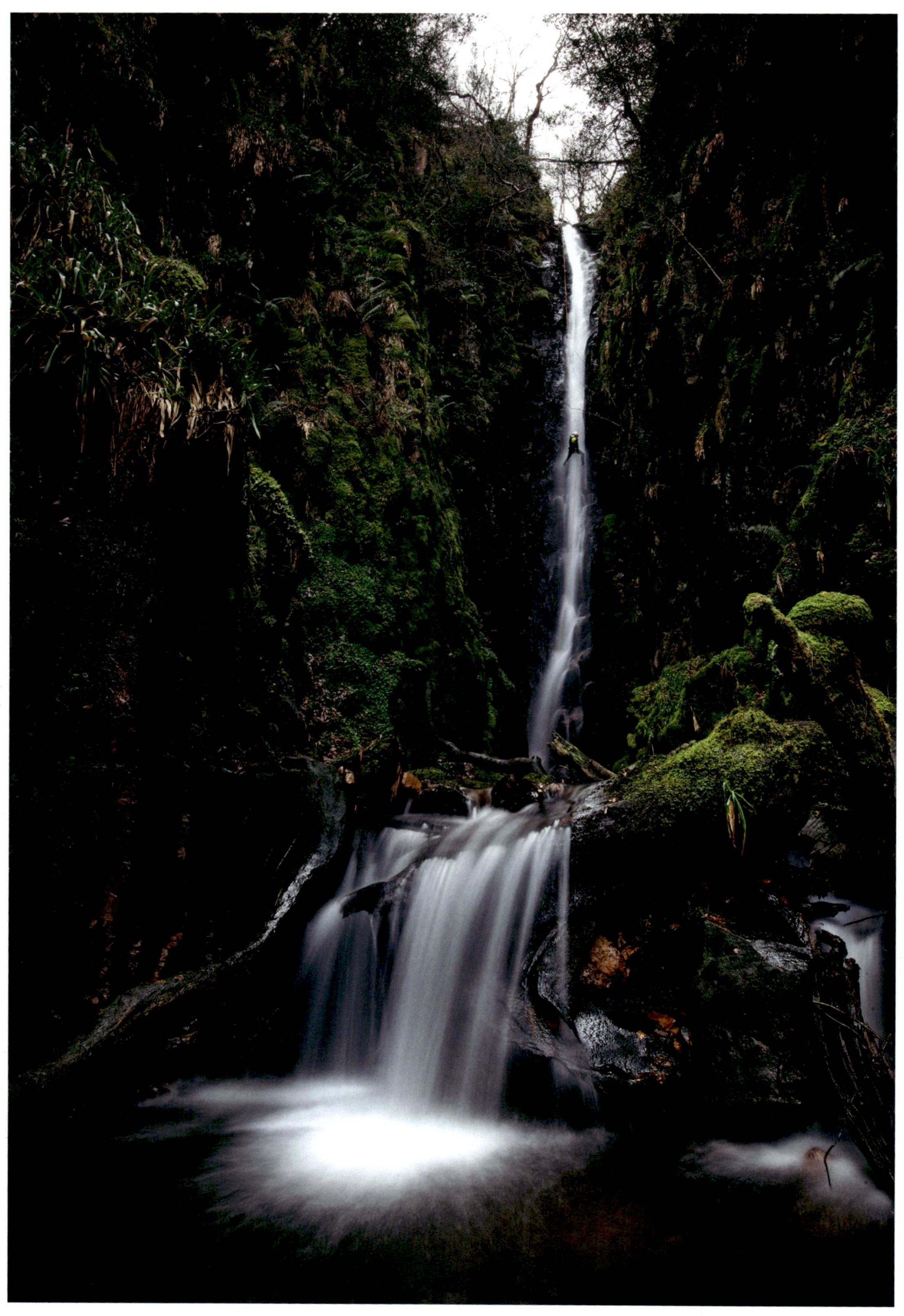

Craig McMahon descends Scale Force, the tallest waterfall in the Lake District. © Tom McNally

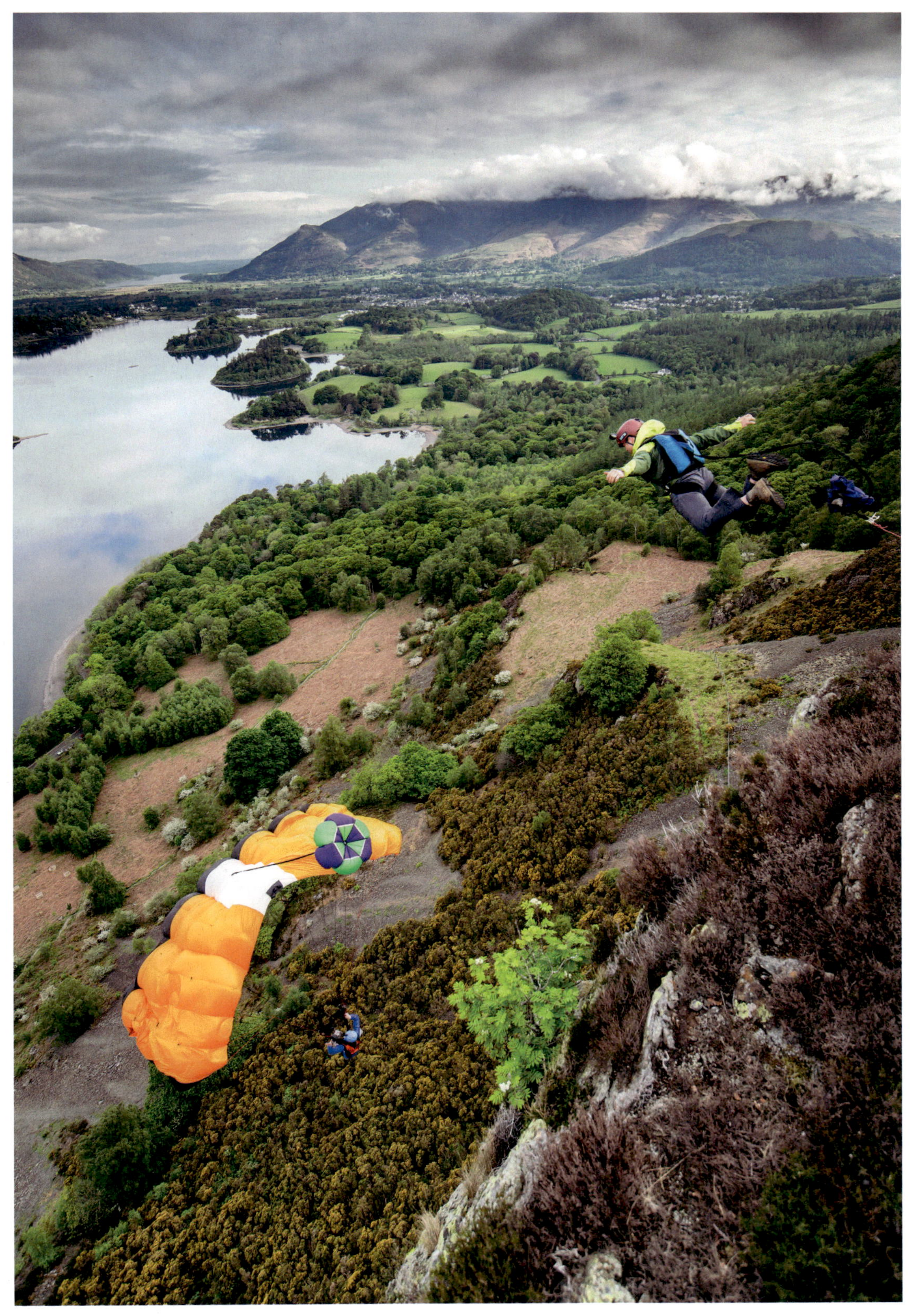

Josh B. and Andrew Ross BASE jump from Falcon Crag, Borrowdale. © Tom McNally

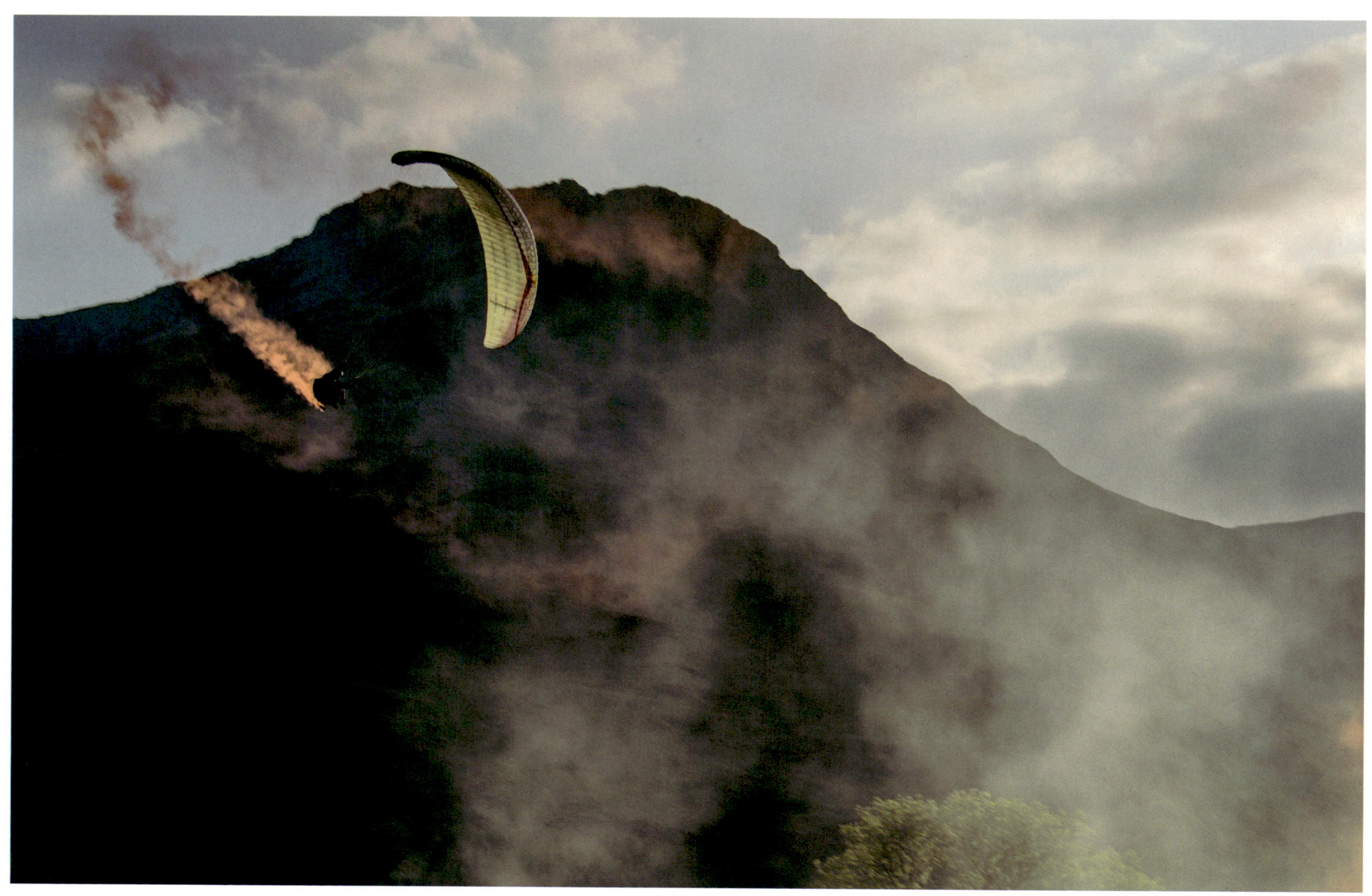

Sebastian Kahn swoops in to land at the Buttermere Bash paragliding festival. © Tom McNally

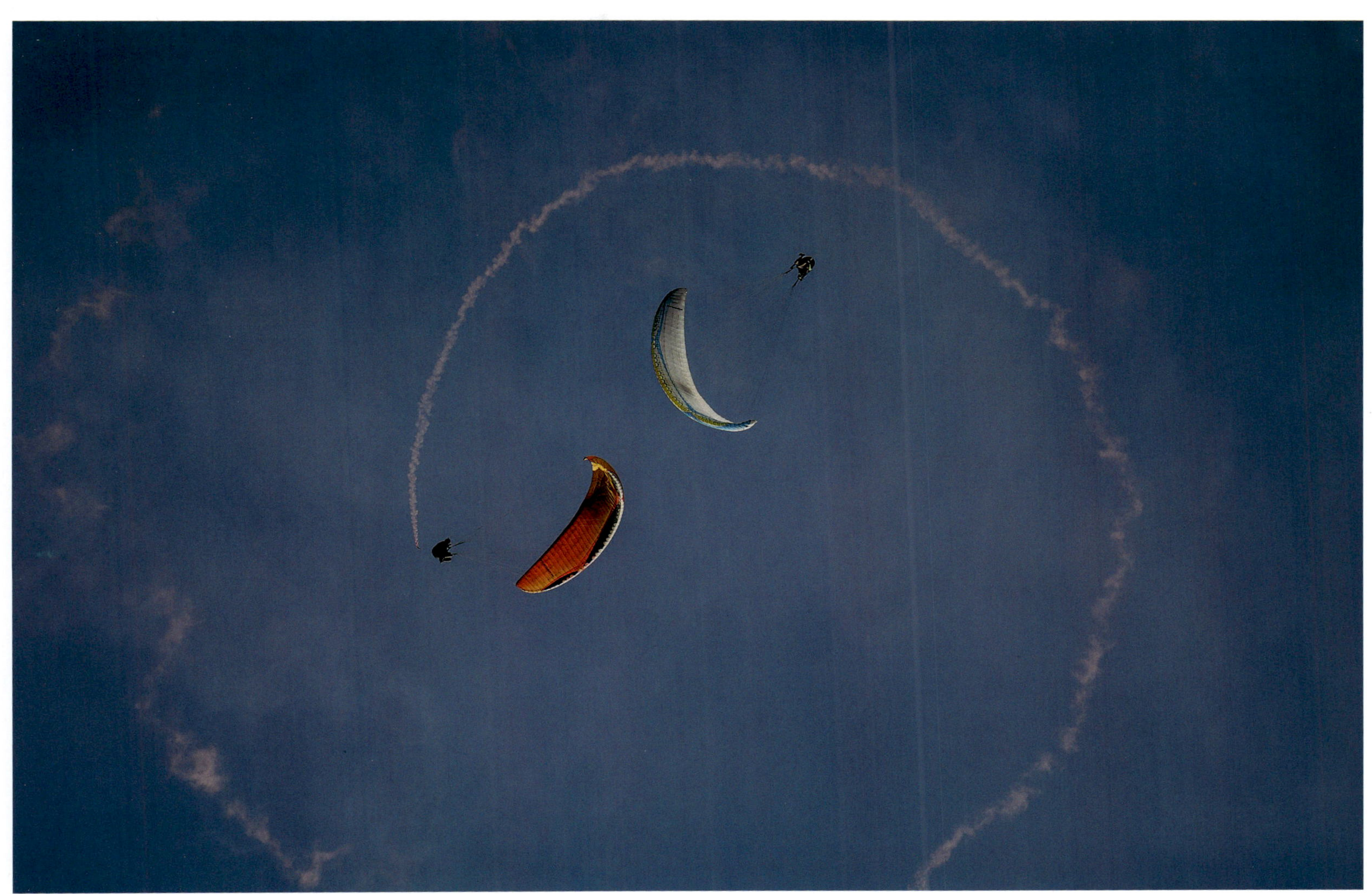

Danny Taylor and Alex Colbeck from the British Acrobatic Paragliding Academy perform during the acro display at the Buttermere Bash. © Tom McNally

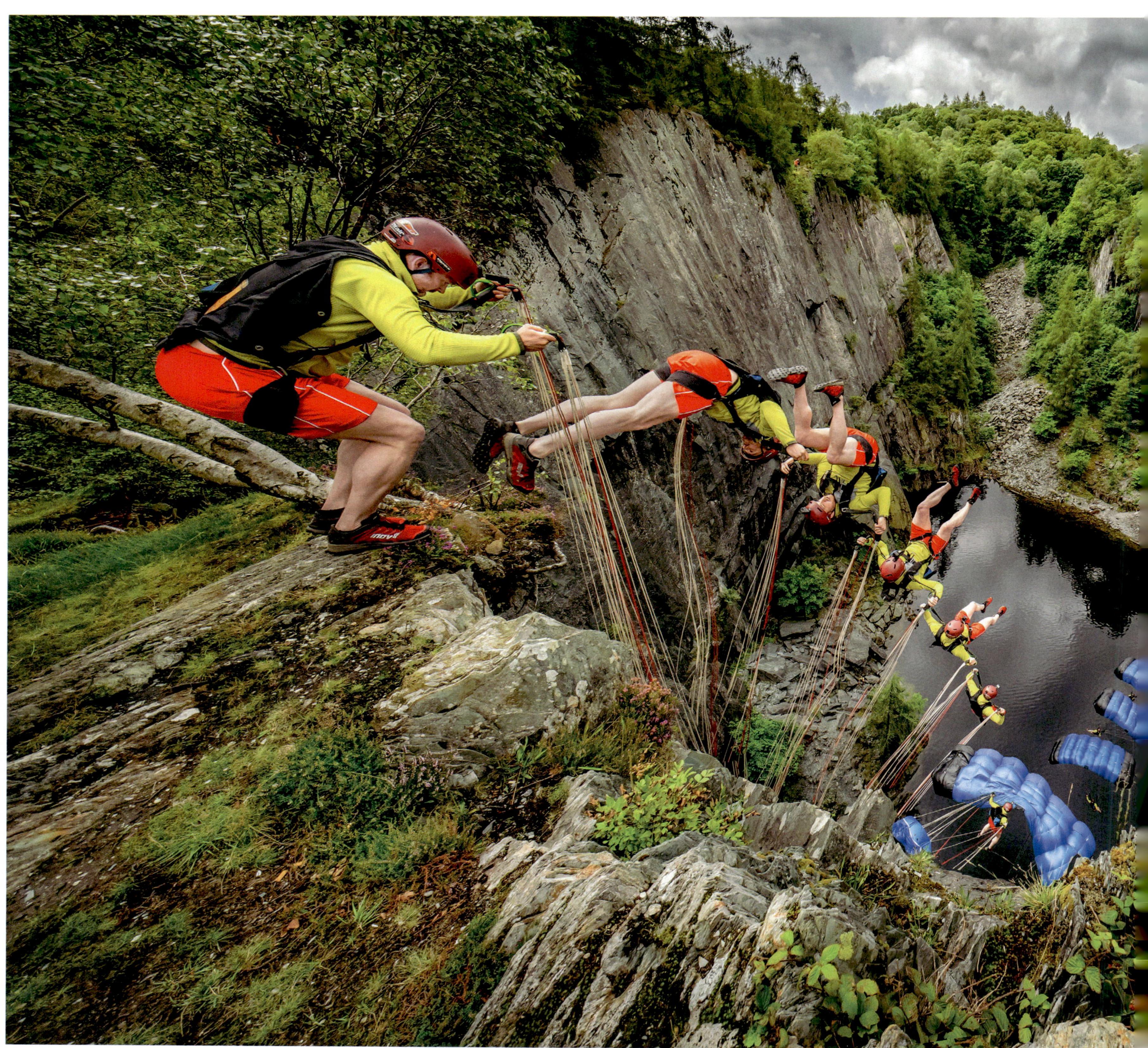

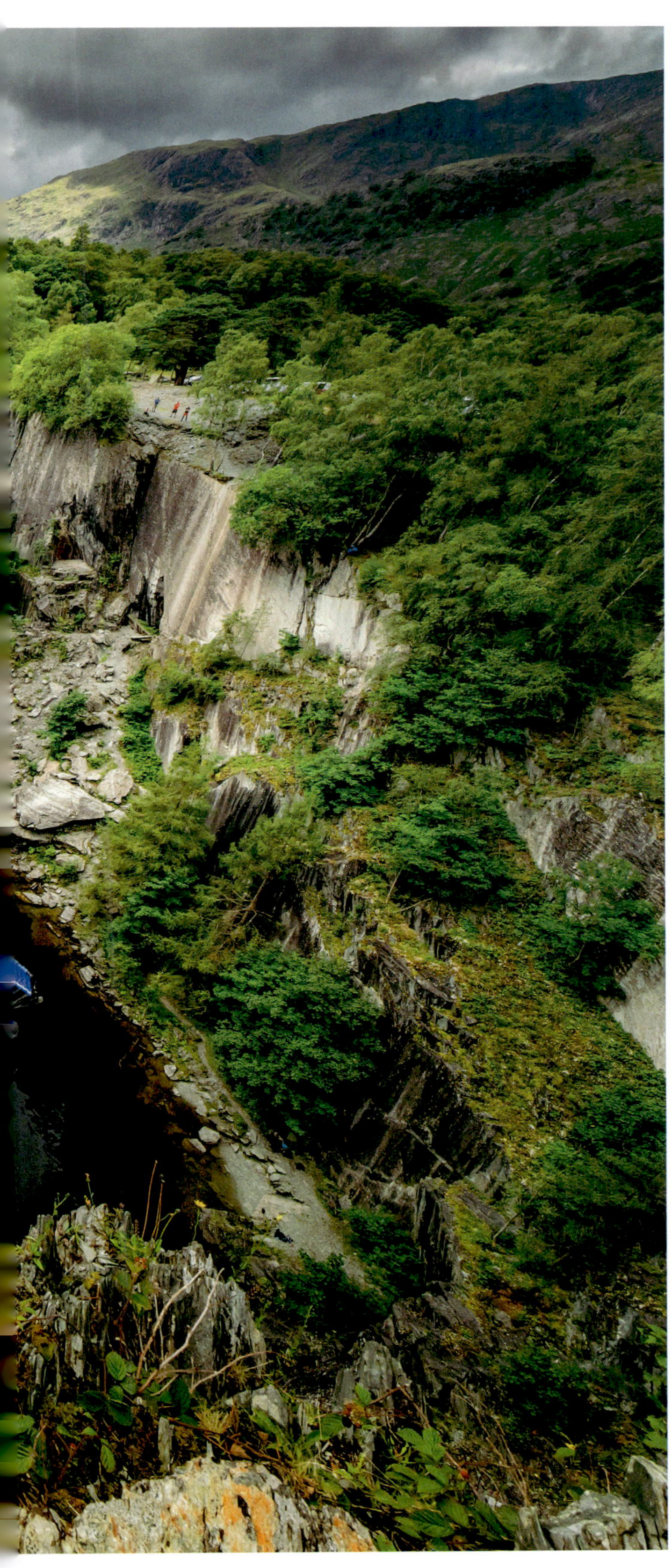

« Josh B. performs a rollover BASE jump into Hodge Close Quarry.
© Tom McNally

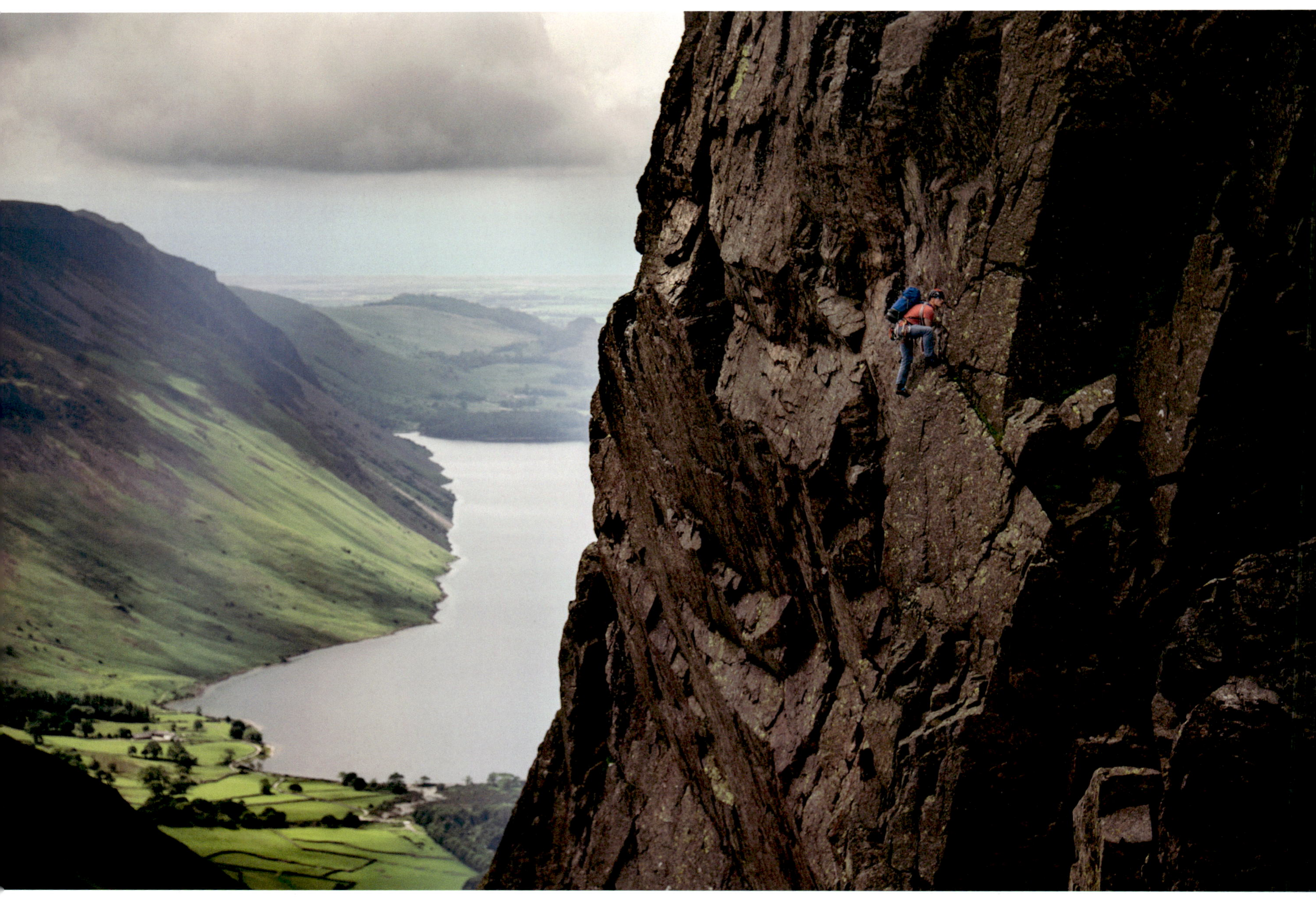

Josh B. and Sam Percival open the first BASE exit from Tophet Wall, Great Gable.
Completed in fine style given it was Josh's first ever climb. © Tom McNally

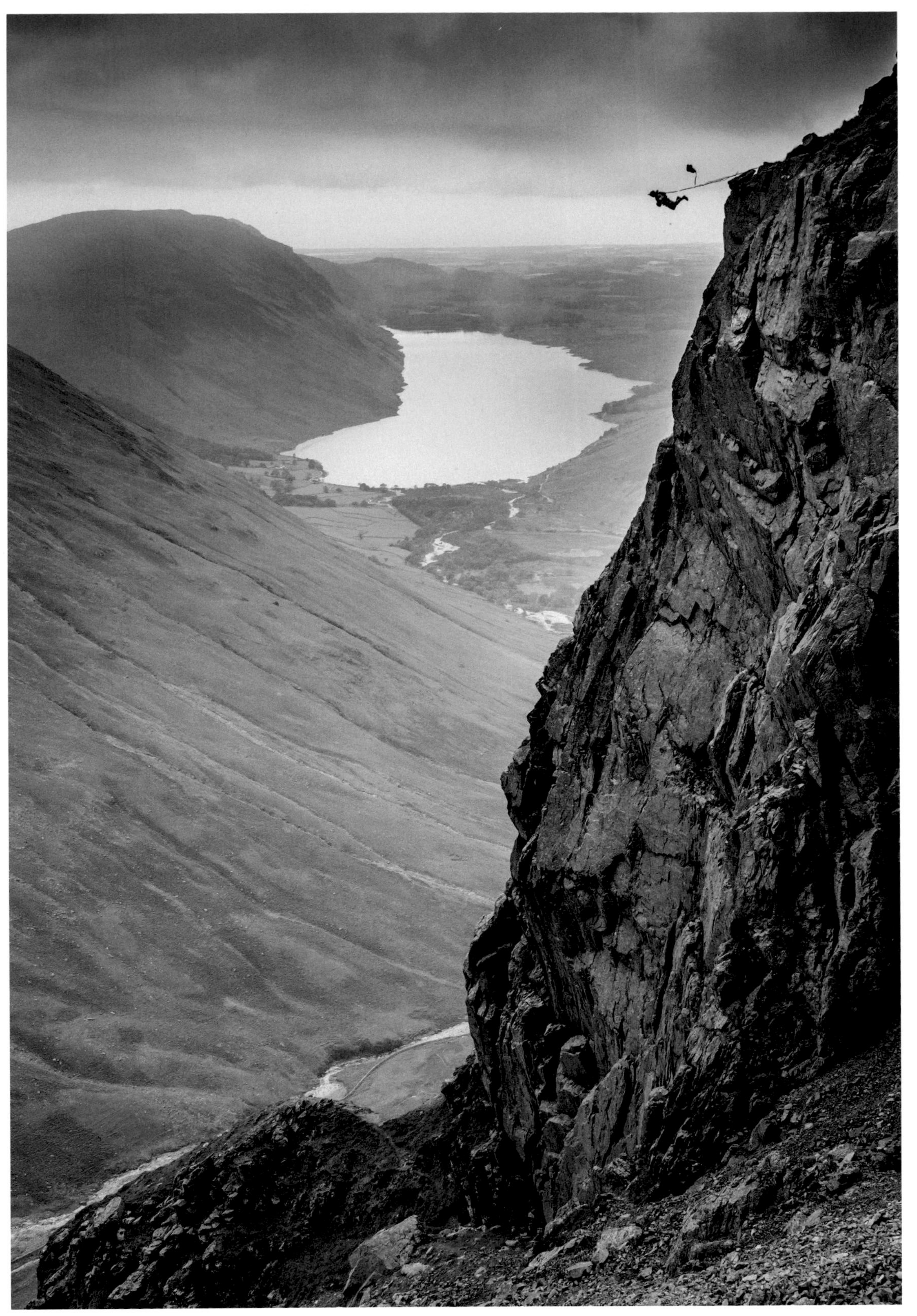

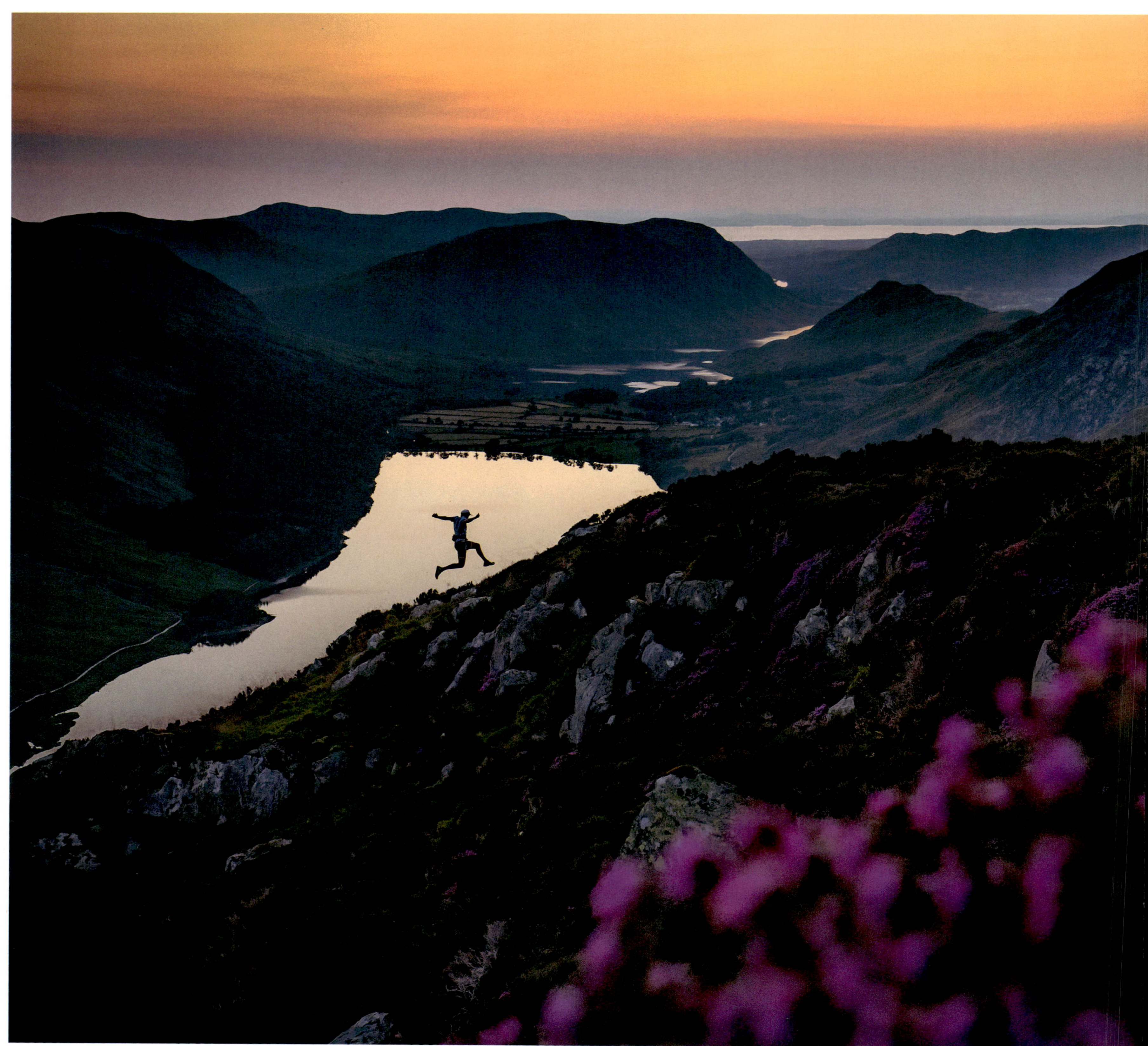

≪ Dava Waterhouse enjoys a summer evening run
on the fells above Buttermere. © Tom McNally

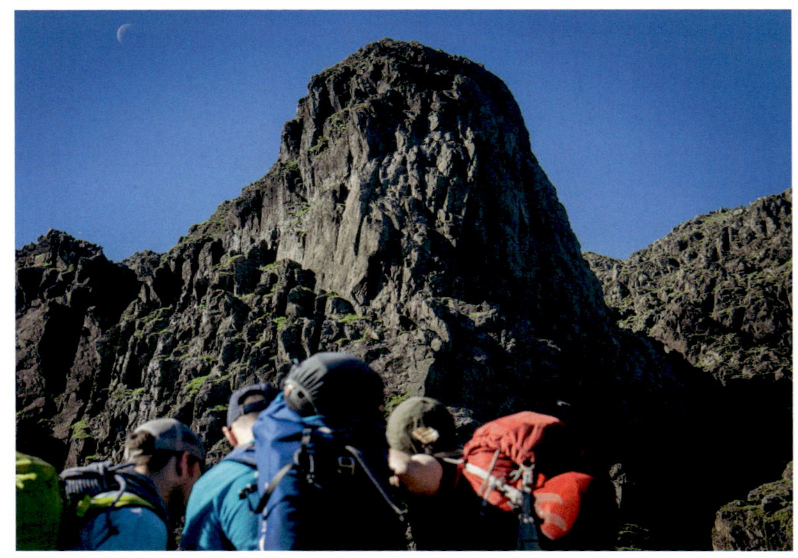

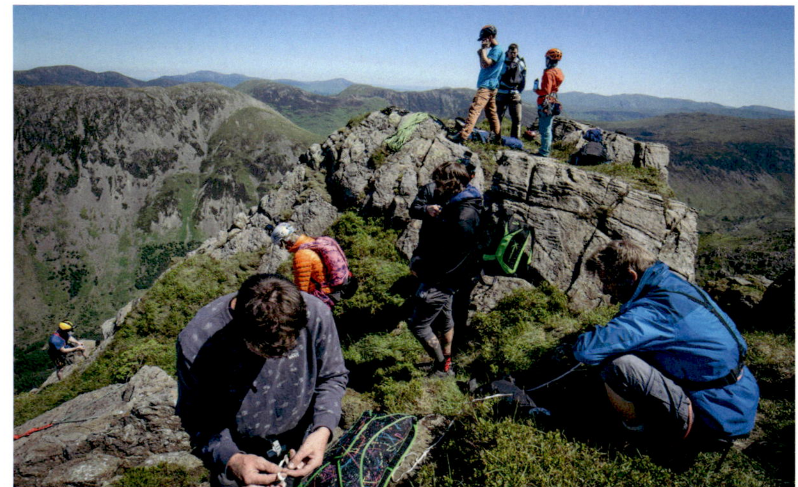

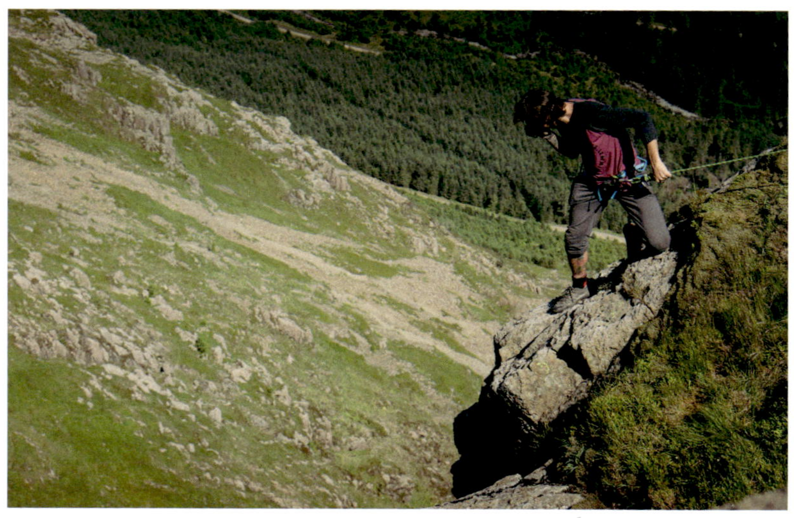

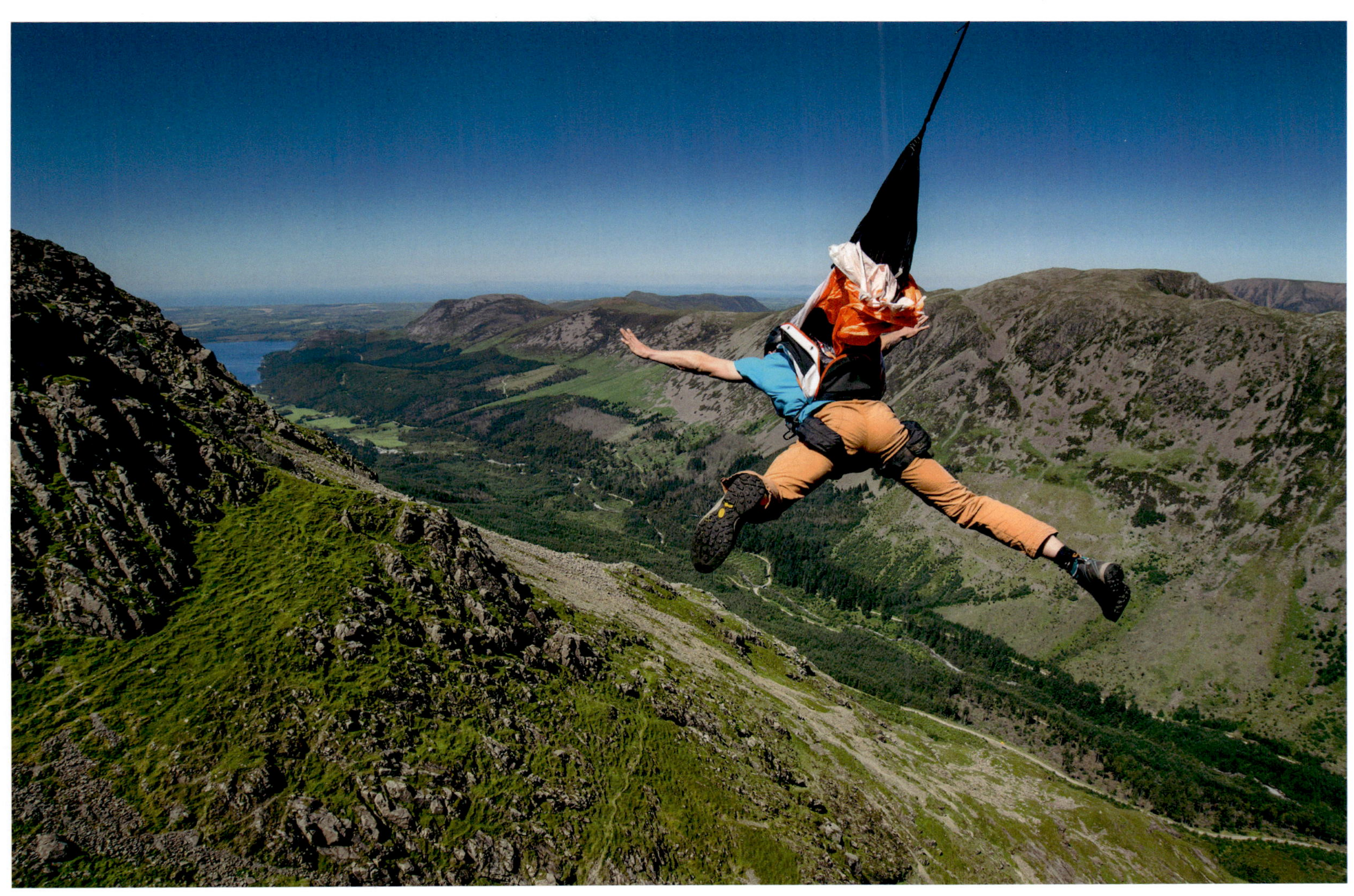

Josh B., Sam Percival, Jamie Harris, Sean Fell, Shaye Byles and Steve Shipman climb Pillar Rock and open the first BASE exit from its summit. © Tom McNally

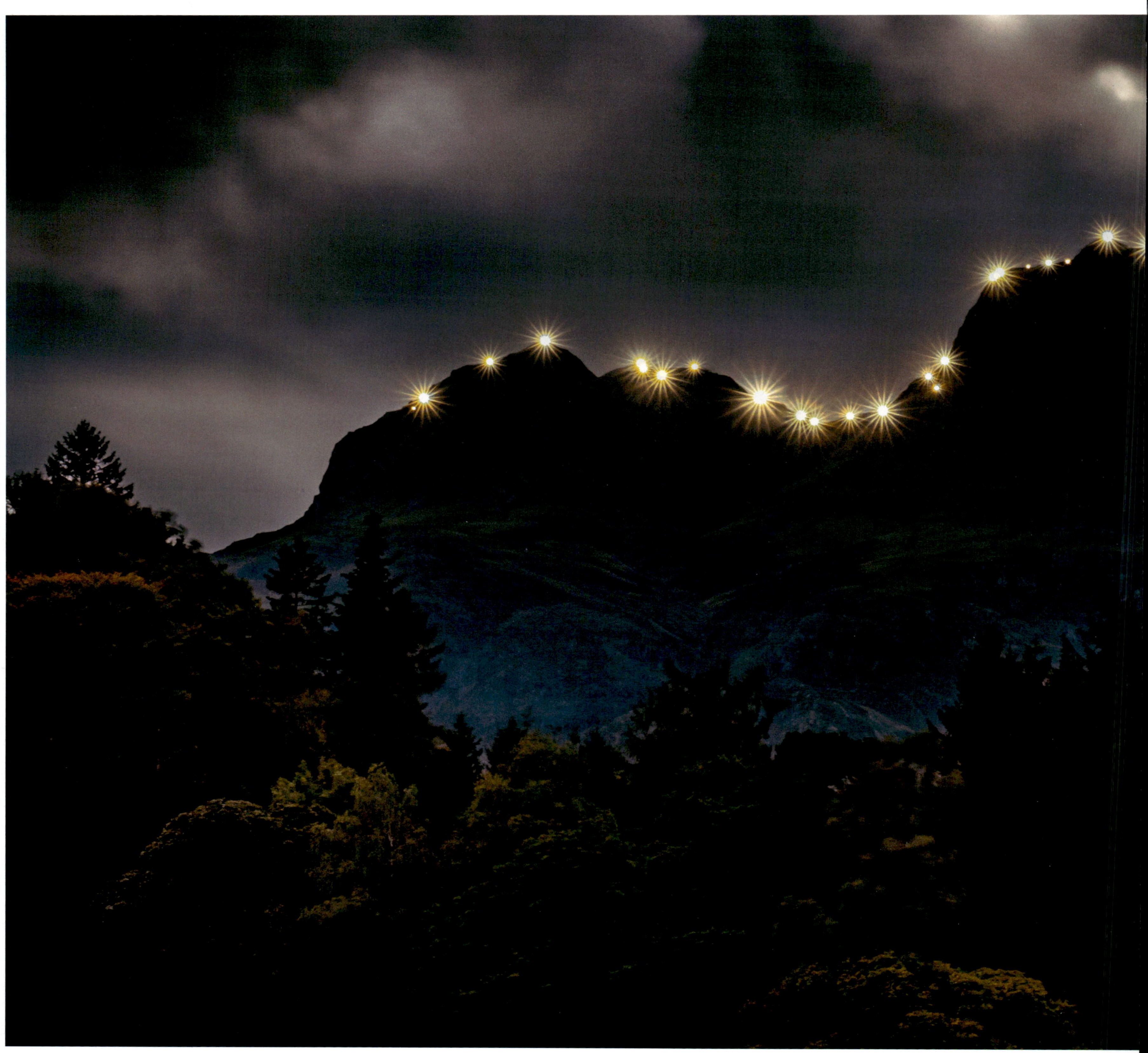

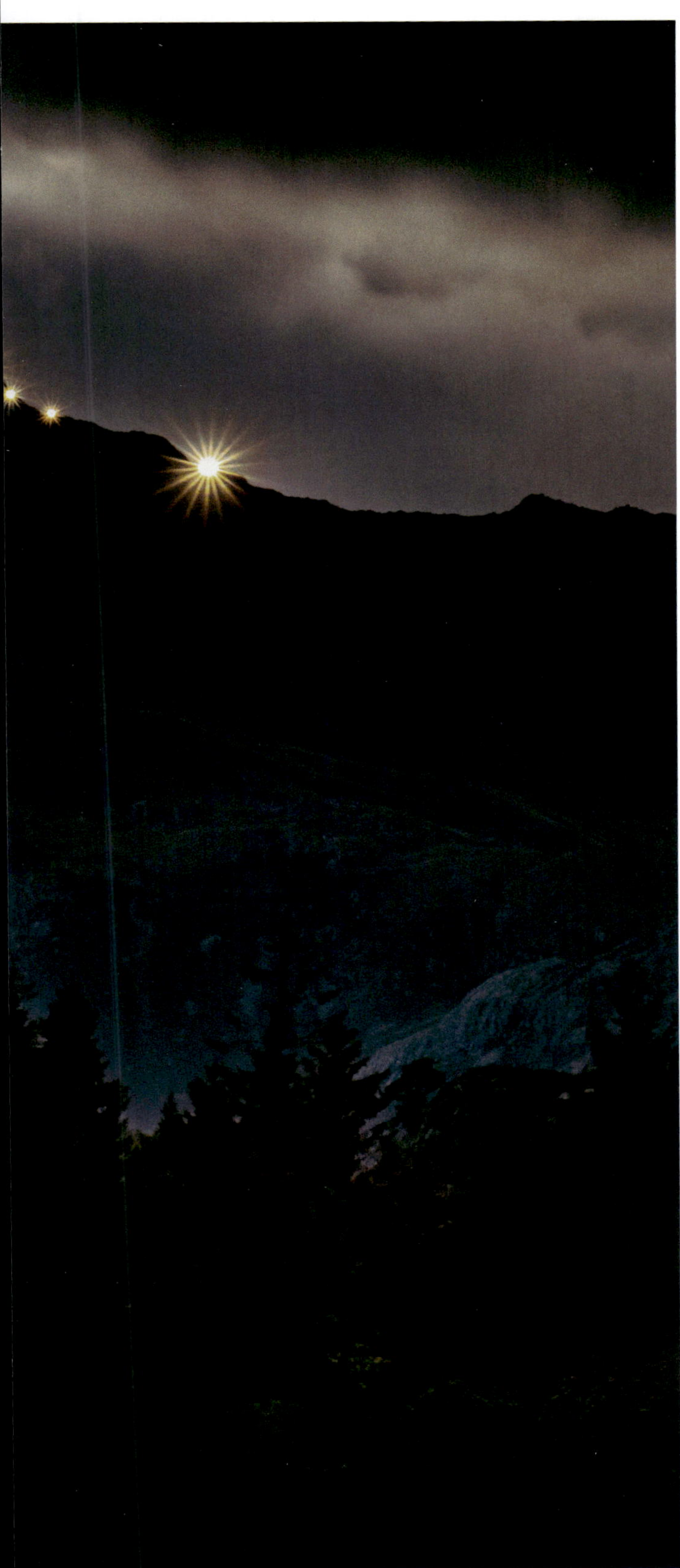

« The Langdale Festival of Light. The Langdale Ambleside
Mountain Rescue Team light up the skyline that makes
up the team logo to celebrate their fiftieth anniversary.
© Tom McNally

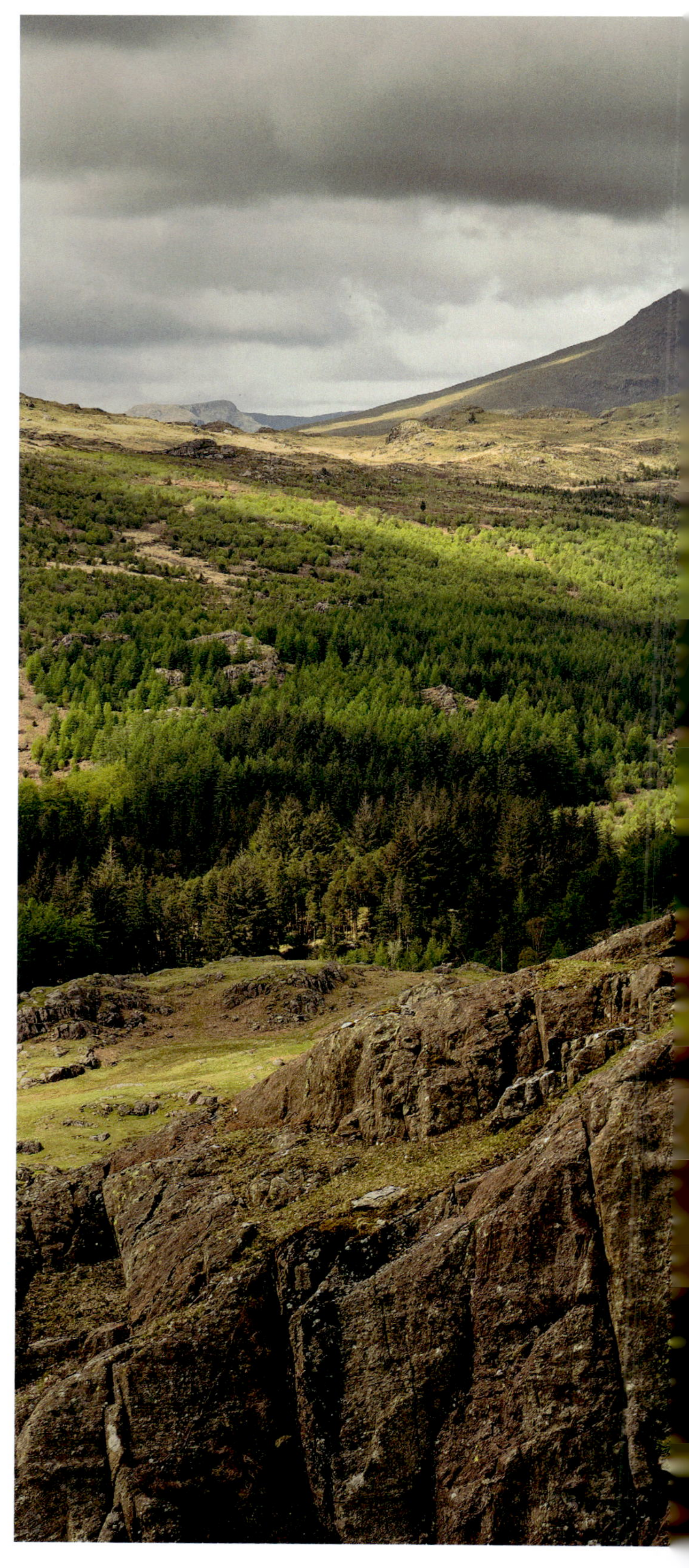

Anna Taylor soloing *May the Foss be with You* (E4 6b) at Foss How Crag in the Duddon Valley – a remote and beautiful valley deep in the Lake District. © Nadir Khan »

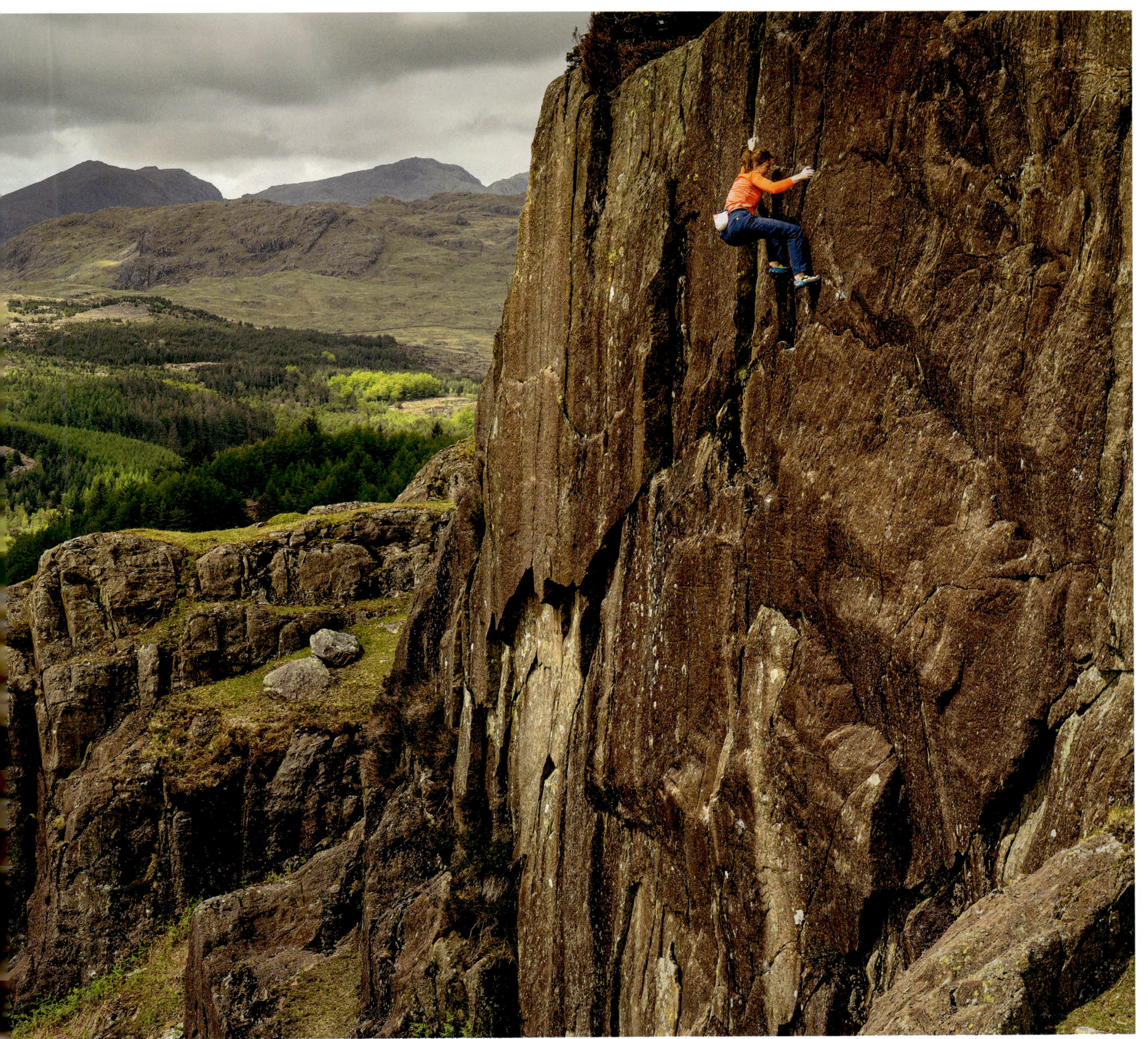

SOLO

BY ANNA TAYLOR

Something's wrong.

I don't know what, but something deep down feels wrong.

Maybe it's the fact that the sky just darkened and the temperature dropped. Maybe I'm just tired. Regardless, I've realised far too late that I don't want to climb this route today. That wouldn't be so bad if I were climbing with ropes and gear, but unfortunately for me, in this moment, I'm climbing solo with no rope for safety. The option of shouting 'Take!' to a belayer and slumping on to a rope does not exist, but something inside is telling me in no uncertain terms that I must not continue upward. I'm slightly baffled by my own brain, as I just soloed a much harder route less than half an hour ago and enjoyed every minute of it, but I've always promised myself that I will listen to any internal feeling when it comes to climbing without a rope. If something doesn't feel right, I need to return to the ground as soon as possible.

That's easier said than done, however. I'm just under halfway up a mountain crag that's over a hundred feet tall. My heart rate picks up as I look over my shoulder and realise just how far above the ground I already am. The steep slope and boulder field below me look distinctly uninviting, and the building burn of lactic acid in my forearms reminds me that I need to move now. Taking a deep breath, I force myself to calm down, get control of my breathing and begin to slowly reverse the set of movements that got me into this fix in the first place.

They're all harder backwards, and my stomach flips as I reach the small horizontal roof that I know full well will be tricky at best to down-climb. It does not disappoint, and for one horrifying second I imagine parting company with the rock and slamming into the ground far below, before my body restores its balance underneath the feature and the hardest part is over.

I continue down-climbing the finger crack to the foot of the crag, cursing myself for … well, I don't really know what. I didn't succeed on the climb, but being able to stay cool and get out of a bad situation without incident is perhaps the most important skill of all when it comes to soloing. I'm disappointed that I didn't reach the top, but I'm confident that I made the right call in retreating.

It's only at times like these (a rarity) that I understand why some people think I'm mad for climbing this way so much. Ninety-nine per cent of my solo climbs go extremely smoothly, but as is the case with most things, problems do sometimes appear when you least expect them to. Perhaps it's a good thing in a way; I've always feared complacency, and the occasional failure and forced retreat are a sharp reminder of the realities of this sport. For a few minutes after climbing down to the ground, as the adrenaline surge slowly eases and my heart rate calms down, I consider giving up, leaving soloing behind and resolving to never partake in it again – but deep down I know it won't last.

The truth is that I love soloing. When things go wrong it can be terrifying, but when everything is right, flowing through the moves of a rock climb without having to worry about dragging ropes and a heavy rack of gear, it's unbeatable. There are no distractions, no pauses; it's just climbing at its most pure and basic level. Fear is present, but it becomes so suppressed that it's barely noticeable. In fact everything seems to become suppressed; there's no real excitement, no rush of adrenaline, nothing apart from hands and feet on holds. Maybe that's what I like about it so much – its simplicity.

It's safe to say that despite the occasional scary moment, some of my most treasured climbing memories have come from ascending routes in this style. I've done the majority of my soloing on my home crags of the Lake District, and each route has offered its own unique charms and causes for concern. In the huge, gaping hole of Hodge Close Quarry, I've started down in the dark and climbed up towards the light, careful not to pull too hard on the many hollow flakes and brittle features that decorate the otherwise clean slate walls and looking down on the spoil heaps and tunnels that are all that remain of the site's years as an active mine. Over on the high crags of Bowfell I've found myself carefully manoeuvring up perfectly formed rhyolite cracks, with the steep slopes beneath me creating dizzying exposure, and with breathtaking views of the Langdale Pikes as a backdrop. Down in the valley of Eskdale the white granite outcrops provide harder, yet shorter-lived challenges, on bullet-hard rock, and in the wooded valley of Borrowdale the soloing options are almost limitless.

Yes, I could just do these climbs with a rope, but the absence of one makes them so much more memorable. Particularly in the easier grades – climbs that if I were traditionally leading, I probably wouldn't be paying much attention to. My mind would stray elsewhere, and I would never remember much about them. With the concentration required to solo, I can look back and appreciate the many beautiful and intricate sequences that I would probably have never noticed had I climbed with a rope, as taking such care to climb as efficiently as possible would not have been so necessary.

My soloing career began when I was still a teenager. At the time I did a lot of bouldering above crash pads, and the climbs I gravitated to slowly began to get higher and higher, until even the biggest stack of pads was not going to help me much in the event of a fall. During this period I learnt the importance of having a good head game. I progressed through the grades quickly, and unsurprisingly it wasn't long before I found myself truly out of my depth in a position where parting company with the rock was unthinkable – three quarters of the way up a holdless sandstone slab. That time I almost let fear take over, but just about held it together and reached the top of the route, albeit with a bit of wobbling.

It was a harrowing experience so early on, but I learnt from it and slowly started developing a better mindset, one where, in the right situation, I can now switch off entirely from the danger and climb without a rope better than I ever could with one. That doesn't mean I'm infallible every time, but it does mean that when things start to go wrong, I can keep my cool long enough to get back to safety.

People often assume that the scariest part of climbing this way must be when I'm on the hardest move or tallest part of a rock face, but to me that's not the case, as the majority of the time I find the psychological crux of a solo to be right at the start, in the few moments of chalking hands and cleaning shoes that precede pulling on to the rock – not the actual climb itself. It's in this time that I usually end up thinking about the 'big' stuff. I can't pretend that soloing isn't entirely selfish. I have friends and a family that I love, and I want to be around for a good while yet and have children of my own some day. That being said, I also want to live my life and do the things that make me happy in the years before I'm responsible for anyone else.

Soloing is dangerous, yes, but it's a very calculated sort of danger. I make sure I know exactly what I'm up against before committing to a climb in this style, and because of this the true danger in my eyes – uncertainty – is removed. I don't tend to do much on-sight soloing (aside from in the very low grades), as to me that's simply a step too far in terms of risk. It's not my own climbing ability I fear, it's the unknowns such as loose rock and wet holds. One hold pulling off the wall unexpectedly would send me cartwheeling off into the abyss, and much as I love soloing, I absolutely do not want to die doing it.

As for the risk that remains, I can think of many situations in everyday life where making a mistake could be fatal, driving being by far the best example, and yet we all still do it. To me, falling off a solo is about as likely as ending up in a pile-up on the motorway; there's always a chance, but it's extremely unlikely to happen. If I drive carelessly and text at the same time, I'm more likely to crash; if I solo routes without the right mindset and preparation, I'm more likely to fall. If care is taken, however, and hazards are not underestimated, I see no point in depriving myself of such rich experiences just to stay safe. The brutal truth of the world is that anyone could die at any time, and despite the occasional moral dilemma, soloing remains a risk I'm willing to take.

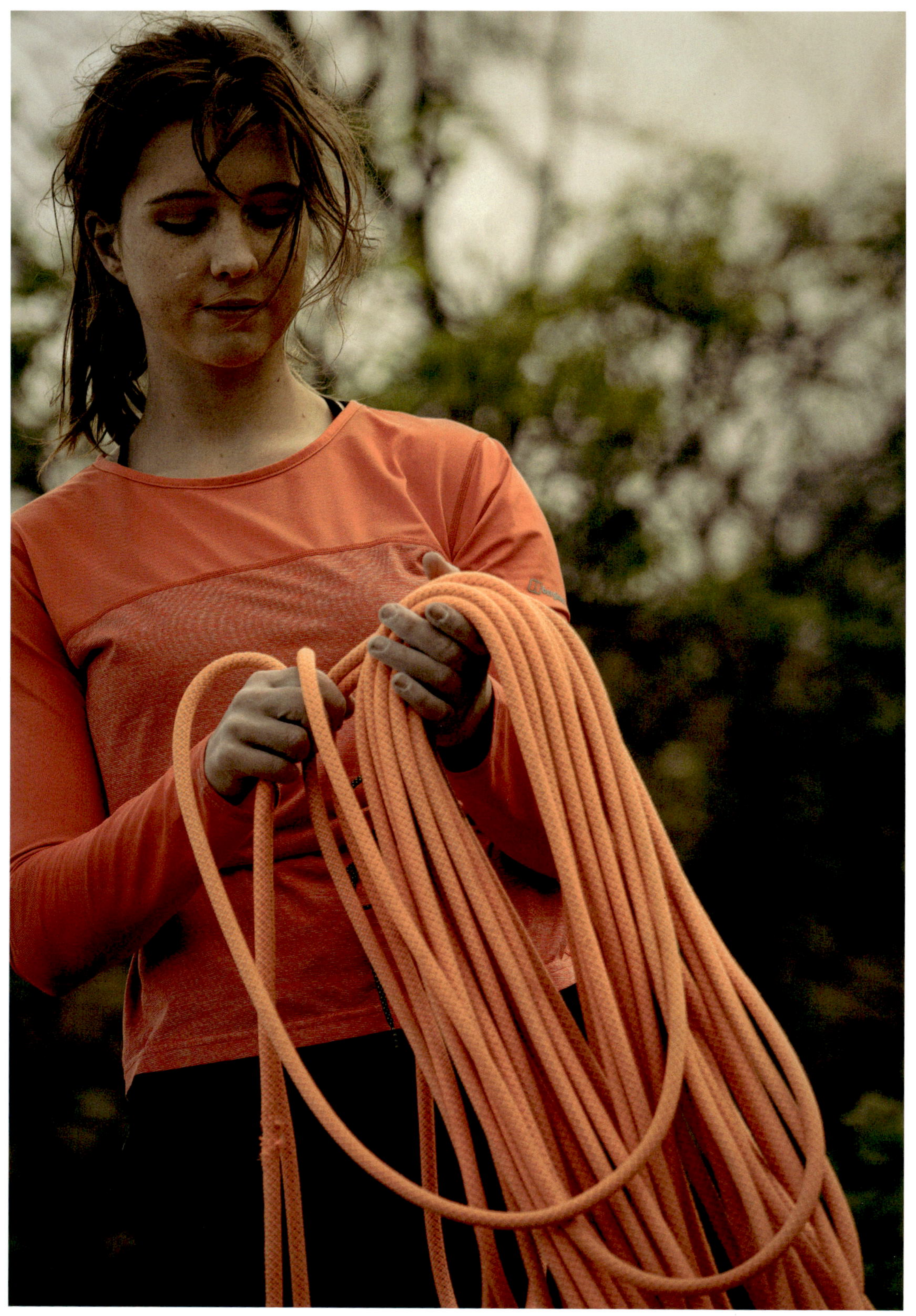

Anna Taylor and rope – rarely seen together. © Nadir Khan

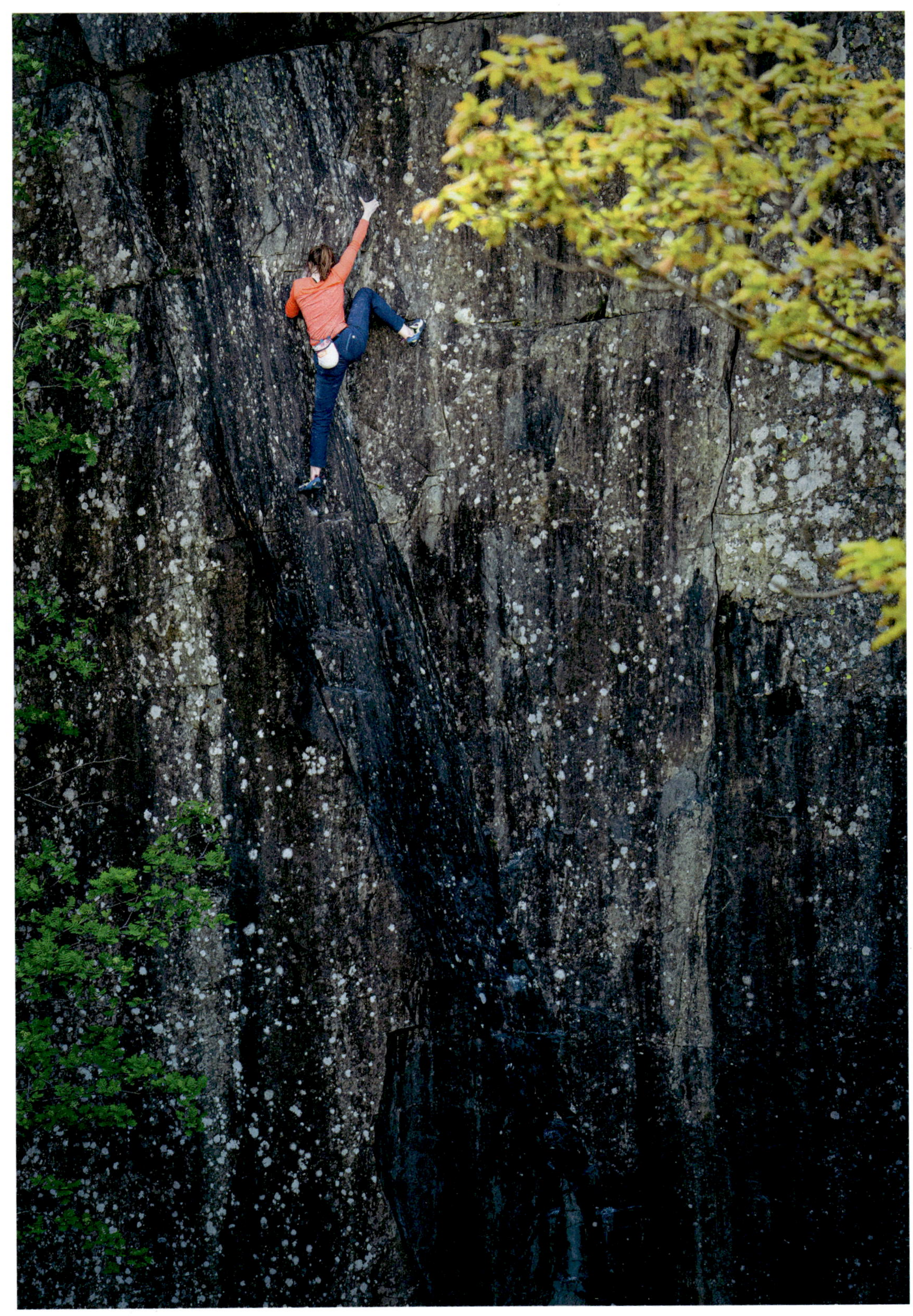

Anna soloing *Treacle Slab* (E3 5c) in Tilberthwaite Quarry. © Nadir Khan

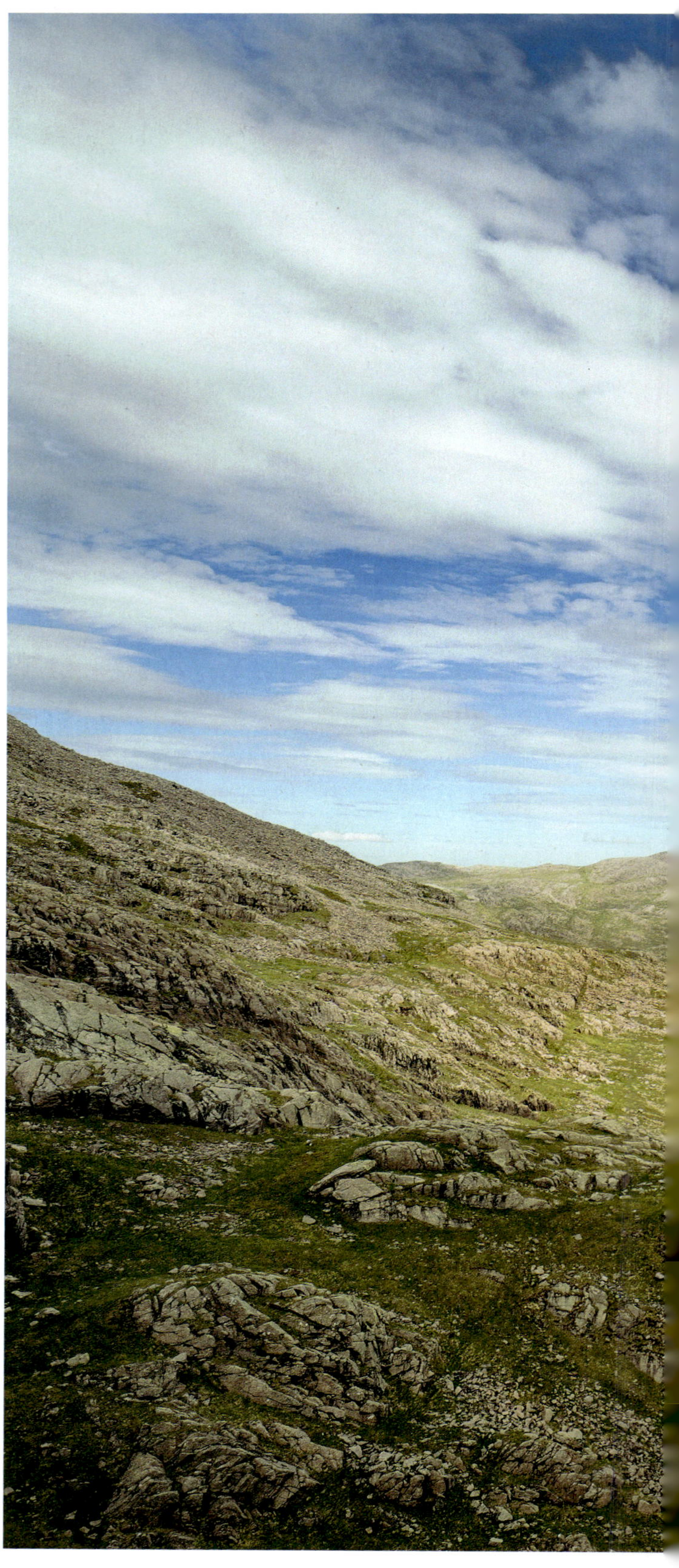

Leo Houlding climbing *Entonox* (E7 6c) on Scafell's East Buttress. © Tom McNally »

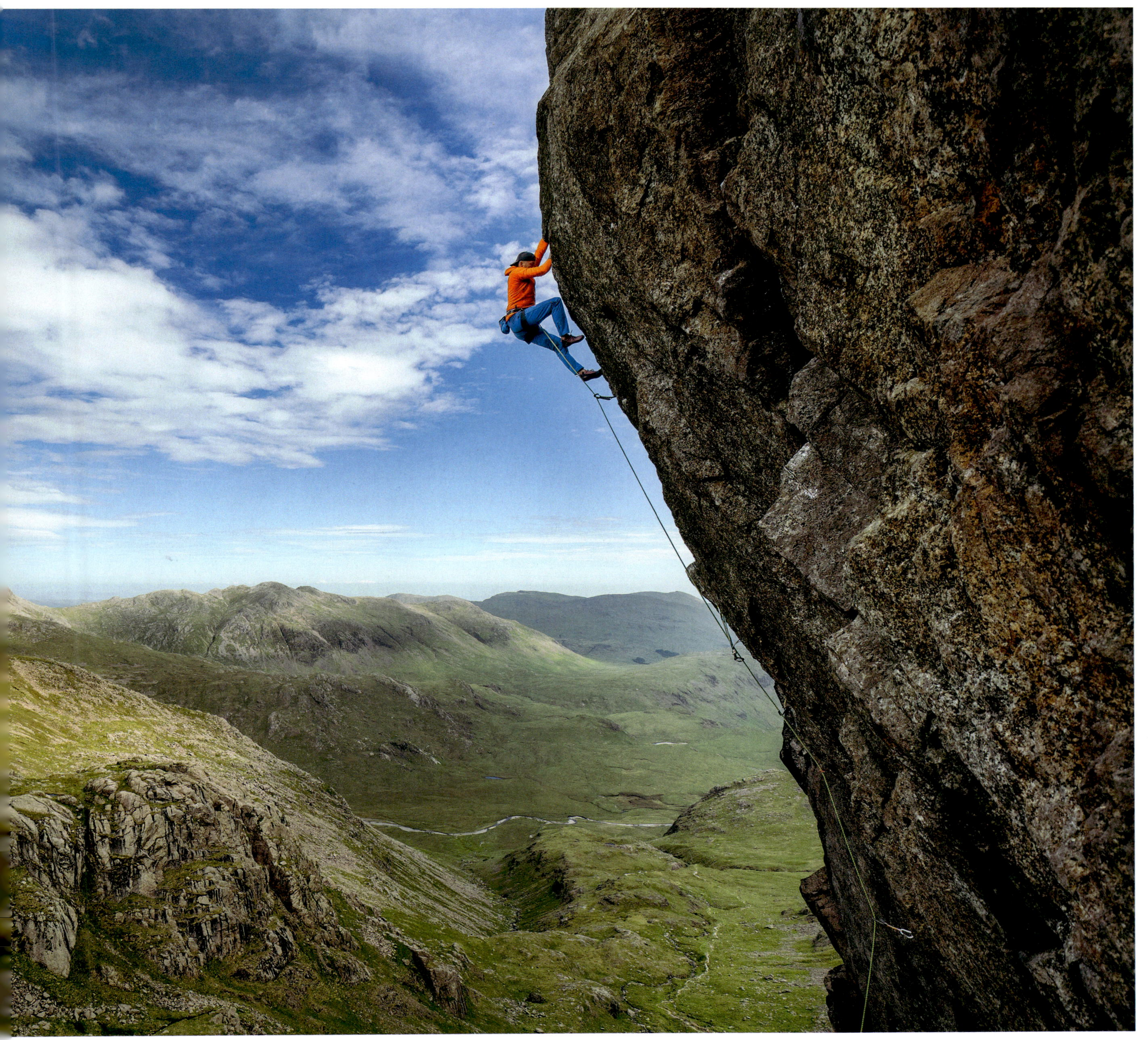

THE LAST

BY KATY FORRESTER

It feels as if it were the last hot day of summer
Sluggish and dopey
Like a bee drunk on nectar

The stream gurgles but slowly
Low
Empty of the winter rains

We walk
Without pace or determination
The easy movement of people who do not mind the time of their arrival

We act as though the day won't end
The happy arrogance of the young and satisfied

The crag beats out the summer heat
Mistakes don't sway our optimism

The movement of the climb is joyful
Brave
Brave
Bravery born from confidence

Dan Varian on *Colonel Hathi* (Font 8a+), Swarthbeck Gill. © Tom McNally »

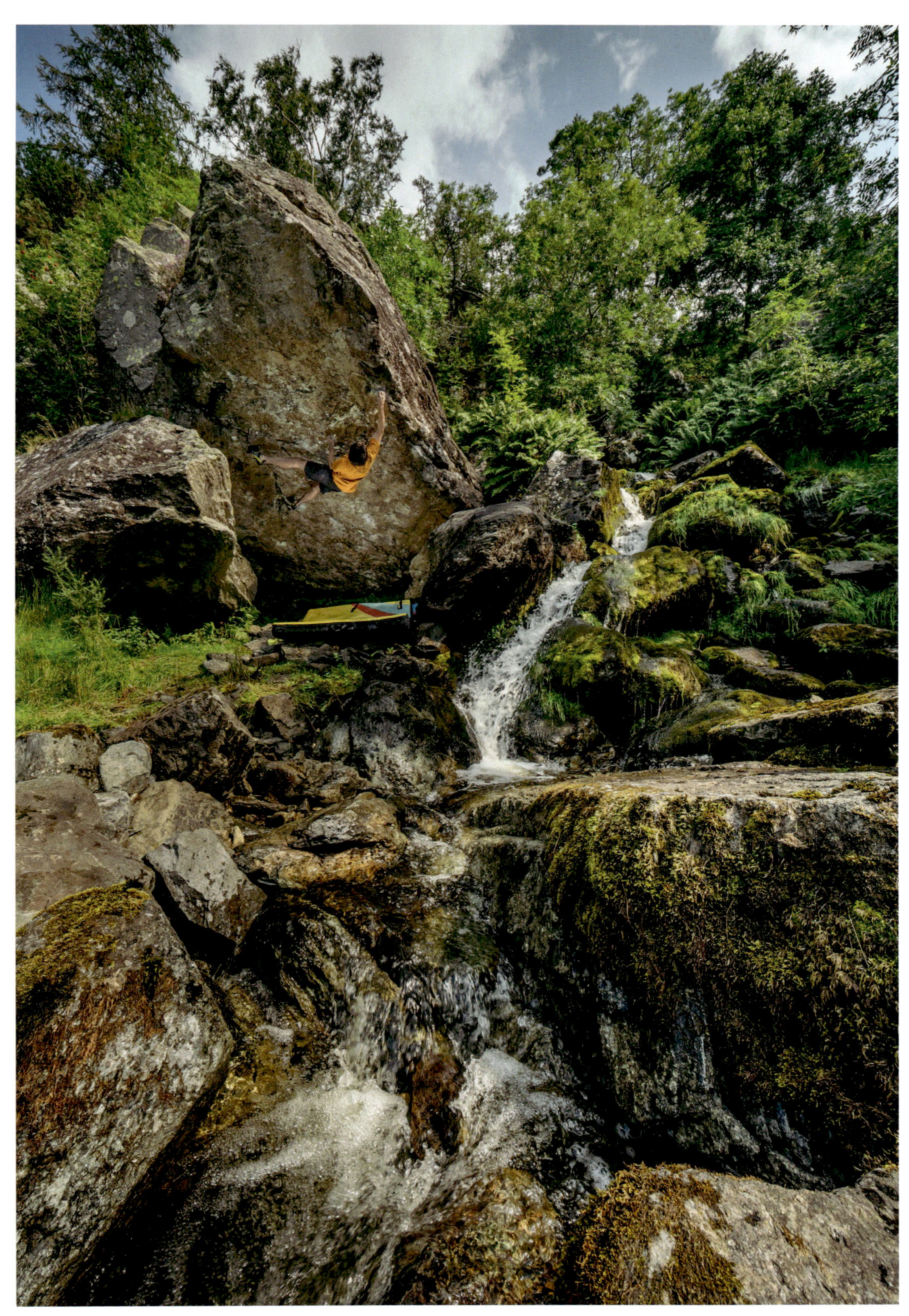

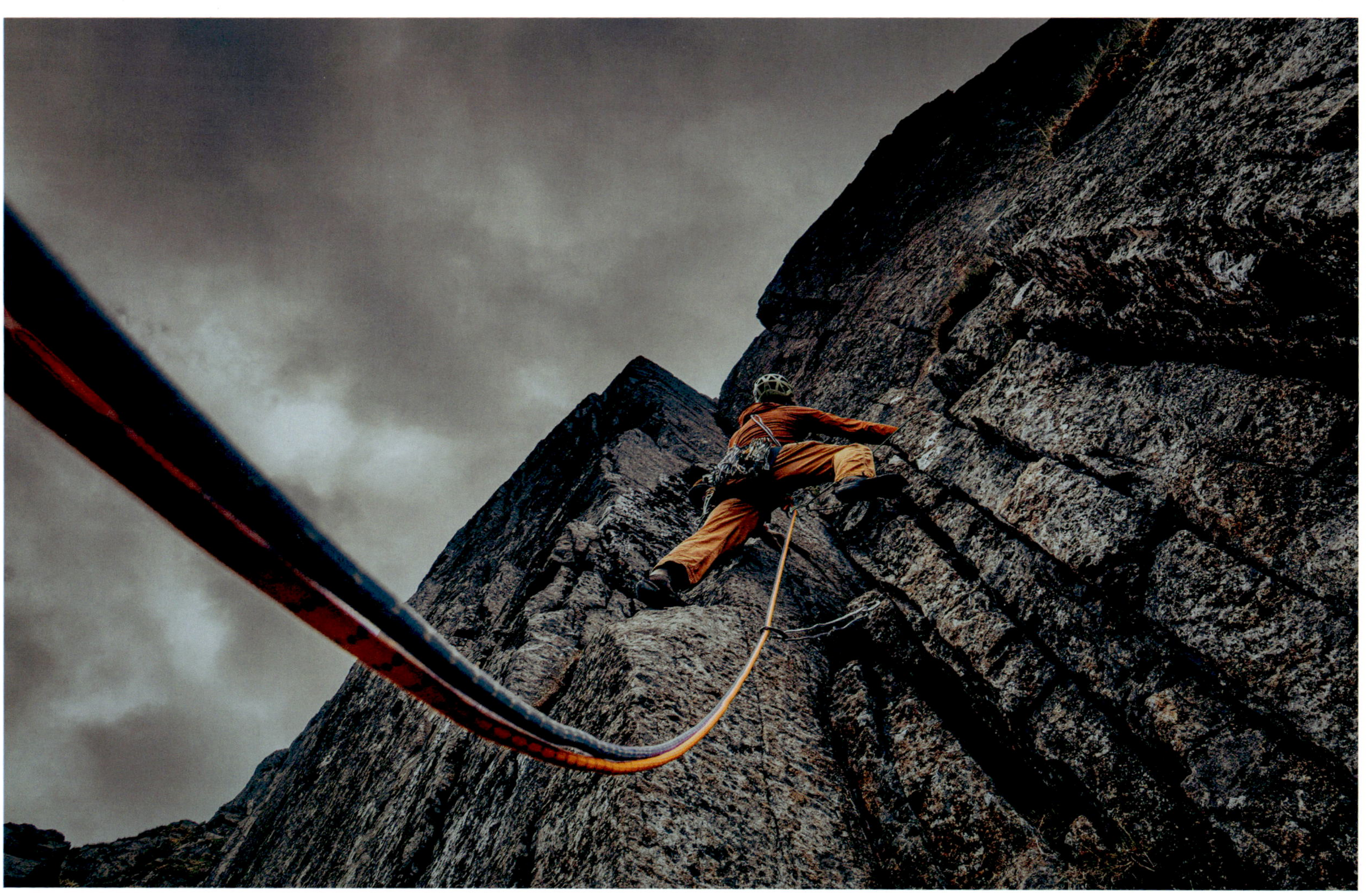

Antony McPhillips on the slabs of *Botterill's Slab* (VS 4c) and *Moss Ghyll Grooves* (VS 4c) on Scafell's Central Buttress.
© Nadir Khan

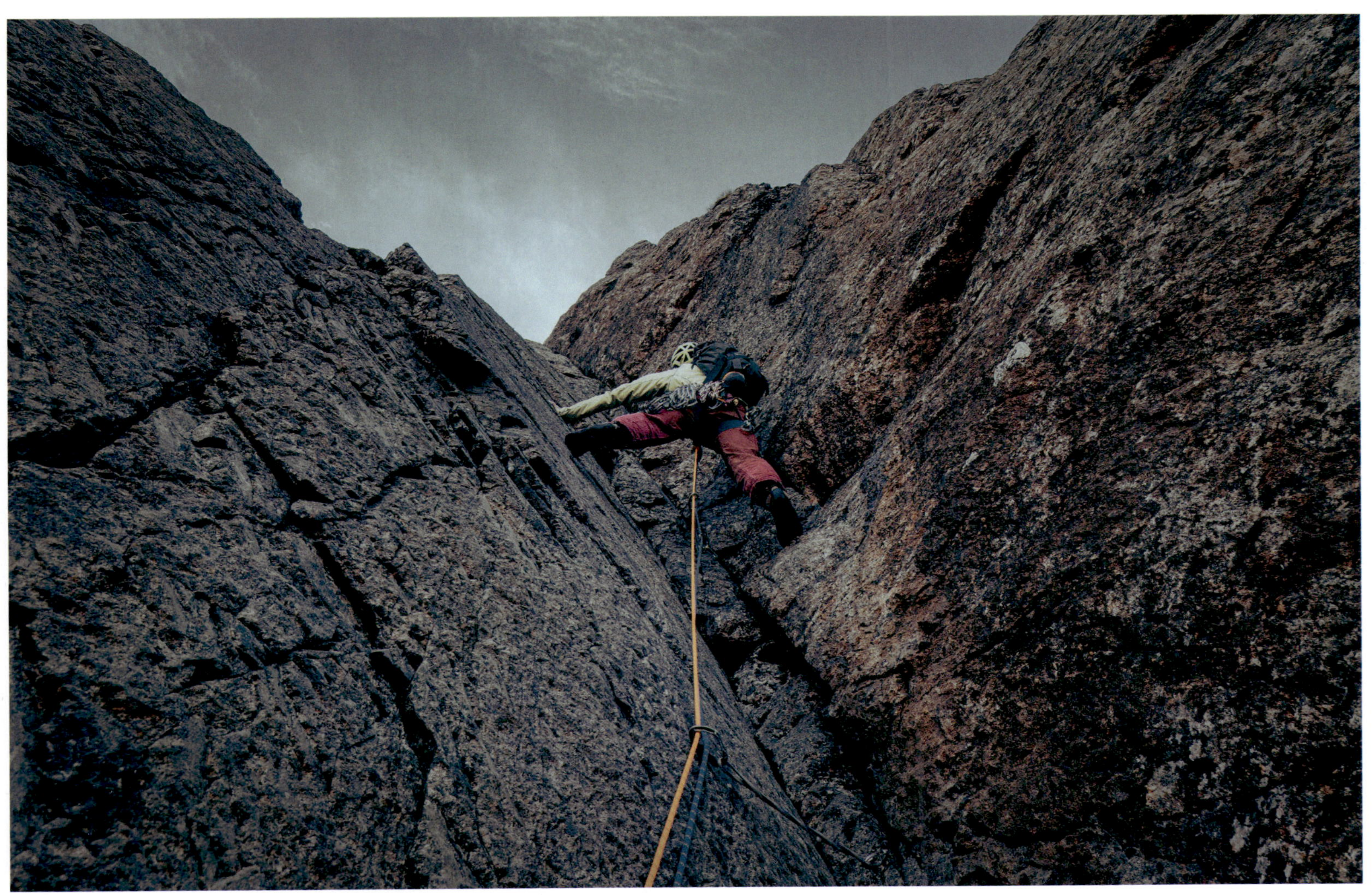

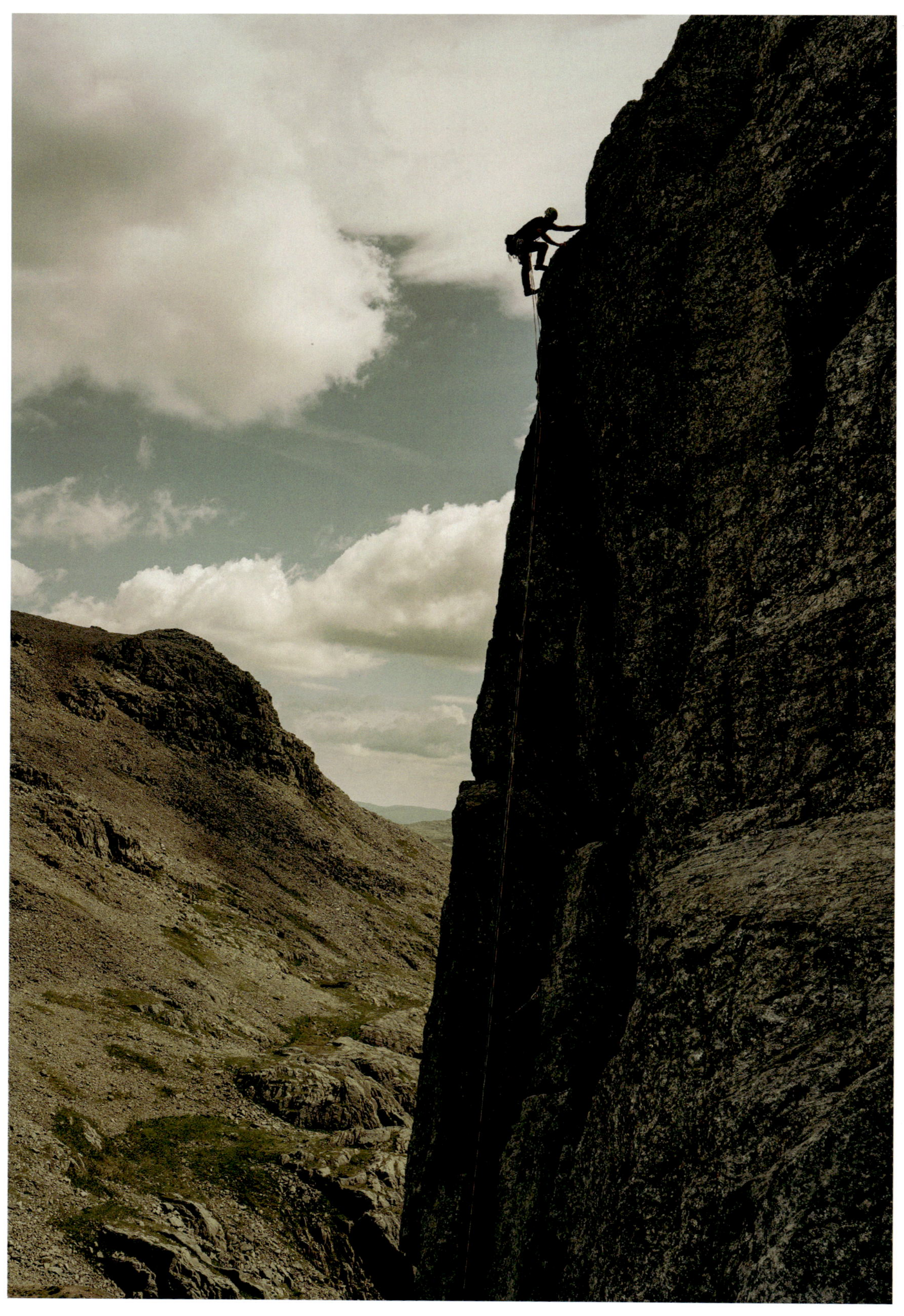

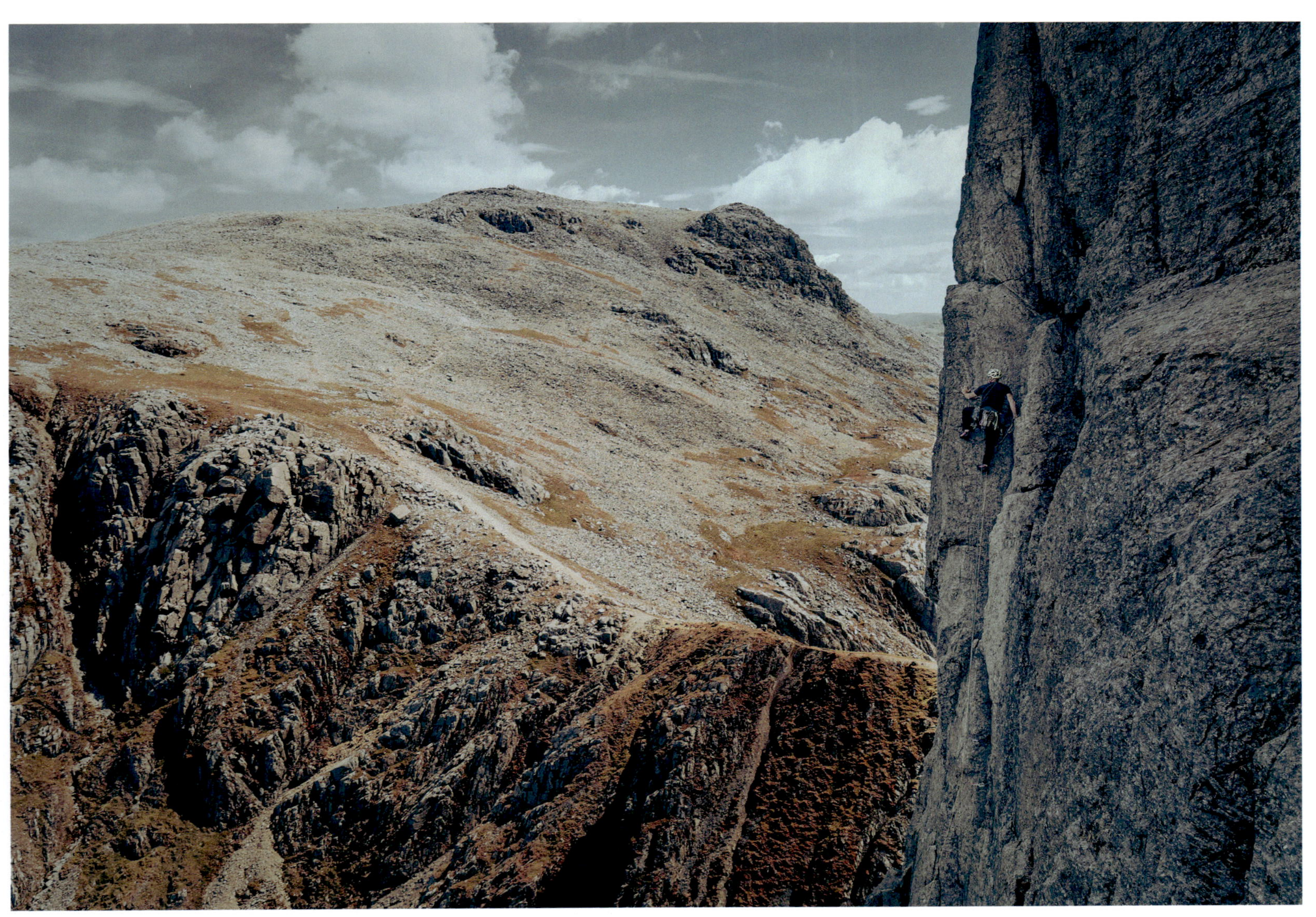

Max Cole on the *Nazgul* finish (E1) to Scafell's *Central Buttress*. © Nadir Khan

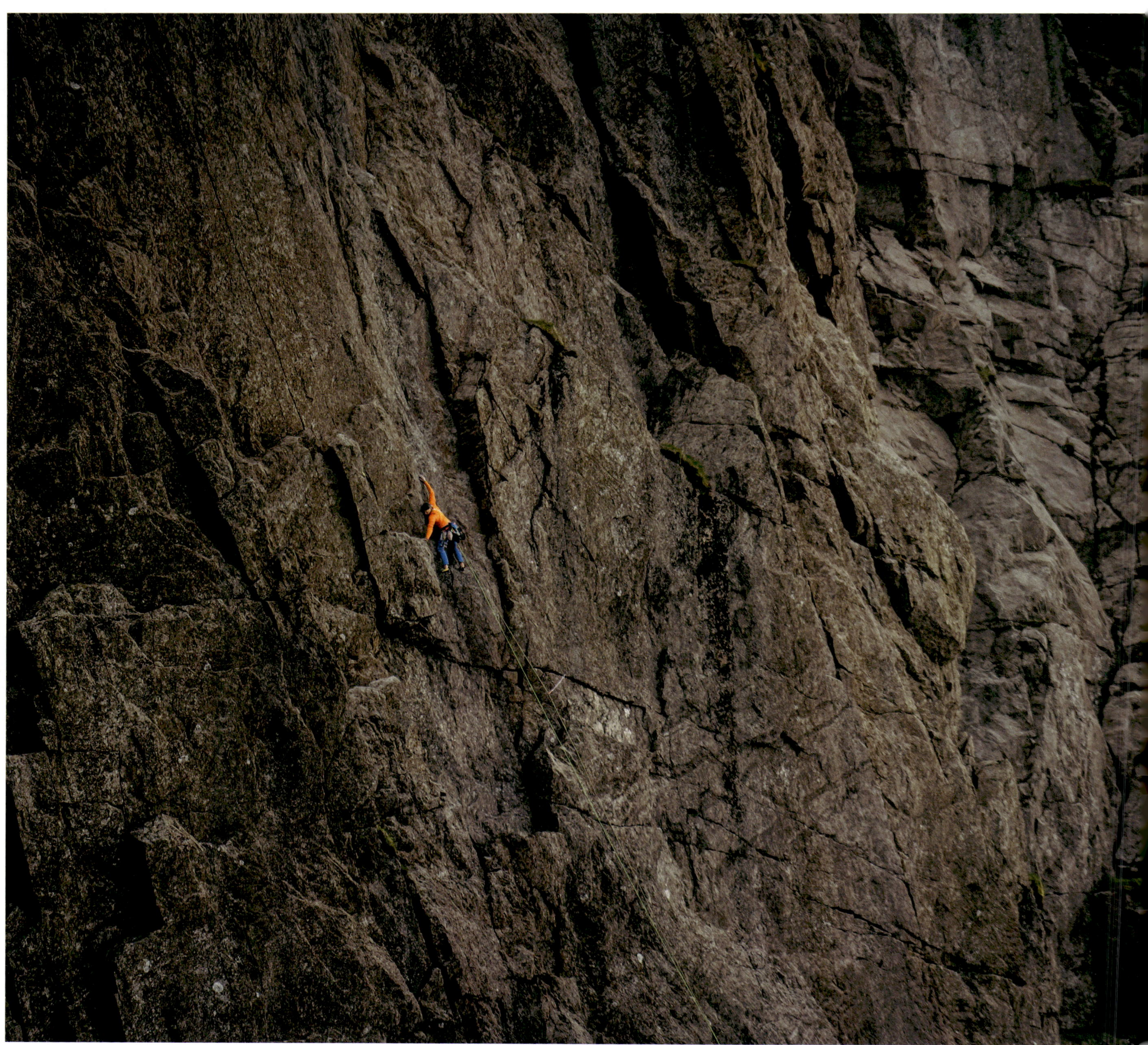

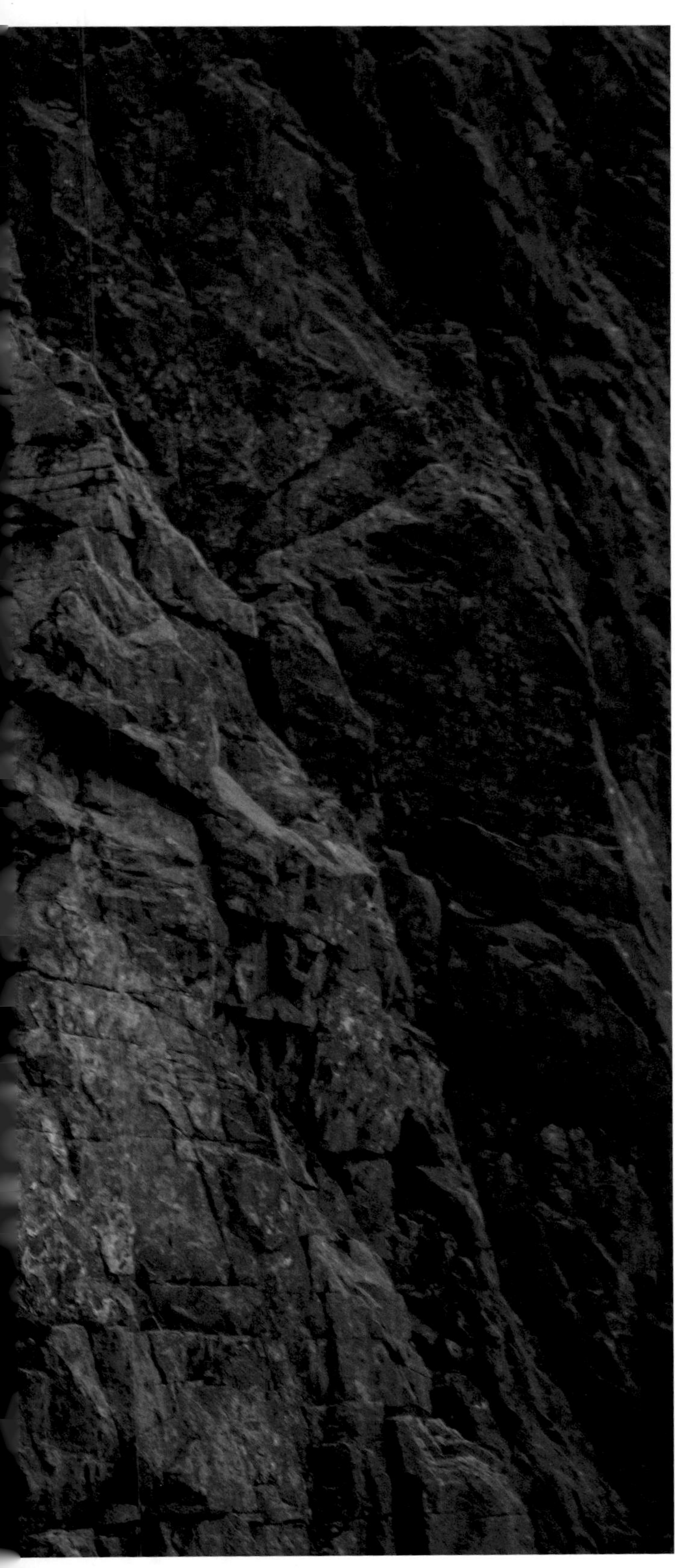

« Leo Houlding on *Central Buttress* (E1 5b), Scafell Crag.
This historic route was first climbed by Siegfried Herford
and George Sansom in 1914. © Tom McNally

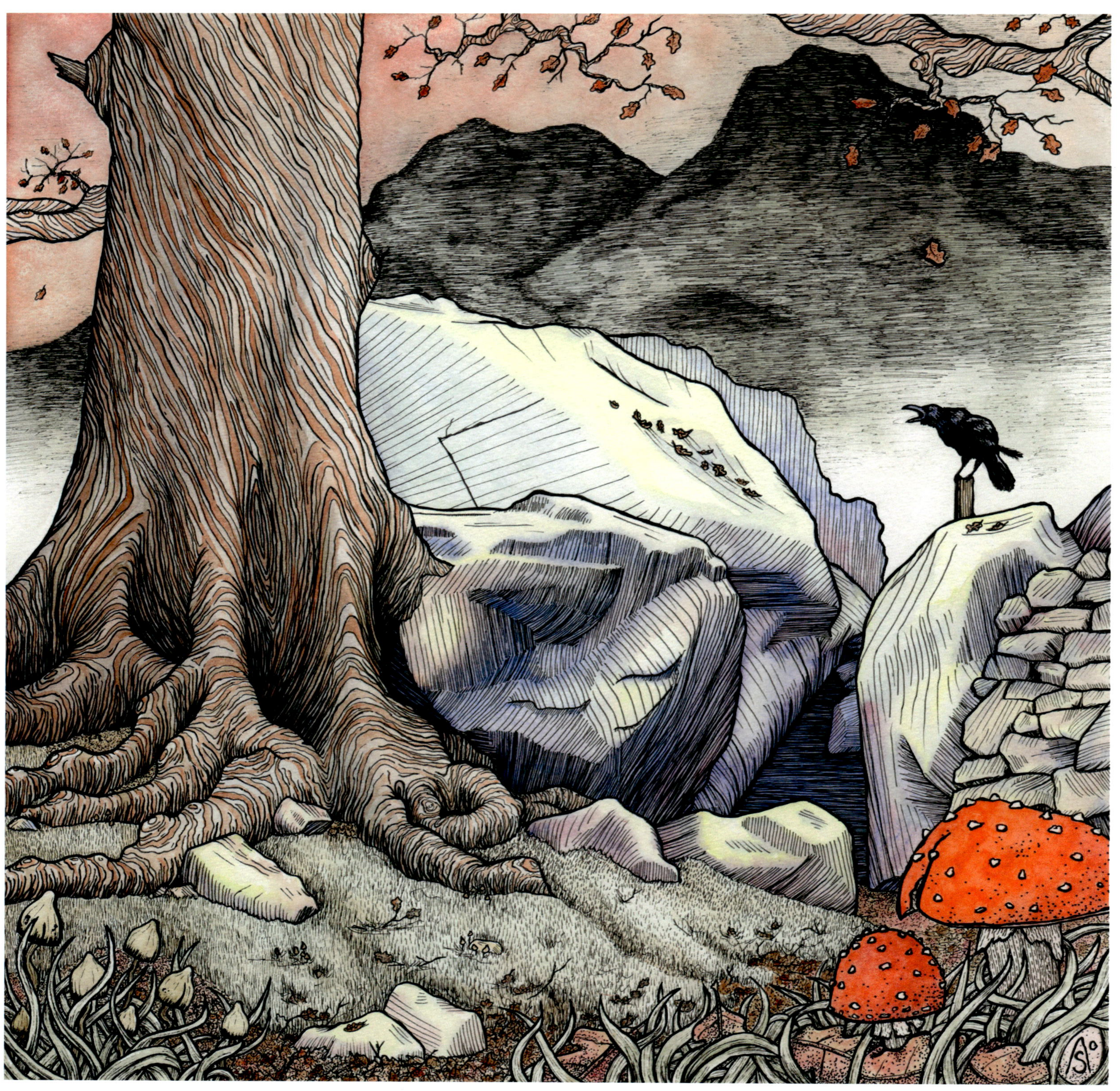

AUTUMN

« *Langdale Boulders.* © Anna Sharpe

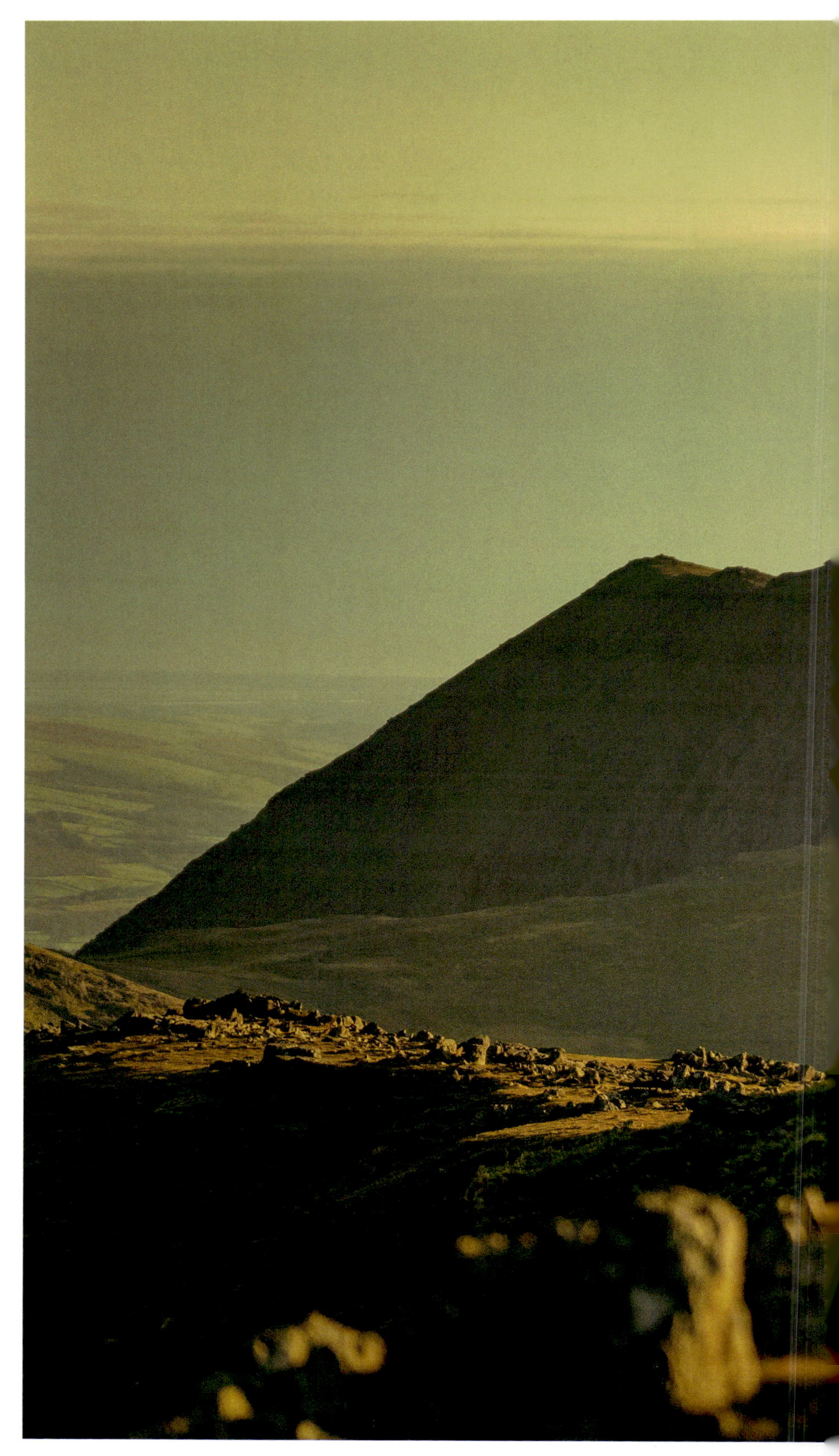

Runners from the OMM team testing new gear
above the Wrynose Pass. © Nadir Khan »

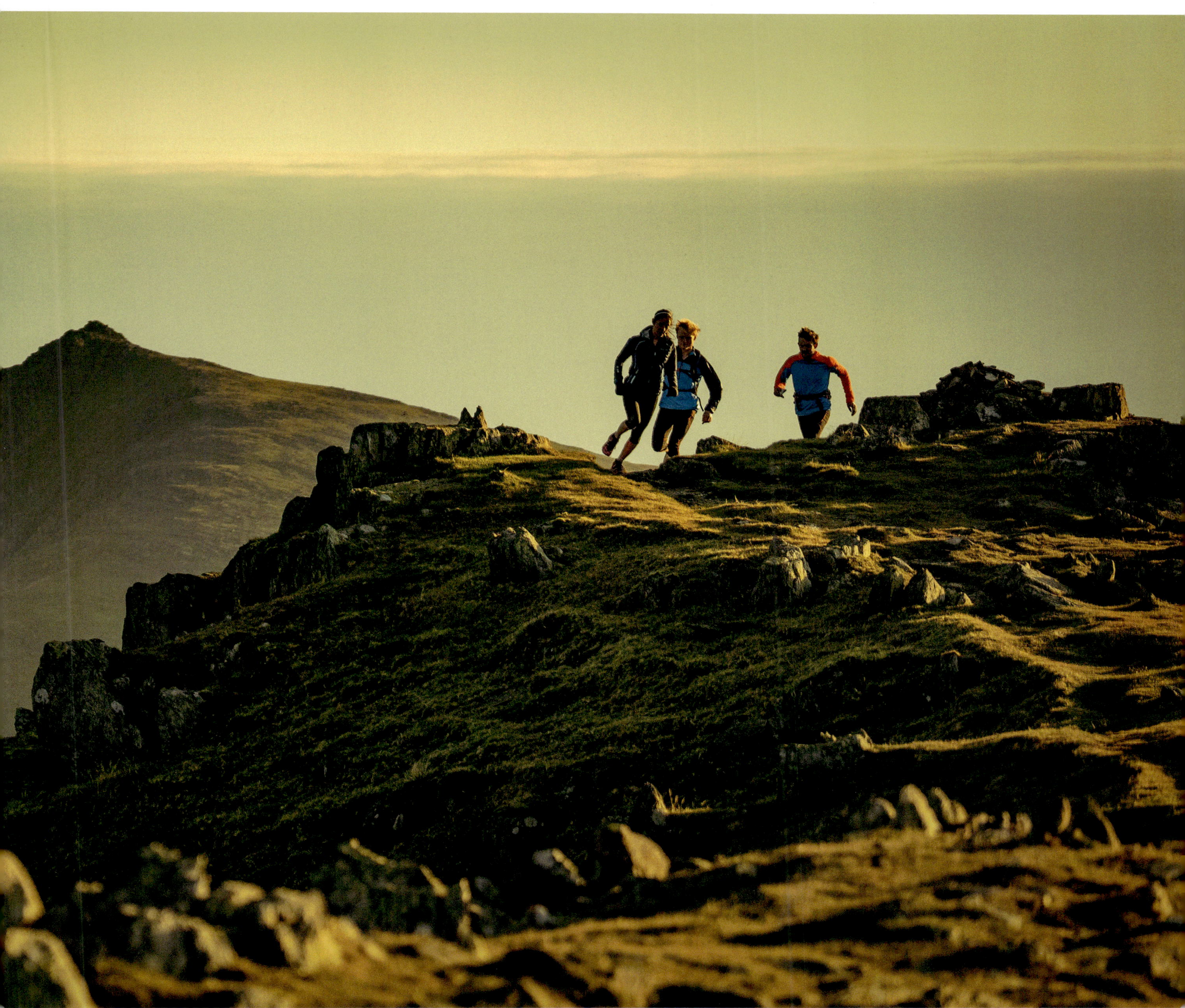

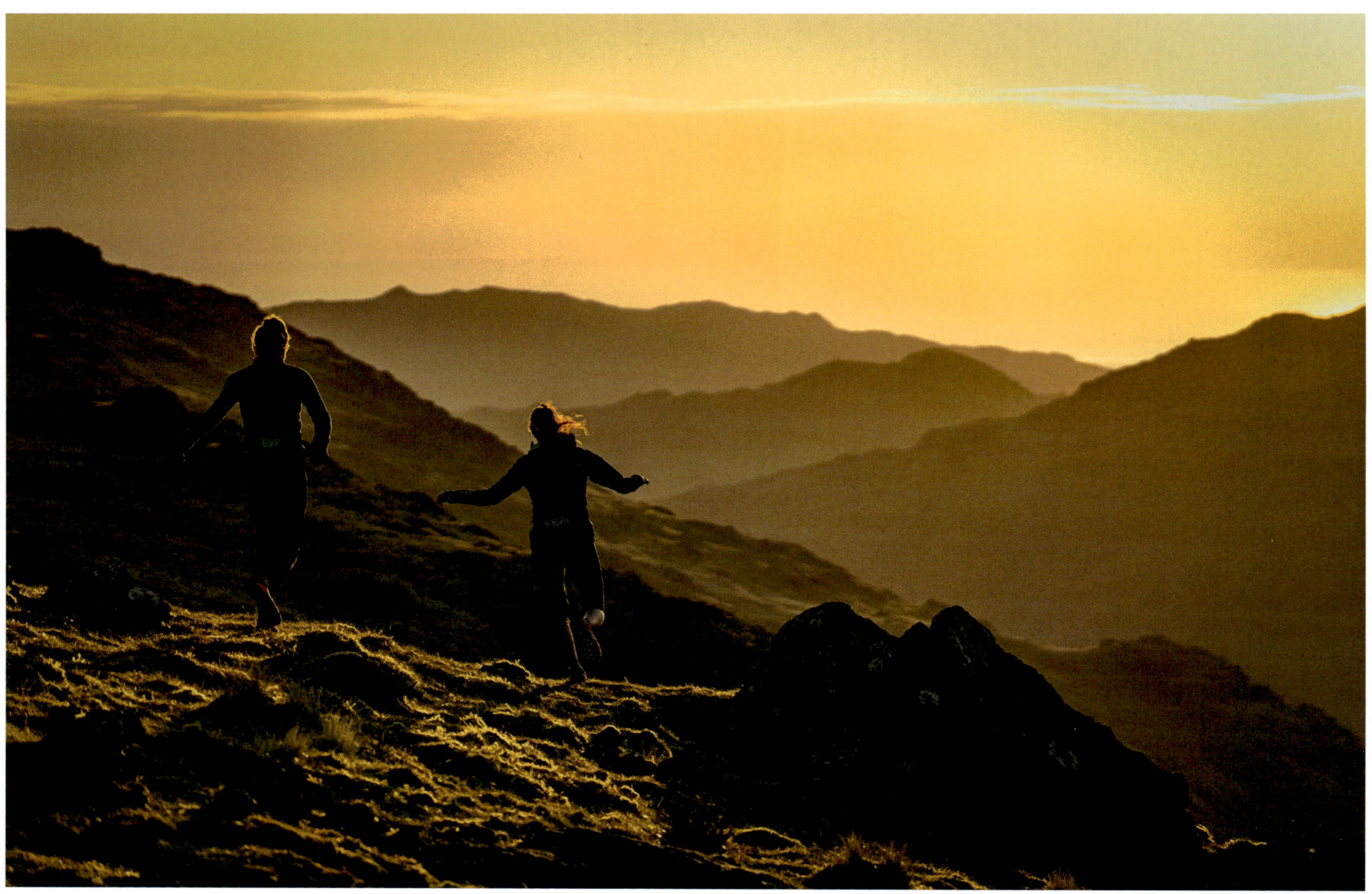

Sunset running above Wrynose Pass. © Nadir Khan

TO BE A FELL RUNNER

BY ELLIS BLAND

What does it mean to be a fell runner in the twenty-first century? To be a true fell runner (in my opinion at least) you must have complete knowledge of the lay of the land, of every contour, and most importantly where the best lines lie. A twenty-first-century fell runner, however, is something altogether quite different; with the meteoric developments in technology it's 'Goodbye, OS map' and 'Hello, Garmin' (other watch brands available).

I'm not saying that a twenty-first-century fell runner can't read a map – just that it's much easier not to. This is partly where the problem lies, though. In a world where getting Instagram 'likes' often outweighs the potential brutality of the fells, there has subsequently been a shift towards reaching these beauty spots just to stock up the social media larder, whatever the risk. Who needs a map when you can just take one of the National Trust's walkers' paths? Great motorways scarring our beloved Wainwrights – easy to navigate, easy to get to and easy to run.

You cannot even begin to imagine the 'Borrowdale Boys' of the day taking the easy route up Glaramara on a training run, only to then have a selfie at the top, one hand each on the cairn like they're showing a prize hound at Crufts. For them it'll have been hard running come rain or shine, and the craic would have had to wait until they were safely off the fell.

Yes, it does in fact rain in the Lake District, not that Instagram would have you believe it.

This is a seemingly cynical account of the twenty-first-century fell runner; however, I'm pleased to say there are still pockets of runners out there who show the Lakeland fells the respect they deserve. Yes, the summits are smaller than our neighbours' in Scotland and Wales but woe betide anybody for thinking that this makes them more forgiving. I'd challenge any top mountain runner to sequence the corridor route off Scafell Pike, at speed, only to reach the foot of Great Gable without having glanced back at least once and let out an audible sigh of relief. Or to drop off the side of Fairfield and take in Cofa Pike before hurtling down to Grisedale Tarn without being just a little bit proud of themselves. For me those sighs of relief and moments of pride are why I adore the pastime of fell running and why the Lakeland fells will forever keep me coming back.

You could say I was born with a curse, that curse being the surname Bland. You only need to sit in the Scafell Hotel, Borrowdale, to see why my name haunts me. On the wall there is a plaque with a list of all previous Borrowdale Fell Race winners. No fewer than fourteen victories to one Bland clan or another in the race's forty-five-year history. I'm certainly not one of them and nor am I ever likely to be. In fact,

I reckon I'd only just be summitting Bessyboot as Billy swatted through the crowds on Scafell Pike.

For me, however, I prefer longer stuff; my 'victories' come when I've sewn together entire quarters of our national park. Long days are what I live for, where I've been the first up Clough Head and last down somewhere over Wasdale way. Chasing sunsets is much more my cup of tea, not Strava crowns. I'd be lying if I said I didn't long to be a little quicker on the down, but at the age of twenty-seven and with aspirations of running into my seventies, I shall have to park this dream. Knees over screes and all that!

Running into my seventies, however, could be unfairly taken from me, on the fells anyway. In a conversation I had back in 2019 with a prominent figure of fell running, I asked what he thought the future of fell running was. He simply stated, 'There isn't one.' I looked at him, perplexed, and he went on to explain how, due to the introduction of the National Trust within the Lakes and their gross spending power, he sees no future for this pastime. For the time being you're free to roam on most Lakeland fells but in a world where everything has a price, how long is it until this ultimately free sport is priced out of the market?

I hope he is wrong and that it's the old man in him talking. For what a crying shame it would be to lose the very thing I think most embodies the fell scene – its free accessibility. Free to bolt out of Grasmere showground on race day, free to curse yourself for not doing enough hill training on the way up and free to petrify yourself on the way down. You cannot put a price on these days. No figure could justify the rush of blood to the legs and pounding heart escaping from behind your garish jersey; the craic at the end of a Lakeland Classic after you've seen your pal trundle in having earlier taken a poor line. These days it just wouldn't be the same if the tariff was more than your daily wage.

You needn't be a statistician to see the influx of numbers on the fells. The recent Covid-19 pandemic has only skyrocketed these figures further; where there is demand there is always financial gain. I am in no way suggesting that the fells should only be for national park residents, or the fell runners within it; I myself live outside the park so wouldn't want this. But the very nature of the park's layout means the infrastructure is too 'weak' to handle the spiralling numbers of visitors. Fells are moated by great lakes, with roads delicately threading between them; without the use of tunnelling or a complex bridge system (I shudder at the thought), the roads will always remain this way.

What of the numbers on the fells themselves? It seems to be almost hourly that a mountain rescue team is called to save the day – heroes, who do this on a voluntary basis. Is it really any surprise that they're seriously looking into jet packs to become even more efficient?

These are complex issues and ones only far cleverer people than myself can solve. Though at the rate at which the national park is being exploited, I expect turnstiles at the bottom of Helvellyn by the time I'm thirty!

Complex issues indeed, but we can all play a role in easing the strain on the national park. Find yourself a remote corner you've never even heard of and just explore it. I can guarantee you'll have a far more spiritual experience. This is why I truly love the English fells. Finding that place which gives you the feeling that you're its first ever conqueror; steep, muscle-burning climbs where you say to yourself, 'Surely I'm the first ever up this!' Leave the mayhem of down below firmly down below and find that escapism.

Instead of the bustling crowds at the foot of Helvellyn, look to Arnison Crag instead. It may only perch at 433 metres but the vistas from its summit (especially at first light) over Ullswater will compensate for any lost elevation. If height is what you crave, though, track west over Birks (622 metres) and St Sunday Crag (841 metres) before the long descent down Sleet Cove back to where you started. If you're lucky you'll not see a soul. If you do, however, happen to cross paths with others, rest assured they're there for the same reason as you – for the tranquillity, not the Instagram likes.

There are sequences like this all around the Lakeland fells; this is just one of my many favourites. All you've got to do is find your own. The irony is, it's sitting in that dusty map you already own, probably acquired off a former conqueror.

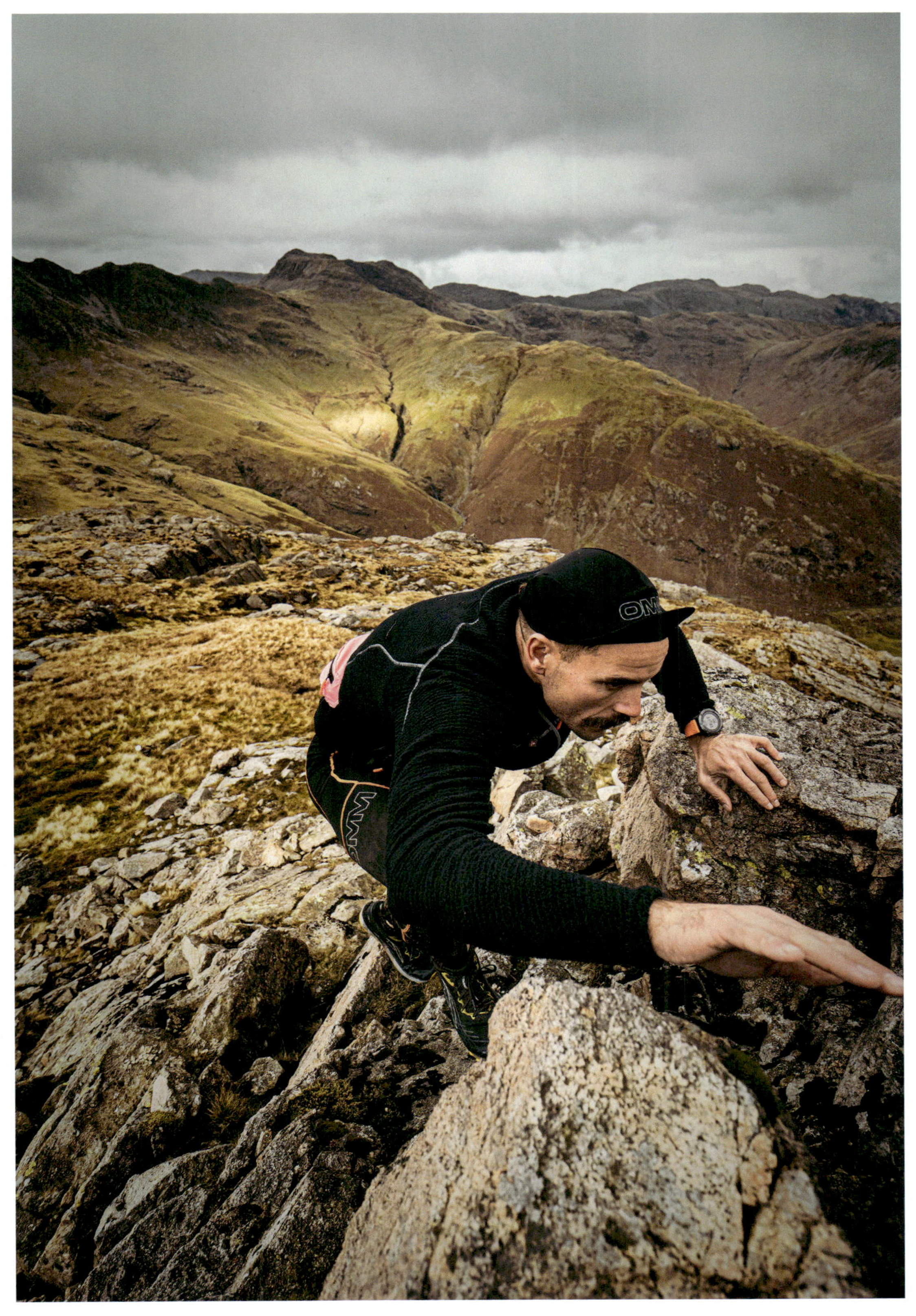

Ellis Bland running above the Wrynose Pass. © Nadir Khan

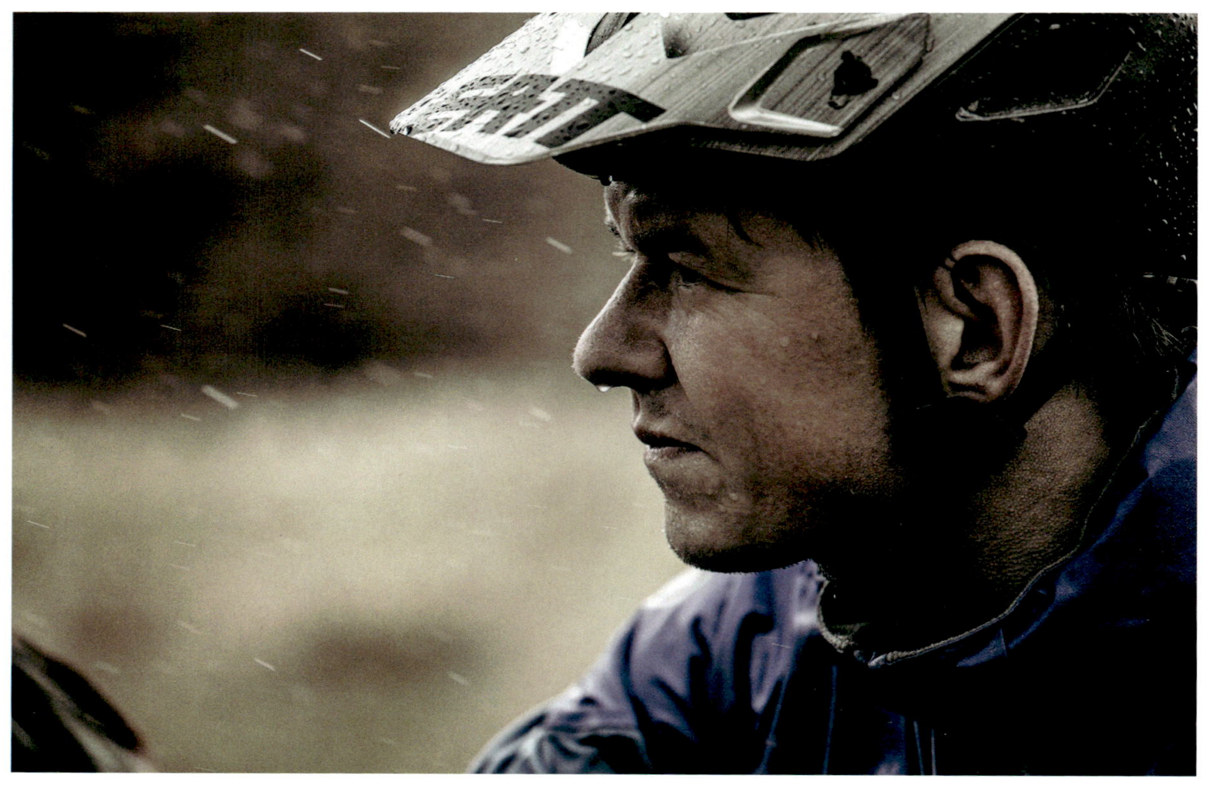

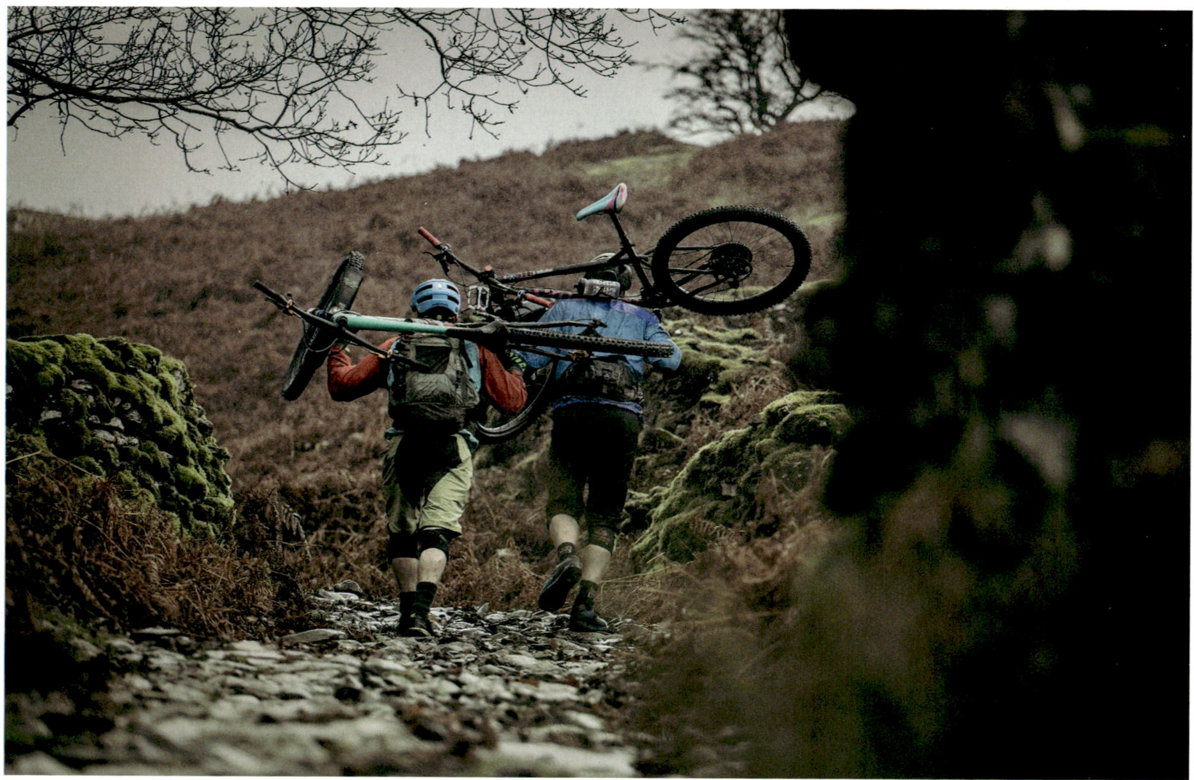

James Vincent and Dan Mead taking in the November rain on the trail from Watendlath to Borrowdale. © Nadir Khan

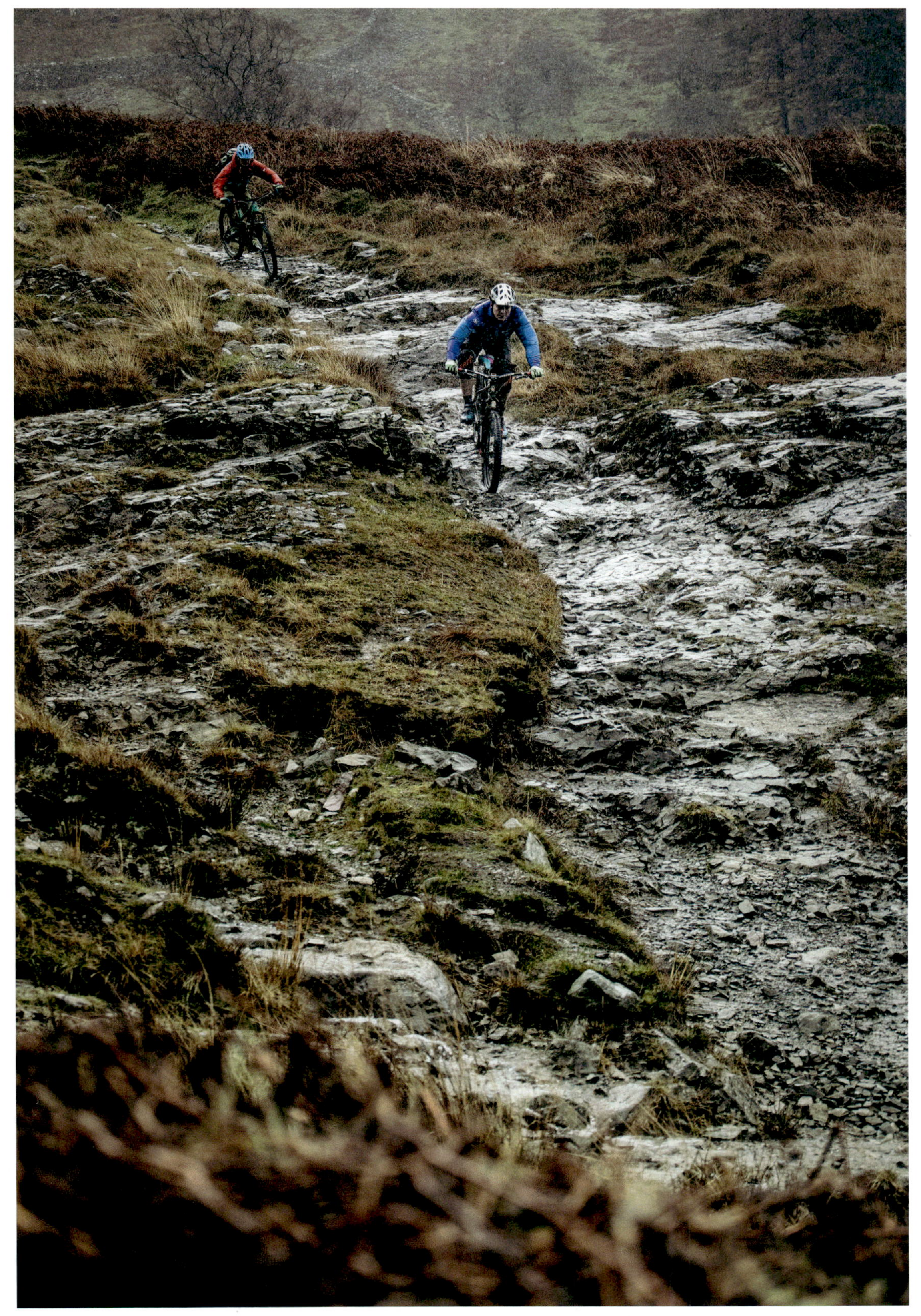

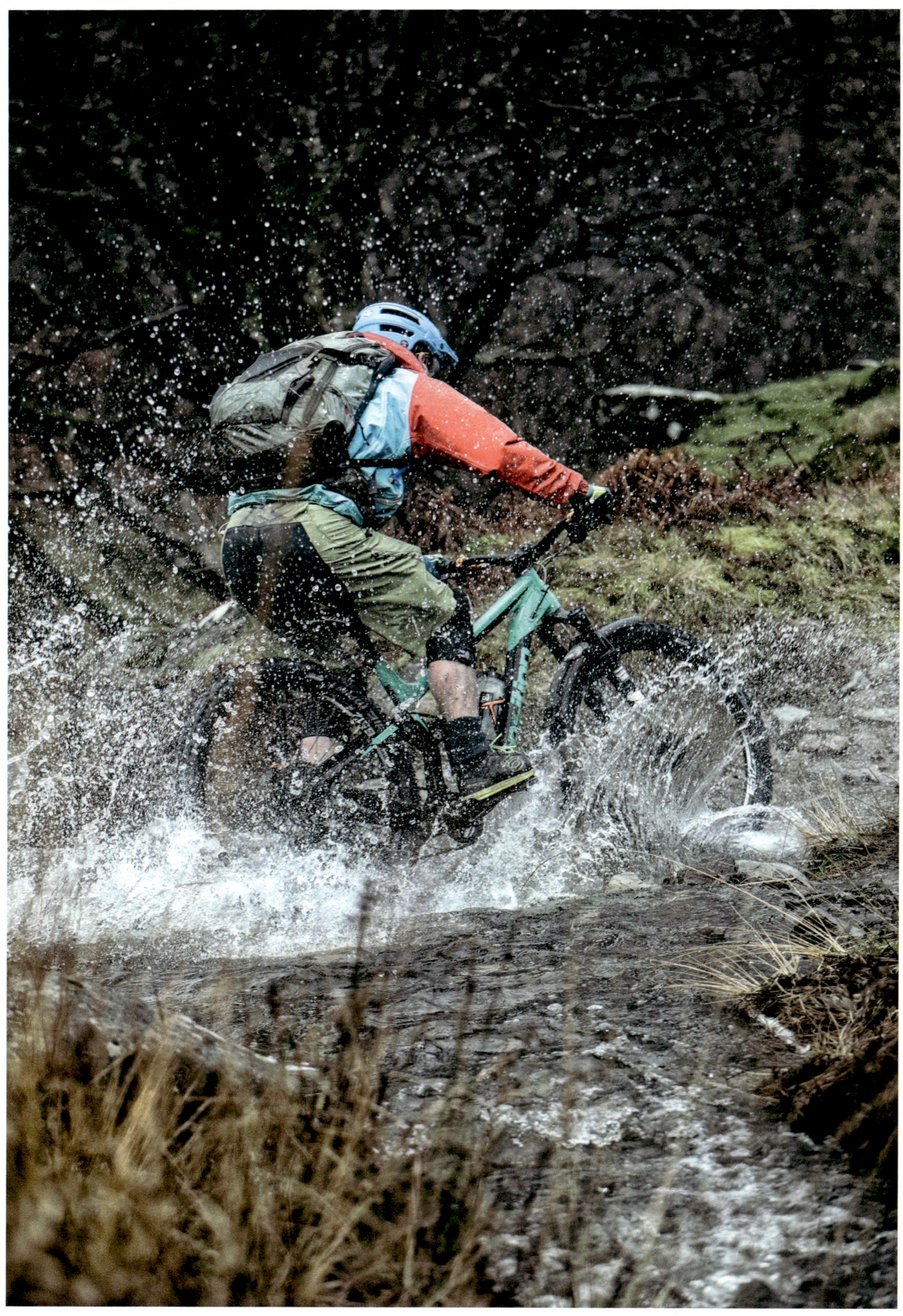

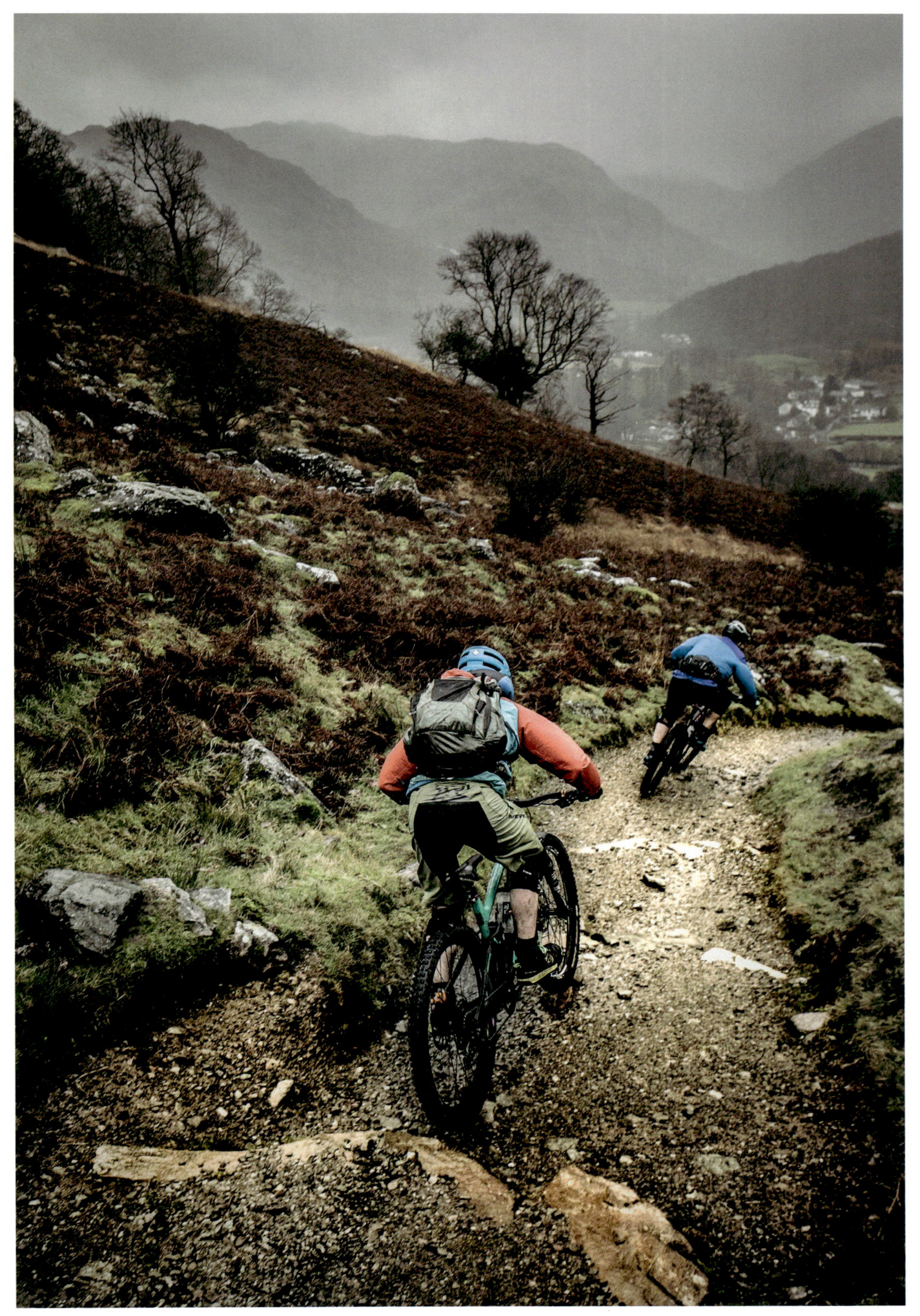

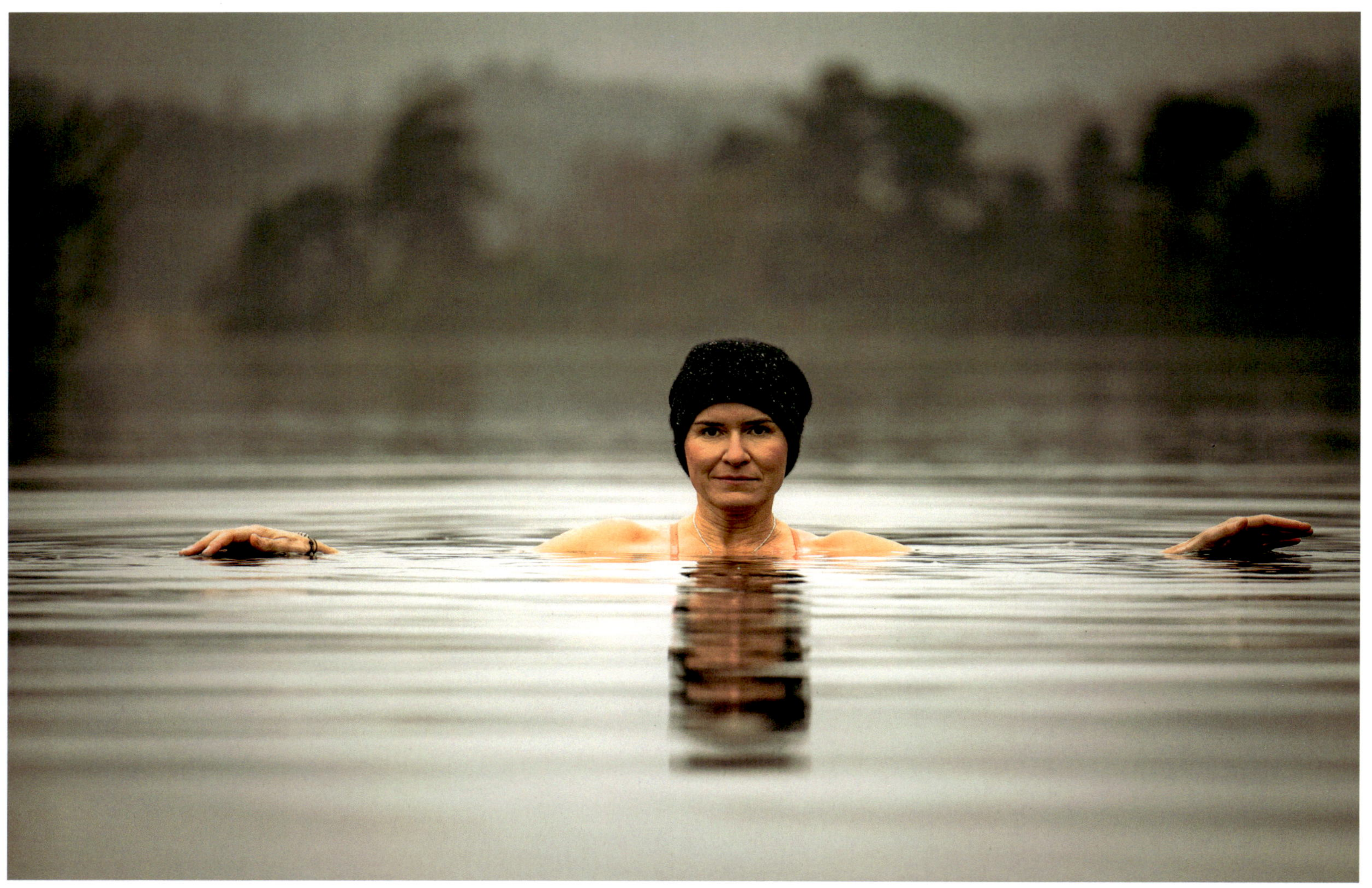

Gilly McArthur in Rydal Water. © Nadir Khan

Ben Atkinson going for full cold-water immersion near Rydal Water. © Nadir Khan »

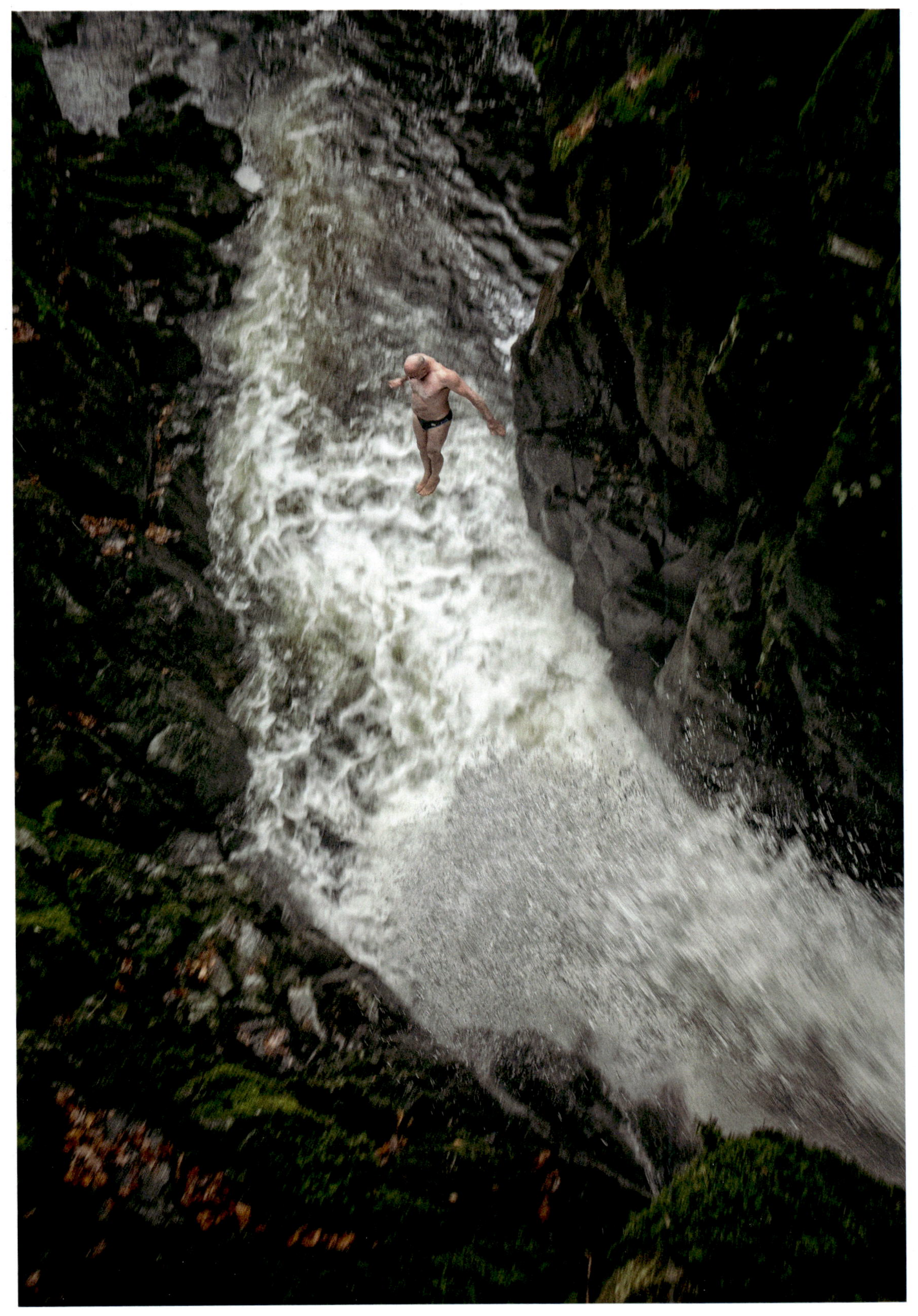

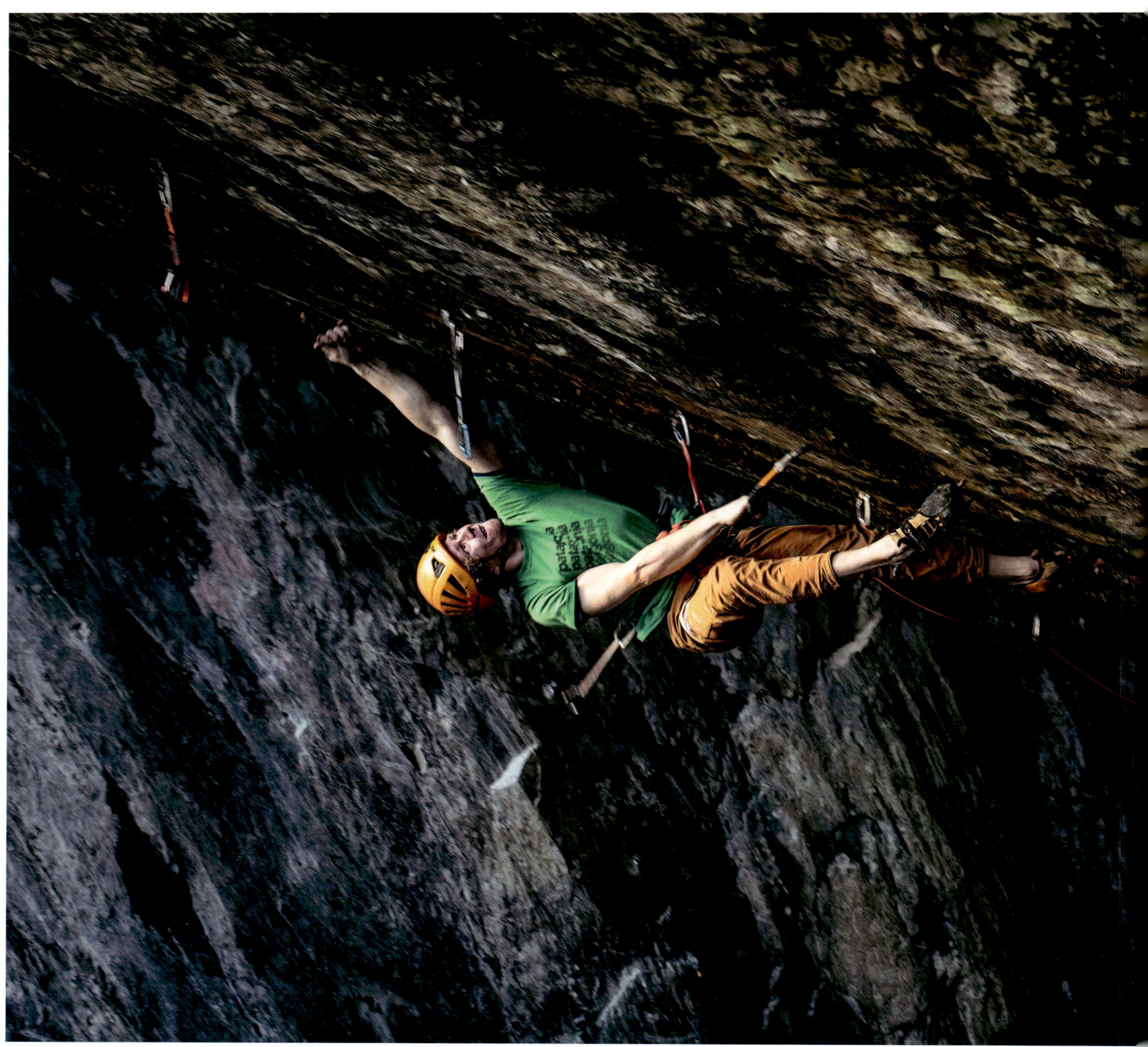

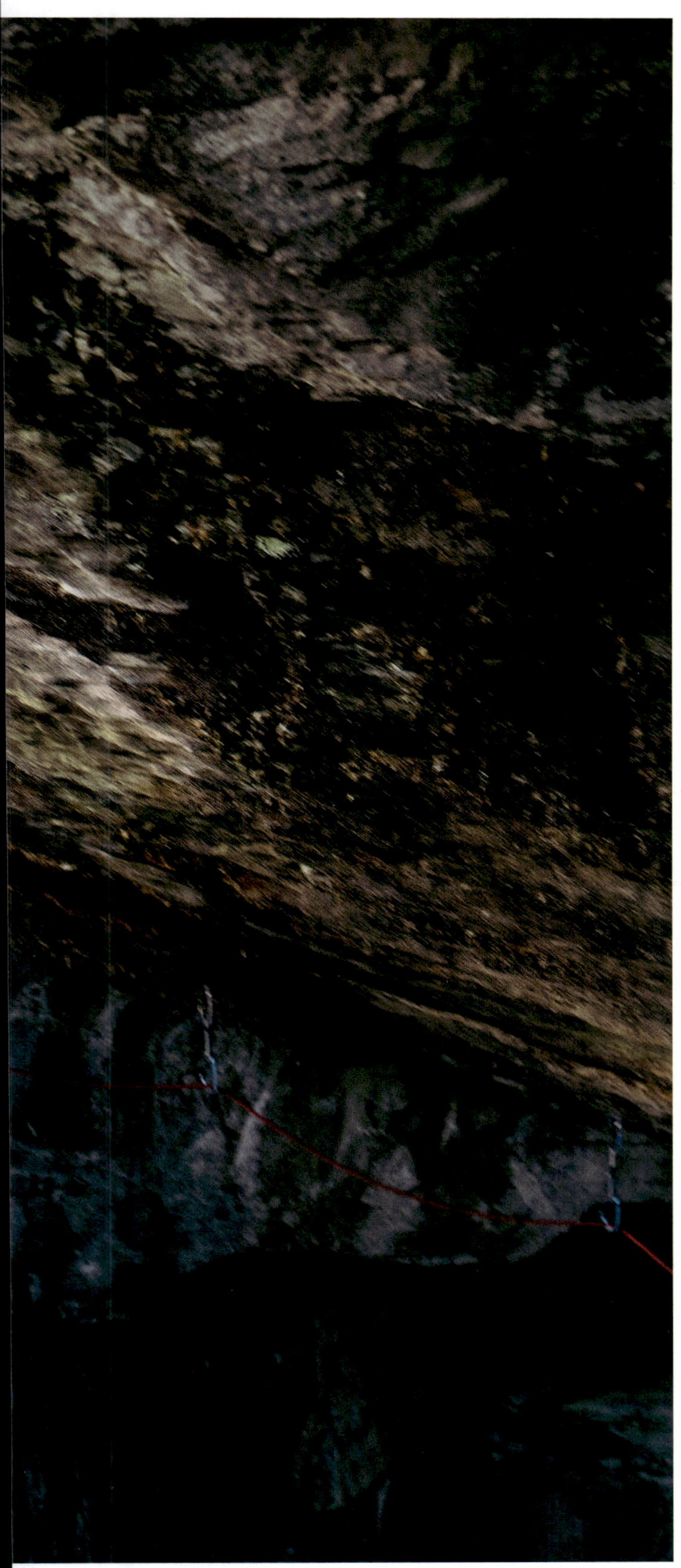

« Matt Foot training on the super-steep *Powerdab* (M13) at Bakestone Quarry. © Nadir Khan

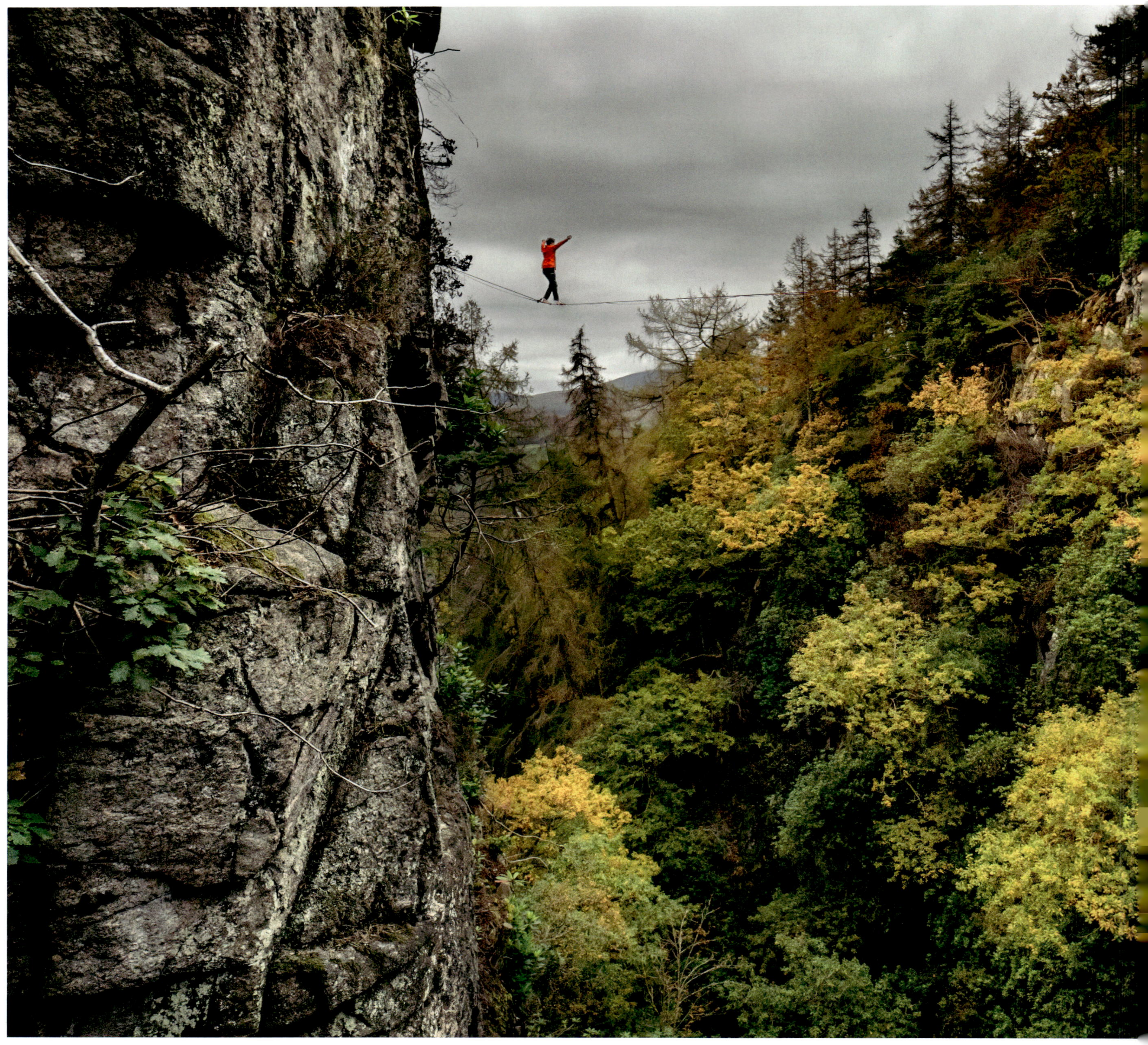

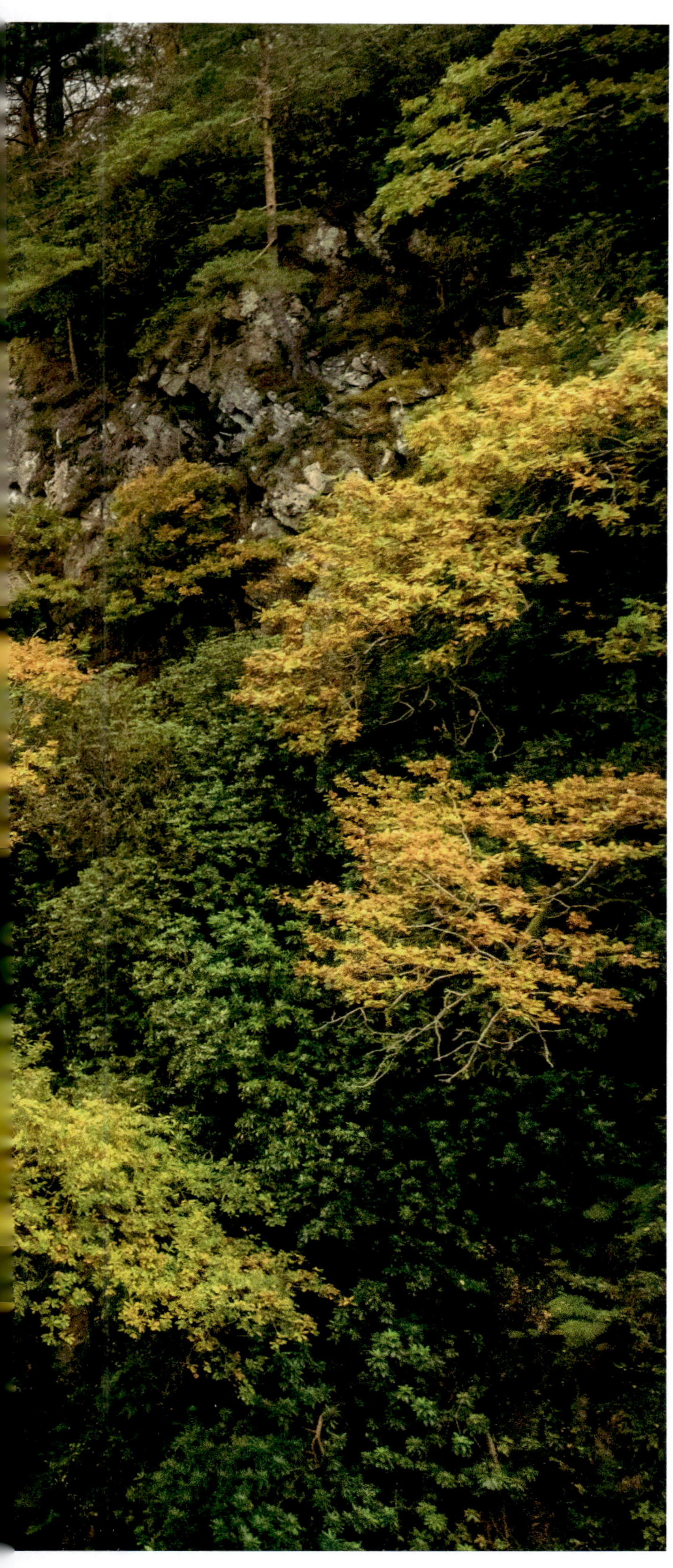

« Jack Chandler slacklines high above Stanley Ghyll in Eskdale.
© Tom McNally

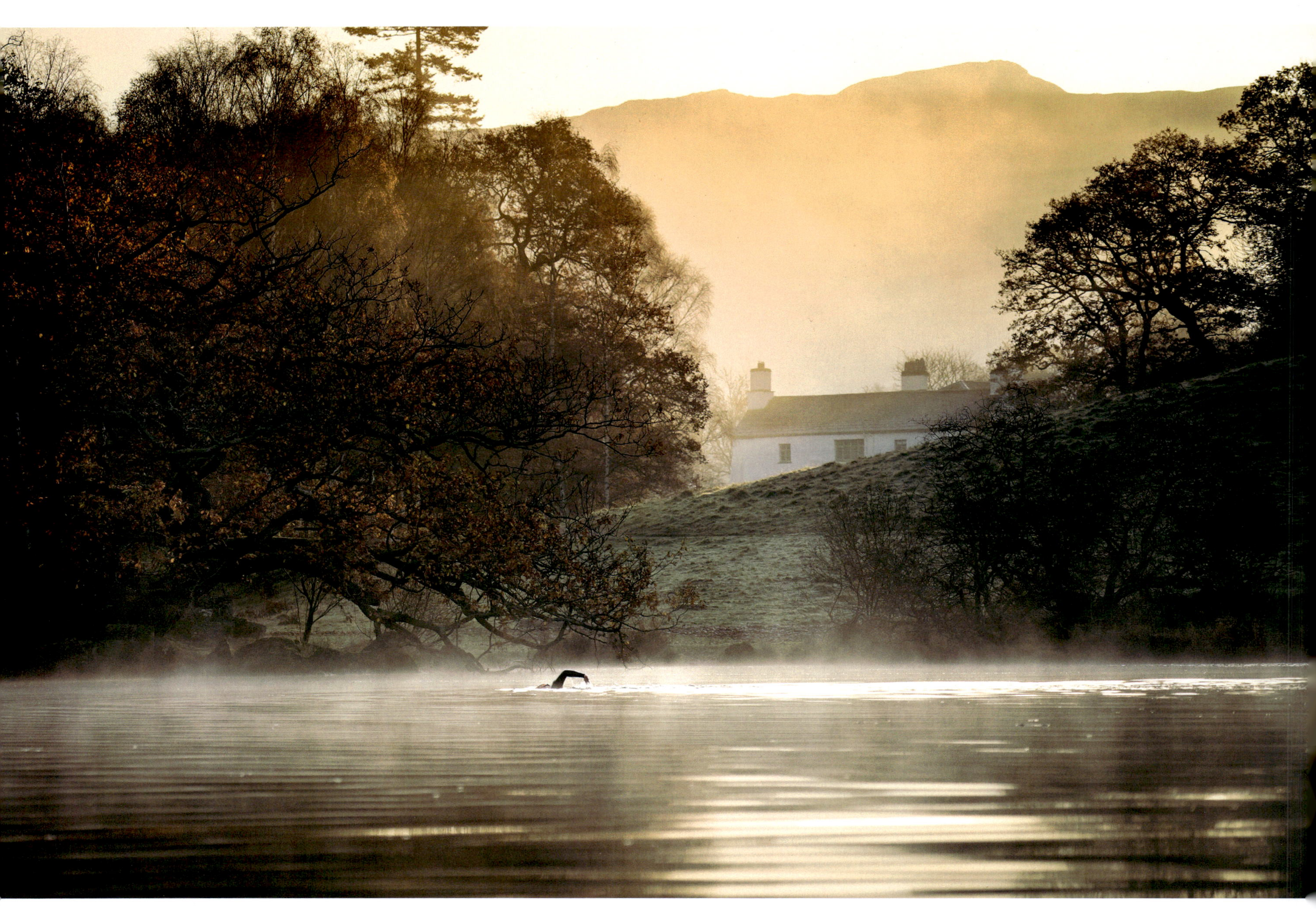

Joanne Richardson enjoys a dawn swim in Rydal Water.
© Tom McNally

Paul Hill canoeing on the Upper Derwent in Borrowdale.
© Tom McNally »

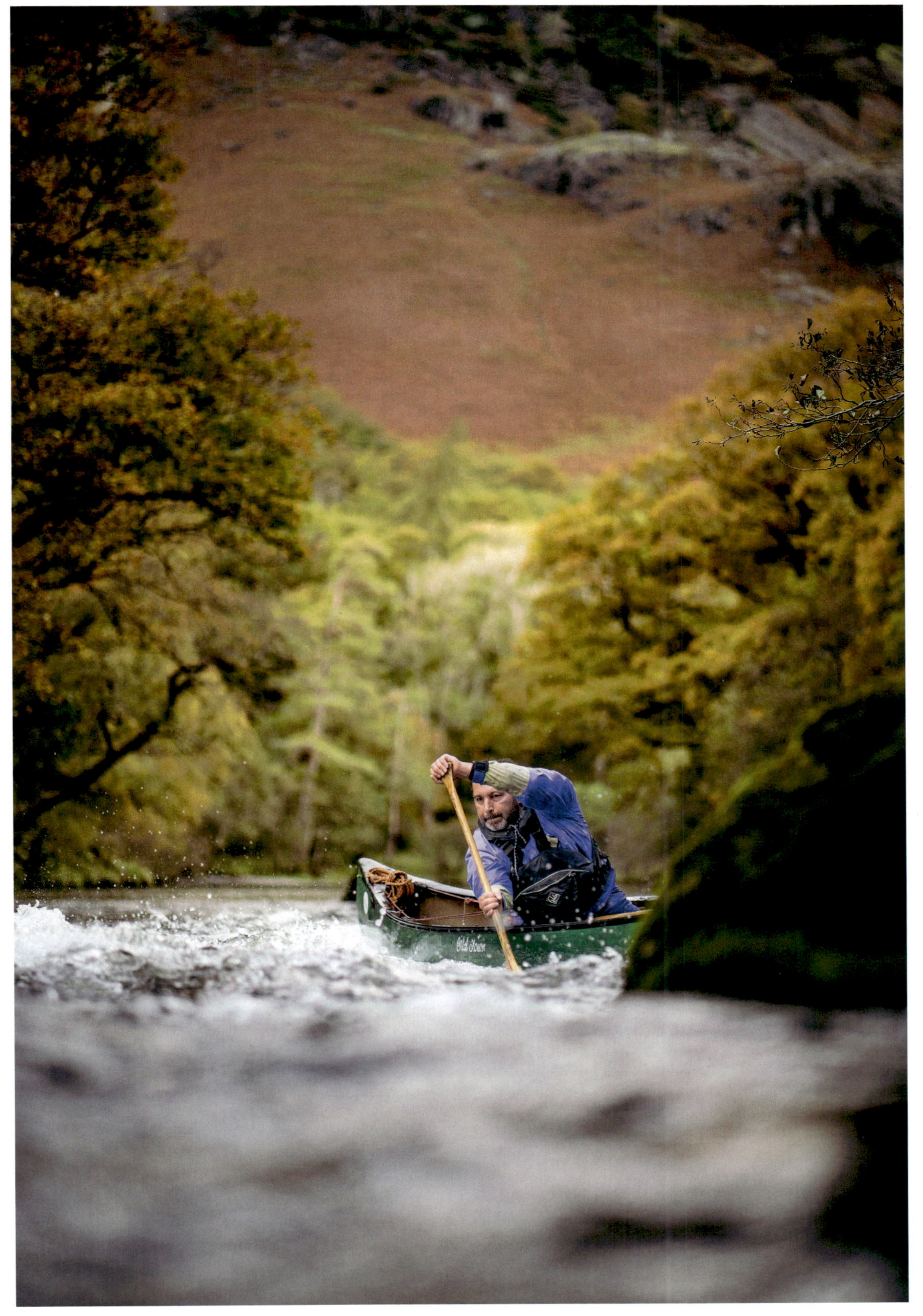

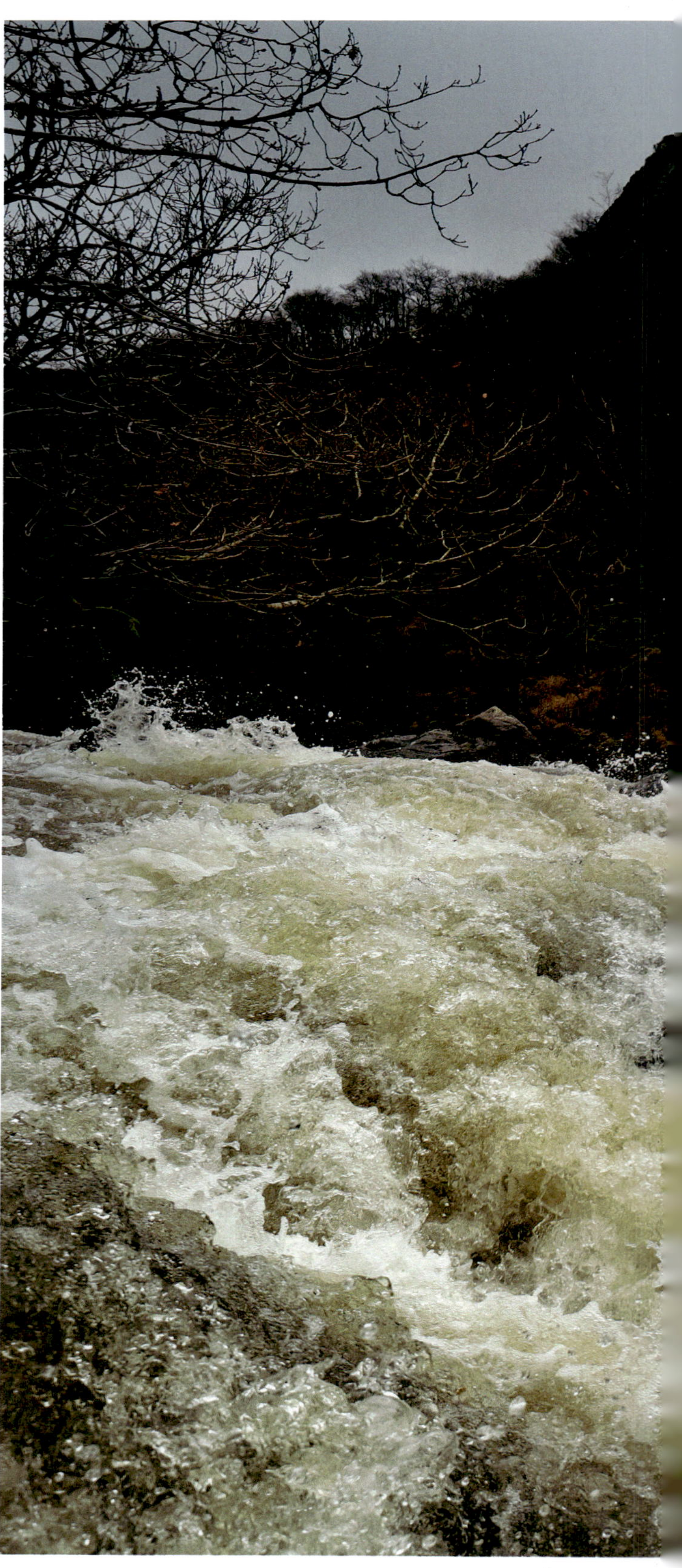

Dan Noblett in Wallowbarrow Gorge (G5)
on the Upper Duddon. © Tom McNally »

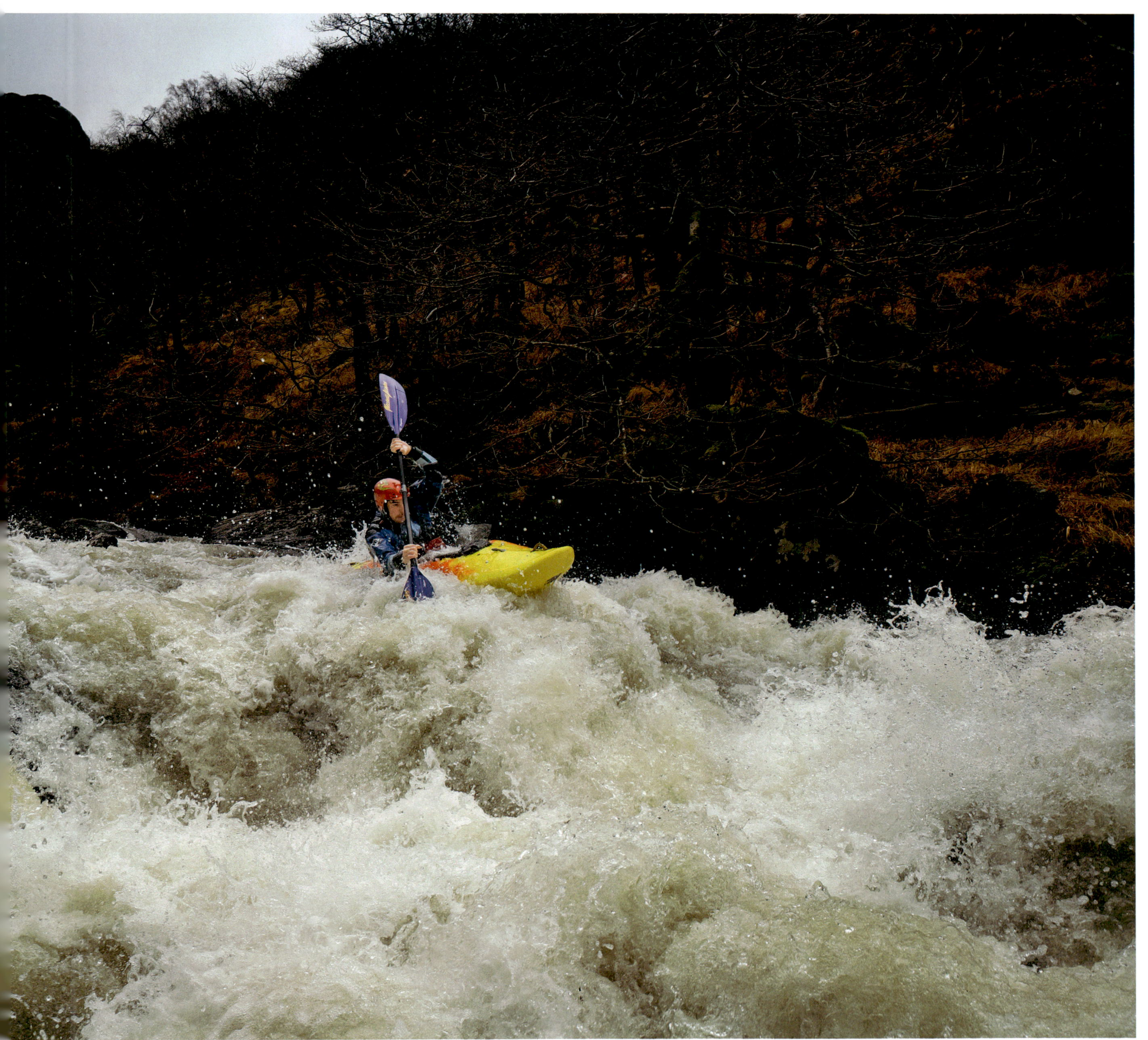

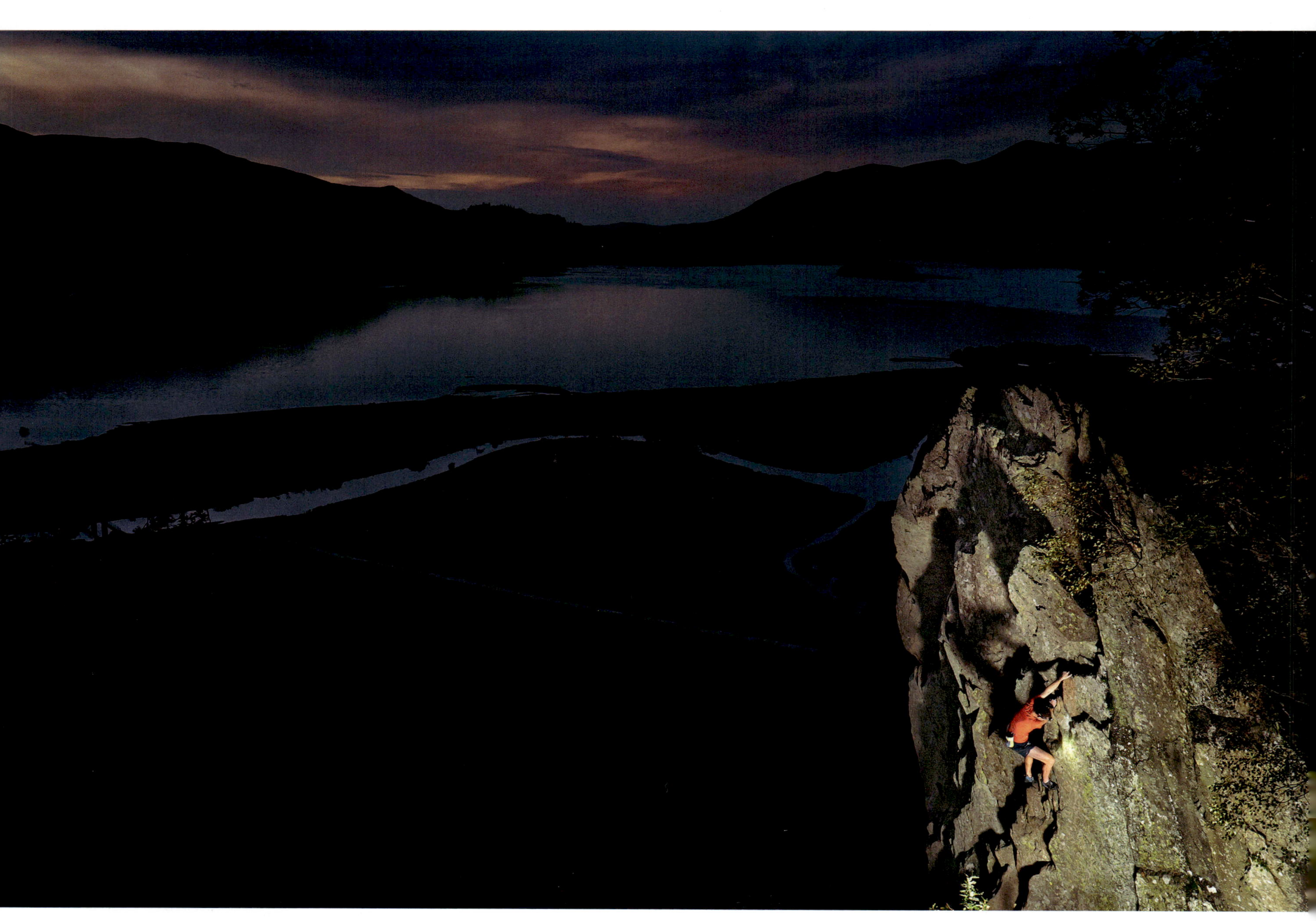

Will Birkett on *Little Chamonix* (VDiff), Shepherd's Crag, at dusk. This route is one of the most regularly climbed in the Lakes and is the final route of the Classic Rock Round. This challenge consists of climbing all fifteen Lakeland rock climbs listed in Ken Wilson's book *Classic Rock*, and running between each one. The summer of 2020 saw a fierce battle between Will Birkett and Tom Randall, with the record changing hands several times. At the time of writing, Will holds the record with a time of 10 hours and 41 minutes. © Tom McNally

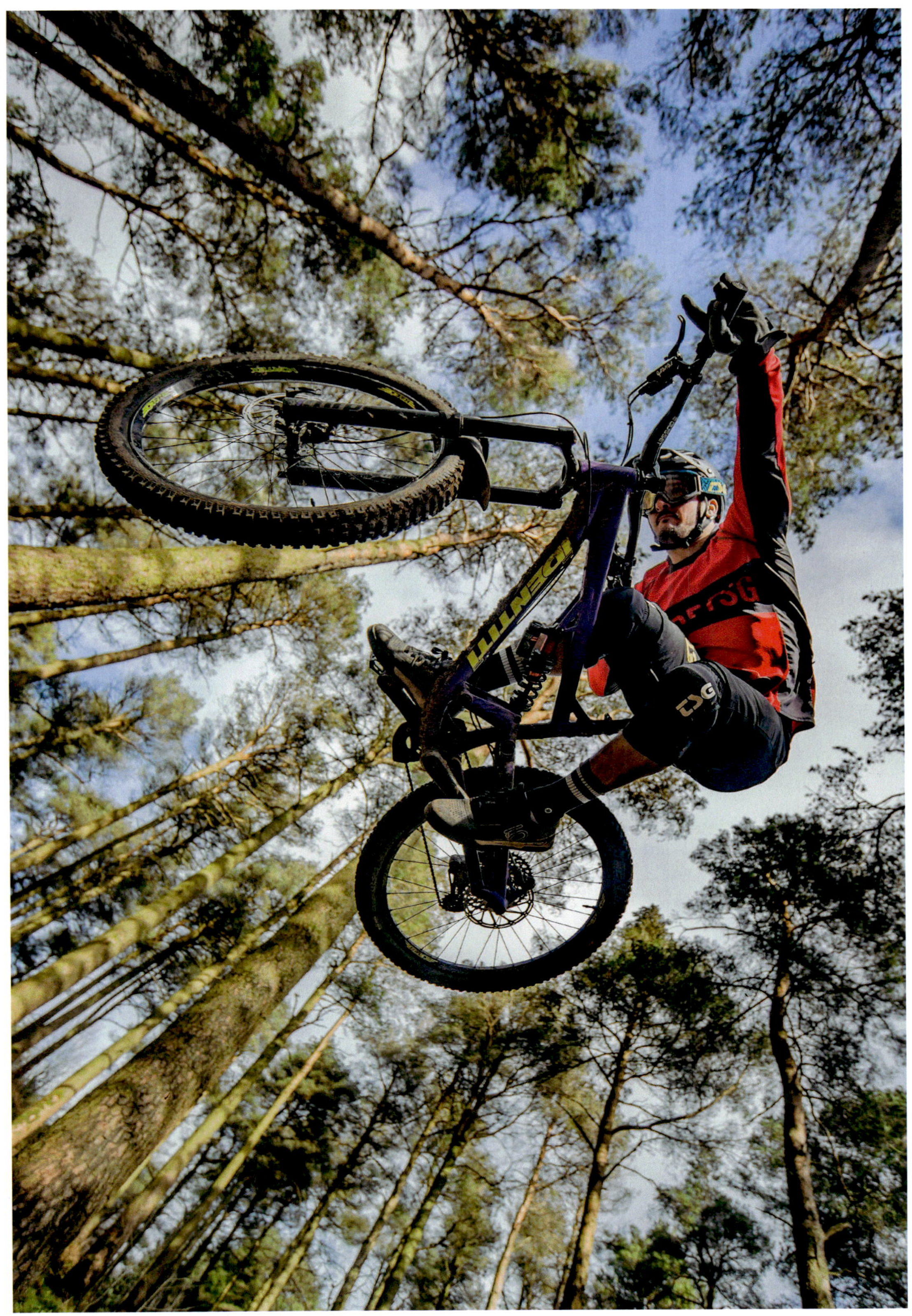

Pat Campbell-Jenner enjoying some airtime in Setmurthy Woods. © Tom McNally

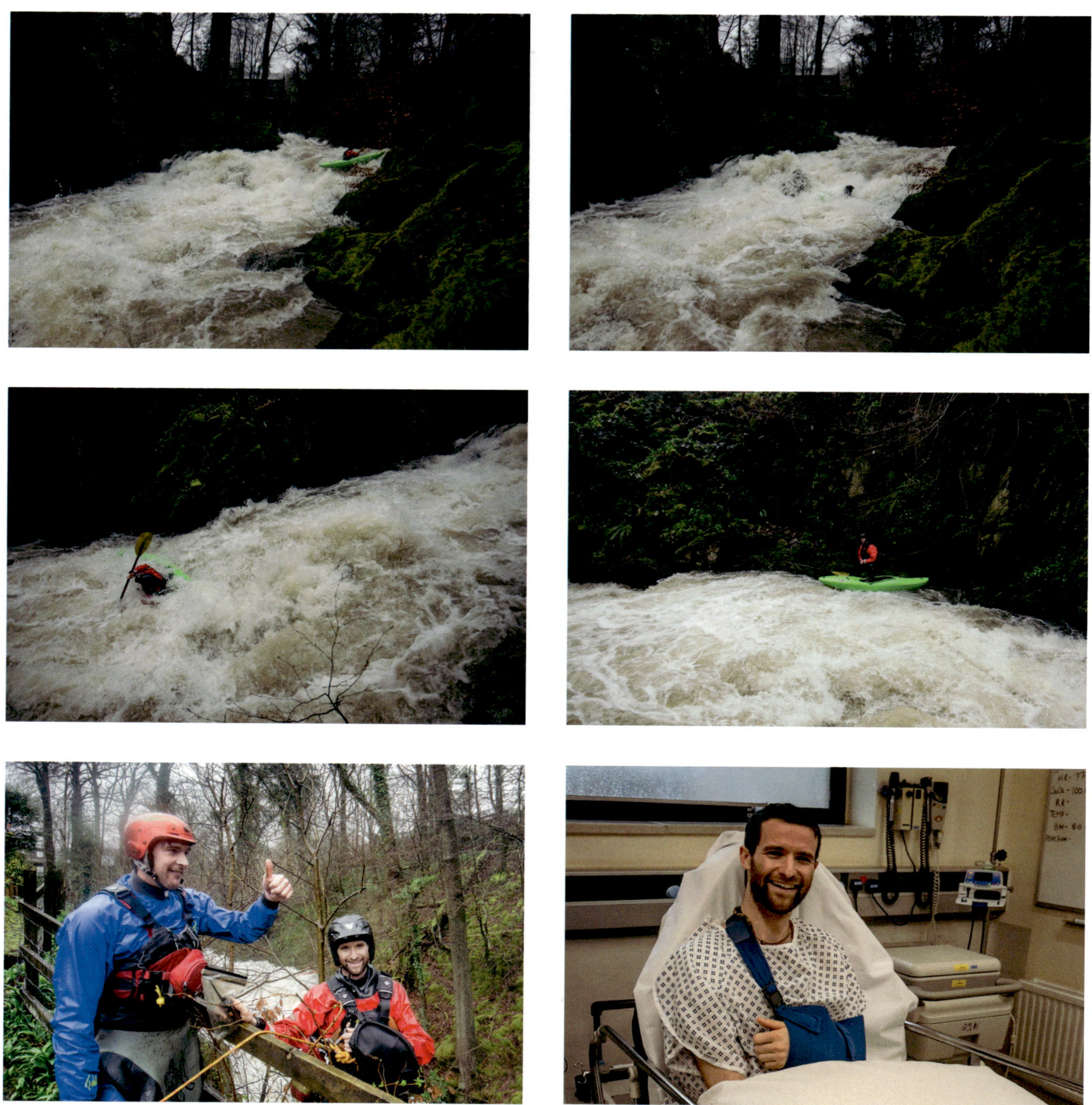

© Tom McNally

NOT EVERYTHING GOES TO PLAN

BY TOM McNALLY

I could hear the roar of the river as soon as I switched off the engine. I opened the van door and it became deafening. I followed the others across the road, and scrambling over the wall I glimpsed Stock Ghyll and felt my jaw drop. Normally a gentle trickle, today it was a thundering brown torrent.

After picking our way steeply down through dripping, mossy trunks, the conversation was brief. A swim here would be unthinkable. Mesmerised once more by the seething water I suddenly felt a surge of relief that I was only taking photographs.

Ten minutes later and I was dangling in place on the end of a rope, water surging up and down around my ankles and drips plopping on my hood. Hampered by the lip of my helmet on the camera's waterproof housing, I peered awkwardly through the viewfinder. The radio crackled into life; they were just about to get on. I checked my settings one last time and waited. Just audible over the roar was a sound like thunder: large rocks and boulders were trundling along the riverbed.

This pause was welcome. It had been raining heavily for days, and while residents and insurance companies were bracing for the worst, we had been pursuing spate river levels in our van convoy laden with brightly coloured plastic boats. Hardcore kayakers chase high rainfall totals in the same way skiers on the continent chase powder snow. The confined geography of the Lake District suits this approach; several rarely paddled classics can be done in a day, particularly if you don't even bother to change out of paddling kit in between.

Dan rounded the corner quickly, barely visible through the crashing white-water. I squeezed the shutter button, and felt the camera whirr, freeze-frames of a desperate battle to stay upright as he shot past me. Trev was next. The current pushed him sideways at exactly the wrong moment and he plunged into a huge recirculating wave, disappearing from view. I swore and kept the shutter held down. After what felt like an age he emerged, still in his boat but again dropping sideways into another big 'stopper'. He absorbed the impact and a skilful brace propelled him into a tiny eddy on the far bank. It was an improbable and impressive recovery.

I turned round and Robin was already on the way down. Between frames I could see him bracing hard but his line was perfect. I looked back through the viewfinder towards Trev, ready to catch him break into the current and continue. Instead, he was out of his boat and breathing heavily, all the colour drained from his face. Something was definitely wrong. We made eye contact and he pointed at his shoulder. It was dislocated.

My jog through Ambleside to reach the opposite bank, wearing full canyoning kit and sopping wet, attracted more than a few puzzled looks. After navigating some backstreets Dom and I approximated which house backed on to that particular section of riverbank and knocked at the door. Nothing. Luckily the back gate was unlocked. At the bottom of the garden we shouted down and could just hear Trev's voice over the river; he was stranded at the foot of a small cliff. After recovering his boat across the river Dan and Robin joined us and we quickly assembled a simple rope rescue. Only a minute later Trev was standing next to us, grey and queasy but smiling.

Our departure was somewhat delayed by Trev's insistence we extract him from his expensive drysuit so the medics wouldn't cut it off him, no mean feat with a dislocated shoulder. Eventually we reached Kendal hospital and his grimace soon turned into a smile with some proper pain relief. The others headed straight off to paddle an equally full-of-water River Sprint while I deposited Trev home to his understandably concerned girlfriend. Dan rang later to check up on him and it sounded like their afternoon had been equally eventful – a tale of snapped paddles and epic swims.

Cracking open a beer when I got home and reflecting on the day's events, I was glad that no one had been more seriously injured. Reviewing the paddling images taken for this book I can't help but feel that they don't fully convey the sheer sensory overload of a kayaker navigating a roaring, tree-infested beck in full spate. Along with the climbers and BASE climbers operating at the cutting edge, for me these paddlers are the epitome of Extreme Lakeland.

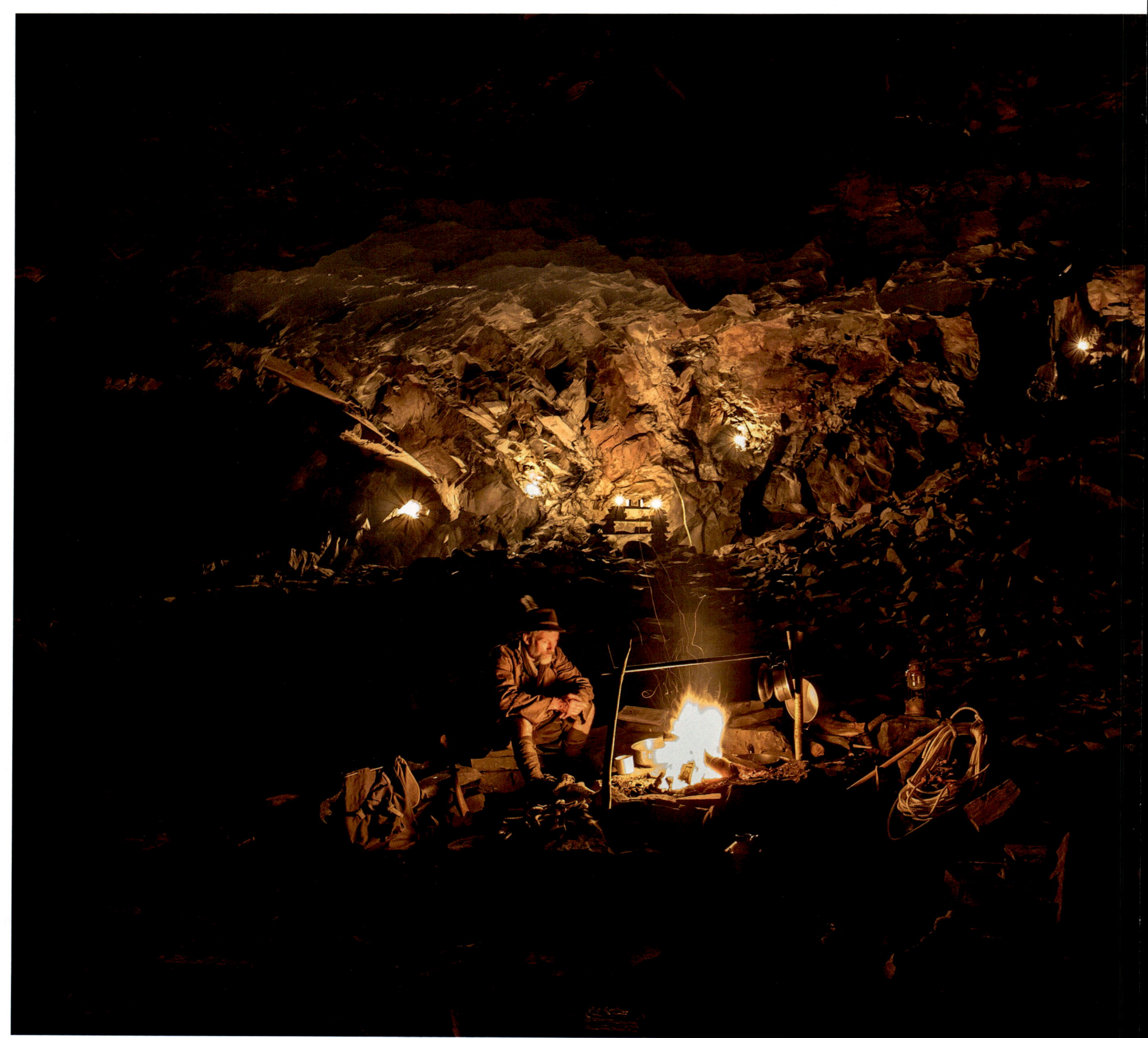

« Opposite and following pages: Matt Sharman as Millican Dalton in a
historic reconstruction at Millican's Cave, Borrowdale. © Tom McNally

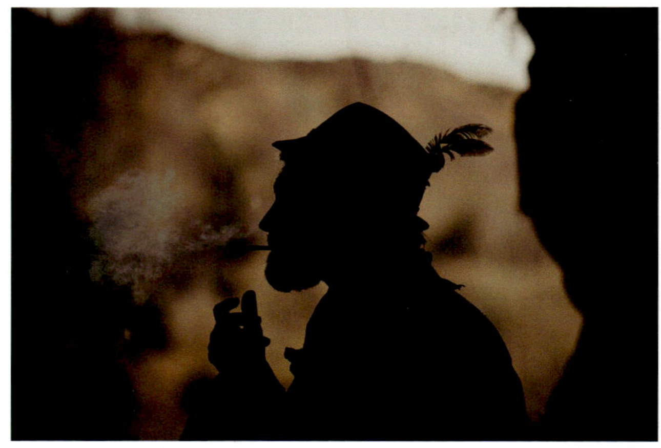

A PROFESSOR OF ADVENTURE

BY TOM McNALLY

Picture a suited insurance clerk in his mid-thirties in the city of London. Tired with the bureaucracy of the insurance industry and feeling trapped by the tedium of a nine-to-five job in the city, he begins to dream of a more rural existence focused on meaningful connections with nature, mindfulness, sustainable living and healthy eating. Eventually he decides to hand in his notice, fully committing to this alternative lifestyle and with aspirations of working as an outdoor instructor. While this may not be an unfamiliar story, in this case it is something of a radical act; the year is 1904 and the outdoor industry as we know it does not exist.

> Free I am as the buzzard mewing by day or the owl hooting at night, Freedom is everything.

After escaping from the drudgery of city life, Millican Dalton concentrated his efforts on becoming a mountain guide, leading many successful trips to the Lake District, Wales, Ireland, Scotland and the Alps. Unlike his contemporaries, he offered clients not just climbing and walking excursions but a variety of outdoor activities, combining ghyll scrambling, white-water rafting, night rambles, open-water swimming and mountaineering into one package. With the multi-activity holiday as his unique selling point, his services were in high demand.

Recognising the opportunities afforded by its diverse landscape and with happy memories of childhood camping trips there, Dalton found the Lake District to be the perfect base from which he could not only introduce others to the excitement of outdoor adventure but also to his then unconventional philosophy.

> After treating life as a chemical experiment, I find that the simplest life is happiest.

Selecting the valley of Borrowdale as his home, he initially lived under canvas at High Lodore before finding more permanent residence in an enormous cave on the wooded flanks of Castle Crag – a relic of the slate-working industry for which the valley is famed. It was to become his summer home for almost fifty years. During the winter months he would migrate south by pedal power to his hut in Buckinghamshire, his bike all but hidden by the mound of belongings festooned to it. His return to the Lakes each year was marked by children running through Keswick exclaiming, 'Millican Dalton's back! Millican Dalton's back!'

His programmes and advertising posters in the shop windows of Keswick promised not only 'Shooting the Rapids, Dangling over the Precipice and Varied Hairbreadth Escapes' but also 'Sunrise Breakfasts by the Lake', 'Midnight Rows on Derwentwater and Lazy Days about Camp'. It is obvious that these itineraries were as focused on fostering genuine connections with the landscape as they were on providing the excitement of outdoor activities. They also highlight Dalton's then somewhat progressive views on women in the outdoors, stating rather wryly that, 'ladies are welcome in the camp … the custom being about 10,000 years old'.

Despite his choice of lodgings, Dalton's character was anything but reclusive. A convivial host, guests and clients alike spoke warmly of the hospitality (and fiercely strong coffee) they received at 'The Cave Hotel'. He spoke eloquently and intelligently on a range of topics and was not afraid of voicing his opinion. A staunch pacifist, his fireside conversations often tackled war, peace and social injustice. He always remained informed on current events, riding into Keswick nearly every day for a newspaper. After being told to extinguish his camp fire in 1941 by an air raid warden, he penned several strongly worded letters to Winston Churchill demanding an end to hostilities as it was impinging on his personal freedoms.

These socialist beliefs were reflected in his frugal existence, and his few possessions were often objects recycled from a nearby tip at Grange. The exception to this rule was his treasured sewing machine, on which he manufactured simple, practical clothes suited to his outdoor way of life.

> Use is everything. We dress too much, we eat too much, almost everything we do is too much. Put a man to it and see what he can come up with.

Dalton always maintained that it was in fact he who invented shorts, not Robert Baden-Powell of British Scout movement fame. Made of corduroy and cut long (to protect the knees while climbing), these were then often rolled up and paired with brown army 'puttees' (reputedly almost indistinguishable in colour to his tanned and weather-beaten knees). A khaki jacket and Tyrolean Alpine hat completed the look. A prolific inventor, he also applied his sewing skills to the design and manufacture of lightweight rucksacks and camping equipment, even producing a two-man tent weighing in at 1.5 kilograms (featherweight even compared with contemporary, hi-tech equivalents).

Dalton's homemade attire and equipment, combined with his tall frame, magnificent facial hair and loping gait made his appearance utterly unmistakable. Keswick and Borrowdale locals soon saw him as a lovable eccentric and he became known by several aliases – 'Robinson Crusoe', 'Buffalo Bill', 'Peter Pan', 'The Wizard of the North' and, most commonly, 'The Borrowdale Hermit'.

Today I live rent free, rate free, tax free. It's the only kind of life worth living.

Food, where possible, was always fresh and foraged – trout from the river with plentiful mushrooms, nuts, berries and greens from the ancient oak woodland surrounding his subterranean home. Highly skilled at catering for his groups, he did rely on the supply of some staples purchased with his guiding fees, mainly potatoes and flour, the latter of which he mixed with raisins to bake his own famed interpretation of wholemeal bread.

The other staple with which it seems Dalton could simply not do without (apart from coffee) was tobacco, purchased from the bar at the Borrowdale Hotel. A self-confessed chain-smoker, all activities were accompanied by an ever-present Woodbine dangling from his mouth, although while stirring food he held it between his toes to keep ash from dropping in the pan.

Give me wholemeal bread, porridge, coffee and cigarettes and I am quite happy.

Despite smoking like a chimney, Dalton remained fit and active for his entire life. He celebrated his fiftieth birthday in style by ascending Napes Needle solo, before lighting a fire to brew some coffee on the sloping, pool-table-sized top. A creature of habit, he repeated this impressive feat every year until at least his mid-seventies. His ease on tricky routes such as this and his close involvement with the Fell & Rock Climbing Club point to him being an accomplished rock climber, but it is his exemplary safety record and skills as a guide for which he is most remembered. In the words of Mabel Barker, his close friend and climbing companion:

He really *taught* his initiates … and his patience with them was wonderful.[1]

While over-wintering in Buckinghamshire during the bitterly cold conditions of 1947, Dalton's wooden hut accidentally burnt down, presumably from an untended candle or errant spark from the fire. Forced to live under canvas in extremely harsh temperatures, he was soon admitted to Amersham hospital

suffering from various bronchopulmonary conditions and died aged seventy-nine on 5 February. On his bedside table lay an uncompleted manuscript titled *Philosophy of Life*. These precious pages have unfortunately been lost to the mists of time, without any trace of their no doubt impassioned contents.

His passing was mourned by many, marked with glowing obituaries in several publications. It is the words of Mabel Barker in the Fell & Rock Climbing Club journal that are most often quoted:

I wonder how many owed to him their first thrills on rock and rope … his picturesque figure and lovable personality have surely become part of the heritage of Lakeland so long as the hills endure and men love them.

Curiously, Dalton's indelible contributions to the lives of so many and the 'outdoor movement' in general are little known outside of the verdant Lake District valleys in which he practised both his craft and philosophy. One has to wonder whether if his manuscript had survived, perhaps his standing as one of the great characters of British outdoor heritage might be more significant. The path of adventure he forged not only demonstrated a profound understanding of the world around him but also greatly benefited others. The word 'legend' is often overused, but in the case of Millican Dalton I feel is entirely apt.

Thanks go to M.D. Entwistle for his wonderful biography *Millican Dalton: A Search for Romance & Freedom*, from which much of the information in this piece, including Dalton's quotations, is gleaned.

1 Barker, Mabel M., 'Memories of My First Leader', *The Journal of the Fell & Rock Climbing Club of the English Lake District*, No. 41, Vol. XV (The Fell & Rock Climbing Club of the English Lake District, 1947).

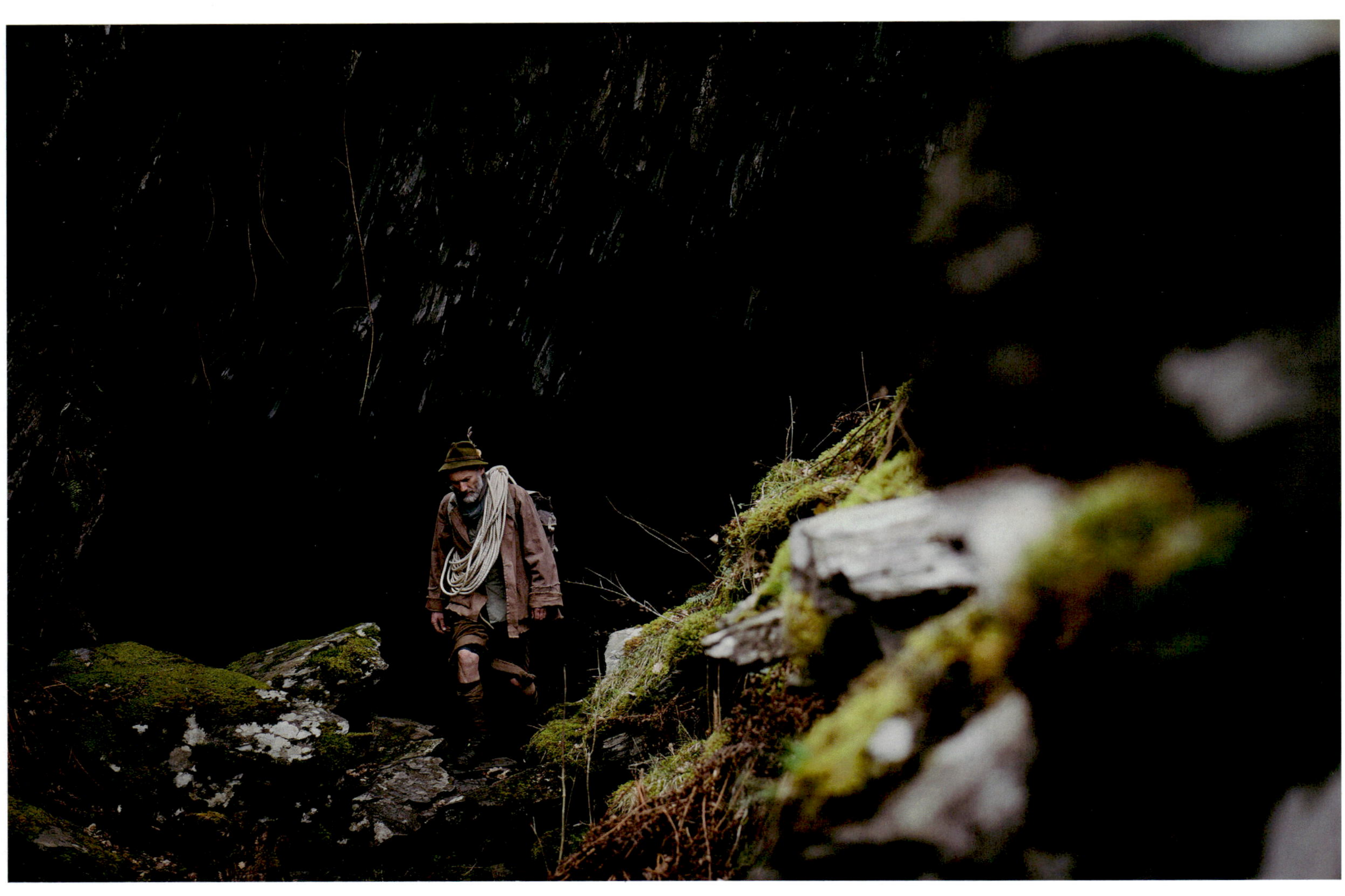

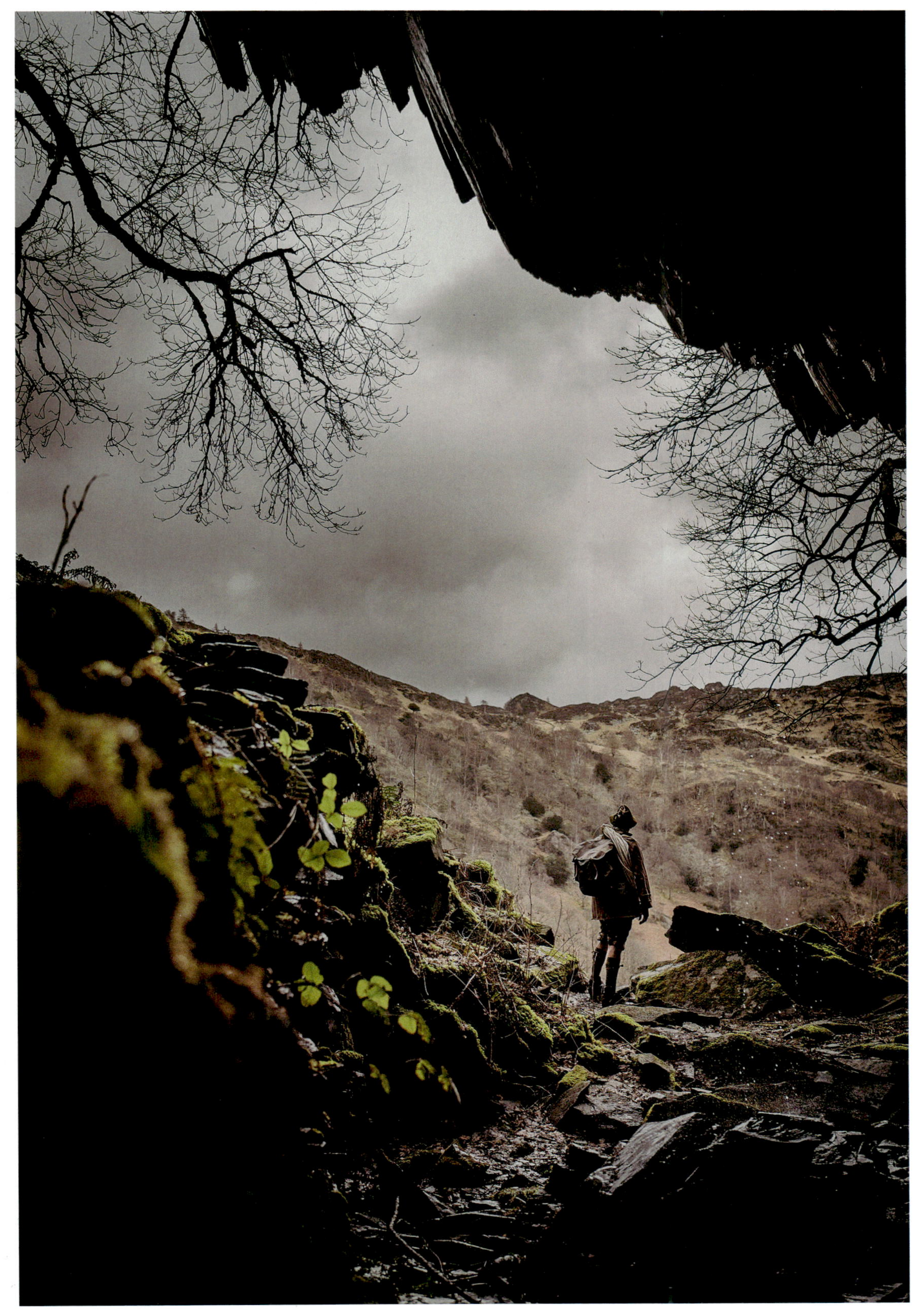

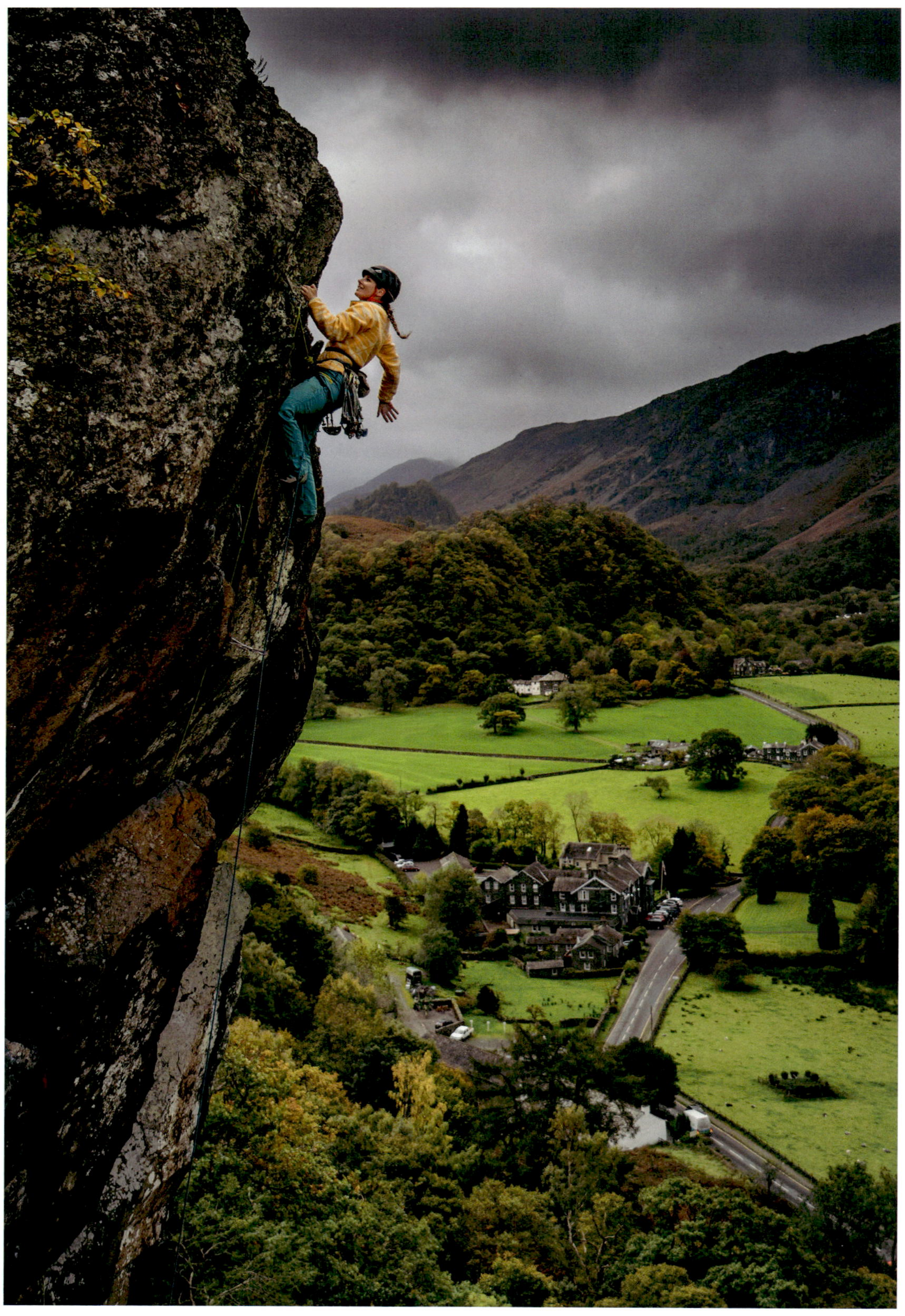

Katie Mackay on the final moves of *The Bludgeon* (E1 5b), Shepherd's Crag, in less-than-optimal autumn conditions. © Tom McNally

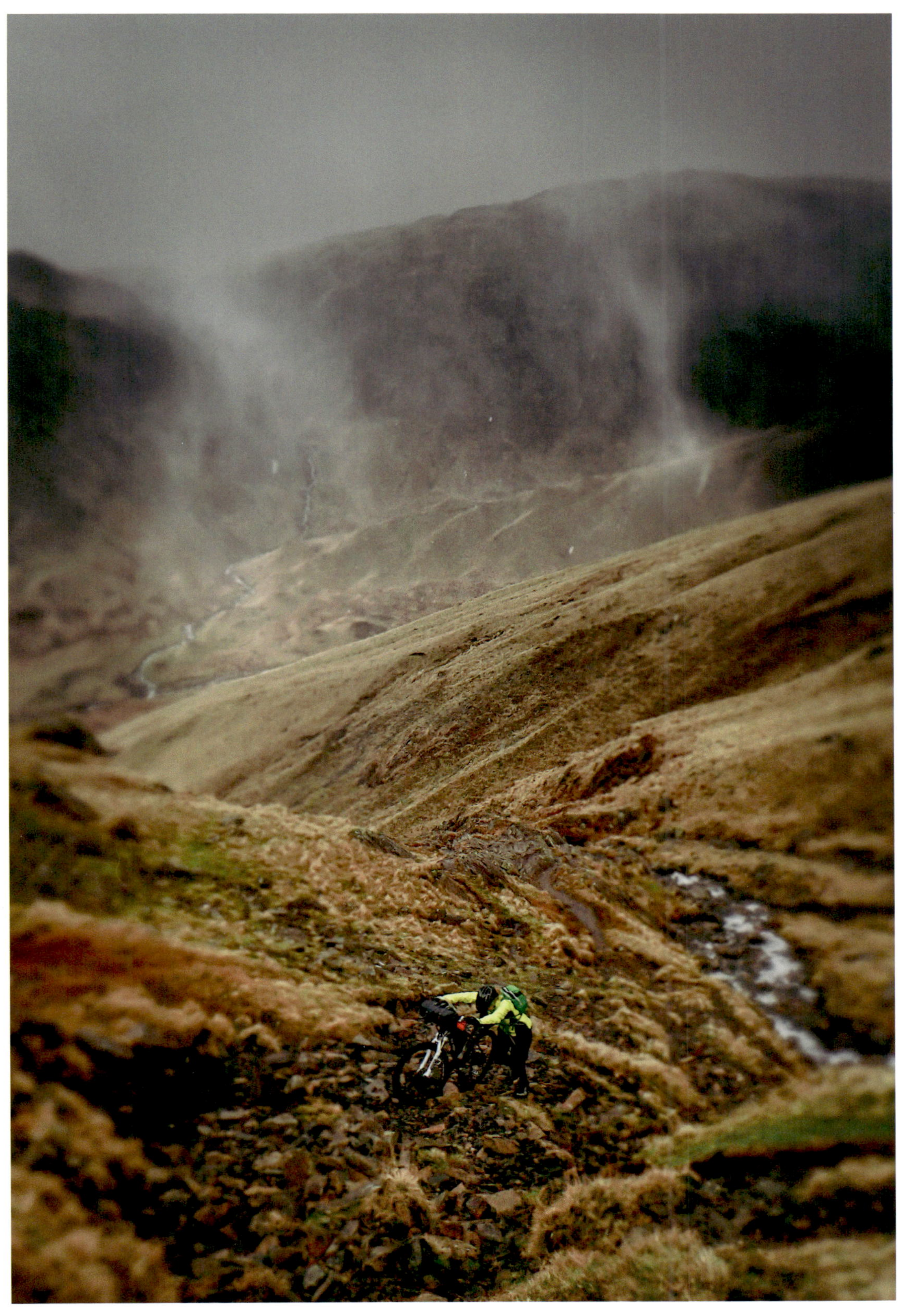

Louise McNally enjoys some type-2 fun negotiating the Black Sail Pass while bikepacking the off-road Coast to Coast route. © Tom McNally

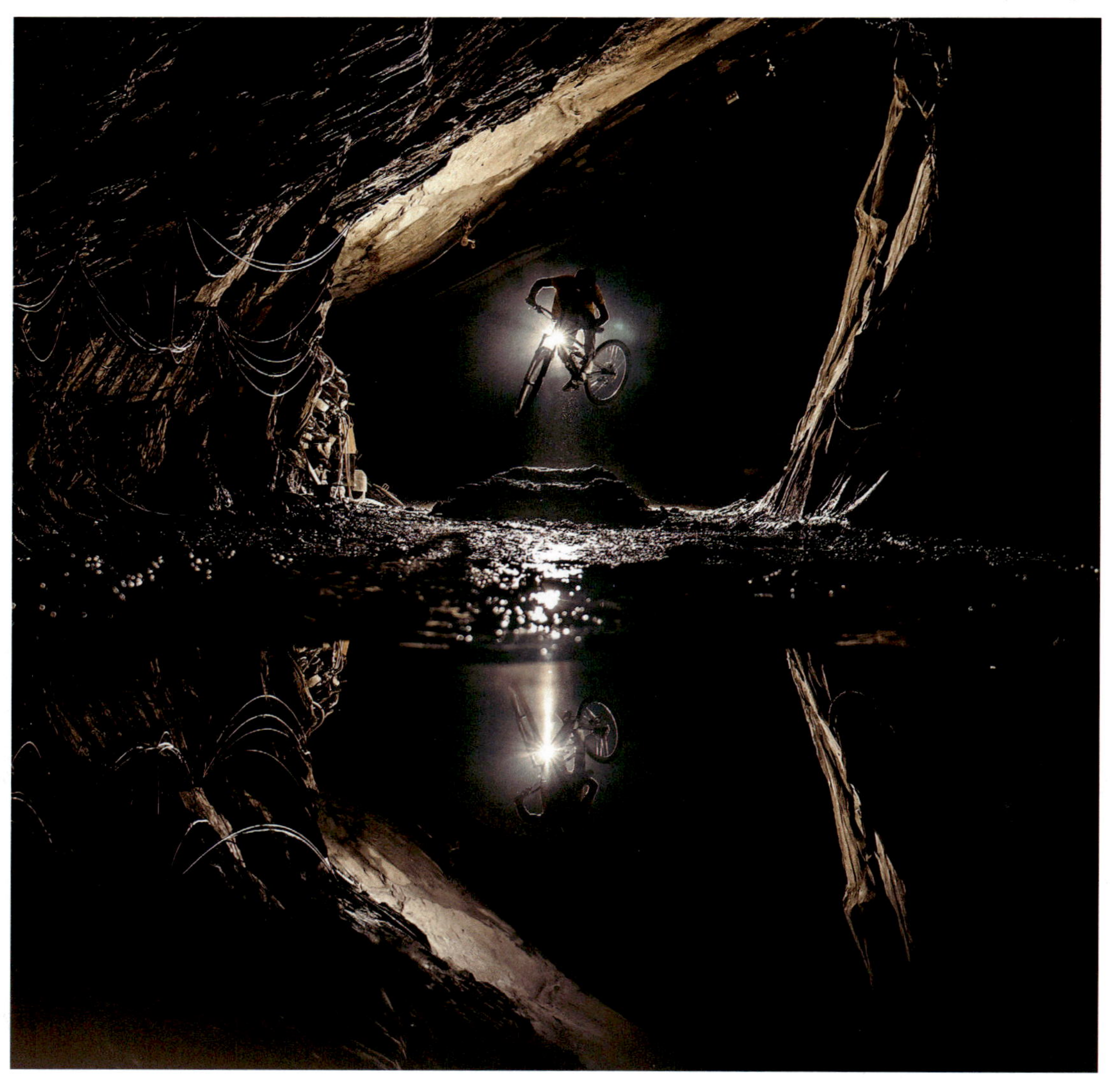

Dave Camus riding deep underground in Honister Slate Mine on a shoot for Cotic bikes. © Tom McNally

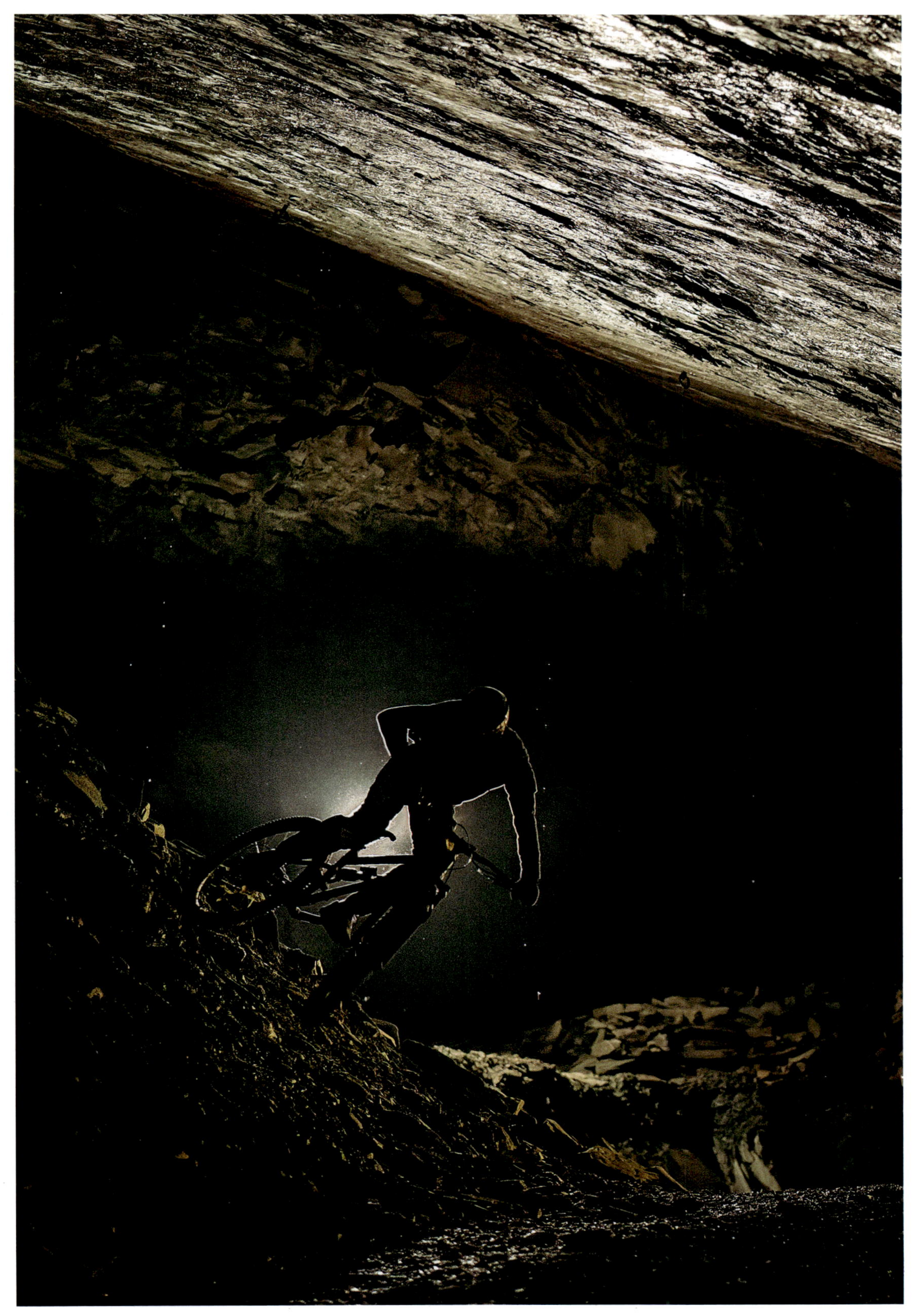

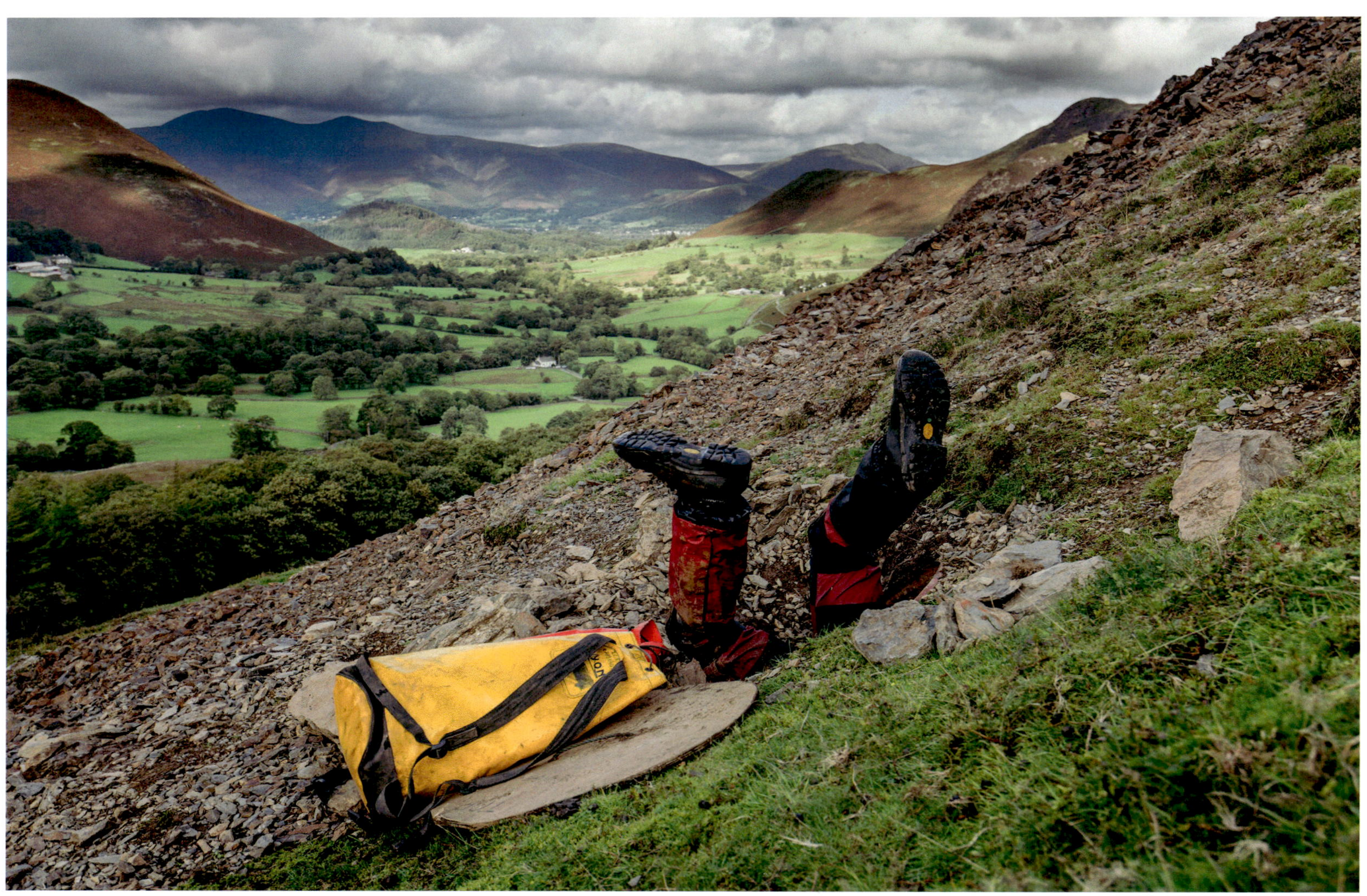

Beneath the well-trodden Lakeland fells is a vast network of spaces, hewn, blasted and carved by hand. Hundreds of miles of caverns and tunnels, some dating back to the medieval era, now lie abandoned; eerie and epic monuments to the sheer physical achievement of the miners that created them. Since 1979 members of the Cumbria Amenity Trust Mining History Society (CATMHS) have been exploring, surveying, digging and stabilising these sites at great personal risk. Through their research it is only now becoming apparent that many of these amazing sites, working in conjunction with the Keswick smelter, may in fact have represented the birth of the wider industrial revolution. © Tom McNally

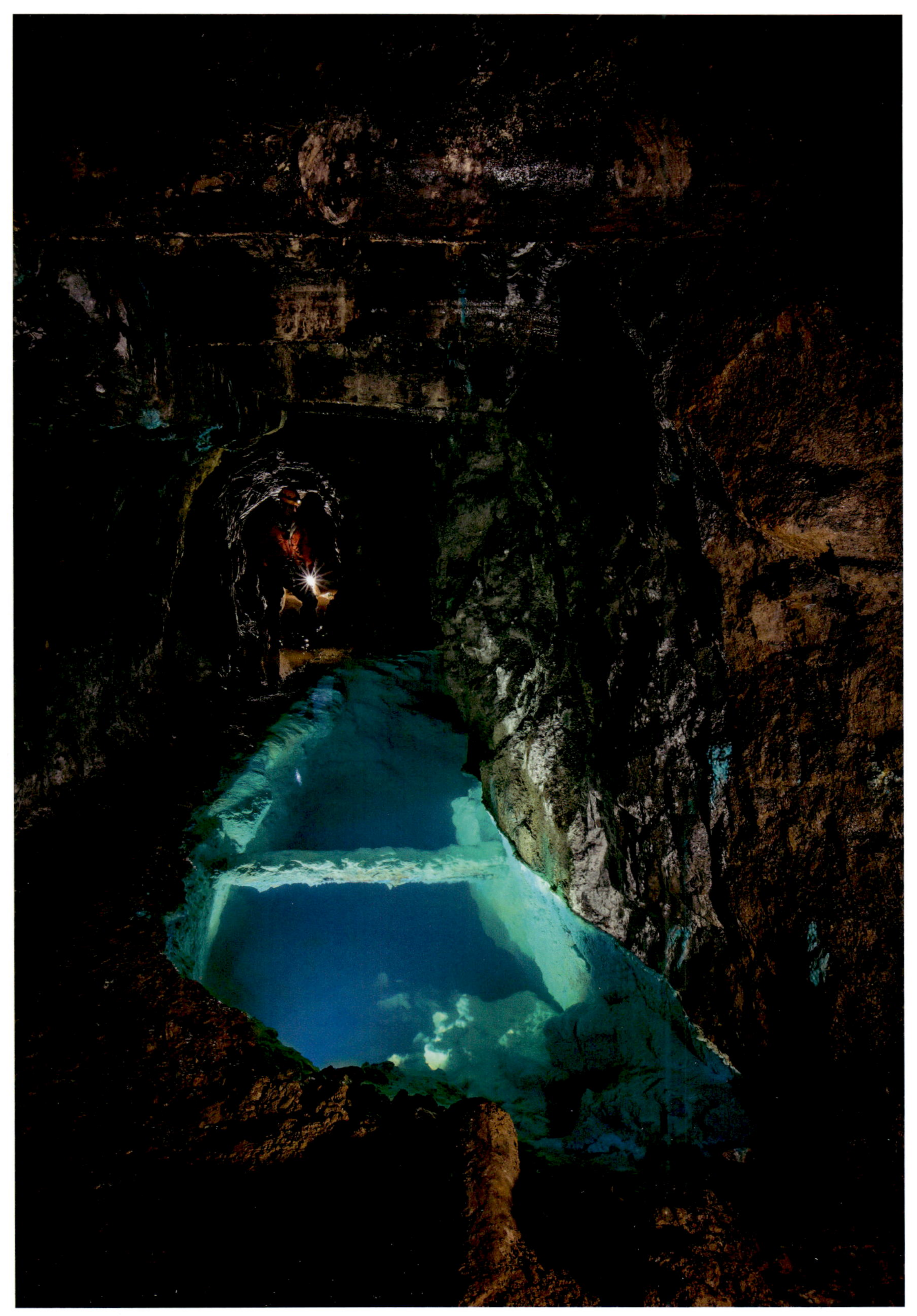

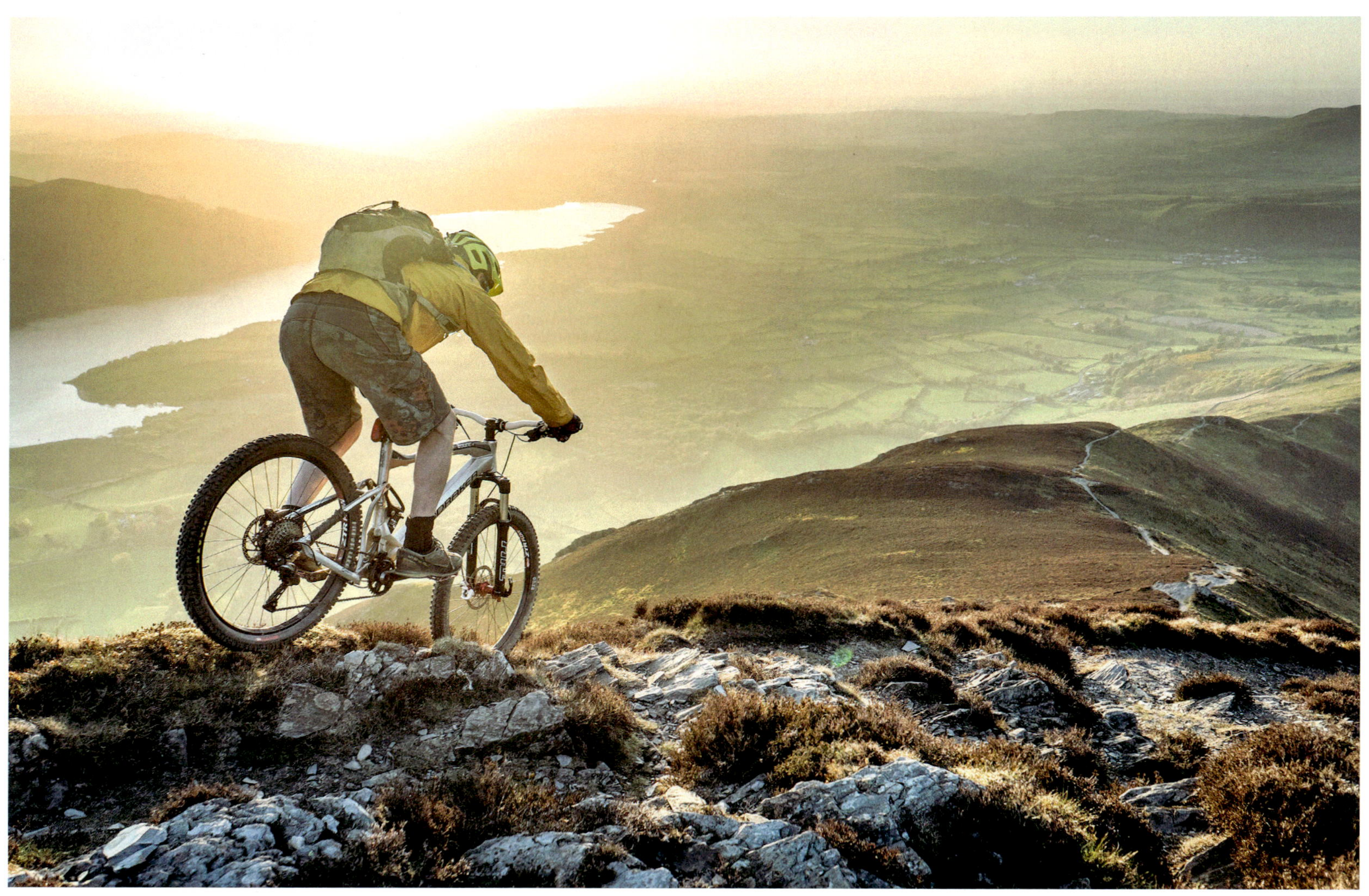
Matt Eaves on two of the best descents in the Lakes. © Tom McNally

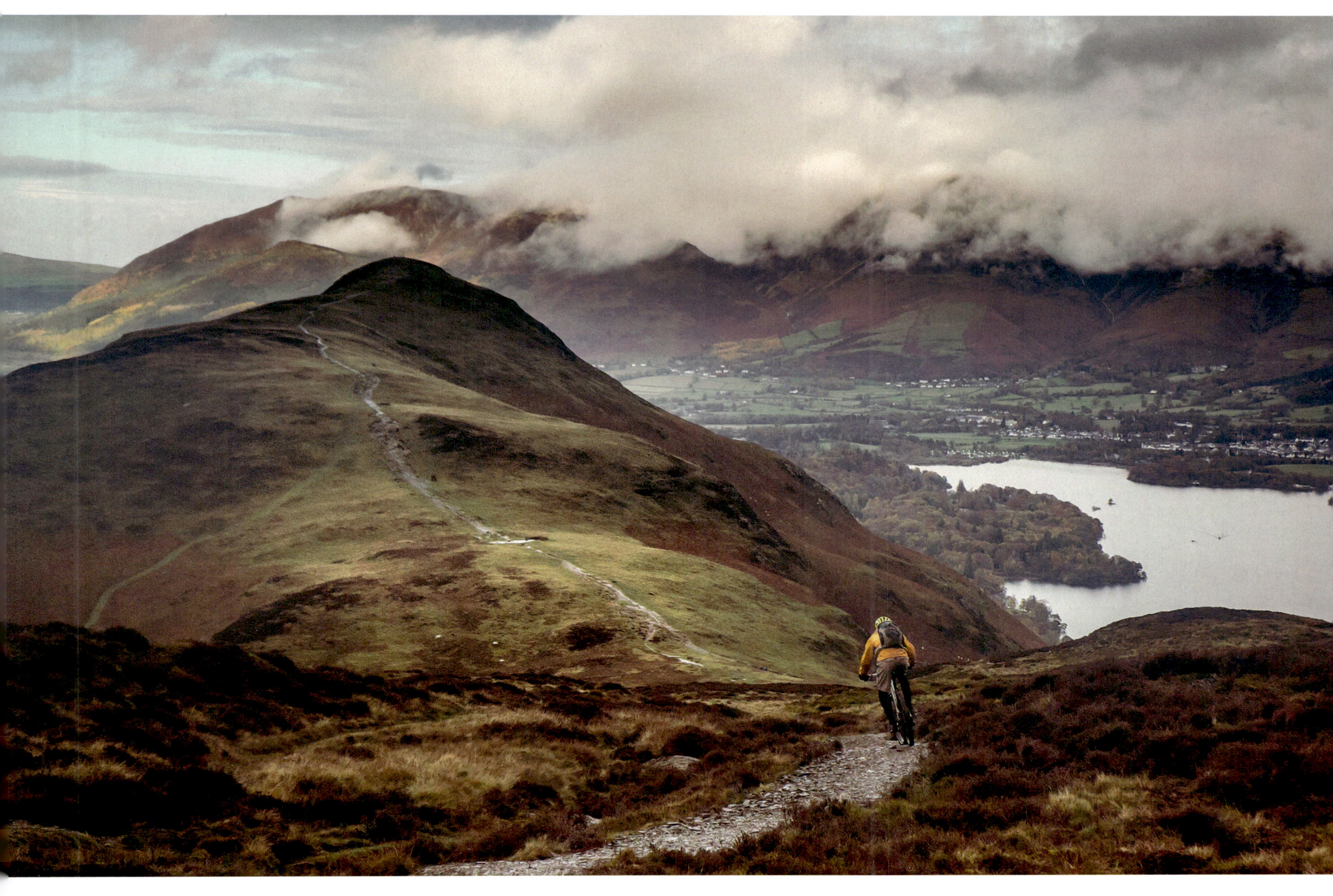

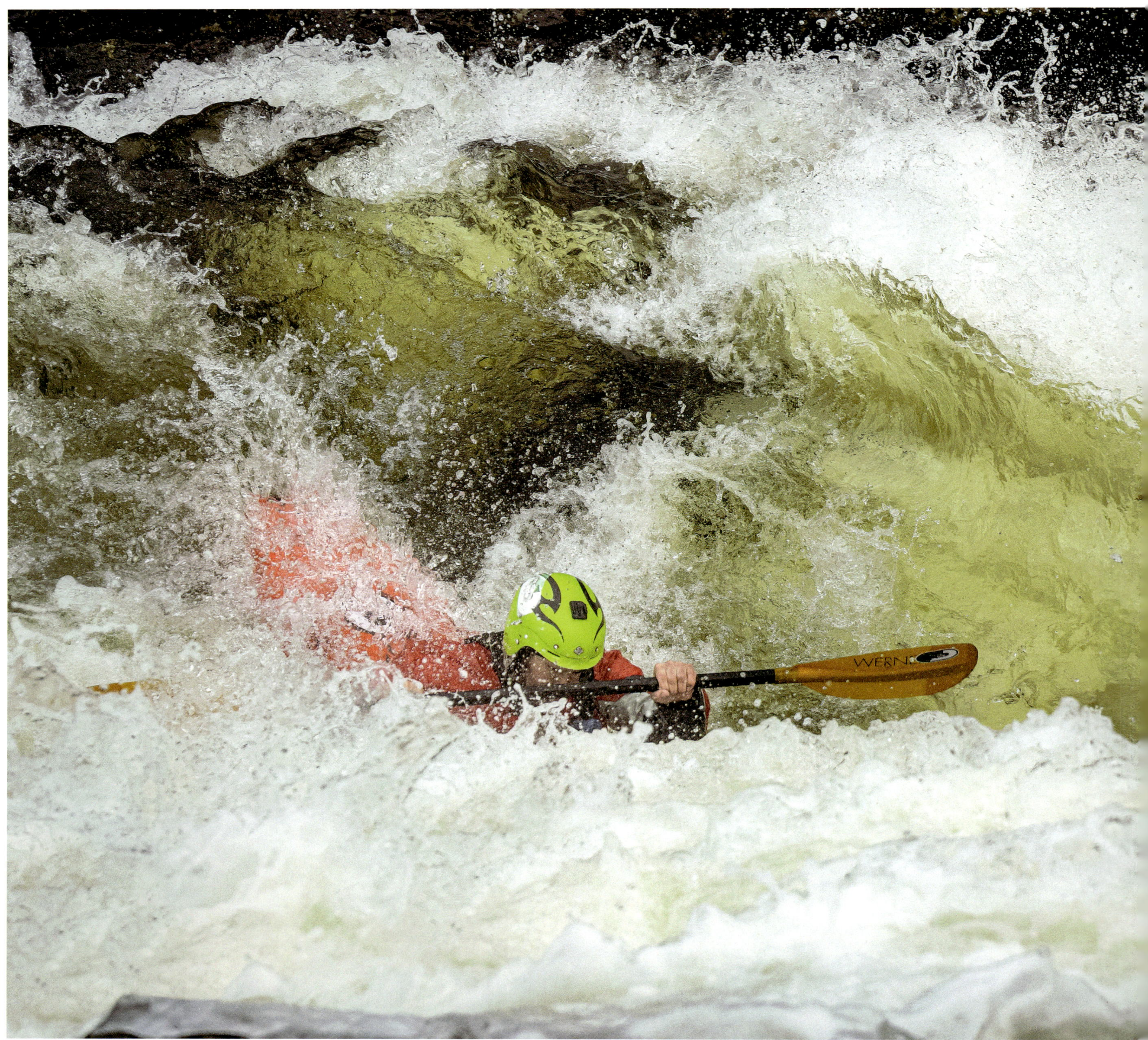

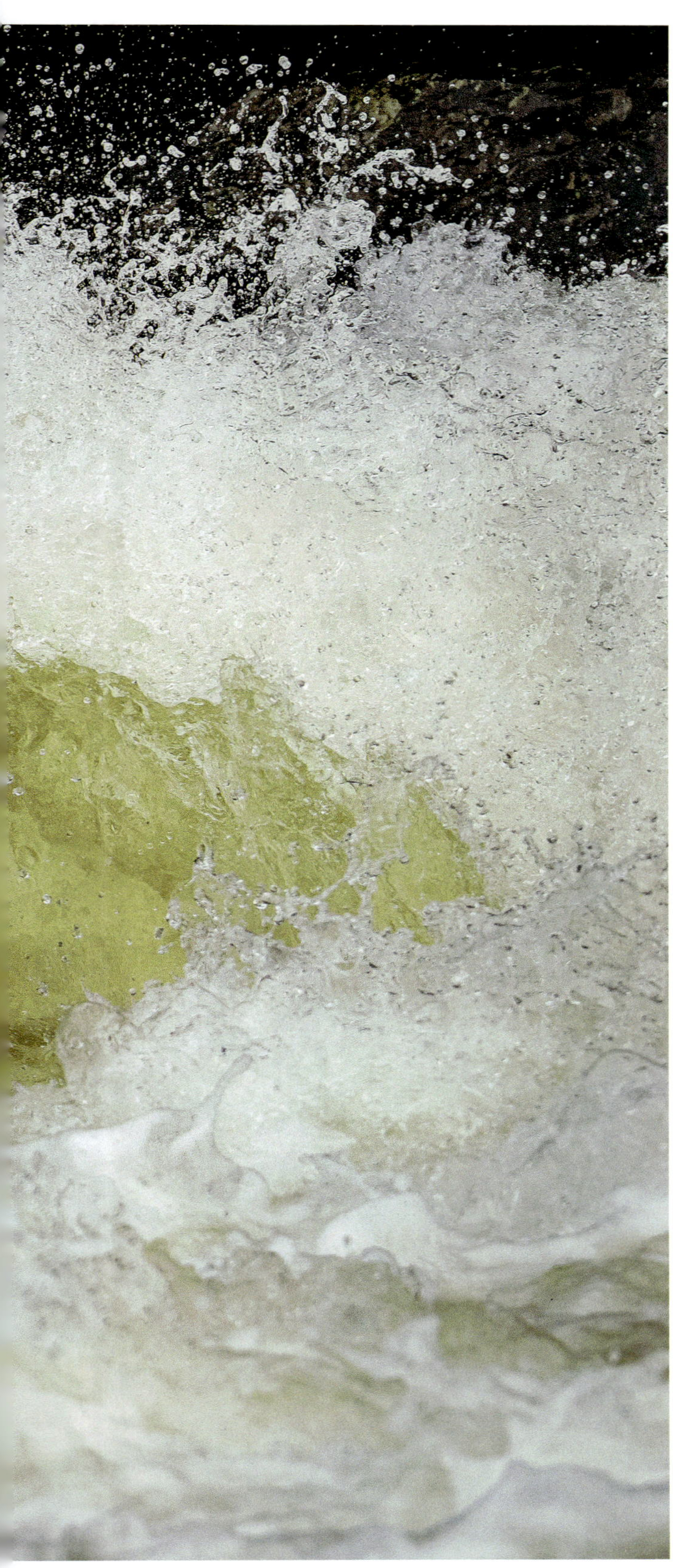

« Dan Fylan-Smith on the grade-IV drop of Force Falls on the River Kent.
  © Nadir Khan

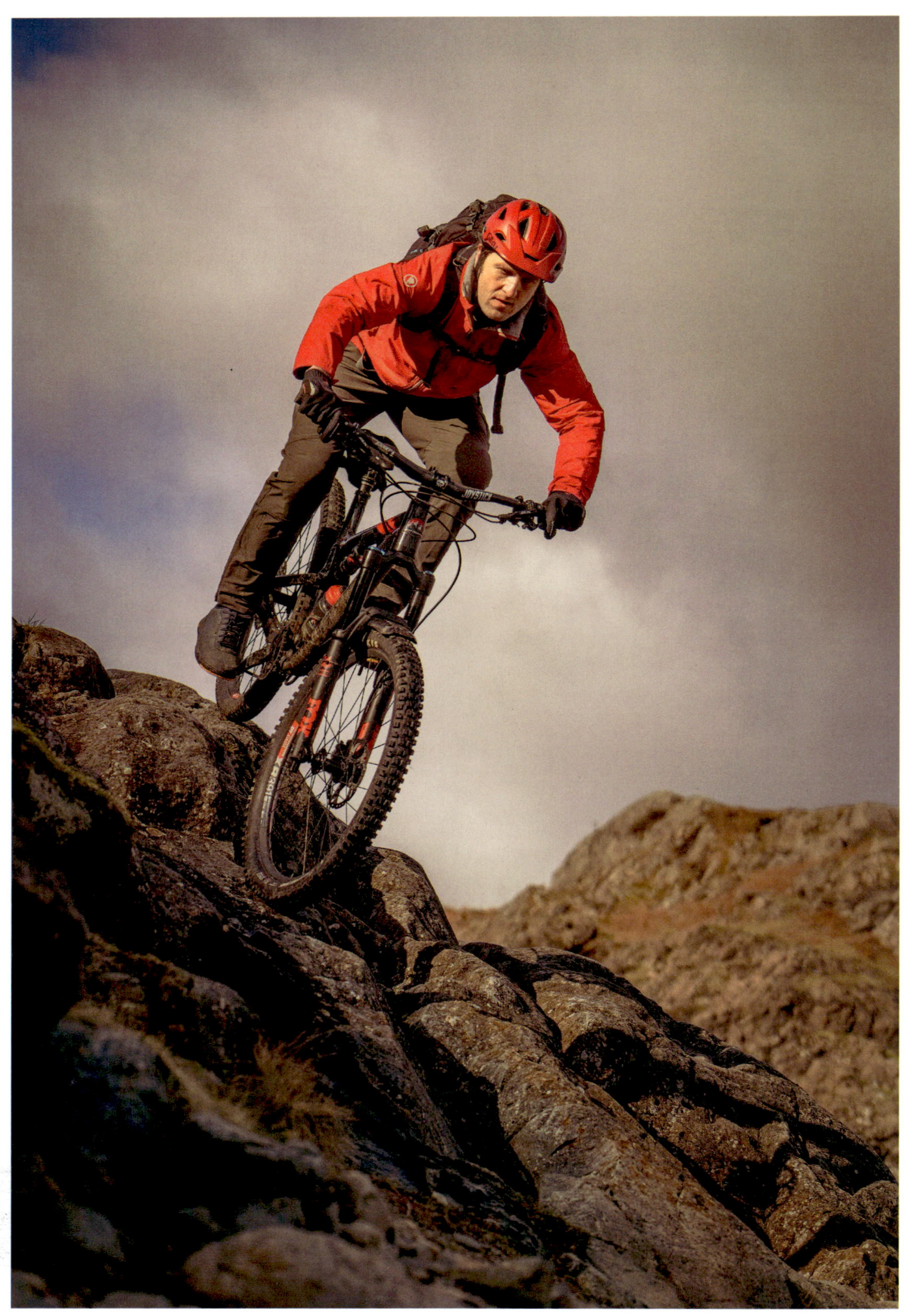

Dan Stringer on the rocky descent to Grasmere from Stickle Tarn. © Nadir Khan

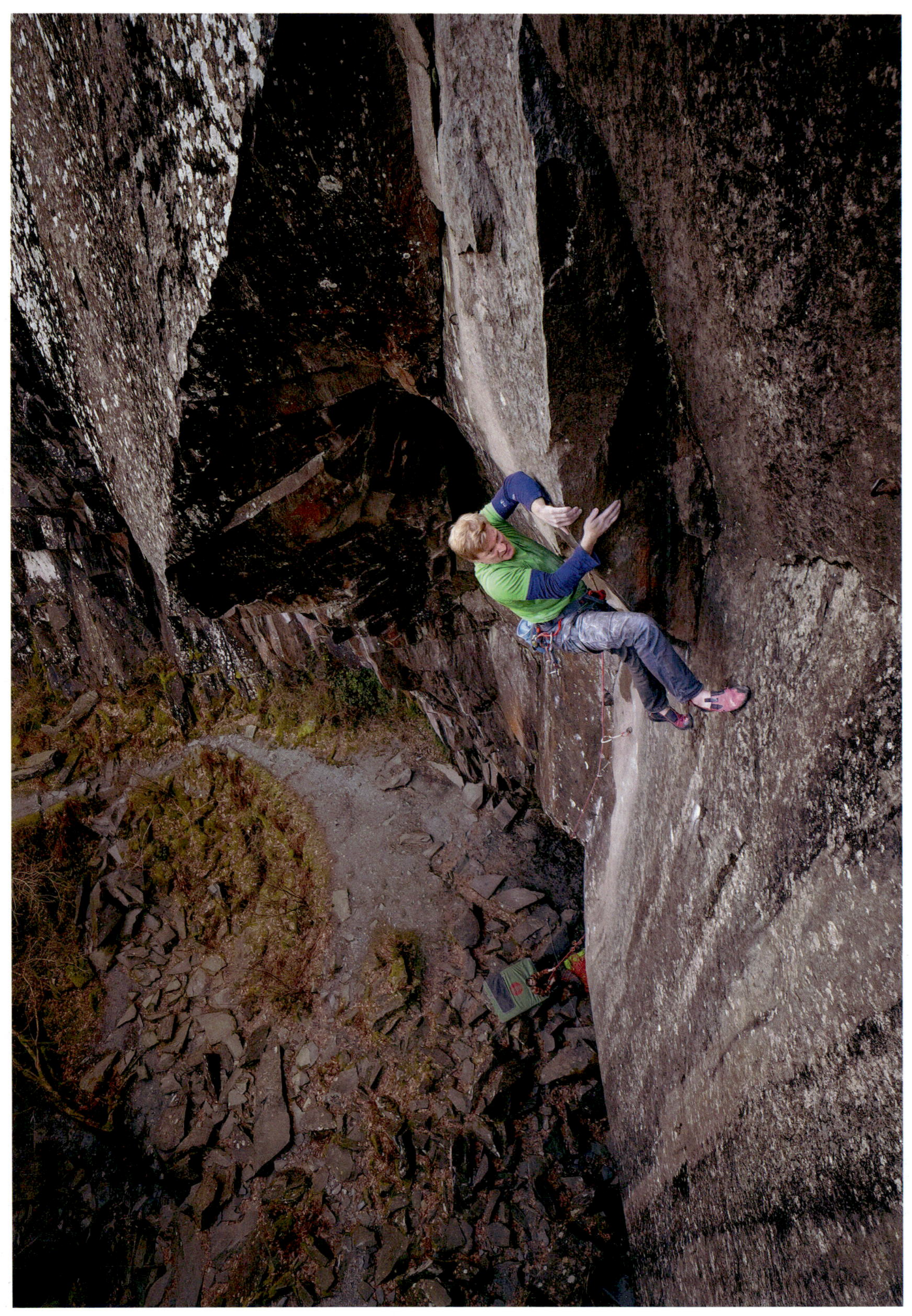

Adam Hocking working hard on *I Got Horribly Sober* (F8b) at Cathedral Quarry. © Tom McNally

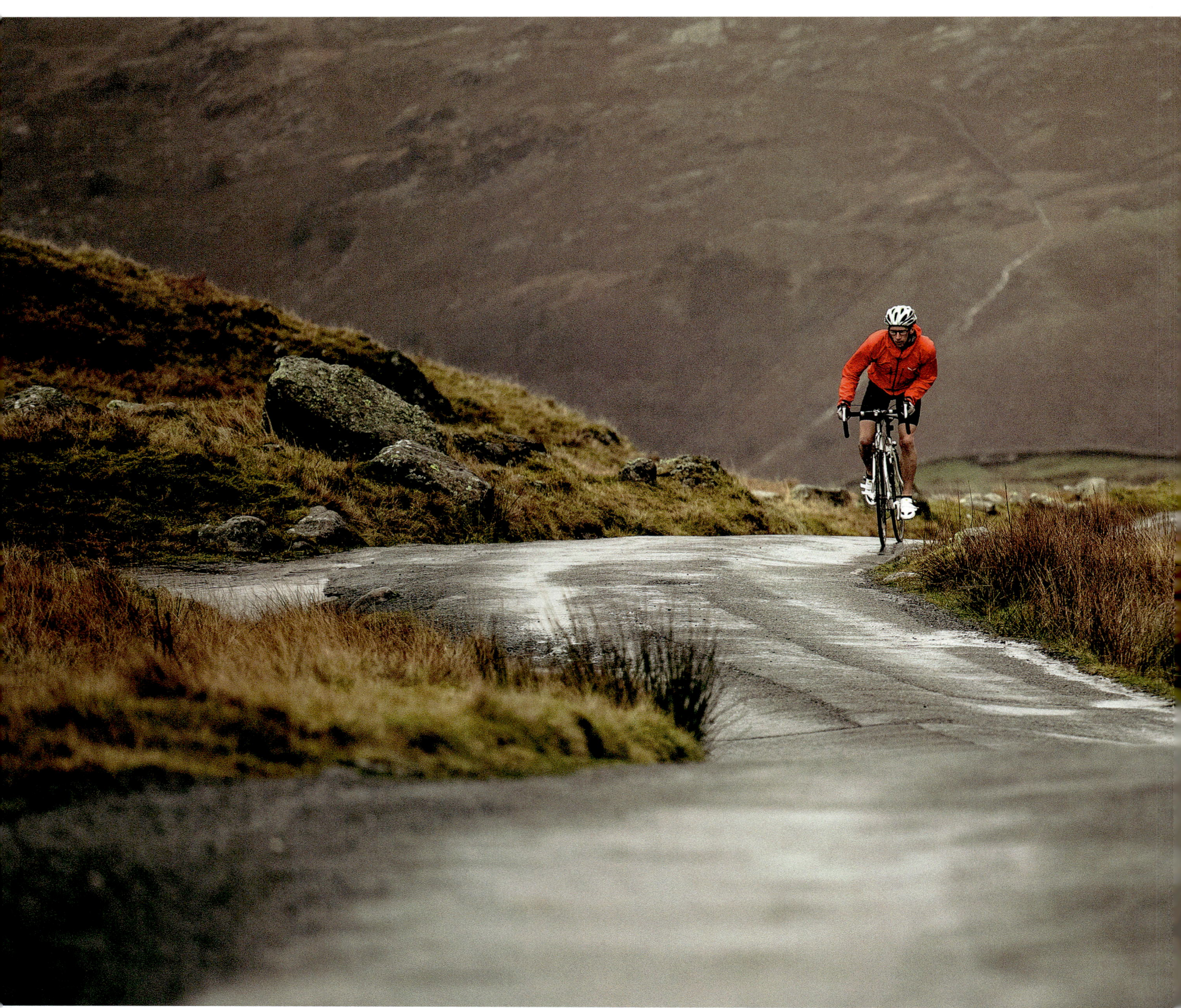

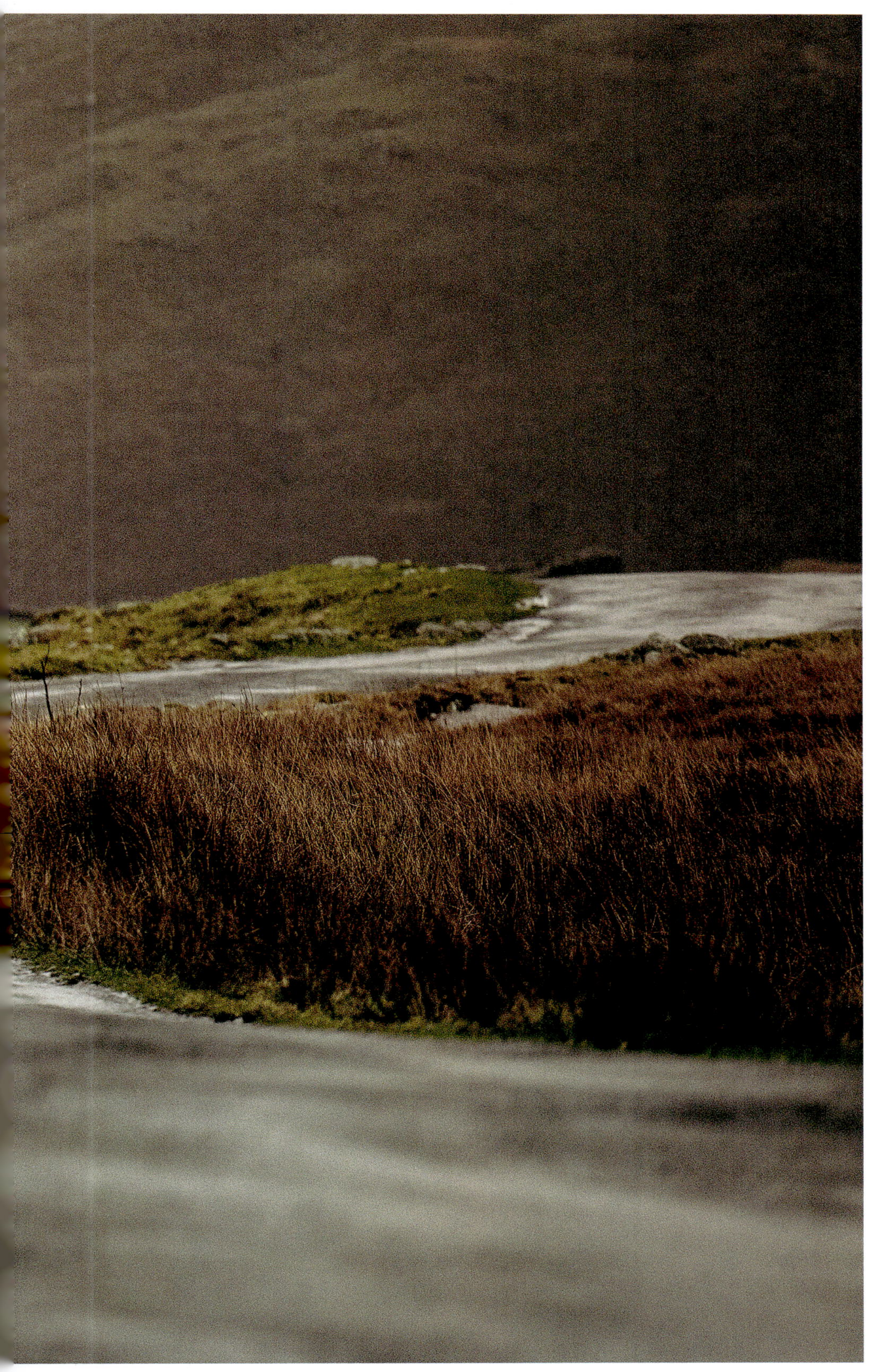

<< Neil Davies endures the pain of climbing the classic Wrynose Pass.
© Nadir Khan

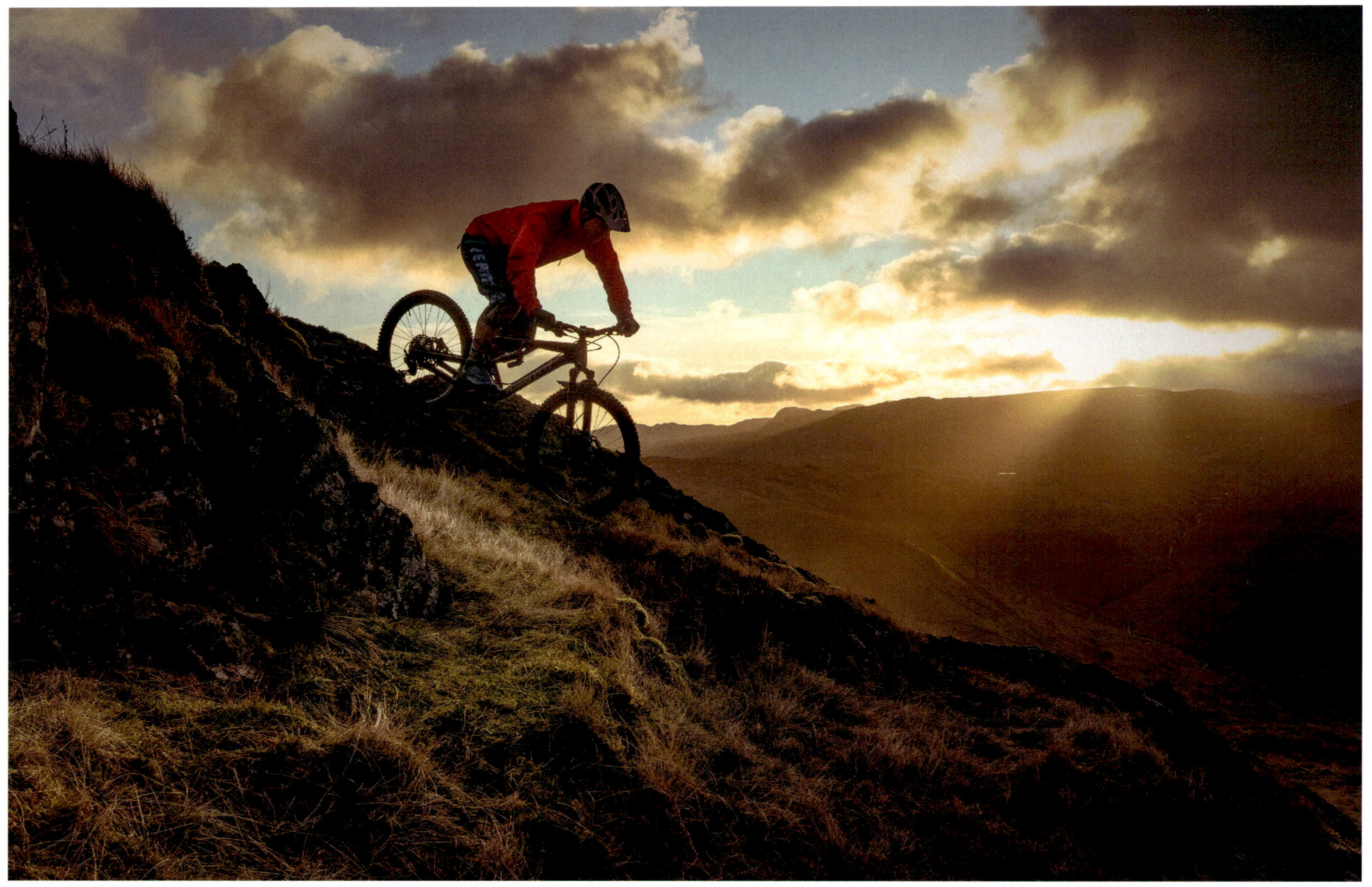

James Vincent descending Helvellyn. © Nadir Khan

Dan Stringer on the hike-a-bike of Black Sail Pass. © Nadir Khan »

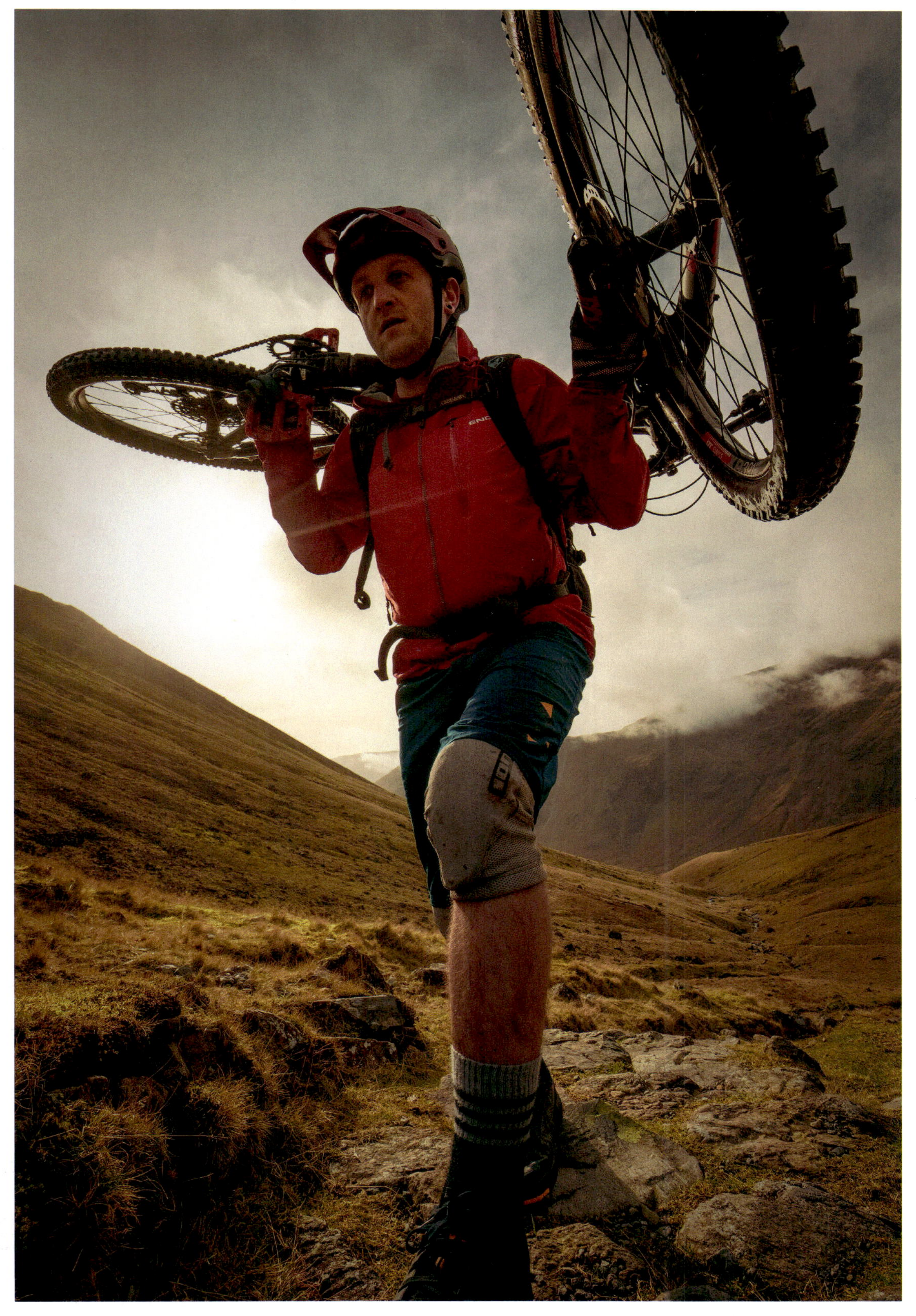

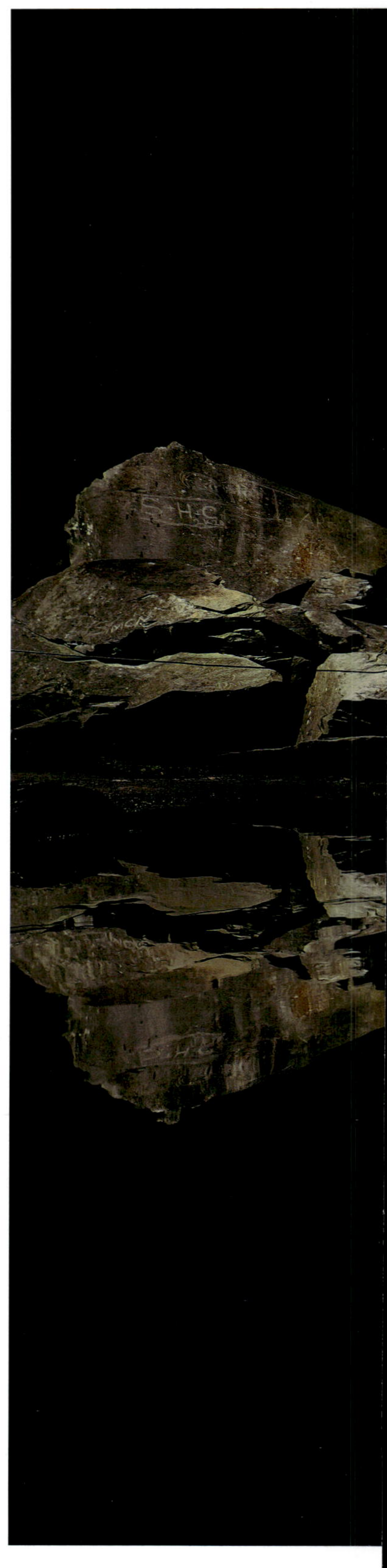

Adam Hocking and Will Jackson on *Quarryman's Arête* (XS),
an old aid route in the underground cavern of Cathedral Quarry.
© Tom McNally »